PgMP: Program Managemen Exam Study Guide

MW00582145

PgMP Exam Objectives

EXAM OBJECTIVE	CHAPTER
1. Defining the Program	
1.1 Perform a program assessment by defining the program objectives, requirements and establishing a high-level road map in order to ensure program alignment with the enterprise strategic plan or mission.	2, 3
1.2 Support business analysis functions in identifying marketplace needs for potential program offering in order to ensure program viability through researching, market analysis, and high-level cost-benefit analysis.	2, 3
1.3 Develop benefits realization plan by estimating the costs and benefits (ROI) of the program in order to establish the program feasibility and obtain funding.	2, 3
1.4 Perform a preliminary stakeholder analysis through RFP, contract, experience, and input from other sources in order to assess their position relative to the program.	2
1.5 Establish alliances with other departments and organizations by recognizing dependencies in order to assess potential partnerships and commitment to the program.	2
1.6 Evaluate the organization's capability by consulting with the groups involved with delivery in order to validate the program priority and alignment to the strategic objectives.	3
1.7 Request authorization to proceed by presenting the program assessment for approval to the governance authorities in order to initiate the program.	2
2. Initiating the Program	
2.1 Define the program mission statement by assembling the stakeholders' concerns and expectations in order to establish program direction and set a baseline for any further action.	3
2.2 Translate strategic objectives into high-level project scope statements by negotiating with stakeholders in order to create a program scope description.	3
2.3 Develop a high-level milestone plan using goals and objectives of the program, applicable historical information, and other available resources in order to align program with expectations of sponsors and stakeholders.	3

Sybex®
An Imprint of
WILEY

EXAM OBJECTIVE	CHAPTER

6. Closing the Program

6.1 Complete a performance analysis report by gathering final values and comparing to planned values for quality, cost, schedule, and resource data in order to determine program performance.   9

6.2 Manage program completion by executing the transition plan (initiate benefits realization measurement, release resources and acknowledge individual performance, perform administrative closure, obtain acceptance, transfer ongoing activities to functional organization) in order to close out the program.   9

6.3 Conduct the stakeholder post-review meeting by presenting the program performance report in order to obtain feedback and capture lessons learned.   9

6.4 Report lessons learned via appropriate methodologies to support future program or organizational improvement.   9

Sybex®
An Imprint of
WILEY

EXAM OBJECTIVE	CHAPTER
4. Executing the Program	
4.1 Consolidate project/program data (documented issues, status reviews, risks, financial reports, resources, etc.), using predefined reporting tools and methods to monitor program performance.	8
4.2 Charter constituent projects by assigning project managers and allocating appropriate resources in order to meet program objectives.	7
4.3 Motivate the team using appropriate tools and techniques in order to increase commitment to the program objectives.	7
4.4 Establish program consistency by deploying uniform standards, resources, infrastructure, tools and processes in order to enable informed program decision making.	7
4.5 Capture program status and data by ensuring the population of the program management information system in order to maintain accurate and current program information for the use of stakeholders.	7, 8
4.6 Execute the appropriate program plans (quality, risk, communication, staffing, etc.) by using the tools identified in the planning phase and by auditing the results of the use of these tools in order to ensure the program outcomes meet the stakeholder expectations and standards.	7
4.7 Approve closure of constituent projects upon completion through appropriate processes and procedures in order to obtain acceptance.	9
5. Controlling the Program	
5.1 Analyze variance of costs, schedule, quality and risks by comparing actual values to planned values from the program plan, trends, and extrapolation in order to identify corrective actions necessary.	8
5.2 Identify potential corrective actions by forecasting program outcomes using simulations, what-if scenarios and causal analysis in order to incorporate corrective actions into the program management plan.	8
5.3 Manage change in accordance with the change management plan to control scope, quality, schedule, cost, and contracts.	8
5.4 Address program level issues by identifying and selecting a course of action by taking into account the program constraints and objectives in order to enable continued program progress.	8

Sybex®
An Imprint of
WILEY

EXAM OBJECTIVE	CHAPTER
2.4 Develop an accountability matrix by identifying and assigning program roles and responsibilities in order to build the core team and to differentiate between the program and project resources.	3, 5
2.5 Establish project management standards within the program (governance, tools, finance and reporting) using industry best practices and enterprise standards in order to drive efficiency and consistency among projects.	3
2.6 Define meaningful measurement criteria for success by analyzing stakeholder expectations and requirements across the constituent projects in order to accurately control program performance.	3, 8
2.7 Obtain senior management approval for the program by presenting the program charter with its high-level costs and benefits for the organization in order to receive authorization to proceed to the next phases.	3
2.8 Conduct program kick-offs with stakeholders by holding a series of meetings in order to familiarize the organization with the program.	3, 7

3. Planning the Program

3.1 Develop a detailed program scope statement by incorporating program vision, objectives, out-of-scope items, schedule, financial milestones and legal/regulatory/safety concerns in order to aid in overall planning.	4
3.2 Develop program scope definition using Work Breakdown Structure in order to determine the program deliverables and tasks.	4, 7
3.3 Establish the program management plan and baseline by integrating the plans for the constituent projects and creating the plans for the supporting program functions including management of scope, schedule, finance, benefits, quality, resource, procurement, risk response, change and communications in order to effectively forecast, monitor, and identify variances during program execution.	4, 5, 6
3.4 Optimize the program plan by reviewing and leveling resource requirements (e.g., materials, equipment, facilities, finance, human capital) in order to gain efficiencies and synergies among projects.	5
3.5 Define project management information system (PMIS) by selecting tools and processes to share knowledge, intellectual property and documentation across constituent projects in order to maximize synergies and savings.	6
3.6 Develop the transition plan by defining exit criteria, policies and processes to ensure all administrative, commercial, and contractual obligations are met upon program completion.	4

Exam objectives are subject to change at any time without prior notice and at PMI's sole discretion. Please visit PMI's website (www.pmi.org) for the most current listing of exam objectives.

Sybex®
An Imprint of
WILEY

PgMP^{SM}:
Program Management
Professional Exam
Study Guide

PgMP^{SM}:
Program Management
Professional Exam
Study Guide

Dr. Paul Sanghera, PMP

BICENTENNIAL
1807
WILEY
2007
BICENTENNIAL

Wiley Publishing, Inc.

Acquisitions Editor: Jeff Kellum
Development Editor: Jim Compton
Technical Editor: Claudia Baca
Production Editor: Elizabeth Campbell
Copy Editor: Candace English
Production Manager: Tim Tate
Vice President and Executive Group Publisher: Richard Swadley
Vice President and Executive Publisher: Joseph B. Wikert
Vice President and Publisher: Neil Edde
Media Project Supervisor: Laura Atkinson
Media Development Specialist: Kit Malone
Media Quality Assurance: Kate Jenkins
Book Designers: Judy Fung and Bill Gibson
Compositor: Happenstance Type-O-Rama
Proofreader: Ian Golder
Indexer: Nancy Guenther
Anniversary Logo Design: Richard Pacifico
Cover Designer: Ryan Sneed
Cover Image: © Pete Gardner/Digital Vision/gettyimages

Sybex®
An Imprint of
WILEY

Dear Reader:

Thank you for choosing *PgMP: Program Management Professional Exam Study Guide*. This book is part of a family of premium quality Sybex books, all written by outstanding authors who combine practical experience with a gift for teaching.

Sybex was founded in 1976. More than thirty years later, we're still committed to producing consistently exceptional books. With each of our titles we're working hard to set a new standard for the industry. From the paper we print on, to the authors we work with, our goal is to bring you the best books available.

I hope you see all that reflected in these pages. I'd be very interested to hear your comments and get your feedback on how we're doing. Feel free to let me know what you think about this or any other Sybex book by sending me an email at nedde@wiley.com. Or, if you think you've found a technical error in this book, please visit http://sybex.custhelp.com. Customer feedback is critical to our efforts at Sybex.

Best regards,

Neil Edde
Vice President and Publisher
Sybex, an Imprint of Wiley

To my son, Adam Sanghera, the lighthouse of my life

Acknowledgments

Each time I get a book published, I re-learn a lesson that transforming an idea into a finished book takes a project (it produces a unique product, that is the book, and it has a beginning and an end) and a project team. As they say (well, if they don't any more, they should), first thing first. Let me begin by thanking Jeff Kellum not only for initiating this project as an Acquisition Editor, but also monitoring it through the planning, executing, and closing stages. Thanks are also due to Jim Compton for playing a very constructive and effective role as Development Editor. With two thumbs up, thanks to Elizabeth Campbell, the Production Editor, for doing an excellent job in managing the copy editing and production activities.

It's my pleasure to acknowledge the hard work of other members of the project team as well: Candace English for copy editing, Ian Golder for proofreading, and Nancy Guenther for indexing. Thanks are also due to the media team (Laura Atkinson, Kit Malone, and Kate Jenkins) to work on the CD & test engine for this book. Thanks to Happenstance Type-O-Rama, the Compositor. My special thanks to Claudia Baca, the Technical Editor of this book, for carefully reviewing all the chapters and offering valuable feedback.

In some ways, writing this book is an expression of the project manager and educator inside me. I thank some great minds from whom I have directly or indirectly learned about management during my journey in the computer industry from Novell to Dream Logic: Chuck Castleton at Novell, Delon Dotson at Netscape and MP3.com, Kate Peterson at Weborder, and Dr. John Serri at Dream Logic. I also thank my colleagues and seniors in the field of education for helping me in so many ways to become a better educator. Here are a few to mention: Dr. Gerald Pauler (Brooks College), Professor David Hayes (San Jose State University), Professor Michael Burke (San Jose State University).

Last, but not least, my appreciation (along with my heart) goes to my wife Renee and my son Adam for not only peacefully coexisting with my projects but also supporting them.

—Paul Sanghera

About the Author

One of the world's leading experts in project and program management, Dr. Paul Sanghera is a manager, educator, technologist, and entrepreneur, and has 15 years of diverse project and program management experience in the computer industry, from Netscape to MP3, and at research labs, from Cornell to CERN. Having worked in various roles, including director of project management, director of software development, software developer, trainer, and scientist, he has a broad view of project and program management. Expertise in multiple application areas including physics, computer science, RFID, and nanotechnology enabled him to climb to the mountaintop of project/program management. Dr. Sanghera has several industry certifications, including PMP, CAPM, Project+, Network+, Linux+, SCJP, and SCBCD, and has contributed to building world-class technologies such as Netscape Communicator and Novell's NDS. As an engineering manager, he has been at the ground floor of several startups and has been a lecturer at San Jose State University and Brooks College. He has authored or coauthored more than 100 technical papers published in well-reputed European and American research journals. Paul is the best-selling author of several books on technology and project management, including *PMP in Depth*. Dr. Sanghera has a Master's degree in computer science from Cornell University and a Ph.D. in physics from Carleton University. He currently lives in Silicon Valley, where he runs an information company, Infonential Inc., that specializes in project management and emerging technologies.

Contents at a Glance

Contents

Introduction

> " 'Begin at the beginning, and go on till you come to the end: then stop.' "
>
> —*Alice in Wonderland* by Lewis Carroll

This book is designed to help you prepare for and pass the Program Management Professional (PgMP) exam administered by the Project Management Institute (PMI). This certification is growing in popularity and demand in all areas of business. The PMI has experienced explosive growth in membership over the last few years, and more and more organizations are recognizing the importance of program management (and project management) certifications.

Since this book has a laser-sharp focus on the exam objectives, expert project managers and program managers who want to pass the PgMP exam can use this book to ensure that they do not miss any objective. Yet it is not an exam-cram book. The chapters and the sections within each chapter are presented in a logical learning sequence: a topic and a chapter depend only upon the previously covered topics and chapters, and there is no hopping from topic to topic. The concepts and topics, both simple and complex, are clearly explained when they appear the first time. This facilitates stepwise learning, prevents confusion, and makes this book useful for both beginners who want to get up to speed quickly to pass the PgMP exam and for experienced professionals. No prior knowledge of program management is assumed. Prior knowledge of project management is helpful but is not required. Chapter 1 presents an overview of project management in the context of program management and portfolio management to help beginners ramp up quickly.

PMI offers the most-recognized certifications in the field of program management and project management, and this book deals exclusively with its processes, procedures, and methods within the scope of the PgMP exam. You will see that program management consists of many processes, each with its own terminology, tools, and methods. The biggest problem with most of the available literature in program management is that it fails to clearly distinguish between program management and project management and often confuses these two concepts. Accordingly, a two-pronged purpose that you should keep in mind while going through this book is to distinguish between program management and project management, and to clearly see the relationship between the two. For example, you will see processes in program management that have identical or similar names to processes in project management. But they are different processes performed at different levels of management.

Like the PgMP exam, this book is largely based on the following three references:

- *The Standard for Program Management—First Edition*
- *A Guide to the Project Management Body of Knowledge (PMBOK® Guide —Third Edition)*
- *PgMPSM Examination Specification*

Even if you're familiar with another organized program management and project management methodology, don't assume you already know the processes discussed in this book. I strongly recommend that you learn all of the processes—their key inputs, tools and techniques, and outputs. Take the time to understand and memorize these elements and the key terms and their definitions, listed in the glossary and at the end of the chapter in which the term is introduced. Just understanding the definition of a term and the input, output, and tools and techniques of the processes will help you answer quite a few questions. It is possible that you've always done that particular task or used the methodology described but called it by another name. Know the name of each process and its primary purpose.

What Is the PMI and Its PgMP Certification?

The PMI is the leader and the most widely recognized organization in terms of promoting project management best practices. The PMI strives to maintain and endorse standards and ethics in this field and offers publications, training, seminars, chapters, special-interest groups, and colleges to further the project management discipline. The PMI is accredited as an American National Standards Institute (ANSI) standards developer and also has the distinction of being the first organization to have its certification program attain International Organization for Standardization (ISO) 9001 recognition.

The PMI boasts a worldwide membership of more than 230,000, with members from 125 countries. Local PMI chapters meet regularly and allow project managers to exchange information and learn about new tools and techniques of project management or new ways to use established techniques. I encourage you to join a local chapter and get to know other professionals in your field.

The PMI, founded in 1969, first started offering the PMP certification exam in 1984, then added the Certified Associate in Project Management (CAPM) exam in 2004 and the Program Management Professional (PgMP) exam in 2007. To pass the PgMP exam is one of many requirements for the PgMP credential, which is developed to acknowledge the qualifications of a professional who leads the coordinated management of multiple projects and ensures the ultimate success of a program. However, CAPM and PMP certifications are not required to become eligible for taking the PgMP exam.

Why Become PgMP-Certified?

The following benefits are associated with becoming PgMP-certified:

- It demonstrates proof of professional achievement.
- It increases your marketability.
- It provides greater opportunity for advancement in your field.
- It raises customer confidence in you and in your company's services.

Demonstrates Proof of Professional Achievement

PgMP certification is a rigorous process that documents your achievements in the field of program management. The exam tests your knowledge of the disciplined approaches, methodologies, and program management practices as described in *The Standard for Program Management*.

You are required to have at least four years of project management experience and four years of program management experience before sitting for the exam. Your certification assures employers and customers that you are well-grounded in the best practices in the disciplines of project management and program management. It shows that you have the hands-on experience and the mastery of the processes in the disciplines necessary to lead the coordinated management of multiple projects in a program effectively and to motivate teams to produce successful results.

Increases Your Marketability

Many industries are realizing the importance of project management and program management and its role in the organization. They are also seeing that simply proclaiming a head technician to be a "program manager" does not make it so. Program management, just like engineering, information technology, and a host of other trades, has its own specific qualifications and skills. Certification tells potential employers that you have the skills, experience, and knowledge to drive successful programs aligned with the strategic business and other organizational objectives and thereby ultimately improve the organization's bottom line.

A certification will always make you stand out above the competition. If you're certified and you're competing against a program manager without certification, chances are you'll come out as the top pick. Certification tells potential employers you have gone the extra mile. You've spent time studying techniques and methods as well as employing them in practice. Furthermore, it shows dedication to your own professional growth and enhancement and to adhering to and advancing professional standards.

Provides Opportunity for Advancement

PgMP certification displays your willingness to pursue growth in your professional career and shows that you're not afraid of a little hard work to get what you want. Potential employers will interpret your pursuit of this certification as a high-energy, success-driven, can-do attitude on your part. They'll see that you're likely to display these same characteristics on the job, which will help make the company successful. Your certification demonstrates your success-oriented, motivated attitude that will open up opportunities for future career advancements in your current field as well as in new areas you might want to explore.

Raises Customer Confidence

Just as the PgMP certification assures employers that you've got the background and experience to handle program management, it assures customers that they have a competent, experienced program manager at the helm. Certification will help your organization sell customers on your ability to manage their projects and programs. Customers, like potential employers, want the reassurance that those working for them have the knowledge and skills necessary to carry out the duties of the position and that professionalism and personal integrity are of utmost importance. Individuals who hold these ideals will translate their ethics and professionalism to their work. This enhances the trust customers will have in you, which in turn will give you the ability to influence them on important program and project issues.

How to Become PgMP-Certified

You need to fulfill several requirements in order to sit for the PgMP exam. The PMI has detailed the certification process quite extensively at its website. Go to `www.pmi.org`, and hover over the

Professional Development & Careers tab to reveal the Certification Program selection, where you can get the latest information on certification procedures and requirements.

As of this writing, to become PgMP-certified, a candidate must successfully complete the following three-step competency evaluation:

1. Eligibility for the exam. You are required to document your experience and education in an application that you can submit online at the PMI website. This application will be reviewed to determine your eligibility for the PgMP exam. You should have at minimum four years of project management experience and a bachelor's degree or high school diploma to qualify for this exam. Furthermore, you must have at minimum four years of program management experience if you have a bachelor's degree, or seven years of program management experience if you hold a high school diploma and no bachelor's degree.

2. The PgMP exam. After you are determined to be eligible for taking the PgMP exam, you'll undergo the second competency evaluation, for which you take an exam based on multiple-choice questions. The exam requires you to demonstrate your ability to apply your knowledge to a variety of situational or scenario-based questions.

3. Multi-rater assessment. After you pass the exam, the third competency evaluation is performed through the multi-rater assessment in which a team of raters will evaluate your competency to perform tasks that are important to program management as determined by the examination specification. You can select the team members who will make this evaluation.

The exam fee at the time this book is being published is $1,500 for PMI members in good standing and $1,800 for nonmembers. Testing is conducted at Thomson Prometric centers. You can find a center near you on the PMI website. You'll need to bring a form of identification such as a driver's license with you on the test day. You will not be allowed to take any materials with you into the testing center. You will be given a calculator, pencils, and scrap paper. You will turn in all scrap paper, including the notes and squiggles you've jotted during the test, to the center upon completion of the exam.

Your exam score is computed immediately; so you will know at the conclusion of the test whether you've passed. You're given four hours to complete the exam, which consists of 170 randomly generated questions. Only 150 of the 170 questions are scored, and the 20 unscored questions will be dispersed randomly throughout the examination. These 20 questions are used by PMI to determine statistical information and to determine whether they can or should be used on future exams. Because you cannot determine which questions are unscored, answer each question under the assumption that it will be scored. All unanswered questions are scored as wrong answers, and there is no penalty for a wrong answer; that is, you do not get a negative score. Therefore, it's to your benefit to guess an answer if you're stumped.

After you've received your certification, you'll be required to earn 60 professional development units (PDUs) every three years to maintain certification. Approximately one hour of structured learning translates to one PDU. (As an example, attendance at a local chapter meeting earns one PDU.) The PMI website details what activities constitute a PDU, how many PDUs each activity earns, and how to register your PDUs with the PMI to maintain your certification.

Some fast facts about the PgMP exam are listed in the following table for your convenience:

Item	Information
Number of questions	Scoreable: 150 Pretest: 20
Maximum time allowed	4 hours
Question types	Scenario-based multiple choice
Minimum educational background	Category 1: Bachelor's degree Category 2: High school diploma
Minimum project management experience	4 years (6,000 hours)
Minimum program management experience	Category 1: 4 years (6,000 hours) Category 2: 7 years (10,500 hours)
Exam fee (given in U.S. dollars; may vary by country)	Member: $1,500 Nonmember: $1,800
Sign code of professional conduct	Yes
Minimum continuing certification requirement	60 professional development units (PDUs) every three years

For detailed and up-to-date information, check out the PMI website: `www.pmi.org`.

Who Should Buy This Book?

If you are serious about passing the PgMP exam, you should buy this book and use it to study for the exam. This book is unique in that it walks you through the program from beginning to end, just as programs (and projects) are performed in practice: initiate, plan, execute, monitor and control, and close. In other words, the book is organized according to process groups, which is consistent with the order followed in the exam specifications by the PMI. Furthermore, the exam objectives covered in each chapter are clearly listed and explained in the beginning of the chapter. All this will avoid confusion and enable you to keep tabs on where you are in your exam prep while studying through this book. As you study, you will learn specific *standard* processes coupled with real-life scenarios that describe how program managers in different situations handle problems and the various issues all program managers are bound to encounter during their careers.

So, with the primary focus on the PgMP exam, this book is designed to serve the following audiences:

- Project management and program management practitioners can use this book to prepare for the PgMP exam.

- Instructors and trainers can use this book as a text book for a course on the PgMP exam prep. Instructional resource material is available from the publisher.

- Program managers and project managers can use this book as a quick and easy reference to the discipline of program management.

How to Use This Book and CD

We've included several testing features, both in the book and on the companion CD. Following this introduction is an assessment test that you can use to check your readiness for the actual exam. If you are not a beginner, take this test before you start reading the book. It will help you identify the areas you may need to brush up on or pay more attention to. Each answer includes an explanation, and a note telling you in which chapter the related material appears.

With the exception of Chapter 1, which is there to help beginners ramp up quickly for the rest of the book, each chapter begins with a list of exam objectives on which the chapter is focused. These objectives are officially called *tasks* by the PMI, and these tasks are organized into *domains*, which are essentially the process groups (except for the first domain, Defining the Program). I have followed the order of the domains published by PMI, but have shuffled around a very few objectives to keep the topics and the subject matter in line with sequential learning and to avoid hopping from topic to topic.

The first section in each chapter is the introduction, in which I establish three main concepts or topics that will be explored in the chapter. Each chapter (after Chapter 1) has the following features:

Exam Objectives. Each exam objective covered in the chapter is fully explained in the beginning of the chapter.

Notes, tips, and warnings. As you read through a chapter, you will find *notes* that present additional helpful material related to the topic being described, *tips* that provide additional quick real-world insight into the topic being discussed, and *warnings* that highlight issues to watch out for.

Real-world scenarios. You will notice various "Real-World Scenario" sidebars throughout the book. These are designed to give you insight into how the various processes and topic areas apply to real-world situations. Also remember that the exam itself contains scenario-based questions.

Summary. The "Summary" section of each chapter provides the big unified picture while reviewing the important concepts in the chapter.

Exam's-eye view. The "Exam's Eye View" section highlights the important points in the chapter from the perspective of the exam: the things that you must comprehend, the things that you should watch out for because they might not seem to fit in with the ordinary order of things, and the facts that you should memorize for the exam.

Exam essentials. This section appears at the end of every chapter to highlight the most essential topics covered in the chapter so that you'll have a solid understanding of those concepts.

Key terms and definitions. This section lists the important terms and concepts introduced in the chapter, along with their definitions.

Review questions. Each chapter ends with a list of questions, which has a two-pronged purpose: to help you test your knowledge about the material presented in the chapter and to help you evaluate your ability to answer the exam questions based on the exam objectives covered in the chapter.

As you finish each chapter, answer the review questions and then check to see whether your answers are right—the correct answer appears after each question. You can go back to reread the section that deals with each question you got wrong to ensure that you answer the question correctly the next time you are tested on the material. If you can answer at least 80 percent of the review questions correctly, you can probably feel comfortable moving on to the next chapter. If you can't answer that many correctly, reread the chapter, or the section that seems to be giving you trouble, and try the questions again.

The accompanying CD consists of the following items:

Bonus exams. In addition to the assessment test and the review questions in the book, you'll find bonus exams on the CD, which add up to a complete practice exam with 171 different questions. Take these practice exams just as if you were actually taking the exam (that is, without any reference material). When you have finished the first exam, move on to the next exam to solidify your test-taking skills. If you get more than 80 percent of the answers correct, you're ready to take the real exam.

Flashcards. You'll also find more than 100 flashcard questions on the CD for on-the-go review. You can download them to your PC, laptop, or Palm or Pocket PC device for quick and convenient reviewing.

Each question in the assessment test, the review questions, and the bonus exams is accompanied by a detailed answer that explains why the correct answer is correct and why the incorrect answers are incorrect. You can use these questions and answers to spot the weaknesses in your preparation and to reinforce important concepts.

Electronic book. The CD contains the whole book in PDF (Adobe Acrobat), so it can be easily read on any computer. For example, if you are going to travel but still need to study for the PgMP exam and you have a laptop with a CD drive, you can take this entire book with you just by taking the CD.

Tips for Taking the PgMP Exam

Here are some general tips for taking your exam successfully:

- Visit the PMI website at www.pmi.org for the latest information regarding certification and to find a testing site near you.

- Get to the exam center early so that you can relax and go through the check-in formalities.

- At the exam station, read the exam questions carefully. Make sure you know exactly what each question is asking, and don't be tempted to answer too quickly.

- Unanswered questions score as wrong answers, so it's better to take your best guess than to leave a question unanswered.

- If you're not sure of an answer, use the process of elimination to identify the obvious incorrect answers first. Narrow down the remaining choices by referring back to the question, looking for key words that might tip you off to the correct answer.

- You'll be given scratch paper to take with into the exam station. As soon as you get to your place but before you start the exam, write down all the formulas and any other memory aids you used while studying. That way, you can relax a little because you won't have to remember the formulas when you get to those questions on the exam—you can simply look at your scratch paper.

The Exam Objectives

Behind every certification exam, you can be sure to find exam objectives—the broad topics in which the exam developers want to ensure your competency.

As mentioned previously, the PgMP exam objectives are largely organized along the process groups, just like this book. As their names suggest, the last five domains in the exam spec are closely related to the corresponding five process groups: Initiating, Planning, Executing, Monitoring and Controlling, and Closing. The first performance domain in the exam spec covers the program definition and tasks, which are largely related to the program initiation. The relative attention given to these six domains in the PgMP exam are listed in the following table:

Domain #	Domain Name	Approximate Percentage Coverage in the Exam	Approximate Number of Scoreable Questions
1	Defining the Program	14	21
2	Initiating the Program	12	18
3	Planning the Program	20	30
4	Executing the Program	25	37
5	Controlling the Program	21	32
6	Closing the Program	8	12
Total		100	150

Exam objectives are subject to change at any time without prior notice and at the PMI's sole discretion. Please visit the Certification page of the PMI's website, www.pmi.org, for the most current listing of exam objectives.

Best wishes for the exam. Go get 'em!

Assessment Test

1. You have been offered a job as a program manager in a company that uses matrix management. Matrix management can be used:

    A. In project management

    B. In program management

    C. In both project and program management

    D. Only at the executive level

2. Which of the following is not included in a program?

    A. Projects

    B. Project portfolio

    C. Operations

    D. Project schedules

3. You are planning to interview the candidates for the project manager positions available in your program. Your manager has told you to make the candidates aware of the culture of your organization. The organizational culture is reflected by:

    A. Work environment, authority levels of the managers, and policies

    B. Policies, values, and annual revenue

    C. Norms, beliefs, and employee turnover rate

    D. Norms, values, and strategic plan

4. A structure that displays the breakdown of project deliverables into more-manageable, smaller work components is called:

    A. Work breakdown structure (WBS)

    B. Project breakdown structure (PBS)

    C. Hierarchical work structure (HWS)

    D. Schedule Network Diagram (SND)

5. You are telling your project managers to prepare the project plans for the projects based on the currently available information and to keep on making it more precise as more information comes in. This technique is called:

    A. Slow start

    B. Continuous improvement

    C. Progressive elaboration

    D. Delphi technique

6. Program life cycle is defined as a combination of:

   A. Five phases

   B. Five process groups

   C. Nine knowledge areas

   D. Seven phases

7. You are preparing to offer a seminar on the themes of program management that run through the program life cycle. Those themes are:

   A. Benefits management, program stakeholder management, and PMO

   B. Benefits realization plan, program stakeholder management, and program governance

   C. Benefits management, program stakeholder management, and program governance

   D. Benefits management, program governance, and program control

8. Your program is in the execution stage. Your manager has asked you to produce a detailed list of the key stakeholders of the program. This list will include:

   A. Project managers, project team members, and customers

   B. Program team members, program sponsor, and facility manager

   C. Program manager, program governance board, and database administrator

   D. Program team members, program director, and chief information officer (CIO)

9. Program Initiating is a:

   A. Phase

   B. Process group

   C. Knowledge area

   D. Process

10. Phase one of a program life cycle is called:

   A. Initiating

   B. Planning

   C. Program setup

   D. Pre-program setup

11. You are at a stage to initiate a program for your company. The program Initiating process group includes:

   A. Initiate Program, Authorize Projects, and Initiate Team

   B. Initiate Program, Authorize Projects, and Develop Program Charter

   C. Initiate Program, Authorize Program, and Initiate Team

   D. Initiate Program, Scope Definition, and Initiate Team

12. You are at a stage to initiate a program for your company. Your manager, Woody Guthrie, walks into your cubicle saying, "You need to work on the business case before performing this process." What process is Mr. Guthrie is referring to?

    A. Authorize Projects

    B. Develop Program Charter

    C. Initiate Team

    D. Initiate Program

13. All of the following are output items of the Initiate Program process except:

    A. Program charter

    B. Detailed program scope statement

    C. Project selection criteria

    D. Benefits realization plan

14. You need to perform a process to determine the program reporting requirements for the projects. Which process is it?

    A. Authorize Projects

    B. Authorize Programs

    C. Initiate Program

    D. Initiate Projects

15. You are the program manager of a program called The Blue Sky. The program sponsor of The Blue Sky has asked for the program team directory. Which process do you need to perform to generate this document?

    A. Authorize Projects

    B. Initiate Team

    C. Initiate Program

    D. Initiate Projects

16. The tools and techniques that are common to most of the program management processes include all of the following except:

    A. Policies and procedures

    B. Delphi

    C. Meetings

    D. Expert judgment

17. You are making a list of tools and techniques that you need to perform the Initiate Program process. The list should include:

A. Benefits analysis, expert judgment, and project selection methods

B. Benefits analysis, expert judgment, and benefits realization plan

C. Benefits analysis, expert judgment, and Ishikawa diagram

D. Benefits analysis, expert judgment, and project selection criteria

18. Phase two of a program life cycle is called:

A. Initiating

B. Planning

C. Program setup

D. Pre-program setup

19. The program Planning processes that belong to Integration Management include:

A. Develop Program Management Plan, Resource Planning, and Transition Planning

B. Develop Program Management Plan, Resource Planning, and Quality Planning

C. Develop Program Management Plan, Plan Program Contracting, and Transition Planning

D. Develop Program Management Plan, Resource Planning, and Integrated Change Control

20. Transition Planning belongs to which of the following knowledge areas?

A. Integration Management

B. Human Resource Management

C. Procurement Management

D. Communication Management

21. The program Planning processes that belong to Scope Management include:

A. Scope Definition and Scope Control

B. Scope Definition and Create Program Work Breakdown Structure (PWBS)

C. Scope Definition and Schedule Development

D. Create Program Work Breakdown Structure (PWBS), and Plan Scope

22. Your program is in the planning stage. You want to determine the resource requirements for the program. What process will you perform?

A. Activity Resource Estimating

B. Resource Planning

C. Create PWBS

D. Resource Management

23. All of the following are input items to the Scope Definition process except:

   A. Program charter

   B. Preliminary program scope statement

   C. Benefits realization plan

   D. Program scope statement

24. You want to develop a scope management plan for your program. Which process do you need to perform?

   A. Scope Planning

   B. Develop Scope Management plan

   C. Scope Definition

   D. Create Program Work Breakdown Structure

25. The Scope Definition process generates:

   A. Program work breakdown structure (PWBS)

   B. Scope management plan

   C. Preliminary program scope statement

   D. Benefits realization plan

26. The components at the lowest level of a program WBS hierarchy are called:

   A. Program packages

   B. Work packages

   C. Schedule activity

   D. Program deliverables

27. You are performing the Interface Planning process for your program. Which of the following is not a tool or technique that can be used for this process?

   A. Organizational theory

   B. Human resource practices

   C. Pareto diagram

   D. Stakeholder analysis

28. A resource histogram is a tool used in which of the following processes?

   A. Resource Planning

   B. Resource Optimization

   C. Interface Planning

   D. Develop Program Management Plan

29. You are going to perform each of the following processes for the first time for your program. Which of these processes will you perform before performing any other one of these processes?

   A. Schedule Development

   B. Transition Planning

   C. Create PWBS

   D. Scope Definition

30. The schedule management plan is an output of which process?

   A. Schedule Planning

   B. Schedule Definition

   C. Schedule Development

   D. Program Planning

31. Walking in the hallway, you overheard Dimitry Lennon, the program sponsor of the We Are the World program that is in the planning stage, saying to a program manager, "You need to perform this process to prepare an organizational chart." Which process was Mr. Lennon referring to?

   A. Resource Planning

   B. Human Resource Planning

   C. Schedule Development

   D. Organizational Planning

32. You are the program manager of the Redwood Forest program, which is at the planning stage. You need to decide whether certain items should be produced in-house or purchased. Which process do you need to perform to make this decision?

   A. Risk Management Planning

   B. Plan Program Contracting

   C. Plan Program Purchases and Acquisitions

   D. Procurement Planning

33. You have figured out the dependencies among the schedule activities. All these dependencies are of type finish-to-start. Which network diagramming method can you use to display these dependencies?

   A. Arrow diagramming method (ADM) only

   B. Precedence diagramming method (PDM) only

   C. Either the ADM or the PDM

   D. Critical diagramming method (CDM)

34. You are in the process of determining the program budget. Which program management process do you need to perform?

   A. Develop Program Budget

   B. Resource Planning

   C. Cost Estimating and Budgeting

   D. Plan Program Purchases and Acquisitions

35. You are managing a book-publishing program. You have decided to procure the book-cover designs from a digital design company for the next fiscal year. At this stage, you are not sure how many books you will publish in the year. What type of contract will be most suitable to sign with the digital design company?

   A. Time and material (T&M)

   B. Cost plus fee (CPF)

   C. Lump sum

   D. Fixed price

36. Risks originate from:

   A. Uncertainty

   B. Constraints

   C. Quality requirements

   D. Strategic plan

37. You are performing the Communication Planning process. All of the following are included in Communication Planning except:

   A. Determine the information needs of the program stakeholders

   B. Determine who needs what information and when

   C. Determine the technology requirements for the communication

   D. Issue a request for information (RFI), a request for proposal (RFP), and a request for quotation (RFQ)

38. You are preparing to perform the Quality Planning process. Before you can perform this process, you will need:

   A. Program scope statement and product description

   B. Program scope statement and operational definitions

   C. Product description and quality checklists

   D. Program cost of quality and quality metrics

xxxviii   Assessment Test

39. Quality metrics are:

   A. Input to Quality Planning

   B. Output of Quality Planning

   C. Output to Perform Quality Assurance

   D. Input to Perform Quality Control

40. A risk response plan for a program is an output of:

   A. Plan Risk Responses

   B. Identify Risks

   C. Risk Management Planning and Analysis

   D. Qualitative Risk Analysis

41. You need to develop a contract statement of work for your program. Which process will you perform?

   A. Plan Program Purchases and Acquisitions

   B. Plan Program Contracting

   C. Develop Program Management Plan

   D. Develop Statement of Work

42. The procurement management plan is an input to which process?

   A. Plan Program Purchases and Acquisitions

   B. Plan Program Contracting

   C. Cost Estimating and Budgeting

   D. Human Resource Planning

43. Phase three of a program life cycle is called:

   A. Initiating

   B. Establish program infrastructure

   C. Program setup

   D. Pre-program setup

44. Which of the following Executing processes belongs to the Integration Management knowledge area?

   A. Direct and Manage Program Execution

   B. Information Distribution

   C. Develop Program Team

   D. Perform Quality Assurance

45. Which of the following processes does not belong to the Executing process group?

  A. Information Distribution

  B. Perform Quality Assurance

  C. Acquire Program Team

  D. Cost Estimating and Budgeting

46. You are preparing to perform the Develop Program Team process. The output that you can expect from this process includes:

  A. Performance assessment and training plan

  B. Updates to training records and staffing management plan

  C. Performance assessment and improvements

  D. Staffing management plan and training records

47. The Acquire Program Team process belongs to which process group?

  A. Initiating

  B. Executing

  C. Human Resource

  D. Planning

48. Work results are output of:

  A. Direct and Manage Program Execution

  B. Develop Program Team

  C. Monitor and Control Program Work

  D. Perform Quality Assurance

49. Contract negotiation is a tool or technique for which process?

  A. Acquire Program Team

  B. Program Contract Administration

  C. Request Seller Responses

  D. Select Sellers

50. Dave Kohli, a senior program manager, is telling Kris Mohali, a junior program manager, to check out the recognition and reward system before performing this process. Which process is Mr. Kohli most likely referring to?

  A. Acquire Program Team

  B. Develop Program Team

  C. Human Resource Planning

  D. Contract Negotiation

51. Phase four of a program life cycle is called:

    A. Deliver incremental benefits

    B. Executing

    C. Program setup

    D. Establish program infrastructure

52. Which of the following Monitoring and Controlling processes belong to the Integration Management knowledge area?

    A. Resource Control, Issue Management and Control, and Monitor and Control Program Work

    B. Resource Control, Issue Management and Control, and Communication Control

    C. Integrated Change Control, Monitor and Control Program Work, and Performance Reporting

    D. Resource Control, Issue Management and Control, and program Contract Administration

53. Performance Reporting is a program process that belongs to:

    A. The Monitoring and Controlling process group

    B. The Communication process group

    C. The Executing process group

    D. The Integration Management knowledge area

54. Program Contract Administration is a program process that belongs to:

    A. The Monitoring and Controlling process group

    B. The Procurement process group

    C. The Executing process group

    D. The Integration Management knowledge area

55. You are preparing to perform the Resource Control process. Which of the following items is not an input to this process?

    A. Program budget

    B. Expenditure reports

    C. Resource management plan

    D. Performance reports

56. You are managing the execution of a program. You want to make forecasts about the expected progress and performance of the program. Which process should you perform to accomplish this?

   A. Direct and Manage Program Execution

   B. Monitor and Control Program Work

   C. Performance Reporting

   D. Extrapolate Performance

57. You are preparing to close the program you have been managing. A program is closed in which phase of the program life cycle?

   A. Phase seven

   B. Phase three

   C. Phase five

   D. Phase six

58. The Closing process group consists of the following processes:

   A. Close Program, Component Closure, and Contract Closure

   B. Close Program, Administrative Closure, and Contract Closure

   C. Contract Closure, Component Closure, and Transition Benefits

   D. Close Program, Close Projects, and Contract Closure

59. You are performing the Close Program process. The outputs of this process include:

   A. Certificate of program completion and project archives

   B. Closure report and contract completion certificate

   C. Final performance review report and program archives

   D. Lessons learned and contract termination documents

60. Lessons learned are an:

   A. Output of the Contract Closure process

   B. Output of the Component Closure process

   C. Output of the Final Performance Review process

   D. Input to and output of the Close Program process

Answers to Assessment Test

1. C.

C is the correct answer because matrix management is the management type that involves a team with members from different functional groups. So it can be used to manage both projects and programs. **A and B** are incorrect because **C** is a more complete and correct answer. **D** is incorrect because matrix management is not limited to the executive level. For more information, see Chapter 1.

2. B.

B is the correct answer because programs are part of a portfolio, not the other way around. **A and C** are incorrect because a program can contain projects and program-related operations. **D** is incorrect because the schedules of the constituent projects are part of the program. For more information, see Chapter 1.

3. A.

A is the correct answer because organizational culture is typically reflected by work environment, management style, policies, and values. **B and C** are incorrect because annual revenues and turnover rates are not elements of organizational culture. **D** is incorrect because the strategic plan may affect the culture but it is not part of the culture. For more information, see Chapter 1.

4. A.

A is the correct answer because the WBS displays the project scope in terms of manageable work components. **B, C, and D** are incorrect because there are no standard structures with these names in project or program management. For more information, see Chapter 4.

5. C.

C is the correct answer because progressive elaboration is the technique used to continually improve and refine a plan in steps as more information becomes available. **A and B** are incorrect because slow start and continuous improvement can be considered elements of the technique, but the proper name of the technique is progressive elaboration. **D** is incorrect because the Delphi technique is used to reach consensus among experts by anonymous participation. For more information, see Chapter 1.

6. A.

A is the correct answer because a program life cycle is composed of five phases: pre-program setup, program setup, establishing program infrastructure, delivering incremental benefits, and closing the program. **B** is incorrect because process groups are closely related to the program phases, but it's the program phases that constitute the program life cycle. **C** is incorrect because a program may use processes from all the nine knowledge areas, but these knowledge areas do not constitute the program life cycle. **D** is incorrect because there are five phases in the program life cycle and not seven. For more information, see Chapter 1.

7. C.

C is the correct answer because the broad management themes that are key to the success of a program and run through the program life cycle are benefits management, program stakeholder management, and program governance. **A** is incorrect because PMO stands for Program Management Office, which is not a management theme. **B** is incorrect because the benefits realization plan is not the same thing as benefits management. **D** is incorrect because it's important to monitor and control a program, but controlling a program is not one of the three broad management themes. For more information, see Chapter 2.

8. A.

A is the correct answer because project managers, project team members, and customers are included in the list of a program's key stakeholders. **B, C, and D** are incorrect because the facility manager, database administrator, and CIO are not key program stakeholders just by virtue of their positions. If one of them is directly involved in the program as a program team member or is on the program governance board, then that individual will be a key stakeholder. For more information, see Chapter 2.

9. B.

B is the correct answer because program Initiating is a process group that contains processes to initiate a program. **A** is incorrect because the five phases of a program life cycle are pre-program setup, program setup, establishing program infrastructure, delivering incremental benefits, and closing the program. **C** is incorrect because Initiating is a process group and not a knowledge area. **D** is incorrect because the Initiating process group contains three processes. For more information, see Chapter 2.

10. D.

D is the correct answer because phase one of the program life cycle is called pre-program setup. **A and B** are incorrect because Initiating and planning are process groups and not phases. **C** is incorrect because program setup is phase two (not one) of the program life cycle. For more information, see Chapter 2.

11. A.

A is the correct answer because the program Initiating process group consists of the Initiate Program, Authorize Projects, and Initiate Team processes. **B** is incorrect because the program charter is developed by using the Initiate Program process. **C** is incorrect because there is no standard process called Authorize Program. The program is authorized during the Initiate Program process. **D** is incorrect because the Scope Definition process belongs to the Planning process group. For more information, see Chapter 2.

12. D.

D is the correct answer because the business case is an input to the Initiate Program process. **A** is incorrect because the business case is not an input to the Authorize Projects process, though the strategic plan is. **B** is incorrect because there is no standard program process called Develop Program Charter. **C** is incorrect because the Initiate Team process does not take the business case as an input. For more information, see Chapter 3.

13. B.

B is the correct answer because the detailed program scope statement is prepared during the Scope Definition process. **A, C, and D** are incorrect answers because all these items are included in the output of the Initiate Program process. For more information, see Chapter 3.

14. A.

A is the correct answer because program reporting requirements is an output of the Authorize Projects process. **B and D** are incorrect because there are no standard program processes called Authorize Programs and Initiate Projects. **C** is incorrect because program reporting requirements are not an output of the Initiate Program process. For more information, see Chapter 3.

15. B.

B is the correct answer because the program directory is an output of the Initiate Team process. **A and C** are incorrect because the program directory is not an output of either of these processes. **D** is incorrect because there is no standard program process called Initiate Projects. For more information, see Chapter 3.

16. B.

B is the correct answer because the Delphi technique, used to reach consensus among experts by having them participate anonymously, is not a common tool used in most of the program management processes. **A, C, and D** are incorrect answers because tools and techniques common to most of the program management processes include expert judgment, meetings, reviews, and policies and procedures. For more information, see Chapter 3.

17. A.

A is the correct answer because benefits analysis, expert judgment, and project selection methods are used as tools and techniques in the Initiate Program process. **B and D** are incorrect because the benefits realization plan and projects selection criteria are outputs of the Initiate Program process. **C** is incorrect because the Ishikawa diagram is a quality tool used in quality control and is usually not used to initiate a program. For more information, see Chapter 3.

18. C.

C is the correct answer because phase two of the program life cycle is called program setup. **A and B** are incorrect because Initiating and Planning are process groups and not phases. **D** is incorrect because pre-program setup is phase one (and not phase two) of the program life cycle. For more information, see Chapter 4.

19. A.

A is the correct answer because the Planning processes in the Integration Management knowledge area are Develop Program Management Plan, Resource Planning, Interface Planning, and Transition Planning. **B** is incorrect because Quality Planning belongs to Quality Management and not to Integration Management. **C** is incorrect because Plan Program Contracting belongs to Procurement Management and not to Integration Management. **D** is incorrect because Integrated Change Control belongs to the Executing process group and not to the Planning process group. For more information, see Chapter 4.

20. A.

A is the correct answer because Integration Management contains the following Planning processes: Develop Program Management Plan, Interface Planning, Resource Planning, and Transition Planning. **B, C, and D** are incorrect answers because Transition Planning belongs to Integration Management. For more information, see Chapter 4.

21. B.

B is the correct answer because the Planning processes in the Scope Management knowledge area are Scope Definition and Program Work Breakdown Structure. **A** is incorrect because Scope Control belongs to the Monitoring and Controlling process group and not to the Planning process group. **C** is incorrect because Schedule Development belongs to Time Management and not to Scope Management. **D** is incorrect because there is no standard program process called Plan Scope. For more information, see Chapter 4.

22. B.

B is the correct answer because the resource management plan and resource requirements are two output items of the Resource Planning process. **A and D** are incorrect answers because Activity Resource Estimating and Resource Management are not standard program management processes. **C** is an incorrect answer because resource requirements is not an output of the create PWBS process. For more information, see Chapter 4.

23. D.

D is the correct answer because the program scope statement is an output of the Scope Definition process. **A, B, and C** are incorrect answers because all of these are input items to the Scope Definition process. For more information, see Chapter 4.

24. C.

C is the correct answer because the scope management plan is an output of the Scope Definition process. **A and B** are incorrect because there are no standard program processes called Scope Planning and Develop Scope Management Plan. **D** is incorrect because the Create Program Work Breakdown Structure (Create PWBS) process is used to develop a PWBS, and it uses the scope management plan as an input. For more information, see Chapter 4.

25. B.

B is the correct answer because the two output items of Scope Definition are the program scope statement and the scope management plan. **A** is incorrect because the PWBS is an output of the Create PWBS process. **C** is incorrect because the preliminary program scope statement is an input to the Scope Definition process. **D** is incorrect because the benefits realization plan is an input to the Scope Definition process. For more information, see Chapter 4.

26. A.

A is the correct answer because program packages are the components at the lowest level of a program WBS (PWBS) hierarchy. B is incorrect because work packages are the components at the lowest level of a project WBS hierarchy. C and D are incorrect because these are not the correct terms for the components at the lowest level of a project or program WBS hierarchy. Work packages can be drawn from deliverables, and can be broken further into schedule activities. For more information, see Chapter 4.

27. C.

C is the correct answer because the Pareto diagram is a quality control tool. A, B, and D are incorrect because these are valid tools and techniques used in the Interface Planning process. For more information, see Chapter 4.

28. A.

A is the correct answer because a resource histogram, a graph that displays resource requirements as a function of some parameter such as time, can be used in the Resource Planning process. B is incorrect because there is no standard program process called Resource Optimization. C and D are incorrect because these processes don't use a resource histogram as a tool. For more information, see Chapter 4.

29. D.

D is the correct answer because Scope Definition generates the program scope statement, which is used to create the PWBS and to perform Transition Planning. A is incorrect because Schedule Development uses the PWBS as an input, which is generated by the Create PWBS process. B is incorrect because Transition Planning uses the program scope statement as an input, which is generated by the Scope Definition process. C is incorrect because Create PWBS uses the program scope statement as an input, which is generated by the Scope Definition process. For more information, see Chapter 4.

30. C.

C is the correct answer because Schedule Development generates a program schedule and a schedule management plan. A, B, and D are incorrect because these are not the names of standard processes in program management. For more information, see Chapter 5.

31. B.

B is the correct answer because the organizational chart is an output of the Human Resource Planning process. A and C are incorrect because the organizational chart is not an output of either of these processes. D is incorrect because there is no standard program process called Organizational Planning. For more information, see Chapter 5.

32. C.

C is the correct answer because make-or-buy decisions are an output of the Plan Program Purchases and Acquisitions process. A and B are incorrect because neither of these processes generate make-or-buy decisions as an output. D is incorrect because there is no standard program process called Procurement Planning. The correct name of the process is Plan Program Purchases and Acquisitions. For more information, see Chapter 5.

33. C.

C is the correct answer because the ADM can be used only to display finish-to-start dependencies, and the PDM can be used to display dependencies of any type: finish-to-start, finish-to-finish, start-to-start, or start-to-finish. **A and B** are incorrect because you can use either the ADM or the PDM to display finish-to-start dependencies. **D** is incorrect because there is no standard network diagramming method called the critical diagramming method. For more information, see Chapter 5.

34. C.

C is the correct answer because the program budget is an output of the Cost Estimating and Budgeting process. **A** is incorrect because there is no standard program process called develop program budget. **B and D** are incorrect because these processes do not generate the program budget as an output. For more information, see Chapter 5.

35. A.

A is the correct answer because this is the most suitable type of contract when you do not know the actual number of items that you will need to procure. **B** is incorrect because you do not know the actual amount of procurement at the time of the contract; so the most suitable contract is T&M. **C and D** are incorrect because you cannot calculate the lump sum or fixed price, as the actual amount of needed items is not known. For more information, see Chapter 5.

36. A.

A is the correct answer because the basic source of risks is uncertainty. **B, C, and D** are incorrect because the basic source of risks is uncertainty. For more information, see Chapter 6.

37. D.

D is the correct answer because issuing an RFI, RFP, and RFQ are part of the Request Seller Responses process. **A, B, and C** are incorrect answers because all these are parts of Communication Planning. For more information, see Chapter 6.

38. A.

A is the correct answer because the program scope statement and product description are inputs to Quality Planning. **B and C** are incorrect because operational definitions and quality checklists are outputs of Quality Planning. **D** is incorrect because the program cost of quality and quality metrics are outputs of Quality Planning. For more information, see Chapter 6.

39. B.

B is the correct answer because quality metrics are an output of Quality Planning. **A** is incorrect because quality metrics are an output of Quality Planning, and not an input. **C** is incorrect because quality metrics are input to Perform Quality Assurance. **D** is incorrect because quality metrics are an input to Perform Quality Assurance and not to Perform Quality Control. For more information, see Chapter 6.

40. C.

C is the correct answer because a risk response plan is an output of the Risk Management Planning and Analysis process. **A, B, and D** are incorrect because there are no standard program processes with these names. However, risk identification, qualitative risk analysis, and risk response planning are all parts of the same process called Risk Management Planning and Analysis. For more information, see Chapter 6.

41. A.

A is the correct answer because the contract statement of work is an output of the Plan Program Purchases and Acquisitions process. **B** is incorrect because the contract statement of work is an input to Plan Program Contracting. **C** is incorrect because the Develop Program Management Plan process does not generate a contract statement of work. **D** is incorrect because there is no standard program process called Develop Statement of Work. For more information, see Chapter 5.

42. B.

B is the correct answer because the procurement management plan is an input to Plan Program Contracting. **A** is incorrect because the procurement management plan is an output of Plan Program Purchases and Acquisitions. **C and D** are incorrect because the procurement management plan is not an input to these processes. For more information, see Chapter 5.

43. B.

B is the correct answer because phase three of the program life cycle is about establishing the infrastructure for the program. **A** is incorrect because Initiating is a process groups and not phase. **C** is incorrect because program setup is phase two (and not three) of the program life cycle. **D** is incorrect because pre-program setup is phase one (and not three) of the program life cycle. For more information, see Chapter 7.

44. A.

A is the correct answer because the Executing process group has only one process that belongs to Integration Management, and its name is Direct and Manage Program Execution. **B** is incorrect because Information Distribution belongs to Communication Management. **C** is incorrect because Develop Program Team belongs to Human Resource Management. **D** is incorrect because Perform Quality Assurance belongs to Quality Management. For more information, see Chapter 7.

45. D.

D is the correct answer because Cost Estimating and Budgeting belongs to the Planning process group. **A, B, and C** are incorrect because these processes belong to the Executing process group. For more information, see Chapter 7.

46. C.

C is the correct answer because the output items of the Develop Program Team process are team performance assessment, team improvement, updates to training records, and updates to team competency assessments. **A and D** are incorrect answers because the training plan and training records are input to the Develop Program Team process. **B** is an incorrect answer because the staffing management plan is an input to the Develop Program Team process. For more information, see Chapter 7.

47. B.

B is the correct answer because the Acquire Program Team process belongs to the Executing process group and the Human Resource Management knowledge area. **A** is incorrect because the team-related process in the Initiating process group is called Initiate Team. **C** is incorrect because there is no process group called Human Resource. There is a knowledge area called Human Resource Management. **D** is incorrect because the Planning process group does not contain the Acquire Program Team process. For more information, see Chapter 7.

48. A.

A is the correct answer because work results are an output of the Direct and Manage Program Execution process. **B, C, and D** are incorrect because work results are not an output of any of these processes. For more information, see Chapter 7.

49. D.

D is the correct answer because contract negotiations are conducted during the process of selecting sellers. **A** is incorrect because contract negotiations is not a standard too used in the Acquire Program Team process. **B** is incorrect because Contract Administration starts after we already have a contract. **C** is incorrect because the Request Seller Response process is too early for conducting contract negotiations. For more information, see Chapter 7.

50. B.

B is the correct answer because the recognition and reward system is a tool or technique used in the Develop Program Team process. **A and C** are incorrect because the recognition and reward system is not used during these processes. **D** is incorrect because there is no standard program process called Contract Negotiation. For more information, see Chapter 7.

51. A.

A is the correct answer because phase four of the program life cycle is called delivering incremental benefits. **B** is incorrect because Executing is a process group and not a phase. **C** is incorrect because program setup is phase two (and not phase four) of the program life cycle. **D** is incorrect because establish program infrastructure is phase three (and not phase four) of the program life cycle. For more information, see Chapter 8.

52. A.

A is the correct answer because the processes of the Monitoring and Controlling process group that map to Integration Management are Integrated Change Control, Monitor and Control Program Work, Resource Control, and Issue Management and Control. **B** is incorrect because Communication Control belongs to Communication Management. **C** is incorrect because Performance Reporting belongs to Communication Management. **D** is incorrect because program Contract Administration belongs to Procurement Management. For more information, see Chapter 8.

53. A.

A is the correct answer because Performance Reporting is part of the Monitoring and Controlling process group. **B** is incorrect because there is no process group called Communication; there is a knowledge area, however, called Communication Management. **C and D** are incorrect because the Performance Reporting process maps to neither the Executing process group nor the Integration Management knowledge area. For more information, see Chapter 8.

54. A.

A is the correct answer because Contract Administration is part of the Monitoring and Controlling process group. **B** is incorrect because there is no process group called Procurement; there is a knowledge area, however, called Procurement Management. **C and D** are incorrect because the Contract Administration process maps to neither the Executing process group nor the Integration Management knowledge area. For more information, see Chapter 8.

55. B.

B is the correct answer because expenditure reports are an output of the Resource Control process. **A, C, and D** are incorrect answers because all these are included in the input to the Resource Control process. For more information, see Chapter 8.

56. B.

B is the correct answer because forecasts are an output of the Monitor and Control Program Work process. **A and C** are incorrect because these processes do not have forecasts as an output. **D** is incorrect because there is no standard program process called Extrapolate Performance. For more information, see Chapter 8.

57. C.

C is the correct answer because closing the program is phase five of the program life cycle. **A and D** are incorrect because the program life cycle consists of five phases. **B** is incorrect because phase three of the program life cycle is establishing program infrastructure. For more information, see Chapter 9.

58. A.

A is the correct answer because the Closing process group consists of the Close Program, Component Closure, and Contract Closure processes. **B** is incorrect because there is no standard program process called Administrative Closure. **C** is incorrect because there is no standard program process called Transition Benefits. **D** is incorrect because there is no standard program process called Close Projects. For more information, see Chapter 9.

59. C.

C is the correct answer because the key outputs of the Close Program process include a final performance review report and program archives. A is incorrect because project archives are an output of the Component Closure process. B and D are incorrect because the contract completion certificate and contract termination documents are an output of the Contract Closure process. For more information, see Chapter 9.

60. D.

D is the correct answer because lessons learned from closing the constituent projects are an input to the Close Program process, and the lessons learned from the program are an output of the Close Program process. A and B are incorrect because lessons learned is not an output of the Contract Closure or the Component Closure process. C is incorrect because there is no standard program process called Final Performance Review. For more information, see Chapter 9.

Chapter 1

Project, Portfolio, and Program: Mind the Gap

LEARNING OBJECTIVES

- ✓ Basic concepts of project management
- ✓ The project life cycle: phases and process groups
- ✓ Project management knowledge areas
- ✓ Project stakeholders
- ✓ Influence of organizational structure on project management
- ✓ Influences of organizational environment on programs
- ✓ Relationships among projects, programs, and portfolios
- ✓ Matrix management

What do project management, portfolio management, and program management have in common? Projects! The basic building blocks that constitute these three disciplines of management are projects. So, it will only be appropriate to start the story of program management by introducing the concepts of projects and project management. Let's start with a simple question: Even given all the required material and the knowledge, how do people really build such immense and complex structures or systems as the Eiffel Tower, the Taj Mahal, and the Internet? The answer is again projects. Through projects, it is possible to build small and big, simple and complex things and systems in an effective and efficient manner. All projects, however, need to be managed. A so-called unmanaged project is simply a poorly managed project and is destined to fail. Therefore, the importance of project management cannot be overstated.

Managing a project means managing the life cycle of a project from the beginning (initiating) to the end (closing), and this is accomplished by using processes that constitute what are called project management *knowledge areas*. While you use your knowledge in terms of processes to manage the projects, the actual management will be greatly influenced by the environment (culture and structure) of the organization in which projects are performed.

Although this chapter is largely focused on providing an overview of project management, I'll be linking some aspects of project management to program management throughout this chapter. After all, the book is about program management. If you are already familiar with project management, you have the option of skipping this chapter. However, you may find it helpful to quickly skim through it—especially if you're more familiar with the practical realities than with the Project Management Institute's (PMI's) terminology. The main goal of this chapter is to present a bird's-eye view of project management before we embark on the subject of program management. To that end, we will explore three avenues: an overview of project management; relationships among projects, programs, and portfolios; and the relationship between project management and program management.

Basic Concepts and Definitions

Each discipline of knowledge builds upon some basic concepts and definitions, and project management is no exception. The terms that refer to or define these concepts make the language of the discipline.

Basic Definitions

Although the emphasis in this chapter is on project management, we also briefly explore the relationships between project management and program management, and the relationships between projects, programs, and portfolios. Therefore, very basic terms in project, portfolio, and program management are described briefly here.

Organization   A group of individuals organized to work for some purpose or mission. Computer companies, energy companies (to whom you pay your electric bills), and cable companies are examples of organizations. An organization may offer products such as books or donuts, or services such as Internet access or online banking. A project is usually performed inside an organization. Different organizations have different structures and cultures, which are discussed further on in this chapter due to their influence on project management and program management.

Project   This is a work effort made over a finite period of time with a start and a finish to create a unique product, service, or result. Because a project has a start and a finish, it is also called a temporary effort or endeavor.

Project stakeholder   This is an individual or an organization that can be positively or negatively affected by the project execution. A project may have a wide spectrum of stakeholders, from the project sponsor to an environmental activist who may oppose it, or a consumer-support group.

Process   This is a set of related tasks performed to manage a certain aspect of a project, such as controlling cost. Each process belongs to a knowledge area.

Management   This is the practice of directing, controlling, coordinating, and using resources, including human, financial, and technological resources to accomplish predetermined tasks with set goals and objectives.

Project management   This is the usage of knowledge, skills, and tools to manage a project from start to finish with the goal of meeting the project requirements. It involves using the appropriate processes.

Knowledge area   In project management a knowledge area is defined by its knowledge requirements related to managing a specific aspect of a project, such as cost, by using a set of processes. *A Guide to the Project Management Body of Knowledge*, also known as the *PMBOK Guide,* is a global standard set by the Project Management Institute (PMI) that recognizes a total of nine knowledge areas such as Cost Management and Human Resource Management.

Performing organization   This is the organization that is responsible for performing the project. In other words, the project work is mostly performed by the employees of the performing organization.

Portfolio   According to *The Standard for Portfolio Management* by PMI, a portfolio is a set of projects, programs, or both that is managed in a coordinated fashion to obtain control and benefits not available from managing them individually.

Portfolio management   This is the centralized management of one or more portfolios. It includes authorizing, controlling, identifying, managing, and prioritizing projects, programs, and other related work. The purpose is to obtain specific strategic business objectives.

Program   According to *The Standard for Program Management* by PMI, a program is a set of related projects managed in a coordinated fashion to obtain control and benefits that would not be available if those projects were managed individually. A program can also include non-project work.

Program management   This is the centralized coordinated management of a specific program to achieve its strategic goals, objectives, and benefits.

Project management office (PMO)   This refers to an entity in an organization that is responsible for providing centralized coordinated management and support for projects in the organization.

Program management office (PMO)   This refers to an entity in an organization that is responsible for providing centralized coordinated management for programs (including the projects in the program) of the organization.

> Although both have the same abbreviation, PMO, the project management office and the program management office are not identical. For example, only an organization that runs programs will have a program management office, whereas the organization that runs individual projects will have a project management office.

This is a minimal set of terms that you need to understand before we start. More terms will be introduced as we continue exploring program management. Now that you know the definitions of projects, programs, and portfolios, let's explore the relationships among these three concepts.

The Triplet Relationship: Project, Program, and Portfolio

The triplet relationship among portfolios, programs, and projects is shown in Figure 1.1, in which an arrow represents containment. As the figure illustrates, all portfolios are composed of programs, projects, or both. A program consists of only projects and not portfolios. The figure also illustrates that both a program and a portfolio can have projects. That means that a project may have membership in a portfolio directly or through a program.

As compared to projects and programs, a portfolio is closer to an organization's business objectives, and therefore this is where most of the investment decisions are made. If you want to learn about an organization's business intent and direction (or strategy), look at its portfolio.

It's also important to note that an operation is not part of a project. However, a program can include non-project work. Similarly, a portfolio can also include work that is not a part of any of its constituent projects and programs.

Now that you understand these basic terms, you can ask a very basic question: What does it mean to manage a project?

FIGURE 1.1 Triplet relationship between projects, programs, and portfolios

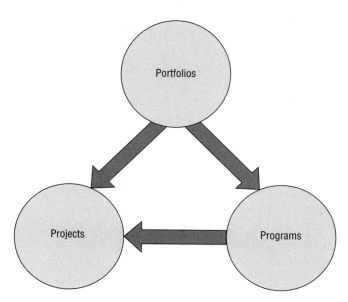

Introducing Project Management

At any organization there are lots of activities being executed every day. Most of these activities are organized into groups of interrelated activities. These groups fall into two categories: projects and operations. An operation is an ongoing and repetitive set of tasks, whereas a project has a life cycle: a beginning and an end.

What Is a Project?

A project is a work effort made over a finite period of time with a start and a finish to create a unique product, service, or result. Because a project has a start and a finish, it is also called a temporary effort or endeavor. In other words, as the *PMBOK Guide* states, a project is a temporary endeavor undertaken to create a unique product, service, or result.

So, a project has two defining characteristics: it is temporary and it creates a unique product. Let's explore further these two defining concepts.

Temporary The temporary nature of projects refers to the fact that each project has a definite beginning and a definite end. A project can reach its end in one of two ways:

- The project has met its objectives; that is, the planned unique product has been created.

- The project has been terminated before its successful completion for whatever reason.

The temporary nature of projects may also apply to two other aspects:

- The opportunity to market the product that the project will produce is temporary; that is, the product needs to be produced in a limited time frame—otherwise it will be too late.
- A project team is temporary; that is, the project team is disbanded after the project ends, and the team members may be individually assigned to other projects.

However, remember that the temporary nature of a project does not refer to the product it creates. The projects can create lasting products such as the Taj Mahal, the Eiffel Tower, or the Internet. The second defining characteristic of a project is that it must create a unique product.

Unique product   The outcome of a project must be a unique product, service, or result. How do product, service, and result differ from each other?

Product   This is a tangible quantifiable artifact that is either the end item or a component of it. The big-screen television set in your living room, the Swiss watch on your wrist, and a wine bottle on your table are some examples of products.

Service   When we say a project can create a service, we mean the capability to perform a service. For example, a project that creates a website for a bank to offer online banking has created the capability to offer online banking service.

Result   This is usually the knowledge-related outcome of a project; for example, the results of an analysis performed in a research project.

 Quite often I will refer to product, service, or result as just *product* for brevity.

Projects are organized to execute a set of activities that cannot be addressed within the limits of the organization's ongoing normal operations. To clearly identify if an undertaking is a project or not, you must understand the difference between a project and an operation.

Distinguishing Projects from Operations

An organization executes a multitude of activities as part of the work to achieve objectives. Some of these activities are to support projects and others are to support operations. An *operation* is a set of tasks that does not qualify as a project. In other words, an operation is a function that performs ongoing tasks: it does not produce a unique (new) product, it does not have a beginning and an end, or both. For example, to put a data center together is a project, but after you put it together, to keep it up and running is an operation.

It is important to understand that projects and operations share some characteristics, such as the following:

- Both require resources, including human resources (people).
- Both are constrained to limited, as opposed to unlimited, resources.
- Both are managed—that is, planned, executed, and controlled.
- Both have objectives.

The distinctions between the projects and operations can be made by sticking to the definition of a project: temporary and unique. Operations are generally ongoing and repetitive. Although both projects and operations have objectives, a project ends when its objectives are met, whereas an operation continues toward attaining a new set of objectives when the current set of objectives has been attained.

Projects may be performed at various levels of an organization; they vary in size, and accordingly may involve just one person or a team. Table 1.1 presents some examples of projects.

TABLE 1.1   Examples of Projects

Project	Outcome (product, service, or result)
Constructing the Taj Mahal	Product
Running a presidential-election campaign	Results: win or lose Products: documents
Developing a website to offer digital music downloads	Service
Setting up a computer network in a company	Service
Working on a research paper	Result: research results Product: research paper
Studying the genes of a group of politicians	Result: data or information Products: documents containing the data

A project, once completed, can leave behind it an operation. For example, constructing the Eiffel Tower is a project, whereas managing it for the tourists visiting it every day is an operation.

So, where do projects come from? In other words, how do you come up with a project? Sure, you have an idea, a concept of some final product, but how exactly do you write it down and declare that it is the project? A project is born and brought up through a procedure called progressive elaboration.

Progressive Elaboration

As the saying goes, Rome was not built in a day, and a project plan isn't either. Usually, first there is a concept and a broad vision for the end product—that is, the outcome of the project. The clearer a vision you have of the unique product that you want from the project, the more accurate the project plan will be. So, you move toward the project plan in incremental steps as the ideas about the final product are refined and as you get more and more information about the requirements in a progressive fashion. This procedure of defining (or planning) a project is called *progressive elaboration*.

Here is an example of progressive elaboration: You wake up one morning with an idea to close the digital gap in your community. You have a concept of the final product (result) of your project: close the digital gap in your community. But what do you really mean by that? It may include many things: build computers in an economical way and provide them at low prices to those who don't have them, raise awareness of the necessity of computer literacy, offer classes, and the like. So, now you are really working to refine your idea of the final product. The second question is, how are you going to do this? Here is where the project plan comes into play. You can see that the project plan and its accuracy and details depends upon how refined the idea of the final product is. The final product or objectives and the plan to achieve them will be developed further and further over the course of several steps.

Uncontrolled changes that make their way into the project without being properly processed are called *scope creep*. Do not confuse progressive elaboration with scope creep.

So, progressive elaboration, in general, means developing something in incremental steps. The project plan will be broadly defined to start with, and will get more accurate, detailed, and explicit in an incremental fashion as better understanding about the project deliverables and objectives develops.

Even after you have an approved final project plan and the project starts executing, progressive elaboration continues to some extent. For example, you will see further on in this chapter that the execution and planning stages of a project interact with each other. Each stage of a project is managed by performing a set of processes.

Processes

Processes are the heart of project management. If you want to think of project management like a project management professional does, think in terms of processes. Almost everything in the world of project management is done through processes.

So, what is a process, anyway? Well, back up a little and look around you; you will see processes everywhere, not only in project management. For example, when you make coffee in the morning, you go through a process. The water, the coffee filter, and the roasted hazelnut coffee made by grinding golden-colored beans are the input items to this process. The coffeemaker is the tool and how you made the coffee is the technique. A cup of freshly brewed hazelnut coffee is an output item from this process. So, a process is a set of interrelated activities performed to obtain a specified set of products, results, or services. A process, as explained in the example and in Figure 1.2, consists of three elements: input, tools and techniques, and output.

Of course, you can come up with other examples of processes that you have been using in your life without realizing it. In project management, you use processes to accomplish things such as develop a project schedule, direct and manage the project execution, and develop and manage the project team.

FIGURE 1.2   The three elements of a process: input, tools and techniques, and output

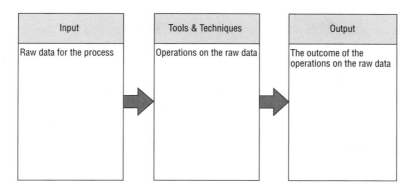

Input   The input to a process consists of the raw data that is needed to start the process. For example, the list of activities that need to be scheduled is one of several input items to the process that will be used to develop a project's schedule.

Tools and techniques   Tools and techniques are the methods that are used to operate on the input to transform it into output. For example, project management software that helps to develop a schedule is a tool used in the Schedule Development process.

Output   The output is the outcome or the result of a process. Each process contains at least one output item; otherwise there is no point in performing a process. For example, an output item of the Schedule Development process is, as you might guess, the project schedule.

Now that you understand what a process is, you can see that you will be using different processes at different stages of a project, such as Planning and Executing. Actually, the whole life cycle of a project can be understood in terms of five stages, with each stage corresponding to a group of processes.

Understanding the Project Life Cycle

From authorization to completion, a project goes through a whole life cycle that includes defining the project objectives, planning the work to achieve these objectives, performing the work, monitoring the progress, and closing the project after receiving the product acceptance. You can look at the life cycle of a project from two perspectives: product-oriented and process-oriented.

From the product-oriented perspective, the project life cycle is a sequence of project phases. A project phase is a project duration characterized by the completion and acceptance of one or more project deliverables. A *deliverable* is a work product that can be measured and verified, such as a design document, a feasibility study, or a computer program. Each phase can be initiated, planned, executed, controlled, and closed. A project may have one or more phases. What if a project has only one phase? Then the product-oriented view of the project life cycle is not very interesting. That's when it could be helpful to look at the project life cycle from the process-oriented perspective.

Exam Spotlight

The PMI standard adopts the product-oriented view of the project life cycle, and therefore defines the life cycle in terms of phases. However, remember that the overall project management approach adopted by PMI is process oriented.

From the process-oriented perspective, a project life cycle consists of Initiating, Planning, Executing, Controlling, and Closing. In a multiple-phase project you will need to go through these stages multiple times. These different process-oriented stages of the project life cycle are shown in Figure 1.3, where the arrows indicate the flow of information.

FIGURE 1.3   Each of the stages in a project's life cycle represents a process group.

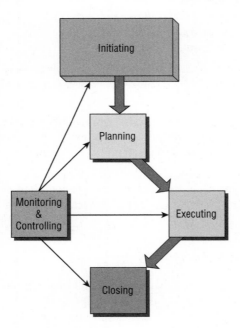

The five stages, called *process groups*, of a project life cycle are described in the following.

Initiating   This stage defines and authorizes the project. The project manager is named and the project is officially launched through a signed document called the *project charter*, which contains items such as the purpose of the project, a high-level product description, assumptions and constraints, a summary of the milestone schedule, and the business case for the project. Another document that is the outcome of this stage is called the *preliminary scope statement*, which describes the characteristics and boundaries of the project. The processes used to perform this stage fall into the Initiating process group.

Table 1.2 presents the processes in the Initiating process group, along with their major outputs.

TABLE 1.2　Processes in the Initiating Process Group

Knowledge Area	Process	Major Output
Integration Management	1. Develop Project Charter 2. Develop Preliminary Project Scope Statement	1. Project charter 2. Preliminary project scope statement

Planning　In this stage, the project manager and the project management team refine the project objectives and requirements and develop the project management plan. This is a collection of several plans that, taken together, constitute a course of action required to achieve the objectives and meet the requirements of the project. The project scope is finalized with the project scope statement. The project management plan, the outcome of this stage, contains subsidiary plans such as the project scope management plan, the schedule management plan, and the quality management plan. The processes used to perform this stage fall into the Planning process group.

Table 1.3 presents the project management processes in the Planning process group, along with their major outputs.

TABLE 1.3　Project Management Processes in the Planning Process Group

Knowledge Area	Process	Major Output
Integration Management	1. Develop Project Charter 2. Develop Preliminary Project Scope Statement	1. Project charter 2. Preliminary Project Scope Statement
Scope Management	1. Scope Planning 2. Scope Definition 3. Create WBS	1. Project scope management plan 2. Project scope statement 3. Work breakdown structure (WBS)
Time Management	1. Activity Definition 2. Activity Sequencing 3. Activity Resource Estimating 4. Activity Duration Estimating 5. Schedule Development	1. Activity list 2. Schedule network diagrams that display the dependencies among the activities 3. Activity duration estimates 4. Project schedule
Cost Management	1. Cost Estimating 2. Cost Budgeting	1. Activity cost estimates 2. Cost baseline (budget with a timeline)

TABLE 1.3   Project Management Processes in the Planning Process Group *(continued)*

Knowledge Area	Process	Major Output
Quality Management	Quality Planning	Quality management plan
Human Resource Management	Human Resource Planning	Staffing management plan and roles and responsibilities
Communication Management	Communication Planning	Communication management plan
Risk Management	1. Risk Management Planning 2. Risk Identification 3. Qualitative Risk Analysis 4. Quantitative Risk Analysis 5. Risk Response Planning	1. Risk management plan 2. Risk register—contains the list of risks 3. Updates to risk register 4. Updates to risk register 5. Updates to risk register and risk-related contractual agreements
Procurement Management	1. Plan Purchases and Acquisitions 2. Plan Contracting	1. Procurement management plan and contract statement of work 2. Procurement documents

Executing   In this stage, the project manager implements the project management plan and the project team performs the work scheduled in the planning stage. You coordinate all the activities being performed to achieve the project objectives and meet the project requirements. Of course, the main output of this project is the project deliverables. Approved changes, recommendations, and defect repairs are also implemented in this stage. But where do these changes and recommendations come from? They arise from monitoring and controlling the project. The stakeholders can also suggest changes, which must go through an approval process before implementation. The project execution is performed by using the processes that fall into the Executing process group.

Table 1.4 presents the project management processes in the Executing process group, along with their major outputs.

TABLE 1.4   Processes in the Executing Process Group

Knowledge Area	Process	Major Output
Integration Management	Direct and Manage Project Execution	Deliverables and work-performance information

TABLE 1.4   Processes in the Executing Process Group *(continued)*

Knowledge Area	Process	Major Output
Quality Management	Perform Quality Assurance	Change requests and recommendations for corrective actions
Human Resource Management	1. Acquire Project Team 2 .Develop Project Team	1. Project staff assignments 2. Team-performance assessment
Communication Management	Information Distribution	Project reports and lessons-learned documentation
Procurement Management	1. Request Seller Responses 2. Select Sellers	1. Qualified-sellers list and proposals 2. Selected sellers and contract management plan

Monitoring and Controlling   You monitor and control the project throughout its life cycle, including the Executing stage. Monitoring and controlling includes defending the project against scope creep (unapproved changes to the project scope), monitoring the project progress and performance to identify variance from the plan, and recommending preventive and corrective actions to bring the project in line with the planned expectations. Requests for changes, such as change to the project scope, are also included in this stage; these requests can come from you or from any other project stakeholder. The changes must go through an approval process and only the approved changes are implemented. The processes used in this stage fall into the Monitoring and Controlling process group.

Table 1.5 presents the project management processes in the Monitoring and Controlling process group, along with their major outputs.

TABLE 1.5   Project Management Processes in the Monitoring and Controlling Process Group

Knowledge Area	Process	Major Output
Integration Management	1. Integrated Change Control 2. Monitor and Control Project Work	1. Approvals and rejections of change requests 2. Forecasts and change requests
Scope Management	1. Scope Verification 2. Scope Control	1. Change requests 2. Change requests and scope update

TABLE 1.5   Project Management Processes in the Monitoring and Controlling Process Group *(continued)*

Knowledge Area	Process	Major Output
Time Management	Schedule Control	Performance measurements, change requests, and schedule update
Cost Management	Cost Control	Performance measurements, change requests, and cost update
Quality Management	Perform Quality Control	Quality control measurements, change requests, and quality baseline updates
Human Resource Management	Manage Project Team	Change requests
Communication Management	1. Performance Reporting 2. Manage Stakeholders	1. Performance reports and forecasts 2. Issue resolutions
Risk Management	Risk Monitoring and Control	Change requests and risk register updates
Procurement Management	Contract Administration	Contract documentation and change requests

Closing   In this stage, you manage the formal acceptance of the project product, close any contracts involved, and bring the project to an end by disbanding the project team. Closing the project includes project review for lessons learned, and possibly turning over the outcome of the project to another group, such as the maintenance or operations group. Don't forget the last but not the least task of the Closing stage: celebration. The terminated projects (that is, the projects cancelled before completion) should also go through the Closing stage. The processes used to perform the closing stage fall into the Closing process group.

Table 1.6 presents the project management processes in the Closing process group, along with their major outputs.

TABLE 1.6   Project Management Processes in the Closing Process Group

Knowledge Area	Process	Major Output
Integration Management	Close Project	Final deliverable: product, service, or result
Procurement Management	Contract Closure	Closure of contracts

Remember that what we refer to as *project stages* here are not the project phases. A *project phase* is part of the whole project in which certain milestones or project deliverables are completed. All these stages can be applied to any phase of a project that is divided into phases.

Table 1.7 presents a summary of the project life cycle. The Initiating stage authorizes a project by naming the project manager, the Planning stage further defines the project objectives and plans the work to meet those objectives, the Executing stage executes the work, the Monitoring and Controlling stage monitors the progress of the project and controls it to keep it in line with the plan, and the Closing stage formally closes the project by obtaining product acceptance. Each of these stages is performed by using a group of processes, and so these stages are called *process groups*.

TABLE 1.7   The Stages of a Project Life Cycle: The Project Process Groups

Stage (Process Group)	Main Goal	Main Output
Initiating	Authorize the project	Project charter and preliminary project scope statement
Planning	Plan and schedule the work to perform the project	Project management plan that contains subsidiary plans, such as scope management plan and schedule management plan
Executing	Perform the project work	Project deliverables: product, service, and results
Monitoring and Controlling	Monitor the progress of the project to identify the variance from the plan and to correct it	Change requests and recommendations for preventive and corrective actions
Closing	Close the project formally	Product acceptance and contract closure

Like project management, program management has five process groups with the same names. However, a process group with the same name in project management and program management does not necessarily have an identical set of processes. Furthermore, if two processes in program management and project management have the same name, they are still different processes performed at different management levels.

The stages of a project life cycle determine when a process is executed, whereas the processes themselves belong to certain knowledge areas of project management.

Understanding Project Management Knowledge Areas

Managing projects means applying knowledge, skills, and tools and techniques to project activities to meet the project objectives. You do this by performing some processes at various stages of the project discussed in the previous section. That means processes are part of the knowledge required to manage projects. Each aspect of a project is managed by using the corresponding knowledge area. For example, each project has a scope that needs to be managed, and the knowledge required to manage scope is in the knowledge area called project Scope Management. To perform the project work within the project scope you need human resources; these resources need to be managed, and the knowledge area used to manage human resources is called Human Resource Management. You get the idea. Each process belongs to one of the nine knowledge areas discussed in the following.

The first few process groups are discussed in more detail than the others. You can always consult the PMBOK Guide for details.

Project Scope Management   The primary purpose of the project Scope Management knowledge area is to ensure that all the required work and only the required work is performed to complete the project successfully. This is accomplished by defining and controlling what is included in the project and what is not. To be specific, project Scope Management includes the following:

Scope plan   Develop the project scope management plan that describes how the project scope will be defined and controlled, and how at the end it will be verified that all the work within the scope has been completed. This is accomplished by using the Scope Planning process.

Scope definition   Develop the detailed project scope statement, which forms the basis for the project scope. This is accomplished by using the Scope Definition process.

Work breakdown structure (WBS)   Decompose the project deliverables into more-manageable smaller work components. The outcome of this exercise is called the work breakdown structure. This is done by using the Create WBS process.

Scope control   Control changes to the project scope: only the approved changes to the scope should be implemented. This is accomplished by using the Scope Control process.

Scope verification   Plan how the completed deliverables of the project will be accepted. Scope verification is planned by using the Scope Planning process and is performed by using the Scope Verification process.

So, the project scope management, in part, defines the work required to complete the project. It's a finite amount of work and will need a finite amount of time, which needs to be managed as well.

Project Time Management   The primary purpose of the Project Time Management knowledge area is to develop and control the project schedule. This is accomplished by performing the following components and their corresponding processes:

Activity definition   Identify all the work activities that need to be scheduled to produce the project deliverables.

Activity sequencing   Identify the dependencies among the activities that need to be scheduled (that is, the schedule activity) so that they can be scheduled in the right order.

Activity resource estimating   For each schedule activity, estimate the types of resources and the quantity for each type.

Activity duration estimating   Estimate the time needed to complete each schedule activity.

Schedule development   Analyze the data created in the previous steps to develop the schedule.

Schedule control   Control changes to the project schedule.

You perform these tasks by using the corresponding processes. It will cost you to get the activities in the schedule completed, and the cost needs to be managed too.

Project Cost Management   The primary goal of project Cost Management is to estimate the cost and to complete the project within the approved budget. Accordingly, the Cost Management knowledge area includes the following components:

Cost estimating   Develop the cost of the resources needed to complete the project, including schedule activities and outsourced work.

Cost budgeting   Aggregate the costs of individual activities to establish a cost baseline.

Cost control   Monitor and control the cost variance in the project execution; that is, the difference between the planned cost and actual cost during execution, and changes to the project budget.

You will use the appropriate processes to accomplish these tasks. The resources needed to complete the project activities include human resources, which need to be managed, as well.

Project Human Resource Management   The primary purpose of the project Human Resource Management knowledge area is to obtain, develop, and manage the project team that will perform the project work. To be specific, project Human Resource Management includes the following components:

Planning human resources   Identify project roles, responsibilities of each role, and reporting relationships among the roles. Also, create the staff management plan that describes when and how the resource requirements will be met.

Acquiring project team   Obtain the human resources.

Developing project team   Improve the competencies of the team members and interaction among them to optimize the team performance.

Managing project team   Track the performance of team members, provide them feedback, and resolve issues and conflicts: all with the goal of enhancing performance; that is, to complete the project in time and within the planned cost and scope.

These components are performed by using the corresponding processes. There will be situations when your organization does not have the expertise to perform certain schedule activities in-house. For this or other reasons, you might want to outsource some of the project work; this outsourcing is called *procurement*, which also needs to be managed.

Project Procurement Management   The primary purpose of the Procurement Management knowledge area is to manage acquiring products (that is products, services, or results) from outside the project team to complete the project. The external vendor that offers the service is called the *seller*. The procurement management includes planning acquisitions, planning contracts with the sellers, selecting sellers, administering contracts with the sellers, and closing contracts. You use the corresponding processes to accomplish these tasks.

Be it procured or in-house work, there are always some uncertainties, which give rise to project risks; these also need to be managed.

Project Risk Management   A *project risk* is an event that if it occurs will have a positive or negative effect on meeting the project objectives. The primary purpose of the Project Risk Management knowledge area is to identify the risks and respond to them should they occur. To be specific, project risk management includes the following:

- Plan the risk management; that is, determine how to plan and execute the risk management tasks.
- Identify risks.
- Perform risk analysis.
- Develop a risk response plan; that is, what action to take should a risk occur.
- Monitor and control risks; that is, track the identified risks, identify new risks, and implement the risk response plan.

These tasks related to risk management are performed by using the corresponding processes. The goal of risk management is to help meet the project objectives. The degree to which the project objectives and requirements are met is called quality, which needs to be managed.

Project Quality Management   *Project quality* is defined as the degree to which a project satisfies its objectives and requirements. For example, a high-quality project is one that is completed in time and all the work in the project scope is completed within the planned budget. The project Quality Management knowledge area includes the following:

- Perform quality planning; that is, determine which quality standards are relevant to the project at hand and how to apply them.

- Perform quality assurance; that is, ensure the planned quality standards are applied.

- Perform quality control; that is, monitor specific project results to ensure they comply with the planned quality standards, and recommend actions to eliminate the causes of unsatisfactory progress.

These tasks of the project Quality Management knowledge area are performed by using the corresponding processes. In order to unify different pieces into a whole project, the different project management activities need to be integrated.

Project Integration Management   A project is planned and executed in pieces, and all those pieces are related to each other and need to come together. That is where integration management comes in. For example, integrating different subsidiary plans into a project management plan needs to be managed. The project Integration Management knowledge area includes developing the project management plan, directing and managing project execution, monitoring and controlling the project work, and closing the project.

So, while managing all the aspects of the project, you, the project manager, will need to coordinate among different activities and groups, and for that you need to communicate.

Project Communication Management   It is absolutely imperative for the success of the project that the project information in generated and distributed in a timely fashion. Communication is the most important aspect of a project and the most important skill for a project manger to have. The Communication Management knowledge area includes the following:

- Plan communication; that is, determine the information and communication needs of the project at hand.

- Distribute needed information to the project stakeholders in a timely fashion.

- Report project performance, including the project status.

- Communicate to resolve issues among the stakeholders.

As you have seen, managing a project largely means performing a set of processes at various stages of the project, such as Initiating and Planning. Accordingly, processes are grouped corresponding to these stages, and these groups are called process groups. Processes are part of the knowledge required to manage projects. So, each of these processes belongs to one of the nine knowledge areas identified in the *PMBOK Guide*. So, a process has a dual membership: one in a process group indicating at what stage of the project the process is performed, and the other in a knowledge area indicating what aspect of the project is managed by using the process. Table 1.8 shows this membership for all the processes identified in the *PMBOK Guide*.

In the parentheses next to each process name in Table 1.8 there appears the letter *Y* or *N*; *Y* indicates that a process with the same name also exists in program management, and *N* means that there is no process in program management with an identical name. The processes with identical names in project management and program management reflect how closely related program management and project management are. However, as noted earlier, having two identically named processes in project management and program management does not mean that they represent one and same process. It means that there are similar tasks to be performed at different levels of management: the program level and the constituent projects level.

TABLE 1.8   Mapping of the Project Management Processes to Process Groups and Knowledge Areas.

Process Groups	Knowledge Areas				
	Initiating	Planning	Executing	Monitoring and Controlling	Closing
Integration Management	1. Develop Project Charter (N) 2. Develop Preliminary Project Scope Statement (N)	Develop Project Management Plan (N)	Direct and Manage Project Execution (N)	1. Monitor and Control Project Work (N) 2. Integrated Change Control (Y)	Close Project (N)
Human Resource Management	—	Human Resource Planning (Y)	1. Acquire Project Team (N) 2. Develop Project Team (N)	Manage Project Team (N)	—
Scope Management	—	1. Scope Planning (N) 2. Scope Definition (Y) 3. Create WBS (N)	—	1. Scope Verification (N) 2. Scope Control (Y)	—
Time Management	—	1. Activity Definition (N) 2. Activity Sequencing (N) 3. Activity Resource Estimating (N) 4. Activity Duration Estimating (N) 5. Schedule Development (Y)	—	Schedule Control (Y)	—
Cost Management	—	1. Cost Estimating (N) 2. Cost Budgeting (N)	—	Cost Control (Y)	—

TABLE 1.8   Mapping of the Project Management Processes to Process Groups and Knowledge Areas. *(continued)*

Process Groups	Knowledge Areas				
	Initiating	Planning	Executing	Monitoring and Controlling	Closing
Procurement Management	—	1. Plan Purchases And Acquisitions (N) 2. Plan Contracting (N)	1. Request Seller Responses (Y) 2. Select Sellers (Y)	Contract Administration (N)	Contract closure (Y)
Quality Management	—	Quality Planning (Y)	Perform Quality Assurance (Y)	Perform Quality Control (Y)	—
Risk Management	—	1. Risk Management Planning (N) 2. Risk Identification (N) 3. Qualitative Risk Analysis (N) 4. Risk Response Planning (N)	—	Risk Monitoring and Control (Y)	—
Communication Management	—	Communication Planning (Y)	Information Distribution (Y)	1. Performance Reporting (Y) 2. Managing Stakeholders (N)	—

Not all the processes are used in all projects. The project management team decides which processes need to be used for the project at hand.

Figure 1.4 shows the big picture of project management: the project, the processes, the project life cycle in terms of project stages, and the project aspects managed by different knowledge areas.

There are nine important aspects of projects, each of which is managed by using the corresponding knowledge area. For example, cost is managed by using the Cost Management knowledge area, and communication is managed by using the Communication Management knowledge area.

Each project is performed by some individuals and it can also affect some individuals or organizations, even if they are not directly (officially) involved in the projects. Now we are talking about the project stakeholders.

FIGURE 1.4   The big picture of project management: the aspects of a project that need to be managed at different stages of the project life cycle by using the processes

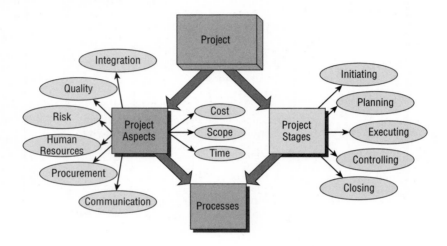

Introducing Project Stakeholders

From the day a project gets into your court, you start meeting a very special class of people called *project stakeholders*. It is very important for the success of the project that you identify these individuals and communicate with them effectively throughout the project.

Identifying Project Stakeholders

Project stakeholders are individuals and organizations whose interests are affected (positively or negatively) by the project execution and completion. In other words, a project stakeholder has something to gain or lose from the project. Accordingly, the stakeholders fall into two categories: *positive stakeholders* who will normally benefit from the success of the project, and *negative stakeholders* who see some kind of disadvantage coming from the project. The implications, obviously, are that the positive stakeholders would like to see the project succeed and the negative stakeholders' interests will be better served if the project is delayed or canceled altogether. For example, your city mayor may be a positive stakeholder in a project to open a megastore such as Safeway or Target in your neighborhood because it brings business to the city, whereas some local business leaders may look at it as a threat to the local businesses and thereby may act as negative stakeholders.

Negative stakeholders are often overlooked by the project manager and the project team, which increases the project risk. Ignoring positive or negative project stakeholders will have a damaging impact on the project. Therefore, it's important that you, the project manager, start identifying the project stakeholders early on in the project. The different project stakeholders may have different and conflicting expectations that you need to analyze and manage.

Identifying all the project stakeholders may be a difficult task, but the following are the obvious ones, starting with you:

Project manager   To start with, include the project manager in the list of the project stakeholders.

Project management office (PMO)   If your organization has a PMO and it is directly or indirectly responsible for the outcome of a project, then the PMO is a stakeholder in that project.

Project management team   These are the members of the project team involved in the project management tasks.

Project team members   The members of the project team that are actually performing the project work are also among the project stakeholders.

Performing organization   The organization whose employees are doing the project work is a stakeholder organization.

Customer/user   These include the individual or the organization for whom the project is being performed and the users that will use the product that will result from a successful completion of the project.

Project sponsor   This is the individual or group that provides financial resources for the project.

Influencers   These are the individuals or groups that are not direct customers or users of the product or service that will come from the project but that can influence the course of the project due to their positions in the customer organization or the performing organization. The influence can be positive or negative—that is, for or against the project.

In addition to these key stakeholders, there can be a number of other stakeholders inside and outside of your organization that may be less obvious to identify. These, depending upon the project, may include investors, sellers, contractors, family members of the project team members, government agencies, media outlets, lobbying organizations, individual citizens, and society at large. Have I left anyone out?

 We will revisit the topic of stakeholders in Chapter 2, "The Program Management Framework," in the context of program management. There will be stakeholders at the program level that are not dealt with at the constituent project level.

It is critical for the success of the project that you identify positive and negative stakeholders early on in the project, understand and analyze their varying and conflicting expectations, and manage those expectations throughout the project.

The Project Manager: A Special Stakeholder

The project manager is a very special project stakeholder. The job (role) of a project manager is extremely challenging and therefore exciting. With the help of the team, it is the project manager's responsibility to bring all the pieces together and make the project happen. The project manager does that by using a multitude of skills, described here.

Communication   The importance of communication in project (and program) management cannot be overemphasized. Even a well-scheduled and well-funded project in the hands of a hard-working team of experts can fail due to the lack of proper communication.

You will be communicating throughout the project. So, for a given project you must develop a communication strategy that should address the following issues:

- What needs to be communicated?
- With whom do you want to communicate? You may need to communicate different items to different individuals or groups.
- How do you want to communicate? That is, what is the medium of communication? Again, this may differ depending on who you are communicating with.
- What is the outcome of your communication? You need to monitor your communication and its results to see what works and what does not, and thereby to improve the communication.

Communication is an ingredient in many other skills, such as negotiation and problem solving.

Negotiation   A negotiation is give-and-take with the goal of generating a win-win outcome for both parties. You, the project manager, may need to negotiate at any stage of the project life cycle. Here are some examples of negotiations:

- Negotiating with the stakeholders regarding the expectations during project planning. For example, the suggested deadline for the project schedule may not be practical, or you may need a certain type or quantity of resources to make that happen.
- Negotiating with the functional managers for obtaining human resources such as software developers.
- Negotiating with the team members for specific job assignments and possibly during conflict resolution among the team members.
- Negotiating the changes to the project schedule, budget, or both because a stakeholder proposed changes to the project objectives.
- Negotiating with the external vendors in procurement. However, in the contract negotiations, representatives from the legal department may be involved.

Sometimes you will be negotiating to solve a problem.

Problem solving   The project-related problems may occur among the stakeholders (including team members) or with the projects. Either way, they are there to damage the project. So, your task is two-pronged: identify the problem early enough and solve it. Here is the general technique for accomplishing this:

1.   Look for the early warning signs by paying close attention to the formal progress reports, and to what the team members say and do regarding the project.

2.   Once you identify a potential problem, do your homework: understand and identify the problem clearly by collecting more information without passing judgment.

3.   Once the problem and its causes are clearly identified, work with the appropriate stakeholders such as project team members to explore multiple (alternative) solutions.

4.   Evaluate the multiple solutions and choose the solution that you will implement.

The key point throughout the problem-solving process is to focus on the problem, and not on the individuals, with the goal of finding the solution to help the project succeed—no finger-pointing.

Sometimes in choosing and implementing the correct solution you will need to exercise your influencing skill.

Influencing   Influencing means getting individuals or groups to do what you want them to do without necessarily having a formal power over them. This is increasingly becoming an essential management skill in today's information economy. In order to exercise influence, you must understand the formal and informal structure of your organization. Again, you may need to use influencing when dealing with any aspect of the project; for example, controlling the changes to the project, negotiating schedule or resource assignments, resolving conflicts, and the like.

Leadership   In the traditional organizational structure, project managers do not have formal authority over the project team members who perform the team work. So you have no other choice than to manage by leadership and not by authority (power). The good news is that managing by leadership is overall more effective and productive than managing by authority. A project team is generally a group of individuals coming together for the lifetime of the project from different functional groups with different skills and experience. They need a leader to show them the vision and excite, inspire, and motivate them toward the goals and the objectives of the project, and you, the project manager, are that leader.

Different organizations have different attitudes and policies toward project management. The structure of the performing organization has a big influence on your job as a project manager.

Influences of Organizational Structures on Projects

A project is typically performed inside an organization, called the *performing organization*. Therefore projects are influenced by many characteristics of the performing organization, such as culture, style, organizational structure, and maturity of the organization.

From the perspective of a project, there are two kinds of organizations: project-based and non-project-based. The project based organizations fall into two subcategories: those that derive their revenue primarily from performing projects for others, and those that do in-house projects to deliver products or services for their own customers. Project-based organizations are well aware of the importance of project management and generally have systems to support project management. The non-project-based organizations generally have a low appreciation and understanding of the importance of project management and often lack systems to support project management.

To do your job efficiently and effectively, you must figure out what kind of organization you are in. Another huge factor that greatly influences the projects and the management is the organizational structure. From the perspective of structure, the organizations fall into three categories: functional organizations, projectized organizations, and matrix organizations.

Functional Organization

A *functional* organization is one that has a traditional organizational structure in which each functional department (such as development, marketing, and sales) is a separate entity. As shown in Figure 1.5, the members of each department (staff) report to the functional manager of that department, and the functional manager in turn reports to an executive, such as the chief executive officer (CEO). Depending on the size of the organization, there could be a hierarchy within the Functional Managers layer shown in the figure; for example, directors of development, QA, and IT operations reporting to the vice president (VP) of engineering, who in turn reports to the CEO.

The scope of a project in a functional organization is usually limited to the boundaries of the functional department. Therefore, each department runs its projects largely independent of other departments. When a communication needs to occur between two departments it is carried through the hierarchy of functional managers.

All the managerial power (authority) in a functional organization is vested in the functional managers, who control the team members' performance evaluations, salary, bonus, hiring, and firing. Project managers are held responsible for the project results even though they have little say over resource assignments and holding team members accountable for their work. As a result, project managers in a functional organization are often frustrated. Their work is, at best, challenging. You, as a project manager in a functional organization, can benefit greatly by maintaining good relationships with functional managers and team members. So, networking and leadership are the key points to your success in a functional organization.

A project manager in a functional organization has the following attributes:

- Part-time (also with part-time project team), that is, the project manager and the project team both can be part-time.

- Little or no authority over anything: resource assignments, team members, and the like

- Reports directly to a functional manager

- Little or no administrative staff to help the project

In functional organizations, a project manager may be called something else, such as a project coordinator or a team leader.

On the other end of the spectrum is the projectized organization.

FIGURE 1.5   An example of the structure of a functional organization. Ovals represent staff involved in a project.

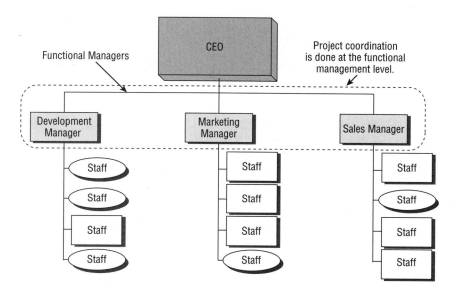

Projectized Organization

A *projectized* organization is one whose structure is organized around projects. Most of the organization's resources are devoted to the projects. As shown in Figure 1.6, the project team members report directly to the project manager, who has a great deal of independence and authority. So along with responsibility comes the high level of autonomy over the projects. The project managers in a projectized organization are happy campers. A functional organization and a projectized organization are on the opposite ends of the spectrum of a project manager's authority.

A project manager in a projectized organization has the following attributes:

- Full-time
- Full authority over the project team
- Full-time administrative staff to help the project

In the middle of the spectrum is the matrix organization.

Matrix Organization

A matrix organization is organized into functional departments, but a project is run by a project team with members coming from different functional departments, as shown in Figure 1.7. On the spectrum of a project manager's authority, matrix organizations are between two extremes: functional and projectized organizations. Matrix organizations are generally categorized into *strong matrix*, which is closer to a projectized structure, *weak matrix*, which is closer to functional structure; and *balanced matrix*, which is between strong and weak.

FIGURE 1.6   An example of the structure of a projectized organization. Ovals represent staff involved in a project under a given project manager.

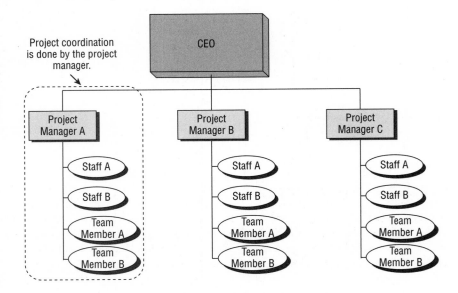

FIGURE 1.7   An example of the structure of a matrix organization. Ovals represent staff involved in a project.

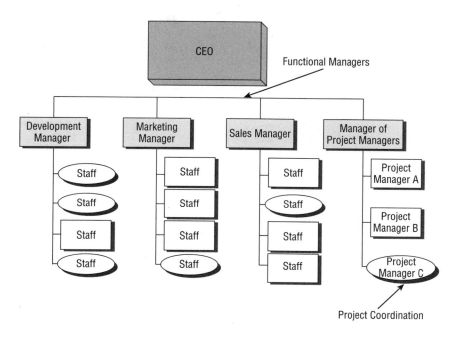

The influences of the different organizational structures on the projects are summarized in Table 1.9.

TABLE 1.9   Influences of the Organizational Structures on Projects

Project characteristic	Organizational Structure		
	Functional	**Matrix**	**Projectized**
Project manager's authority	None to low	Low to high	High to full
Project manager's role	Part-time	Part-time to full-time	Full-time
Project management administrative staff	None to part-time	Part-time to full-time	Full-time
Project budget controlled by:	Functional manager	Functional manager, project manager, or both	Project manager
Resource availability	Low	Limited to high	High to full

So, you have learned how the five process groups (the different stages in the project life cycle), and nine project management knowledge areas constitute the project management framework. The actual implementation of project management is greatly influenced by the facts on the ground; the organizational structure, for example. Throughout this book, you will be exploring the details of project management and getting introduced to some advanced concepts up front will make that journey more pleasant and smoother. The management in a matrix organization is called matrix management, which is further discussed later on in this chapter.

The organizational structures and culture influence the programs in very much the same way as they influence the projects.

Influences of Organizational Culture and Structure on Programs

Both projects and programs are affected by the organizational culture and structures.

Influence of Organizational Culture

Each organization often develops its own unique culture that depends on many factors, such as the application area of the organization and the general management philosophy implemented in the organization. The organizational culture includes the following elements:

Work environment   The organizational culture is reflected in work ethics and work hours. For example, do the employees work strictly from 8:00 AM to 5:00 PM, or do they work late into the night and on weekends?

Management style   Do the managers manage by authority or by leadership? How much feedback is taken from the employees in making management decisions? How do the employees view the authority of the management?

Policies   The organizational policies and procedures also reflect the organizational culture. For example, they can reflect how formal or informal the work environment is and how much room there is for entrepreneurship and innovation.

Values   A significant part of organizational culture lives in the set of values, norms, beliefs, and expectations shared within the organization. For example, a nonprofit organization will have different values than a for-profit organization. One organization may encourage an entrepreneurial approach while another organization may be rigidly hierarchical and take an authoritarian approach in making decisions on what to do and what not to do.

Organizational culture influences multiple aspects of a program, including the following:

Program and project selection   The organizational culture will creep into the selection criteria for program and projects. For example, a rigidly hierarchical and authoritarian organization may not be very adaptive to programs and projects with high risk.

Program management style   The program manager should adapt his management style to the organizational culture. For example, an authoritarian style may run into problems in an entrepreneurial organization that has a participative culture.

Team performance assessments   While making the team-performance assessment the program manager should keep in mind the established norms and expectations within the organization.

Program policies and procedures   The program policies and procedures will be influenced by the organizational policies and procedures because the two should be consistent with each other.

   The organizational structure also influences the programs.

Influence of Organizational Structure

The influences of different organizational structures on a program are very much the same as on projects, discussed in a previous section. For example, a program manager will have the least authority in a functional organization and the greatest authority in a projectized organization. Other aspects of a program that are influenced by the organizational structure and environment include the following:

Benefits realization plan   A program is run to create a set of benefits. The benefits realization plan describes those benefits and determines how those benefits will be achieved. Obviously this plan will be influenced by the organizational structure and culture. For example, the organizational structure may influence the way in which the benefits will be achieved. So, a program manager should adapt the benefits realization plan to the organizational environment.

Program governance   Some aspects of program governance are also influenced by the organizational structure. For example, in a functional organization some project managers may be directly reporting to a functional manager rather than to the program manager.

   The projectized organizational structure is the most suitable structure to run programs. However, there is always some matrix management built into a program.

Matrix Management

Management of a matrix team is called *matrix management*. A matrix team is a team of individuals from different groups and departments. For example, a project manager in a matrix organization will most often be managing a matrix team, and the project management in that matrix environment is an example of matrix management.

   Matrix management can be challenging due to the following:

- It involves managing individuals from different departments and groups with different and sometimes conflicting agendas.
- Quite often it requires leading by example rather than by authority.

   Matrix management has its advantages and disadvantages.

Advantages of Matrix Management

The following are the some of the advantages of matrix management:

Information sharing   In a matrix team, members can share information and work together without the functional boundaries (that is, the management boundaries) between different functional departments.

Organizational synergy   It facilitates interaction among employees from different departments, and if properly managed, this interaction can help develop organizational synergy, which in turn contributes to the success of the organization.

Resource optimization   In a matrix management environment the resources from across different departments are allocated to accomplish a task or project. This allows optimal use of resources.

Career opportunities   In a matrix environment, the employees are exposed to multiple tasks and opportunities. It can help employees to transition to a different career path within the same organization.

Of course, there is the other side of this coin too.

Disadvantages of Matrix Management

Disadvantages of matrix management include the following:

Confusion   In a matrix management environment, quite often employees report (informally or formally) to different managers. For example, an employee working on three projects will report her work progress to three project managers, and yet her functional manager will be largely responsible in assessing her performance and determining bonuses, etc. So, employees can get confused about their loyalties. However, this problem can be solved through proper management.

Functional gap   There is always a cultural and methodological gap between different functional departments of the same organization. Team members from different departments will have different perspectives on the project, and even different lingo. These differences, if not properly managed, can lead to misunderstandings and conflicts and thereby decrease the team productivity. This problem can be prevented or solved through team-development and conflict-resolution techniques.

Different objectives   Team members from different departments may have different objectives and priorities. So, it's very important that the project manager keep the project team focused on the big picture and the project members on their specific assignments. It is also important that the team members interact with each other in a constructive way and try to understand and respect their objectives. In other words, communication becomes even more important.

Matrix Management in a Program

In a previous section we explored the relevance and implications of matrix management for projects. How about programs? Programs by their definition support matrix management; that is, matrix management to some extent is built into the definition of programs. A program is run to meet some strategic business objectives of an organization. A program needs individuals with different functional expertise, such as engineering, marketing, and sales. So, even in a functional organization, a program team will obviously be a matrix team, whereas in a projectized organization, a program team will have matrix characteristics due to the different functional expertise of the team members.

The other aspect of the program structure relevant to matrix management is that the program consists of multiple projects. These projects may have different objectives, priorities, and functionalities at their own levels. So, while managing these projects from the program level, the program manager ends up dealing with a matrix environment.

Advanced Concepts

Throughout this book, you will encounter concepts such as probability, baseline, project team, and project management team. Those concepts are introduced here.

Probability

The theory of probability has its roots in the investigations of games of chance, such as roulette and cards, early in the 17th century. Since then a multitude of mathematicians and scientists has contributed to the development of the theory of probability. Today, the concepts of probability appear in almost every discipline, ranging from physics to project management. In the modern age, probability has already entered into the folk psyche through phrases such as "what are the odds that this is going to happen?"

Probability is defined as a chance that something will happen. For example, when you play the lottery and you wonder about your odds of winning, you are thinking of probability. The simplest example of probability is a coin toss. The question is, when you toss a coin, what is the probability that the coin will land with the head up? Now, when you toss a coin there are only two possibilities: it will land either head up or tail up. Each possibility is equally likely if you are not cheating. Therefore the probability that the coin will land head up is $1/2 = 50$ percent or 0.5. In general, if there are n possible outcomes of an event and each outcome is equally likely, then the probability of a specific outcome is $1/n$.

Another useful concept in probability is the combined probability of several events. For example, if you toss two coins, the probability that first coin will land head up and the second coin will land face down is $0.5 \times 0.5 = 0.25$. In general, to calculate the combined probability, you multiply the individual probabilities. If the probability that an event X will happen is a, the probability that event Y will happen is b, and the probability that event Z will happen is c, then the probability that all the three events (X, Y, and Z) will happen is $a \times b \times c$.

Random variable This is a variable that may acquire any value within a given range or out of a set of values. For example, you can use a random variable to represent the results of rolling a fair die, which has six sides that display from one to six dots each. The possible outcome of rolling a die could be any number form the set of outcomes: { 1, 2, 3, 4, 5, 6 }.

Expected value This is the expected value of an outcome. As an example, assume you get into a bet that you will win $10 if a coin toss results in a head, and you will lose $5 if it results in a tail. Given that the probability for a head and a tail is 0.5 for each, the expected value for the money that you will win is $10 × 0.5 = $5, and the expected value for the money that you will lose is $5 × 0.5 = $2.5.

Variance The variance of a random variable is the deviation from the expected value. It is computed as the average squared deviation of each number from its mean. For example, assume that the values of a random variable are 2, 4, 5, 7, and 2 in five measurements. The mean value for these measurements is (2 + 4 + 5 + 7 + 2)÷ 5 = 4.

The variance of the spread of these values is as follows:

$$V = \sigma^2 = [(2 - 4)^2 + (4 - 4)^2 + (7 - 4)^2 + (2 - 4)^2] \div 5 = 3.4$$

Standard deviation This is the square root of the variance, represented by the symbol σ. So, in our example, the standard deviation is the square root of 3.4; that is, 1.84.

Algebraic equations Project/program management and some questions in the CAPM, PMP, and PgMP exams will assume that you can do simple mathematical calculations. You should also have a very simple understanding of algebraic equations. You should be able to make simple manipulations such as the following:

CPI = EV ÷ AC implies EV = CPI × AC

CV = EV − AC implies EV = AC + CV

Project Team and Project Management Team

In order to avoid confusion, make sure you can distinguish the project team from the project management team. The project management team for a project consists of the individuals who perform the project management activities for the project. The project team consists of all the individuals directly involved in the project: the individuals that perform the schedule activities, the members of the project management team, and some other stakeholders, such as the project sponsor.

Baseline

The project *baseline* is defined as the approved plan for the cost, schedule, and scope of the project. The project baseline is also referred to in terms of its components: cost baseline, schedule baseline, and scope baseline. How do we know how the project is performing? We compare the performance against the baseline.

Approved changes in cost, schedule, and scope will also change the baseline.

The Three Big Takeaways

The three most important takeaways from this chapter are the following:

- As compared to projects and programs, a portfolio is closer to the business strategy of an organization. A portfolio consists of programs and projects, whereas a program consists of projects.

- The project processes that are performed to manage projects constitute nine project management knowledge areas: Communication Management, Cost Management, Human Resource Management, Integration Management, Procurement Management, Quality Management, Risk Management, Scope Management, and Time Management. These processes also map to five process groups: Initiating, Planning, Executing, Monitoring and Controlling, and Closing.

- Like project management, program management also has nine knowledge areas and five process groups with identical names. Identical names do not mean that program management and project management have the same set of processes, however.

Summary

Projects, programs, and portfolios have a triangular relationship. This is where this relationship comes from: The activities inside an organization are generally organized into groups, which fall into two categories: operations and projects. Operations usually consist of ongoing routine work, whereas a project has a goal to generate a unique product, service, or result in a finite time; that is, it has a planned beginning and a planned end. To obtain some benefits, multiple projects can be grouped together into a program. Both projects and programs can be grouped together into a portfolio, which is real reflection of the organization's business strategy.

Organizations launch projects for different reasons, such as to meet a business or legal requirement, or to take on an opportunity offered by the market. A project, like anything else in an organization, needs to be managed. Project management is the application of knowledge and skills to project activities in order to meet the project objectives. It involves performing a set of processes that constitute nine knowledge areas of project management: Communication Management, Cost Management, Human Resource Management, Integration Management, Procurement Management, Quality Management, Risk Management, Scope Management, and Time Management. Each process is part of a knowledge area and has a membership in one of five process groups: Initiating, Planning, Executing, Monitoring and Controlling, and Closing. Program management also has these knowledge areas and process groups with identical names.

Each project has a set of individuals or organizations that it influences positively or negatively, and they are accordingly called positive and negative stakeholders. Some of these stakeholders may influence the project. Therefore, you must identify all the project stakeholders, positive and negative. The different project stakeholders may have different and conflicting expectations that you need to analyze and manage.

Another big influence on project management is the structure of the performing organization, which could be functional, projectized, or matrix. On one end of the spectrum, a project manager is usually part-time, with little or no authority in a functional organization. On the other end, the project manager is full-time with high to full authority in a projectized organization. In the middle of the spectrum is the matrix organization, in which a project manger has low to high authority.

Projects are grouped together into programs, and the programs need to be managed just as the individual (constituent) projects do. Programs are managed by using the processes in program management. We'll explore the program management framework in the next chapter.

Exam's-Eye View

Comprehend

- According to the project management standard developed by the PMI, the discipline of project management is composed of nine knowledge areas such as project Cost Management, project Scope Management, and project Human Resource Management.

- Depending upon which stage of the project life cycle they are executed, the processes are grouped into five process groups, such as Initiating and Planning.

- The project manager's authority is none to low in a functional organization, low to high in a matrix organization, and high to full in a projectized organization.

- The organizational environment also affects the programs.

Look Out

- In order for a work effort to be qualified as a project, it must be temporary (that is, have a start and a finish), and the outcome must be a unique product, result, or service. A routine ongoing work is an operation and not a project.

- Any individual or organization that is positively or negatively affected by a project is the project stakeholder. So, stakeholders can exist outside of the performing organization.

- You must identify both positive and negative stakeholders for your project, and must not ignore the negative stakeholders.

- Regardless of the structure of the performing organizations, project managers are responsible for the project results.

- Project phases and process groups are not the same thing.

> **Memorize**
>
> - The life cycle of a project has five stages called process groups: Initiating, Planning, Executing, Monitoring and Controlling, and Closing. Program management also has these five process groups with the same names.
>
> - All the processes that are executed at different stages of a project belong to nine knowledge areas: Communication Management, Cost Management, Human Resource Management, Integration Management, Procurement Management, Quality Management, Risk Management, Scope Management, and Time Management. A given process belongs to only one knowledge area. Program management also has these nine knowledge areas with identical names.

Key Terms and Definitions

knowledge area   A knowledge area in project management is defined by its knowledge requirements related to managing a specific aspect of a project, such as cost, by using a set of processes. PMI recognizes a total of nine knowledge areas, such as Cost Management and Human Resource Management.

matrix management   Management of a matrix team; that is, a team composed of individuals from different functional groups and departments.

organization   A group of individuals organized to work for some purpose or mission.

performing organization   The organization that is performing a project.

process   A set of interrelated activities performed to obtain a specified set of products, results, or services.

program   A set of related projects managed in a coordinated fashion to improve their overall efficiency and effectiveness.

program management   The centralized coordinated management of a specific program to achieve its strategic goals, objectives, and benefits.

progressive elaboration   A technique to develop a plan in steps as more information becomes available. The detail and accuracy of the plan improves as it progresses with time.

project   A work effort made over a finite period of time with a start and a finish to create a unique product, service, or result. A process consists of three elements: input, tools and techniques, and output.

project management   Application of knowledge, skills, and tools and techniques to project activities in order to meet the project objectives. You do this by performing some processes at various stages of the project.

project management office (PMO)   An entity in an organization that is responsible for providing centralized coordinated management for projects in the organization.

project portfolio   A set of projects, programs, or both that is managed in a coordinated fashion to obtain control and benefits that would not be achieved if these projects and programs were managed individually.

project stakeholder   An individual or an organization that is positively or negatively affected by the project.

scope creep   The phenomenon of introducing uncontrolled changes, such as adding or modifying a feature, without going through the planned change-control system for approval.

Review Questions

1. Which of the following is not a project management knowledge area?
   A. Project Integration Management
   B. Project Risk Management
   C. Project Stakeholder Management
   D. Project Time Management

2. Which two of the following are the essential characteristics that make a group of activities a project?
   A. It takes multiple individuals to perform the activities, and the outcome is a new product.
   B. The work is managed by a project manager.
   C. It has a start date, finish date, and a budget.
   D. It has a start date and a finish date, and its outcome will be a new product.

3. Which of the following is a project?
   A. Running a library
   B. Building another school in your area
   C. Keeping a data server up and running
   D. Running a childcare center

4. Which of the following are included in the project process groups?
   A. Initiating, Planning, and Implementing
   B. Monitoring and Controlling, Closing, and Designing
   C. Designing, Implementing, and Running
   D. Initiating, Planning, and Closing

5. Which of the following is the best definition of progressive elaboration?
   A. Taking the project from concept to project management plan in steps
   B. Taking the project from conception to completion
   C. Taking the project from phase one to Closing
   D. Decomposing the project objectives into smaller, more manageable work pieces

6. In which of the following organizational structures does the project manager have the greatest authority?

   A. Functional

   B. Projectized

   C. Matrix

   D. Leveled

7. In which of the following organizational structures does the project manager have the least authority?

   A. Functional

   B. Projectized

   C. Matrix

   D. Programized

8. Which of the following is not included in a program?

   A. Project

   B. Non-project work

   C. Portfolio

   D. Benefits realization plan

9. Organizational environment can influence:

   A. Projects

   B. Programs

   C. Both projects and programs

   D. Neither projects nor programs

10. The probability for completing a project within budget is 0.7, and the probability for completing the same project according to the schedule is also 0.7. What is the probability that the project will be finished within cost and according to the schedule?

    A. 0.7

    B. 0.35

    C. 0.49

    D. 1.4

Answers to Review Questions

1. C.

   C is the correct answer because stakeholder management is part of the Managing Stakeholders process and is not a knowledge area.

   A, B, and D are incorrect because these are three of nine project management knowledge areas.

2. D.

   D is the correct answer because the defining characteristics of a project are that it must be temporary (have a start and finish date), and it must produce a unique (new) product.

   A and B are incorrect because it's possible to have a project that will involve only one person, and there could be a project without an individual called the project manager. The only two defining characteristics of a project are that it is temporary and unique.

   C is incorrect because it leaves out the third essential condition: that the project produces a unique product.

3. B.

   B is the correct answer because building a school is temporary; that is, it will have a start and a finish date, and it will produce a new school.

   A, C, and D are incorrect because running a library, keeping a server up and running, and running a childcare center are all ongoing operations.

4. D.

   D is the correct because the five process groups of a project are: Initiating, Planning, Executing, Monitoring and Controlling, and Closing.

   A is incorrect because there is no process group in project management called Implementing.

   B and C are incorrect because there are no process groups in project management called Implementing or Designing.

5. A.

   A is the correct and the best answer because the project plan is developed starting from the concept and going through progressive elaboration.

   B and C are incorrect because B includes project life cycle and C is the life cycle. Progressive elaboration does not include the life cycle of the project; its goal is to plan the project. Because project planning may develop (or change) throughout the project life cycle, progressive elaboration may continue through the project life cycle, but it does not include the work of the life cycle.

   D is incorrect because progressive elaboration can be used in decomposing, but is not itself the decomposing technique.

6. B.

    B is the correct answer because the projectized organization provides the greatest authority for the project manager.

    A and C are incorrect because the authority of the project manager is none to low in a functional organization, and low to high in a matrix organization.

    D is incorrect because there is no organizational structure called leveled.

7. A.

    A is the correct answer because the project manager's authority is none to low in a functional organization.

    B and C are incorrect because the authority of the project manager is high to full in a projectized organization, and low to high in a matrix organization.

    D is incorrect because there is no organizational structure called programized.

8. C.

    C is the correct answer because programs are part of a portfolio, not the other way around.

    A and B are incorrect because a program can contain projects and non-project work.

    D is incorrect because a program is run to generate some benefits.

9. C.

    C is the correct answer because organizational environment (structure and culture) can impact both projects and programs.

    A, B, and D are incorrect because the organizational environment (structure and culture) does impact the projects and the programs.

10. C.

    C is the correct answer because the combined probability is $0.7 \times 0.7 = 0.49$

    A is not correct because the combined probability is not the average of the two.

    B is incorrect because the combined probability is not achieved by division.

    D is incorrect because the combined probability is not the sum of two probabilities; it's the multiplication.

Chapter 2

The Program Management Framework

THE PGMP EXAM CONTENT FROM THE DEFINING THE PROGRAM PERFORMANCE DOMAIN COVERED IN THIS CHAPTER INCLUDES THE OBJECTIVES LISTED AND EXPLAINED IN THE FOLLOWING:

- ✓ **1.1 Perform a program assessment by defining the program objectives, requirements and establishing a high-level road map in order to ensure program alignment with the enterprise strategic plan or mission.**
- ✓ **1.2 Support business analysis functions in identifying marketplace needs for potential program offering in order to ensure program viability through researching, market analysis, and high-level cost-benefit analysis.**
- ✓ **1.3 Develop benefits realization plan by estimating the costs and benefits (ROI) of the program in order to establish the program feasibility and obtain funding.**
- ✓ **1.4 Perform a preliminary stakeholder analysis through RFP, contract, experience, and input from other sources in order to assess their position relative to the program.**
- ✓ **1.5 Establish alliances with other departments and organizations by recognizing dependencies in order to assess potential partnerships and commitment to the program.**
- ✓ **1.7 Request authorization to proceed by presenting the program assessment for approval to the governance authorities in order to initiate the program.**

When an organization runs multiple projects and those projects are related to each other, the organization should look into the possibility of grouping these projects together into what is called a *program*. A program is managed under program management like a project is managed under project management. You can imagine that just like a project, a program has stakeholders. Whereas a project is focused on its product, service, or result, a program is focused on the benefits that it will deliver in line with the strategy of the organization. A program is a larger venture than a project; so it needs to be governed in addition to managed. Therefore, there are some broad management themes that run through the life cycle of a program.

The goal of this chapter is to offer a high-level view of the program management framework. To accomplish that goal, I will explore three avenues: program-related basic concepts, the life cycle of a program, and three management themes running through the life cycle of a program—benefits management, stakeholder management, and program governance.

The Big Picture of Program Management

The previous chapter presented an overview of project management. The goal of this chapter is to present an overview of program management. This overview is required by the exam objectives covered in this chapter.

Exam Roadmap

The following table presents each PgMP exam objective covered in this chapter, along with its explanation:

Exam Objective	What It Really Means
1.1 Perform a program assessment by defining the program objectives, requirements and establishing a high-level road map in order to ensure program alignment with the enterprise strategic plan or mission.	Know the definitions of a program enterprise strategic plan, business objectives, mission statements, vision, business objectives, and how these elements are related to each other. You must understand the big picture of program life cycle and the relationship between the program and the strategic plan of the performing organization. Understand the importance of program alignment with the strategic plan of the organization. You should also know how an organization's structure and culture influence its programs and projects (This issue is covered in Chapter 1, "Project, Portfolio, and Program: Mind the Gap.")

Exam Objective	What It Really Means
1.2 Support business analysis functions in identifying marketplace needs for potential program offering in order to ensure program viability through researching, market analysis, and high level cost-benefit analysis. 1.3 Develop benefits realization plan by estimating the costs and benefits (ROI) of the program in order to establish the program feasibility and obtain funding.	Understand benefits management, one of the three central themes of program management. You must understand that a benefits realization plan contains a definition of each program benefit and how it will be realized. It also maps the program outcome to the benefits. You must know the program metrics such as return on investment (ROI), value realization, and balanced scorecard that can be used to establish the viability of the program and to measure the program benefits. You should also be able to identify key performance indicators (KPIs) at the organization level and at the program level to support business analysis for the program. Some components of these objectives are covered in Chapter 3, *"Initiating a Program."*
1.4 Perform a preliminary stakeholder analysis through RFP, contract, experience, and input from other sources in order to assess their position relative to the program.	Understand the stakeholder management theme of program management, including a stakeholder management plan. You must be able to identify the key stakeholders of a program. You should understand the role of communication strategy in stakeholder management. You must be able to identify the stakeholder analysis and characterization techniques to perform stakeholder analysis, such as collecting requirements, understanding the stakeholder needs, and determining the stakeholder positions relative to the program.
1.5 Establish alliances with other departments and organizations by recognizing dependencies in order to assess potential partnerships and commitment to the program.	Understand the impact that enterprise structure and capabilities have on program management. Also understand the potential effects of organizational culture and environment on the program. Know how to manage the program dependencies to execute a program successfully.
1.7 Request authorization to proceed by presenting the program assessment for approval to the governance authorities in order to initiate the program.	Understand the program governance structure, including program board and program management office (PMO). Other elements of these objectives are covered in Chapter 3.

As in project management, most of the tasks in program management are also performed by using processes.

Understanding Program Management Processes

Just like project management, program management is performed through processes that fall into five process groups. These process groups are independent of areas of application and industry focus of the programs. They are discussed in the following.

The Initiating process group This includes defining and authorizing the program and the projects within the program, and generating the benefits statement and benefits realization plan for the program.

The Planning process group This includes developing the program plans to deliver benefits.

The Executing process group This includes using projects and resources in an integrated fashion to execute the plan for the program in order to deliver benefits.

The Monitoring and Controlling process group This involves monitoring and controlling the progress of the program and the constituent projects, which includes making performance measurements against the planned benefit delivery, identifying variances from the plan, and implementing corrective actions to stay the course to deliver expected benefits.

The Closing process group This includes accepting products, services, and results from the constituent projects, and benefits delivery from the program, plus bringing the program and the program components (e.g., projects) to a formal closure.

Note that these process groups have the same names as the project process groups discussed in Chapter 1. Just like in project management, the processes in these process groups map to nine knowledge areas, listed in Table 2.1 in order of their appearance in this book. In the parentheses next to each process name is the number of the chapter that covers the process.

In Table 2.1 and throughout the book, the names of processes, knowledge areas, and process groups are taken from the PMI standards such as The Standard for Program Management.

The processes within a process group are not performed in a linear fashion: they do overlap. For example, the processes in the Monitoring and Controlling group can be executed along with the processes from the Executing group. The processes within the same process group and from different process groups can interact with each other. For example, the output of one process can become the input to another process.

That said, it is convenient, at least for learning purposes, to see some degree of linearity among the process groups. For example, a program is first initiated (defined and authorized), and then planned. It is executed before it is closed, and so on. In that spirit, the presentation of program management in this book is organized along what I call five stages of a program: Initiating, Planning, Executing, Monitoring and Controlling, and Closing. Each of these stages corresponds to the process group of the same name. For example, you can say the processes in the Initiating process group are performed in the initiating stage of a program. You can see some relationship between stages and phases, but they are not one and the same thing.

TABLE 2.1   Mapping of the Program Management Processes to Process Groups and Knowledge Areas

Knowledge Areas	Process Groups				
	Initiating	Planning	Executing	Monitoring and Controlling	Closing
Integration Management	1.Initiate program (3) 2. Authorize projects (3)	1. Develop program management plan (4) 2.Interface planning (4) 3.Transition planning (4) 4. Resource planning (4)	Direct and manage program execution (7)	1. Integrated change control (8) 2. Resource control (8) 3. Monitor and control program work (8) 4. Issue management and control (8)	1. Close program (9) 2. Component closure (9)
Human Resource Management	Initiate team (3)	Human resource planning (5)	1. Acquire program team (7) 2. Develop program team (7)	—	—
Scope Management	—	1. Scope definition (4) 2. Create program work breakdown structure (4)	—	Scope control (8)	—
Time Management	—	Schedule development (5)	—	Schedule control (8)	—
Cost Management	—	Cost estimating and budgeting (5)	—	Cost control (8)	—
Procurement Management	—	1. Plan program purchases and acquisitions (5) 2. Plan program contracting (5)	1. Request seller (7) responses 2. Select sellers (7)	Program contract administration (8)	Contract closure (9)

TABLE 2.1   Mapping of the Program Management Processes to Process Groups and Knowledge Areas *(continued)*

Knowledge Areas	Process Groups				
	Initiating	Planning	Executing	Monitoring and Controlling	Closing
Quality Management	—	Quality planning (6)	Perform quality assurance (7)	Perform quality control (8)	—
Risk Management	—	Risk management planning and analysis (6)	—	Risk monitoring and control (8)	—
Communication Management	—	Communication planning (6)	Information distribution (7)	1. Communication control (8) 2. Performance reporting (8)	—

The process groups (or *project stages*, as defined in this book) do not have a direct one-to-one relationship with program phases. PMI standard looks at the program life cycle in terms of phases, and not in terms of stages (process groups).

Basic Program Concepts

Each discipline of knowledge builds upon some basic concepts. The terms that refer to or define these concepts make up the language of that discipline. Part of becoming an expert is to master those terms and concepts. The very basic terms in program management are described briefly here:

Program   A program is a set of interrelated projects and can also include non-project work. Under a program, the constituent projects can be managed in a coordinated fashion to obtain benefits and control that might not be achieved by managing them individually.

Program life cycle   The *program life cycle* is the span of five well-defined program phases: pre-program setup, program setup, establish program management and technical infrastructure, deliver benefits, and close the program. These phases are described throughout the book.

Benefit   A *benefit* is a positive contribution or improvement to the running of an organization, such as increased revenues, reduced costs, and improved employee morale.

Control   This refers to a set of techniques used to control projects and programs by activities such as analyzing variances, assessing trends to improve processes, evaluating alternatives, comparing actual performance with planned performance, and recommending appropriate corrective and preventive actions and changes in order for the program or the project to succeed. Most of these techniques also facilitate monitoring, as you cannot control anything successfully without monitoring it.

Benefits management   This is the part of management that includes activities and techniques for defining, creating, maximizing, and sustaining benefits from a program.

Program management   *Program management* is the centralized coordinated management of a specific program to achieve its strategic goals, objectives, and benefits.

Program office   This is the entity designed to handle the program administration functions of a program centrally by providing support to the program management team and the program manager.

Program Management Office (PMO)   Typically, PMO is responsible for defining and managing program-related governance procedures, processes, templates, and so on for all the programs in the organization.

Note the difference between program office (PO) and program management office (PMO). The PO manages a specific program, whereas the PMO provides support to all the programs in the organization. Depending on the organizational structure, the functionalities of the PMO and the PO may be unified into one office.

This is a minimal set of terms that you need to understand before you can start exploring the world of program management. These terms will be explained further and more terms will be introduced as you continue exploring the discipline of program management in this book.

A program may include elements of the work related to the program; e.g., ongoing operations, which are outside the scope of all individual projects included in the program.

Now that you understand these basic terms, you can ask a very basic question: What's involved in managing a program? The first step in understanding program management is to understand what a program is.

Understanding Programs

The definition of a program may differ from one organization to another. However, for almost all organizations, a program is a set of multiple projects. Furthermore, almost all organizations will agree that projects and therefore programs are run to do something more effectively and efficiently and to achieve some kind of benefits for the organization. These agreements can be put together into the following standard definition of a program:

> "A program is a group of related projects managed in a coordinated way to obtain benefits and control not available from managing them individually."
>
> —The Standard for Program Management by PMI

Some organizations may consider any large project as a program. According to our standard definition of a program, a large project will not qualify to be a program. However, if you divide this large project into more manageable smaller projects, then we have a set of related projects and therefore a program. As an example, consider a large project in a training company that includes developing syllabi, developing content, and producing content for a number of courses, such as computer basics, system administration, network administration, and network security. If this is one project with a project manager and a project team, this may be a large project, but it's not a program. Now let's assume that the training company realizes that it is to their benefit to split this large project into multiple projects with each project handling only one course. Now, do not jump to a conclusion that we will need more project managers and more project team members to run these multiple projects. It depends: people do work on multiple projects simultaneously. The point to note here is, now these interrelated multiple projects can be managed under one umbrella called a program.

Note the following about a program:

- A program may include work that is related to the program but is out of the scope of any individual project included in the program.

- Programs, like projects, are means of achieving organizational goals and objectives, which are often in the context of a strategic plan of the organization.

- Programs, like projects, offer benefits to organizations in several ways, including improving existing capabilities and adding new ones.

- A project within a program can offer discrete benefits of its own, as well as contribute to the consolidated benefits of the program of which it's a part.

 Ongoing and repetitive operations in an organization are neither projects nor programs according to the standard definitions of a project and a program.

Like a project, a program needs to be managed. I'll discuss program management in the next section.

Understanding Program Management

No, program management is not about managing multiple projects simultaneously; that would be project management. Project management and program management are two different (but related) beasts. For many organizations, project management and program management have been synonymous, but it should be easy for you to realize the difference between the two once you clearly distinguish a program from a project: project management involves managing a project, whereas program management involves managing a program.

Yes, a program consists of multiple projects and each of those projects is managed under project management. To understand the need for program management, the question to ask is, what aspects of multiple projects are not being managed under individual project management? Here are a few:

- Dependencies among projects
- Prioritizing issues arising from different projects
- The strategic goals and objectives of the organization for which the projects are being executed

This is an incomplete list of aspects that are managed under program management. This suggests that program management is not about managing the details of individual projects, but rather involves managing the big picture. So, the standard definition of program management is the following: Program management is the centralized coordinated management of a program to achieve the program's strategic benefits and objectives.

So, the keywords in the definition of program management are *centralized*, *coordinated*, and *benefits*. Program management also supports the following broader management themes:

Benefits management   This refers to activities and techniques used to define, create, maximize, and sustain benefits from a program.

Program governance   Program governance is a management method that is used to develop, communicate, implement, and monitor the organizational structures, policies, procedures, practices, and other acts to run a program.

Stakeholder management   This includes understanding and managing the influence and expectations of the program stakeholders.

Once you develop a basic understanding of a program and program management, you can immediately see the following benefits:

- Optimization and integration of cost, schedule, and efforts over multiple projects in a program
- Optimal use of staff and other resources over multiple projects in the overall context of a program
- Capability of producing integrated deliverables across multiple projects in a program

Program management involves coordination between related or interdependent projects in a program. What makes the projects interdependent or related? In other words, what links the projects together into a program? Here are two obvious and general links:

Common attribute   Projects may be related because they share a common attribute. For example, multiple projects are being performed for the same customer.

Collective capability   Projects may be related because together they can deliver a collective (or integrated) capability or a product. For example, consider a training company's diploma or certification program that consists of several courses and each course is being managed as a separate project. Therefore each project (course) delivers its own results, and the whole program delivers a diploma: the integrated product or result. All the projects in the program contribute to this integrated capability.

These are two obvious ways of grouping projects into programs. Depending upon the number of projects, the nature of the projects, and the performing organization, there may be many other criteria that can be used to link the projects together into a program. Some of them are listed here:

Escalation level   Projects can be linked together into a program based on the escalation level of various factors, such as scope changes, quality, communication, risks, and other issues.

Organizational change in direction   If an organization changes its direction, it will certainly affect the projects and their relationship to each other. The effect on the relationship between the projects will in turn have an impact on how the projects will be grouped together into programs.

Resource constraints   Resource constraints can play a significant role in grouping projects into a program. The goal here is to group the projects together into a program to make wise and optimal use of limited resources.

Risk mitigation   Risk mitigation means reducing the probability of risk occurring, reducing the impact of the risk if it does occur, or both. This may be a factor in grouping the projects into a program.

Task dependency   The projects in a program may have a set of identical or similar tasks. Or perhaps a task in one project cannot be started until a task in another project is completed. By combining such projects into a program, you optimize the schedule and cost by eliminating duplication of efforts and by handling dependencies efficiently.

 Real World Scenario

Identifying Relationships among Projects

Your training company offers training in specific areas such as network administration and computer programming. Encouraged by the growth of the project management field, your manager has put together the following list of project management courses:

- PM 101: Basics of project management
- PM 201: Certified Associate in Project Management (CAPM) training
- PM 202: Project Management Professional (PMP) training
- PM 301: Program Management Professional (PgMP) training
- PM 302: Managing project risks

You are going to propose that each of these courses should be handled as a project and all these projects should be executed under a program. Identify some of the relationships (links) among these projects and determine the category of each relationship.

Dependency	Category
PM 101 may be a prerequisite for all other courses.	Task dependency
A Guide to the Project Management Body of Knowledge (PMBOK Guide) will be used for both PM 201 and PM 202.	Common attribute
A student has to pass all these courses to get a project management certification from your company.	Common attribute
If the enrollment is low, you can combine the PM 201 and PM 202 courses into one class section.	Risk mitigation

The dependencies among the projects play a major role in determining which projects should be grouped together into a program, and once we have a program, the program management focuses on these dependencies. Yet the underlying motivating factors for grouping projects into a program remain shared resources, strategic benefits, and optimal results by coordinated planning and management. As Figure 2.1 shows, each project in a program may have discrete benefits; it often also contributes to the consolidated benefits of the program.

FIGURE 2.1　　Relationship between project management, program management, and benefits

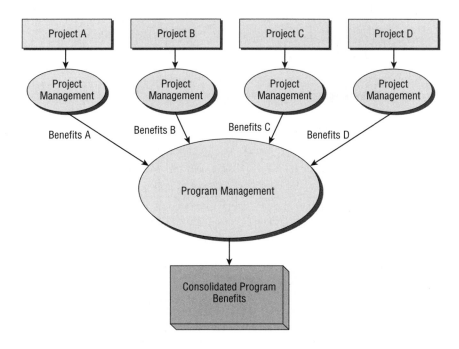

Although each project in a program may have discrete benefits, it often also contributes to the consolidated benefits of the program.

So, project management refers to managing a project, whereas program management refers to, well, managing a program, which is a collection of related projects. You also understand by now that project management and program management are different but related disciplines. How exactly are project management and program management related to each other? Let's explore.

Comparing Project Management and Program Management

Just as a project is managed by a project manager, a program is managed by a program manager, who oversees the projects and provides high-level guidance to the project managers. In other words, a program manager oversees projects and coordinates efforts between projects, but does not manage the projects: the project managers manage the projects.

Identification, monitoring, controlling, and rationalization of the dependencies among the projects in a program is an essential responsibility of a program manager.

The following are the main responsibilities performed by program management:

- Identification, monitoring, controlling, and rationalization of the dependencies among the projects in a program
- Playing a role in determining which issues among the projects in the program should be escalated
- Dealing with the escalated issues
- Tracking the contribution of each project to the consolidated program benefits
- Tracking the contribution of the program-related non-project work to the consolidated program benefits

The program manager uses the program management processes, and the integrative nature of these processes involves coordinating processes for each of the projects in the program. The interaction between the program-level processes and project-level processes is iterative. This interaction uses the top-down approach during the planning stage of a program, and then a bottom-up approach at later stages. For example, a program is designed and projects are selected in the early stage of a program. These decisions are made at the program level and the information is passed down to the projects. Later, detailed planning and scheduling of projects happen at the project level, and the information is passed up to the program. This cycle of information continues through the life cycle of a program.

 Information typically flows from a program to its projects during early stages (or phases), such as initiating and planning, and from projects to program during later stages, such as executing, controlling, and closing.

Table 2.2 presents a comparison between some characteristics of a project and a program.

TABLE 2.2 Comparison between a Project and a Program

Characteristic	Project	Program
Change	Project manager tries to keep changes to a minimum.	Program manager expects changes and thrives on them if they help maximize the strategic benefits and objectives of the program.
Leadership style	Focuses on monitoring the execution of the project and delivery of the project objectives.	Focuses on managing relationships and conflict resolution. Program managers handle the political aspects of stakeholder management.
Management skills	Project managers are team players who use their skills and knowledge to motivate the team.	Program managers provide overall vision and leadership.
Monitoring	Project manager monitors and controls the project activities (tasks) to produce the products or results of the project.	Program manager monitors projects and program-related non-project work through governance structure.
People management	Project managers may manage the project team members and possibly other staff, such as specialist and technicians.	Program managers manage project managers.
Planning	Project managers are responsible for creating detailed plans for their projects.	Program managers are responsible for performing high-level planning and providing guidance to project managers for their detailed planning.

TABLE 2.2   Comparison between a Project and a Program *(continued)*

Characteristic	Project	Program
Scope	A project has a narrow scope limited to delivering its product or results.	A program has a wider scope dedicated to meeting the benefit goals of the organization. The scope can change to meet the goals.
Success	Success relates to a project and is measured generally by the criteria of completing the project within the planned budget, cost, and scope.	Success relates to the overall program, and is measured in terms of ROI, benefit delivery, and new capabilities produced by the program.

From the table, you may wonder about the apparent conflict of the project manager trying to keep the changes to a minimum, whereas a program manager thrives on changes. This reflects the different perspectives and responsibilities of project managers and the program manager. A project manager is focused on meeting the goals and objectives of one project among many in the program. There is not much room to move around. A program manager is focused on the big picture: meet the strategic objectives of the organization and maximize the overall program benefits. The changes often provide the program manager the flexibility to move around to serve this ultimate goal.

In a nutshell, an organization starts a program to deliver benefits and meet some predetermined objectives. The program is executed in terms of multiple projects. A project manager is focused on the project to assure that the project delivers its product, service, or results, and meets its objectives and requirements. The program manager keeps one eye on the outcome of each project and the other eye on the desired program benefits and ensures that the outcomes from multiple projects will meet the desired benefits and objectives expected from the program. This relationship is depicted in Figure 2.2.

If an organization is running multiple programs, they can be composed into what is called a portfolio.

Comparing Program Management and Portfolio Management

A portfolio is a set of projects, programs, or both that is managed in a coordinated fashion to obtain control and benefits not available from managing them individually.

Portfolio management is the centralized management of one or more portfolios, and it includes identifying, prioritizing, authorizing, managing, and controlling projects, programs, and other related work in order to obtain specific strategic business objectives. Just as a program is managed by a program manager, a portfolio is managed by a portfolio manager.

To understand the relationship of a portfolio with projects and programs, note the following:

- Even if an organization does not have any programs but it has only individual projects, all these projects can be grouped into one or more portfolios.

- If an organization has programs and no individual project out of programs, all these programs can be grouped into one or more portfolios.

- If an organization has some programs and some individual projects, all these programs and projects can be grouped into one or more portfolios.

FIGURE 2.2   Relationship between organizational benefits, a program, and projects

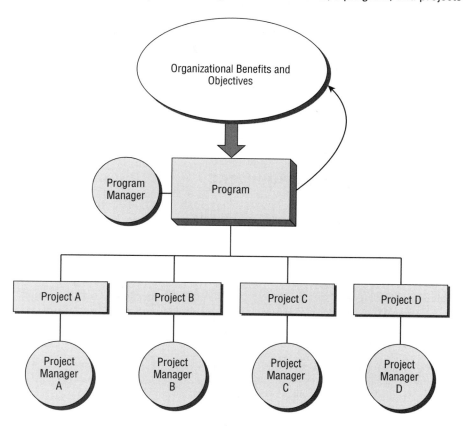

Portfolio management focuses on making sure that programs and projects are prioritized for resources to serve the organization's strategy. Therefore, investment decisions are usually made at the portfolio level. Program management focuses on achieving the benefits that would be aligned with the portfolio and hence with the strategic objectives of the organization. So, a portfolio is part of the interface between programs and strategic business objectives of the organization for which the programs are run.

A program is run and program management is performed within the context of business strategy of an organization that includes benefits and objectives. This gives rise to some common themes that will run through all the program activities.

Understanding Program Management Themes

Theme in literature means a unifying idea of a literary piece such as a story. Program management encompasses several areas, but the following three themes ring through the whole story of program management:

- Program benefits management
- Program stakeholder management
- Program governance

These themes help unify the program efforts to meet the strategic benefits and objectives for which the program is designed.

Program Benefits Management

A benefit is a positive contribution or improvement to the running of an organization, such as increased revenues, reduced costs, and improved employee morale. Benefits can be broadly grouped into two categories:

Tangible benefits   A tangible benefit is a quantifiable benefit which may be directly related to the financial objectives, such as a 10 percent increase in revenue.

Intangible benefits   An intangible benefit is a benefit that may not be easy to quantify, such as improved employee morale or increased customer satisfaction. However, most intangible benefits eventually end up contributing to tangible benefits. For example, improved high morale leads to increased productivity, which in turn may result in increased revenue.

Benefits management refers to defining and formalizing the benefits that the program is expected to deliver. This involves planning, modeling, and tracking the intermediate and final results throughout the program life cycle.

Formalizing means making something official and putting it in the framework of proper rules and procedures.

Because programs are run to realize benefits, benefits management starts before a program is initiated, runs through the program, and lasts until after the program is closed. Usually, the benefits will be defined and formalized before being delegated to a program for realization. During the conclusion of the program, the program manager transfers the responsibility for sustaining the benefits in the framework of ongoing operations.

To be specific, benefits management includes the following tasks:

- Assess the value of the program in terms of benefits and capabilities, and also its overall impact on the organization.

- Ensure that the expected benefits are realistic, specific, measurable, and can be realized within a specified time period.

- Examine the contributions of multiple projects in the program to the consolidated program benefits to identify the interdependencies of benefits resulting from different projects.

- Whenever a program change is planned, analyze its potential impact on the realization of benefits, or benefits outcome.

- Assign accountabilities and responsibilities for the actual benefits expected (required) from the program.

Things in project management and program management are done through proper planning. Benefits management is no exception. A benefits realization plan is drafted in the early phases of a program life cycle, and is maintained throughout the program. It includes the following elements:

- **Communication plan.** This plan determines how to use communication to support benefits management.

- **Definitions.** The benefits realization plan contains a definition of each benefit along with a description of how the benefit will be realized.

- **Mapping.** This element of the plan maps the program outcomes to the expected benefits of the program.

- **Metrics.** The benefits realization plan determines which metrics will be used to measure benefits.

- **Roles and responsibilities.** Benefits management is to be performed by some individuals. So the benefits realization plan determines the roles required to facilitate benefits management and assigns responsibilities to each role.

- **Transition.** The benefits management needs to be transitioned at the end of the program. So the benefits realization plan states how the transition of responsibilities regarding benefits sustainment from the program into ongoing operations will be performed.

Figure 2.3 illustrates the benefits management life cycle, which runs through all the stages of a program life cycle.

Although benefits management is an important theme running through a program life cycle, it is not a subset of program management. It starts before the program and continues after the program is concluded. The benefits realization plan also determines which techniques (or procedures) will be used to measure the benefits. Some of these techniques are described in the following:

Value realization   Generally speaking, value realization means obtaining value from the investment. As an example, assume you buy a software tool that lets you perform a task in five minutes that you will otherwise perform in one hour. The saving of 55 minutes is a value that you have realized as a result of investing in this tool. Value realization can be used to measure benefits of a program.

FIGURE 2.3   An outline of the benefits management approach

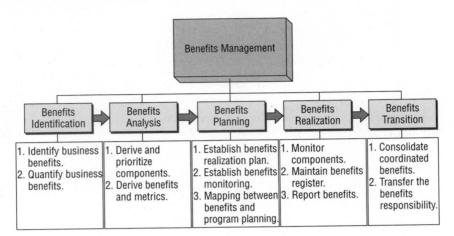

Balanced scorecard   According to the balanced scorecard technique, developed by Robert Kaplan and David Norton, strategic goals are partitioned into four dimensions: customer, financial, internal operations, and learning and innovation. So, you can measure benefits by answering the following questions related to these dimensions:

- How does your program help increase customer satisfaction? Example: Customer satisfaction rating rose to 90 percent.
- What are the finance and the accounting outcomes of the program? Example: 12 percent increase in revenue.
- How will you describe the process and functional performance of the core competence? Example: Inventory turns of 5 or better.
- How are we doing in application of technology to increase productivity, new product development, and organization learning and skill development? Example: 6 percent increase in revenue through new sales channel or methodology.

These four dimensions are listed in Table 2.3.

TABLE 2.3   The Four Dimensions of the Strategic Goals in the Balanced Scorecard Technique

Goal Dimension	Question To Be Asked
Customer	How do our customers see us?
Financial	What financial gains do we obtain from our investment?
Internal operations	What is our core competency?
Learning and innovation	How do we continue to improve and create value?

Other metrics   Value realization and the balanced scoreboard discussed earlier are examples of *metrics*. You can also use some other standard metrics, such as ROI, to measure benefits. Those metrics are discussed further on in this chapter.

So, benefits management is the part of management that includes activities and techniques for defining, creating, maximizing, and sustaining benefits from a program. The benefits and other outcomes of the program can affect individuals and organizations. Those individuals and organizations are called program stakeholders, and they need to be managed.

Program Stakeholder Management

Right from the day you assume responsibility for managing a program, you start meeting a very special class of people called *program stakeholders*. It is very important for the success of the program that you identify these individuals (or organizations) and communicate with them effectively throughout the life cycle of the program.

Program stakeholder management (the second major theme of program management) means identifying the program stakeholders, resolving their issues, and understanding, analyzing, satisfying, and managing their needs and expectations.

Analyzing Stakeholders

Stakeholder analysis is the procedure used to identify and understand the stakeholders and their needs and expectations. Some of the tools and techniques that can be used to perform the stakeholder analysis are discussed in the following.

Consultation   This refers to techniques such as interviews, surveys, and social maps. A social map is a map of a geographical area that displays the social structures and institutions found in the area. It contains important information such as the economy, ethnicity, and religion of the people living in the area and their views about the institutions in the area. Social maps can also help establish a starting point for conducting effective interviews and surveys and to analyze the collected data. This technique helps identify the stakeholders, such as some interest groups, and helps collect information about their interests, needs, and expectations.

Procurement documents   These are the documents used to get part of the program work done by an individual or an organization outside of the performing organization. These documents contain important information that can be used in stakeholder analysis. This set of documents includes the following:

Contract   A mutually binding agreement between a buyer and a seller that obligates the seller to provide the specified product, service, or result and obligates the buyer to make the payment for it

Contract statement of work (SOW)   A document that describes the products or services to be delivered by the seller

Request for proposal (RFP) or request for quotation (RFQ)   A document that is distributed to potential sellers out of the buyer's organization and contains the information about the needs and requirements of the buyer

For example, for a seller the buyer is a stakeholder and the needs and expectations of this stakeholder can be found in these documents.

 As the program progresses, the list of program stakeholders and their interests may vary. Therefore, program stakeholder analysis should be an ongoing iterative activity (not just a one-time task) whose results can be used throughout the life cycle of the program.

Communication   Communication is an important tool and technique to collect the requirements and understand the needs of the stakeholders. It will also help in detecting changes such as identifying new stakeholders, change in level of interests, change in the expectations, and so on.

Organizational process assets   The organizational process assets that can be used in stakeholder analysis include historical information, including lessons learned. The knowledge database of your organization may have some information about the potential stakeholders.

Enterprise environmental factors   The enterprise environmental factors that are relevant to stakeholder analysis include the following:

- Company work authorization system
- Organizational culture and structure
- Stakeholder risk tolerances
- Management information system to store, retrieve, analyze, and retrieve the information

Characterization and classification   This refers to characterizing and classifying (categorizing) the stakeholders based on the collected information. The stakeholders can be characterized by using the following criteria:

Interests   Based on their interests, the stakeholders can be grouped into two categories: *positive stakeholders*, whose interests will be positively affected by the program, and *negative stakeholders*, whose interests will be negatively affected.

Involvement levels   The stakeholders can also be grouped based on their level of involvement in the program. For example, program manager and customer are examples of a group of stakeholders called k*ey stakeholders*.

Management levels   Another criterion for grouping stakeholders is based on the levels of management hierarchy. You will probably need different ways of communication and different content for communication for stakeholders in different management levels because their needs will be different.

The main purpose of characterization and classification of stakeholders is to group them according to their needs, interests, and expectations so that they can be managed efficiently and effectively. You use these techniques to accomplish the following:

- Identify the stakeholders

- Understand their interests and needs and, based on that, understand their position relative to the program
- Manage the stakeholders

As you can see, you need to identify the stakeholders before you can manage them.

Identifying Program Stakeholders

Program stakeholders are individuals and organizations whose interests may be affected—positively or negatively—by the outcomes of program execution and completion. In other words, a program stakeholder has (potentially) something to gain from the program or something to lose to the program. Accordingly, the stakeholders fall into two categories: positive stakeholders, who will normally benefit from the success of the program, and negative stakeholders, who may see some kind of disadvantage coming from the program. The implications are that the positive stakeholders would like to see the program succeed and the negative stakeholders' interests will be better served if the program is delayed or canceled altogether. For example, your city mayor may be a positive stakeholder in a program that involves opening a private college in your neighborhood because it brings business to the city, whereas the residents in the neighborhood may see it as a threat to the peace and harmony in the community because it brings traffic, noise, and the possibility of many other problems. The residents thereby may act as negative stakeholders.

WARNING   There is a natural tendency to ignore the negative stakeholders. Do not ignore or overlook the negative stakeholders—doing so will increase the program risk. Identify them and deal with them along with the positive stakeholders.

Negative stakeholders are often overlooked by the program managers, which increases the program risk. Ignoring positive or negative program stakeholders will have a damaging impact on the program. Therefore, it's important that you, the program manager, start identifying the program stakeholders early in the program. Identifying all the program stakeholders may be a difficult task, but the following are the obvious ones, starting with you:

Program manager   Include yourself, the program manager, in the list of the program stakeholders.

Project managers   The project managers for all the projects in the program.

Program office (PO)   The organization designed to handle the program administration functions of a program centrally by providing support to the program management team and the program manager.

Program management office (PMO)   As stated earlier in this chapter, the PMO is responsible for defining and managing the program-related governance procedures, processes, templates, and so on for all the programs in the organization.

Program team members   The members of the program team that are actually performing the program activities.

Project team members   Each project of a program has a project team whose members are actually performing the project work. The project team members belonging to all the projects in the program are the program stakeholders.

Performing organization   The organization that is performing the program work through projects.

Customer   The individual or organization that will utilize the new capabilities or results of the program and will receive the benefits expected to be delivered by the program.

Program sponsor   The individual or group that champions the program initiatives, holds responsibility for providing resources to perform projects in the program, and often holds the ultimate responsibility for delivering the program benefits.

Program director   An executive who owns the program in the organizations. A program director may, of course, own multiple programs.

Program governance board   An organizational body responsible for assuring that the program goals are achieved. It provides support for addressing program risks and other issues.

In addition to these obvious key stakeholders, there can be a number of other stakeholders, which may be less obvious to identify, inside and outside of your organization. The stakeholders inside the performing organization are called *internal stakeholders* and those outside the organization are called *external stakeholders*. The following are some examples of potential external stakeholders:

- Competitors that may be affected by the outcome of your program

- Groups and organizations representing the interests of consumers, investors, environmentalists, and so on

- Government regulatory agencies who will be interested to ensure that your program complies with all the existing regulations relevant to your program, and may come up with new policy or regulation that might affect your program

- Suppliers who may be affected by the product of your program

- Media outlets that can have interest in your program and have, in this information age, the potential to make it or break it

- Individual citizens and society at large that can potentially be affected by your program

The different program stakeholders may have different and even conflicting expectations that you need to analyze and manage.

Managing Program Stakeholders

It is critical for the success of a program that you identify positive and negative stakeholders early on in the program, understand and analyze their varying expectations—including conflicting expectations—and manage those expectations throughout the program. The following are some of the important aspects of program stakeholder management:

Additional levels of stakeholders   The first thing to understand about program stakeholder management is that it extends beyond project stakeholder management. Program stakeholder management must look for additional levels of stakeholders arising from dependencies among the projects in the program and from the whole of the program: the consolidated benefits and capabilities.

Stakeholder management plan   You must have a clear stakeholder management plan that should include the stakeholder communication plan to deliver needed, accurate, and consistent information to all the relevant stakeholders in a timely fashion. This would help in managing stakeholder expectations, developing a clear understanding of the issues, and reducing the number of conflicts and misunderstandings. The stakeholder management plan should include the following elements:

Positive and negative stakeholders   Program stakeholder management must identify both kinds of stakeholders, negative and positive, and determine how the program will affect them. For example, a program may affect an organization's culture, current major issues, barrier to change, and so on.

Communication strategy   The communication strategy (that includes the communication approach) can greatly affect the stakeholder management. Based on the identification of stakeholders and the effects that the program will have on them, stakeholder management must develop a communication strategy aimed at managing the stakeholders' expectations and improving their acceptance of the program objectives. The right communication strategy will help resolve issues, manage expectations, and resolve conflicts effectively and thereby contribute to the success of the program. The communication approach should be proactive and targeted. Other elements of the right communication strategy include delivering the needed information to the right stakeholder at the right time, applying a direct, collaborative, professional, and respectful communication approach, and using an appropriate communication technique for the task at hand. For example, to resolve a conflict, a face-to-face meeting (or a teleconference in the case of a virtual team) will be a better technique than emails.

Change management   As a program manager, you have to keep your eye on the ball, and the ball in program management is the benefits the program will deliver. Sometimes to keep the benefits ball going in the right direction, you will need to make other changes. Stakeholder management is crucial to the successful implementation of program changes. The program plans in this case should clearly show how the change complies and integrates with the generally accepted methods of the organizational change management. To successfully manage a change, you need to take some steps.

First, identify the key stakeholders that will be affected by the change and ensure that they are aware of and supportive of the change. Make them part of the change process.

Second, communicate to the stakeholders a clear vision of the need for change, specific objectives of the change, and the resources required for the change.

Third, set goals, assess readiness, and develop a plan for the change. You must also monitor the change as it is implemented.

Fourth, obtain and evaluate feedback from stakeholders who are affected by the change and also address the issues of stakeholders who are not embracing the change.

The third major theme that runs through program management is program governance.

Program Governance

Program governance is a practice of developing, communicating, implementing, and monitoring policies, procedures, organization structure, and acts associated with the program. Program governance provides the following:

- A framework for efficient and effective decision making
- A consistent delivery management focused on achieving program goals
- An appropriate mechanism to address risks and stakeholder requirements

 The term *governance* refers to procedures, processes, and systems used by an organization (or society) to operate. The word *governance* has a Latin origin that means to steer.

Program governance is performed in the context of corporate (organizational) governance. Corporate governance is the practice of developing, implementing, and monitoring the processes, policies, procedures, and organizational structure, and following the relevant laws of the land to run a corporation or an organization. Corporate governance also includes managing the relationships among the stakeholders and the goals for which the corporation is governed.

Program governance should fit into corporate governance, and into the big picture of the organization. The big picture is formed by the three key concepts: mission, vision, and strategy, as described in the following:

Mission   The mission of an organization is a summary of its goals and objectives. It is what an organization does: the purpose for the organization to exist. The mission is expressed in the mission statement, such as the following: "Our mission is to level the playing field in education by providing affordable and quality education to low-income families."

Vision   This refers to a description, in graphic terms, of where the goal setters want to see the organization in the future. Unlike a mission statement, which is true in the present, the vision statement points to the truth in the future. Here is an example of a vision statement: "Our goal is to become the number-one education provider in the world."

Strategy   This refers to a long-term plan of action designed to achieve the organization's goals and objectives; that is, its mission and vision.

Program/project selection decisions are made in context of the strategic plan of the organization developed through a rigorous process. As a program manager, you may not be involved in the strategic planning of the organization, but because the program benefits must be aligned with the strategic plan, you must have the knowledge of the strategic planning process. This process, performed by the executive management team, accomplishes the following:

- Investigate current strategy in the context of the current environment and market trends.
- Resolve ongoing business issues.

- Define the organization's future in terms of mission, strategic goals, and vision.
- In light of the mission, goals, and vision, provide a framework in which the enterprise analysis will be conducted to make investment decisions.

A strategic plan changes with the business needs.

Exam Spotlight

Understand the relationships between strategic plan, mission, vision, and strategic objectives. The purpose of the strategic plan is to achieve the mission, and to that end it defines business objectives.

Figure 2.4 shows the big picture of which program governance is a part. Program governance is generally implemented through two bodies: the program board and the program management office.

FIGURE 2.4   The context of program governance

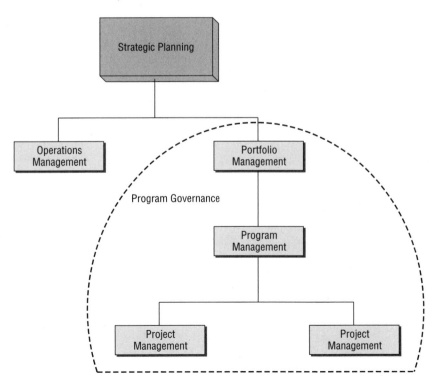

Corporate Governance

The program board   A program is executed in the context of an organization. So, program governance will be affected by constraints and guidance offered by the following:

- Strategic management
- Practices related to program management, such as portfolio management and project management
- Processes and structures that are in place to execute and control the operations in the organization

This connection is addressed through a program board, which provides an executive-level forum to manage the issues of a program. Note the following defining characteristics of a program board:

- It is the body responsible for the governance and quality assurance of a specific program.
- It is typically a cross-functional group composed of senior stakeholders.
- It exists throughout the life of the program.
- It is also sometimes referred to as a *governance board* or *steering committee*.

Functions of a program board include the following:

- Approving the program plans and changes in the plans
- Collecting input for strategic progress reporting
- Ensuring compliance with corporate and legal policies, procedures, requirements, and standards
- Ensuring the availability of resources for the program
- Guiding the program manager on issues where guidance is needed
- Reviewing the program's progress, cost, and benefits delivery
- Establishing the framework to facilitate and limit decision making on investments in the program
- Initiating the program

The program board includes a program director and an executive sponsor, who is responsible for creating an environment that will ensure the program's success. The program board is not always a one-vote, one-person consensus committee when it comes to decision making. Usually, the executive sponsor is the key decision maker who takes into consideration the input from other board members and the program management team. The board may include key stakeholders, from both inside and outside of the organization. The board members usually do not work full-time on the program, and therefore they rely heavily on the program management team.

In addition to a program board, some organizations decide to set up a program management office to manage a specific program.

The program management office (PMO) The program management office is an entity within an organization that holds the responsibility for defining and managing program-related governance elements such as processes, procedures, and templates for all programs in the organization. All the programs in the organization must comply with these processes and procedures. Figure 2.5 shows the relationship between program board and the PMO.

As the program progresses, program governance is largely concerned with monitoring and controlling two factors: the organization's investment and benefits delivery.

This control is achieved and maintained by monitoring the progress reports and reviews on a regular basis throughout the life cycle of the program. These reviews are even more important at the end of each phase of the program because they help the senior management to determine if the program should go to the next phase, and if a new project should be started in a program.

FIGURE 2.5 The program governance framework and structure

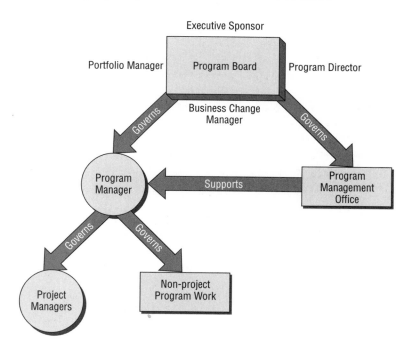

Understanding the Program Life Cycle

From authorization to completion, a program goes through a whole life cycle that includes defining the program objectives, planning the work to achieve those objectives, performing the work, monitoring the progress, and closing the program. You can look at the life cycle of a program in terms of program phases or in terms of process groups (discussed at the beginning of this chapter). The PMI standard looks at the program life cycle in terms of five program phases.

Program Phases

Just like a project, a program is also better managed and controlled by dividing it into phases. The different phases of a program life cycle are shown in Figure 2.6, where the arrows indicate the flow of information and progress.

FIGURE 2.6   The typical program life cycle

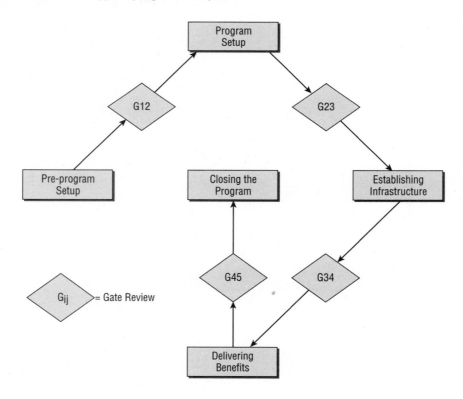

The phases of a program life cycle are discussed in the following:

Pre-program setup   The main function of the pre-program setup phase is to establish a firm foundation of support and approval for the program. This involves understanding the strategic value of the program, defining the program objectives, identifying the key stakeholders and decision makers, developing a high-level business case for the program, obtaining approval for the program, and appointing the program manager. After getting the approval, the program proceeds to the next phase: program setup.

Program setup   The main purpose of the program setup phase is to build a detailed roadmap by defining the key deliverables and planning how the program will be managed to produce these deliverables. The outcome of this phase is the detailed program management plan and the approval to execute it. After the successful completion of this phase, the program manager, along with the program management team, needs to establish infrastructure in which the program work will be performed.

Establishing infrastructure   The main function of this phase is to establish program management and technical infrastructure to support the program and its constituent projects. This infrastructure includes program facilities, program board, program-specific tools, and so on. After successful completion of this phase, the program is ready to execute and deliver benefits.

Delivering benefits   The main purpose of this phase is to initiate the constituent projects and coordinate the interproject activities to create the incremental benefits. When all the program work is completed, the program moves to its closure.

Closing the program   The main function of the closing the program phase is to perform a controlled closedown of the program. This includes the shutdown of the program infrastructure, including program organization and transition of benefits monitoring to appropriate groups in the organization.

The G_{ij} numbers in Figure 2.6 represent gate reviews between phases. The main purpose of a gate review is twofold:

- To check the program performance against the planned criteria for exit from the phase that has just been completed.
- To determine the readiness for proceeding to the next phase.

So, each gate review is a decision point for the program as a whole: go or no go.

Throughout the program life cycle, you need to monitor the program to ensure it's on track. This is where metrics come into the picture.

Understanding Metrics

How do you know if your program is headed for success or failure? How do you even know whether a process in a program is working well or not? The answer is, measure it. If you cannot measure something, you don't know it. This is important because if you can't measure it, you can't control it, and if you can't control it, it is more likely than not headed for a failure. So, how do we measure things in program management? This question has a one-word answer: *metrics*. In this section I'll discuss metrics in general, and a special set of metrics called *key performance indicators (KPIs)*.

The term *metrics* can refer to the whole system or to parameters within the system. However, it should be clear from the context which meaning is intended.

The Metrics System

Metrics refers to a system used to evaluate an entity quantitatively. It specifies a set of parameters that will be measured, a procedure to measure them, and a way to interpret the measurements. Table 2.4 presents different components of a metrics system. There can be multiple parameters in a metrics system and each parameter in general has its own measurement procedure, measurement frequency, threshold value, target value, and units of measurements.

TABLE 2.4   Mapping of the Program Management Processes to Process Groups and Knowledge Areas

Metrics Component	Description	Example
Metric	A parameter in the metrics system that is to be measured	Revenue
Measurement procedure	The procedure used to measure the parameter	Add up the money made by selling the product.
Measurement frequency	How frequently a given parameter will be measured	Once at the end of each quarter
Measurement controls	The controls in place to detect and account for the uncertainties in the measurements introduced by factors such as bias, and to remove the uncertainty if possible	A clear definition of the measurement procedure. Specify date and customer of each sale figure counted in the revenue.
Threshold value	The acceptable minimum (or maximum) value of the parameter below (or above) which a failure will occur	10,000 (minimum) Any amount less than 10,000 represents failure.
Target value	Best value for the parameter that you wish to achieve	50, 000
Units	The units in which the measured value is expressed	U.S. dollars

I used the term *entity* in defining the metrics system. In this context, some examples of entities are: process, performance, and progress. You can use a metrics system to evaluate a process; that is, to evaluate whether the process is working effectively. You can also use a metrics system to evaluate the performance of a team, a team member, a project, or the whole program. In a metrics system set up to evaluate performance, the set of parameters (metrics) will contain key performance indicators, which will mostly depend upon the application area. You can see that it's hard to come up with a general global standard for metrics because the metrics highly depend on the application areas. However, some general metrics (parameters) can be used in project/program management and are relevant to most application areas, if not all. I will be introducing those metrics throughout this book. Here are some general properties of a good metric:

Measurement   The metric (parameter) must be measurable and not vague. For example, a 40 percent increase in revenue is measurable, whereas a *substantial* increase in revenue is not.

Standardization   The metric must be standardized; that is, it is measured and interpreted in a well-defined, standard way throughout the organization.

Clarity   The role of a metric must be clear.

Precision and consistency   Precision refers to the consistency of measurements. This means the repeated measurements of a metric at a given point should, ideally, yield the same values. In other terms, the definition of a metric is not subjective: Regardless of whether John measures it or Mary measures it, it should yield the same value.

Accuracy and reliability   Accuracy refers to how close the true value is to the measured value. The closer it is, the more reliable it is. You must include the degree of accuracy with every measurement; that is, the uncertainty. For example, in the value 70 ± 10, the value 10 is the uncertainty on the measured value 70. This means the true value is between 60 and 80.

Examples of Metrics

Here are some examples of strategic-plan metrics:

Earnings before interest and taxes (EBIT)   EBIT is used to refer to an organization's earning, and is also called *operating income*. It reflects the organization's basic earning potential.

Market share   This refers to the proportion of the total available market (or a market sector) being serviced by this organization. There are several ways of calculating the market share—for example, by the number of customers or by the revenue. For instance, assume that 10,000 customers buy a specific product from your company, whereas a total of 50,000 customers buy that product from any company. Then, your share of that market is 20 percent. In other words, the market share can be calculated by dividing the company's unit sale volume by the total units sold in the market. It can also be calculated by dividing the company's sale revenue from a product by the total sales revenue in the market for that product. Increasing market share is a common business objective.

Return on investment (ROI)   ROI refers to the rate of return on an investment. For example, if you earn $50 interest on a $1,000 investment, the ROI is 50/1000 = 0.05 or 5 percent. However, note the following about ROI:

- It does not factor in how long the investment is held.
- A company with higher ROI does not necessarily earn more, because to calculate the earning from ROI you also need the value for the investment amount.

ROI can also be used at the program level.

Value realization   Value realization means obtaining value from the investment. This metric has already been discussed as a technique in this chapter.

Balanced scorecard   The balanced scorecard focuses on four dimensions: customer, financial, internal operations, and learning and innovation. This metric has already been discussed as a technique in this chapter.

You already know that your program should support the strategic plan of your organization; that is, program benefits should be aligned with the organization's business objectives. This is the point that links the program metrics with the strategic-plan metrics of the organization. The program metrics measure the progress and performance of a program, whereas the strategic-plan metrics measure the progress of the implementation of the strategic plan. In general, strategic-plan metrics serve the following purposes:

- Measure overall achievement; that is, implementation of the strategic plan.
- Link the program benefits to the big picture (strategic plan).
- Provide accountability and credibility.
- Provide a framework for collecting and analyzing data, deriving conclusions, making decisions, and taking actions.

There are some metrics whose purpose is to measure the performance at different levels; for example, at the project, program, and strategic plan levels.

Key Performance Indicators

Key performance indicators (KPIs) are the metrics used to measure performance at different levels, such as strategic plan, program, and project levels. Some KPIs can be used only at one level, and others can be used at more than one level. The KPIs at the strategic-plan level are typically used to quantify business objectives in order to measure the strategic performance of an organization. KPIs at the strategic-plan level are used to accomplish the following:

- Assess the current state of the organization's business and recommend appropriate actions.
- Monitor the business activity in real time.
- Measure activities that are otherwise difficult to measure, such as customer satisfaction and benefits from employees' skill development.

KPIs are typically closely tied to the organization's business strategy, or strategic plan. In other words, KPIs differ from organization to organization depending on the organization's nature and strategy. The KPIs are defined within the framework established by the strategic business plan of the organization. They help make a business objective measurable. A measurable business objective consists of the following:

Direction   The basic definition of the objectives that takes the organization in a certain direction.

Benchmark   Something standard to which the objective is compared or against which it is measured.

Target and time frame   What needs to be achieved and by what time.

KPI   A numerical representation of the performance to achieve the objective.

So, a KPI can be considered as a part of a measurable objective. It is commonly said that when you are defining KPIs for your organization, you must remember that the KPIs need to be SMART—specific, measurable, achievable, realistic, and timely:

Specific   If a KPI is not specific, it will introduce inconsistencies in its measurements and in its use.

Measurable   If it's not measurable, it's not a metric, and hence it's not a KPI.

Achievable   The target value of a KPI must be achievable.

Realistic   A KPI must be realistic to the extent that it can be measured and it can be achieved. A fantasy is not a KPI. However, a fantasy can be broken into KPIs.

Timely   You could almost always achieve your objective if the deadline weren't there. An untimely achievement is a non-achievement.

> Recently, there has been a trend to replace the acronym SMART with SMARTA in which the last A means align. This is to emphasize that the strategic level KPIs must be aligned with the strategic business objectives of the organization.

 Real World Scenario

Measurable Business Objective

The Mind the Gap company has the following as one of its business objectives:

Increase the number of homes in the community connected to the Internet from the current 10 percent to 60 percent by the year 2009.

Note that this is a measurable objective with the following elements:

Direction   It's aimed at eliminating the digital gap between the rich and the poor.

> **Benchmark**   The benchmark in this objective is rather subtle. The assumption is that other communities in the area are better connected to the Internet.
>
> **Target and time frame**   Target is 60 percent of homes connected, and the time frame is the year 2009.
>
> **KPI**   The KPI is the percentage of homes in the community connected to the Internet, that is:
>   Connectivity = (Nc/Nt) 100
> where Nc is the number of homes connected to the Internet and Nt is the total number of homes in the community.

KPIs at the program level are used to measure and monitor the progress and performance of the program. I will discuss those KPIs in the upcoming chapters. However, to ensure the approval of the program, you must ensure that the KPIs and other metrics that you decide to choose for your program are aligned with the strategic-plan metrics. This is part of the gap analysis discussed in the next chapter.

> ## The Three Big Takeaways
>
> The three most important takeaways from this chapter are the following:
>
> - Program management focuses on the dependencies among the projects in the program.
>
> - Three broader management themes that run through the life cycle of a program are program benefits management, program stakeholder management, and program governance.
>
> - Program processes map to nine knowledge areas and five process groups. The names of these knowledge areas and process groups are the same as those in project management.

Summary

Why do organizations run programs? An organization launches a program to deliver some benefits and meet some objectives in the context of its business strategy. A program is defined as a group of related projects managed in a coordinated way to achieve benefits and control that is not available from managing them individually. So, program management is the centralized and coordinated management of a program to achieve the strategic benefits and objectives for which the program is designed. Individual projects in the program are still managed under project management, and program management focuses on dependencies among those projects.

The three broad management themes that run through all the activities of program management are program benefits management, program stakeholder management, and program governance. These themes help unify the program efforts to meet the strategic benefits and objectives for which the program is designed. A program life cycle goes through five stages: pre-program setup, program setup, establishing infrastructure, delivering benefits, and closing. Just like project management, program management is performed through processes that map to five process groups and nine knowledge areas. The names of these process groups and knowledge areas are the same as those in project management.

Before a program can be launched it needs to be defined and authorized. This is accomplished during initiation, which is the topic of the next chapter.

Exam's-Eye View

Comprehend

- A program is defined as a group of related projects managed in a coordinated way to achieve benefits and control that is not available from managing them individually.

- Programs, like projects, are a means of achieving organizational goals and objectives, which are often in the context of a strategic plan of the organization.

- Projects produce deliverables such as product, service, or results, whereas programs deliver benefits and capabilities that the organization can utilize to sustain, enhance, and deliver organizational goals.

- Program managers coordinate efforts between projects, which includes coordinating processes for each of the projects in the program.

Look Out

- A program may include elements of the work related to the program, e.g. ongoing operations, which are outside the scope of all individual projects included in the program.

- Ongoing and repetitive streams of operations in an organization are neither projects nor programs, according to the standard definitions of a project and a program.

- Program stakeholder management extends beyond project stakeholder management. The program stakeholder management must look for additional levels of stakeholders arising from dependencies among the projects in the program and from the wholeness of the program: the consolidated benefits and capabilities.

- Program stakeholder management must identify both kinds of stakeholders, negative and positive, and determine how the program will affect them.

Memorize

- The following three themes run through all the activities of program management: program benefits management, program stakeholder management, and program governance.

- Although each project in a program may have its own discrete benefits, it often also contributes to the consolidated benefits of the program.

- All the processes which are executed at different stages of a program belong to nine knowledge areas: Communication Management, Cost Management, Human Resource Management, Integration Management, Procurement Management, Quality Management, Risk Management, Scope Management, and Time Management. A given process belongs to only one knowledge area.

- The program processes are grouped into five process groups: Initiating, Planning, Executing, Monitoring and Controlling, and Closing.

Exam Essentials

The relationship between the strategic plan and the program Program benefits and requirements must be aligned with the strategic plan: requirements are derived from the strategic plan. The progress at the project, program, and plan levels can be measured by carefully chosen suitable metrics.

The strategic planning process The strategic planning process includes determining the mission, strategic goals, and vision for the organization. It provides the framework for making investment decisions and selecting programs and projects.

Key performance indicators (KPIs) KPIs are the metrics used to measure performance at different levels, such as the strategic plan, program, and project levels. The KPIs at the strategic-plan level are typically used to quantify business objectives in order to measure the strategic performance of an organization. The KPIs are defined within the framework established by the organization's strategic business plan. They help make a business objective measurable.

Stakeholder analysis Stakeholder analysis involves identifying the stakeholders and their needs, and analyzing the needs to determine the stakeholder positions relative to the program. You use stakeholder-analysis techniques such as consultation and procurement documents to collect the stakeholder requirements. Based on those requirements and needs, you characterize the stakeholders into different groups, such as positive and negative stakeholders, to best serve their needs for the success of the program.

Program management themes The following three management themes run through the life cycle of a program:

Benefits management This includes activities and techniques for defining, creating, maximizing, and sustaining benefits from a program. The benefits realization plan contains a definition of each program benefit and how it will be realized. It also maps the program outcome to the benefits.

Program governance   This is the governance that is responsible for developing, communicating, implementing, monitoring, and assuring the policies, procedures, practices, and organizational structures associated with a given program.

Stakeholder management   This includes understanding and managing the influence and expectations of the program stakeholders.

Key Terms and Definitions

benefit   A positive contribution or improvement to the running of an organization such as increased revenues, reduced costs, and improved employee morale.

benefits management   Part of management that includes activities and techniques for defining, creating, maximizing, and sustaining benefits from a program.

control   Set of techniques used to control projects and programs by activities such as analyzing variances, assessing trends to improve processes, evaluating alternatives, comparing actual performance with planned performance, and recommending appropriate corrective and preventive actions and changes in order for the program or the project to succeed. These control activities include the monitoring element.

executive sponsor   An executive who is the key decision maker in the program board and is responsible for creating an environment that will ensure the program success.

formalization   Making something official and putting it in the framework of proper rules and procedures.

gate review   A program review, also called *phase-gate review*, that checks against the exit criteria of the phase that has just been completed and determines the readiness of the program for entering the next phase.

intangible benefit   A benefit that may not be easy to quantify, such as improved employee morale or increased customer satisfaction.

program   A group of inter-related projects that are managed in a coordinated fashion to achieve benefits and control that is not achievable from managing these projects individually.

program board   An executive-level forum to manage the issues of a program.

program governance   A management method that is used to develop, communicate, implement, and monitor the organizational structures, policies, procedures, practices, and other acts to run a program.

program management   The centralized management of a specific program performed in a coordinated fashion to achieve the strategic goals, objectives, and benefits of the program.

program management office (PMO)   An entity within an organization that holds the responsibility for defining and managing program-related governance elements such as processes, procedures, and templates for all the programs in the organization.

program office (PO)   An entity within an organization designed to handle the program administration functions of a program centrally by providing support to the program management team and program manager.

program stakeholders   Individuals, organizations, or both whose interests may be affected—positively or negatively—by the outcomes of program execution and completion.

program stakeholder management   Understanding and managing the influence and expectations of the program stakeholders.

risk mitigation   A technique for reducing the probability of risk occurring, reducing the impact of the risk if it does occur, or both. The risk-mitigation activities that impact the direction and delivery of multiple projects can play an important role in determining which project should go into a program.

social map   A map of an area that displays the social structures and institutions found in the area.

stakeholder analysis   The procedure used to identify and understand the stakeholders and their needs and expectations.

tangible benefit   A quantifiable benefit that may be directly related to the financial objectives, such as a 10 percent increase in revenue.

Review Questions

1. All of the following statements about a program are true except:

   A. A program is a group of related projects managed in a coordinated way to achieve benefits and control that are not available from managing them individually.

   B. A program can include only those tasks that are parts of the projects included in the program.

   C. A program delivers benefits to the organization by enhancing current or developing new capabilities for the organization to use.

   D. Programs are means to achieve organizational goals and objectives.

2. Program management is the:

   A. Collective distributed management of multiple projects.

   B. Centralized coordinated management of a program to complete the projects in the program in the minimum possible time.

   C. Centralized coordinated management of a program to achieve strategic benefits and objectives of the program.

   D. Management of a project whose work is spread out at multiple locations.

3. Program management supports the application of all of the following broad management themes except:

   A. Portfolio management

   B. Benefit management

   C. Program governance

   D. Stakeholder management

4. Program management includes all of the following responsibilities except:

   A. Identifying dependencies among the projects in a program

   B. Dealing with the escalated issues

   C. Creating a work breakdown structure (WBS) for each project

   D. Tracking the contribution of the program-related non-project work to the consolidated program benefits.

5. Benefits management includes all of the following except:

    A. Ensure the availability of resources for the program.

    B. Ensure that the expected benefits are realistic, specific, measurable, and can be realized within a specified time period.

    C. Assign accountabilities and responsibilities for the actual benefits expected (required) from the program.

    D. Whenever a program change is planned, analyze its potential impact on the realization of benefits, or benefits outcome.

6. Which of the following is not a key stakeholder of a program?

    A. Program management office

    B. Project managers

    C. Government regulatory agencies

    D. Performing organization

7. All of the following are true statements about program board except:

    A. It is typically a cross-functional group composed of senior stakeholders.

    B. It exists throughout the life of the program.

    C. It is also sometimes referred to as a steering committee.

    D. It is not responsible for quality assurance of a program.

8. All of the following are the phases of a program life cycle except:

    A. Pre-program setup

    B. Program setup

    C. Monitoring and Controlling

    D. Closing

9. Which of the following is not a program process group?

    A. Initiating

    B. Program setup

    C. Planning

    D. Monitoring and Controlling

10. The nine program management knowledge areas include all of the following except:

    A. Team Management

    B. Integration Management

    C. Cost Management

    D. Risk Management

11. Which of the following are the elements of a strategic plan? (Choose one.)

    A. Vision, mission, and program benefits

    B. Vision, mission, and business objectives

    C. Mission, vision, and project portfolio

    D. Vision, goal, and ROI

12. The analysis performed to verify that the program metrics are aligned with the strategic-plan metrics is called:

    A. Gap analysis

    B. Alignment analysis

    C. Benefits analysis

    D. Stakeholder analysis

13. The program life cycle consists of how many phases?

    A. One

    B. Five

    C. Three

    D. Seven

14. Before exiting a phase, a program goes through a review, which is called:

    A. Exit review

    B. Exit gate review

    C. Phase review

    D. Phase gate review

15. The metric that refers to organization earning is called:

    A. EBIT

    B. ROI

    C. Market share

    D. KPI

Answers to Review Questions

1. B.

   B is the correct answer because a program may include work that is related to the overall program but is not part of any individual project included in the program.

   A, C, and D are incorrect answers because these are the correct statements about programs.

2. C.

   C is the correct answer because it states the definition of program management.

   A, B, and D are incorrect answers because none of these are the correct definition of program management.

3. A.

   A is the correct answer because portfolio management is different from program management.

   B, C, and D are incorrect answers because program management facilitates the application of benefit management, program governance, and stakeholder management.

4. C.

   C is the correct answer because creating a WBS for a project is the responsibility of project management.

   A, B, and D are incorrect answers because all these responsibilities are included in program management.

5. A.

   A is the correct answer because ensuring the availability of resources for the program is a function of the program board.

   B, C, and D are incorrect answers because all these are included in benefits management.

6. C.

   C is the correct answer because government regulatory agencies may be stakeholders in a program, but not key stakeholders.

   A, B, and D are incorrect answers because all these are key stakeholders in a program.

7. D.

   D is the correct answer because the program board is the body responsible for the governance and quality assurance of a specific program.

   A, B, and C are incorrect answers because all these are true statements about the program board.

8. C.

C is the correct answer because Monitoring and Controlling is a process group and not a phase of the program life cycle.

A, B, and D are incorrect answers because the five phases of a program life cycle are pre-program setup, program setup, establishing infrastructure, delivering benefits, and closing.

9. B.

B is the correct answer because program setup is a phase of a program life cycle, and not a process group.

A, C, and D are incorrect answers because the five program process groups of a program life cycle are Initiating, Planning, Executing, Monitoring and Controlling, and Closing.

10. A.

A is the correct answer because there is no knowledge area called Team Management. The teams are managed as part of Human Resource Management.

B, C, and D are incorrect answers because the nine program management knowledge areas are Communication Management, Cost Management, Human Resource Management, Integration Management, Procurement Management, Quality Management, Risk Management, Scope Management, and Time Management.

11. B.

B is the correct answer because vision, mission, and business objectives are the basic elements of a strategic plan.

A and C are incorrect because program benefits and project portfolio are not elements of the strategic business plan. They are created to support (fulfill) the plan.

D is an incorrect answer because ROI is a strategic-plan metric, not a basic element of the plan.

12. A.

A is the correct answer because one of the goals of gap analysis is to verify that the program metrics are aligned with the strategic-plan metrics of the performing organization.

B and C are incorrect because these are the wrong names for this analysis.

D is incorrect because stakeholder analysis is performed to identify the stakeholders and to understand their needs.

13. B.

B is the correct answer because a program consists of five phases: pre-program setup, program setup, establishing infrastructure, delivering benefits, closing the program.

A, C, and D are incorrect because each program has five phases.

14. D.

D is the correct answer because a phase gate review is performed to check the program performance against the planned criteria for exit from the phase that has just been completed, and to determine the readiness for proceeding to the next phase.

A, B, and C are incorrect because the correct term is phase gate review.

15. A.

A is the correct answer because earning before interest and taxes (EBIT) refers to an organization's earning, and is also called *operating income*.

B is incorrect because ROI refers to return on investment.

C is incorrect because market share refers to the proportion of the total available market (or a market sector) being serviced by an organization.

D is incorrect because KPI refers to a key performance indicator.

Chapter

3

Initiating a Program

THE PGMP EXAM CONTENT FROM THE
INITIATING THE PROGRAM PERFORMANCE
DOMAIN COVERED IN THIS CHAPTER
INCLUDES THE FOLLOWING OBJECTIVES:

- ✓ **1.1 Perform a program assessment by defining the program objectives, requirements and establishing a high-level road map in order to ensure program alignment with the enterprise strategic plan or mission.**

- ✓ **1.2 Support business analysis functions in identifying marketplace needs for potential program offering in order to ensure program viability through researching, market analysis, and high-level cost-benefit analysis.**

- ✓ **1.3 Develop benefits realization plan by estimating the costs and benefits (ROI) of the program in order to establish the program feasibility and obtain funding.**

- ✓ **1.6 Evaluate the organization's capability by consulting with the groups involved with delivery in order to validate the program priority and alignment to the strategic objectives.**

- ✓ **2.1 Define the program mission statement by assembling the stakeholders' concerns and expectations in order to establish program direction and set a baseline for any further action.**

- ✓ **2.2 Translate strategic objectives into high-level project scope statements by negotiating with stakeholders in order to create a program scope description.**

- ✓ **2.3 Develop a high-level milestone plan using goals and objectives of the program, applicable historical information, and other available resources in order to align program with expectations of sponsors and stakeholders.**

- ✓ **2.4 Develop an accountability matrix by identifying and assigning program roles and responsibilities in order to build the core team and to differentiate between the program and project resources.**

✓ 2.5 Establish project management standards within the program (governance, tools, finance, and reporting) using industry best practices and enterprise standards in order to drive efficiency and consistency among projects.

✓ 2.6 Define meaningful measurement criteria for success by analyzing stakeholder expectations and requirements across the constituent projects in order to accurately control program performance.

✓ 2.7 Obtain senior management approval for the program by presenting the program charter with its high-level costs and benefits for the organization in order to receive authorization to proceed to the next phases.

✓ 2.8 Conduct program kick-offs with stakeholders by holding a series of meetings in order to familiarize the organization with the program.

As you learned in the previous chapters, you manage projects and programs through processes. A process is composed of at least one input, tools and techniques, and at least one output. You use the tools and techniques on the input of a process to generate its output. Some input, output, and tools and techniques items are common to most of the program processes. The program initiation is triggered by the activities of the pre-program setup phase. You manage the initiation of a program through the Initiating process group, which consists of three processes: Initiate Program, Authorize Projects, and Initiate Team. Before you can initiate a program, the program (or its concept) must originate form somewhere. It's like asking, where do you come from?

So, the central question in this chapter is, how is a program initiated? In search of the answer, you will explore three avenues with me: origin of a program; initiating processes; and common input, output, and tools and techniques.

The Big Picture of Initiating a Program

The big picture of program initiation consists of the program origin, the pre-program setup, and the initiating processes. All of these topics are included in the exam objectives covered in this chapter.

Exam Roadmap

The following table presents each PgMP exam objective covered in this chapter, along with its explanation:

Exam Objective	What It Really Means
1.1 Perform a program assessment by defining the program objectives, requirements and establishing a high-level road map in order to ensure program alignment with the enterprise strategic plan or mission.	Understand phase one of the program, called pre-program setup. You must understand the importance of phase gate reviews in the life cycle of a program, discussed in Chapter 2, "The Program Management Framework." You must also understand how to develop a high-level program roadmap that includes high-level program milestones and high-level business plan, and its relationship to the organization's strategic business objectives. Also understand the selection criteria and selection methods of the program and its constituent projects.
1.2 Support business analysis functions in identifying marketplace needs for potential program offering in order to ensure program viability through researching, market analysis, and high level cost-benefit analysis.	You must know how market-trends analysis, research, and strategic analysis techniques are important in verifying the viability and feasibility of the program, and also in developing the high-level business plan for the program. Understand the Initiate Program process, including the relationship between organizational environment and the benefits realization plan.
1.3 Develop benefits realization plan by estimating the costs and benefits (ROI) of the program in order to establish the program feasibility and obtain funding.	
1.6 Evaluate the organization's capability by consulting with the groups involved with delivery in order to validate the program priority and alignment to the strategic objectives.	Understand the relationship of the origin of a program with the organization's strategic objectives. You must know how to perform a gap analysis to ensure the proposed program benefits are aligned with the business objectives of the performing organization. You must understand that organization's capabilities should also be factored into the gap analysis.

Exam Objective	What It Really Means
2.1 Define the program mission statement by assembling the stakeholders' concerns and expectations in order to establish program direction and set a baseline for any further action.	Understand the origin of programs and how to perform pre-program setup. You must know how to use the Initiate Program process to generate the program initiating documents, such as program charter and preliminary program scope statement. You should also be able to identify the information-gathering techniques and know the project-selection methods.
2.2 Translate strategic objectives into high-level project scope statements by negotiating with stakeholders in order to create a program scope description.	You must be able to identify the techniques to develop a benefits realization plan and the techniques to measure the program benefits.
2.3 Develop a high-level milestone plan using goals and objectives of the program, applicable historical information, and other available resources in order to align program with expectations of sponsors and stakeholders. 2.7 Obtain senior management approval for the program by presenting the program charter with its high level costs and benefits for the organization in order to receive authorization to proceed to the next phases.	You must understand the importance of phase gate reviews in the life cycle of a program (discussed in Chapter 2). You must understand how to develop the high-level program milestones plan and its relationship to the program business objectives. Also, understand the program governance structure (discussed in Chapter 2) to obtain the program approval. To this end, you must know how to perform a gap analysis to ensure the proposed program benefits are aligned with the business objectives of the performing organization.

Exam Objective	What It Really Means
2.4 Develop an accountability matrix by identifying and assigning program roles and responsibilities in order to build the core team and to differentiate between the program and project resources.	Understand the Initiate Team process. You must know the tools and techniques used to assemble the core program team. You must know how to conduct an effective and successful kickoff meeting. You must understand the team-development techniques as well.
2.8 Conduct program kickoffs with stakeholders by holding a series of meetings in order to familiarize the organization with the program.	
2.5 Establish project management standards within the program (governance, tools, finance, and reporting) using industry best practices and enterprise standards in order to drive efficiency.	Thoroughly understand the Authorize Projects process. You should also understand the project management framework within a program. You must know how the projects are selected and what the relationships are between a program and its constituent projects. You should also know how program office and program management office (discussed in Chapter 2) work.
2.6 Define meaningful measurement criteria for success by analyzing stakeholder expectations and requirements across the constituent projects in order to accurately control program performance and consistency among projects.	Understand that you need to identify and select suitable measurement techniques and metrics to monitor and control the performance of your program and the constituent projects. (This issue is discussed in Chapter 2 and will be discussed in the forthcoming chapters as well.)

Some items the pre-program setup phase described in this section are accomplished by using the processes from the Initiating process group.

Program Initiation Processes

Most of the tasks of the program initiation are performed by using the processes of the program Initiating process group. These processes are mapped to the knowledge areas in Table 3.1:

TABLE 3.1   The Processes of the Program Initiating Process Group Mapped to the Knowledge Areas

Program Initiating Process	Knowledge Area	Major Output
Initiate Program	Integration Management	Program charter Benefits realization plan
Authorize Projects	Integration Management	Project charter
Initiate Team	Human Resource Management	Core program team

Before you can begin the program initiation, someone in the organization must say, we need a program. So, where do the programs originally come from? All the programs basically come from the same grand origin.

Understanding the Grand Origin of Programs

A program in an organization delivers benefits and capabilities that the organization can use to meet and enhance its strategic objectives. In other words, programs are means of achieving an organization's goals and objectives in the context of the organization's strategic business plan. So, there is the origin of programs: call it organizational goals and objectives, organization's strategy, or strategic business plan.

To survive, advance, or change, organizations do the following:

- Plan strategic business initiatives and objectives
- Launch programs to take those initiatives and deliver those objectives

As an example, assume that your organization, in its strategic business plan, has identified the following three strategic initiatives:

- Launch a new product line: nanoAssistant
- Open new revenue channels for existing products
- Modify an existing product

All of these strategic initiatives in the business plan can be accomplished by performing some programs. Let's assume that the new product line has the priority over other objectives. As shown in Figure 3.1, this objective can be met by performing two programs: developing the new product and marketing the new product.

FIGURE 3.1   An example of the relationship between a strategic business plan and programs.

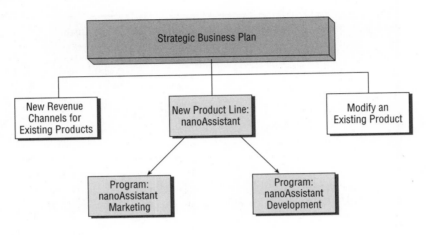

    To get the best results out of its programs, an organization must ensure that the programs are aligned with its strategic goals, consist of the optimal mix of project investments, and make the optimal use of resources.

So, the grand origin of programs in an organization is the strategic business plan of the organization. Not only does a program originate from the strategic objectives of an organization, it's also important to keep it aligned with those objectives during its life cycle. A strategic decision-making body such as a program board or an executive program sponsor initiates the program by summarizing the strategic objectives the program will meet. This is part of what is called *pre-program setup*: phase one of the program life cycle.

Performing Pre-Program Setup

Just like the project life cycle, the program life cycle starts with the program being assessed, selected, and approved as a result of a business-based selection process, which is conducted by a strategic decision-making body such as a program board, a portfolio management group, or an executive program manager. The purpose of the pre-program setup phase is to establish a firm foundation of support and approval for the program. This is accomplished by the following:

- Focusing on preparing for the selection process and venturing through it

- Developing a high-level roadmap that includes program milestones and a high-level business plan
- Performing a gap analysis, conducting kickoff meetings, and using information-gathering techniques

The Selection Process

You, the program manager, need to support business analysis functions in identifying marketplace needs in order to ensure program viability through researching, market analysis, and high-level cost-benefit analysis. These analyses are part of the selection process.

The overall selection process consists of several activities, including the following:

1. Understand the strategic value of the proposed initiative (or change) from where the program is originating.

2. Define the program objectives and align them with the strategic objectives that the program will meet.

3. Identify the key decision makers and stakeholders relevant to the selection process of the program, and also understand their expectations and interests related to the program.

4. Develop a high-level business case that demonstrates the following about the program:
   - Feasibility
   - Justification
   - Need

5. Develop a plan to initiate the program.

6. Hold program kickoff meetings at appropriate times.

7. Appoint the program manager.

8. Get the approval for the program charter by getting signatures of the key stakeholders or by following the approval process that is in place in the organization.

One thing you should realize is that programs are more strategy-oriented than projects are. In other words, a program is at least one level (in the hierarchy) closer to the strategic business plan than the projects are. Therefore, it's important during the pre-program setup phase to show how the projects in the program will be aligned to map to the consolidated program objectives or benefits.

To survive and succeed, organizations need to advance and change. Advancement also has a change element to it. Therefore, organizations often undertake programs to support or facilitate a change at some level. In this case, the program plans should clearly reflect an understanding of generally accepted methods used by the organizational change management and integrate with those methods.

Somewhere during the selection process a question must be answered: can we meet this strategic objective with a project or do we need a program?

Program versus project   Let's step back and focus on the main purpose of a program: to deliver benefits that will help the organization to meet its strategic objectives. Theoretically speaking, there are three possible means to deliver these benefits:

- A project
- Multiple projects
- A program

So, you will need to make a case for why the benefits will be better delivered through a program as opposed to through one or multiple projects without the overhead of a program. The rationale used for launching a program rather than a set of projects can include the following:

- In a program, you can make optimal use of resources (e.g., share them) across multiple constituent projects in the program.
- When the interrelated projects are being managed as a program, you can make optimal resolution and use of dependencies among them.
- A program allows you to coordinate the participation in constituent projects from across different departments in the organization to improve efficiency and performance.
- Programs are more strategic than projects, and therefore they help keep the projects properly aligned to realize the strategic benefits for which the program (and the projects) is being performed.

The stakeholder identification should start during the selection process.

Stakeholder identification   The role that stakeholders play at this phase is generally different from that at later phases because the orientation of the selection committee and the information required may be significantly different from those of the stakeholders that will eventually be affected by the program. So, the most important stakeholders at this phase are those who are in a position to influence the selection of the program for approval. However, you must start identifying those stakeholders as well who can influence the success of the program in case it is selected.

Once the origin of the program in the strategic business plan is identified and understood and the stakeholders are identified, it's time to develop a high-level business plan for the program.

The high-level business plan   The high-level business plan for the program must reflect that the strategic initiative acting as a stimulus for the program is clearly understood. It should align the program objectives with the strategic objectives for which the program is being proposed. It should clearly state the following components:

Mission   The mission states what the program will achieve and why that achievement is important.

Vision   The vision shows how the end state resulting from the program looks and how the organization will benefit from it. In other words, it states where the program will take the organization.

Values   This refers to what's important to the program; that is, how the program will evaluate necessary tradeoffs to strike a balance between different options.

> Recall that the organization has its own mission and vision, as discussed in Chapter 2. In addition to this, each program in the organization has a mission and a vision that should be aligned with the mission and vision of the organization.

The mission, vision, and values of the program must be integrated into the program scope statement.

In a nutshell, the high-level business plan develops a high-level business case that demonstrates the following about the program:

- Feasibility
- Justification
- Need

This can be accomplished through a *feasibility analysis*, which is conducted to verify the viability of the program by assessing its need, value, and practicality. Depending on the program, that analysis may involve studying different aspects of feasibility, including the following:

Financial feasibility   The program will be considered financially feasible if its anticipated benefits outweigh its estimated cost. Cost-benefit analysis, metrics, and other tools can be used to analyze the financial feasibility of a program.

Technical feasibility   The program is considered technically feasible if the performing organization has (or can arrange) the required expertise and infrastructure.

Operational feasibility   A program is operationally feasible if it meets the needs and expectations of the organization. Note that financial feasibility and operational feasibility are not one and the same thing. For example, consider a program in a nonprofit organization that is chartered to improve the graduation rate in a disadvantaged community. The program will be operationally feasible if it meets the needs and expectations of the organization, reflecting from the program objectives and benefits, which may not include any profit.

In evaluating the program viability, you should also consider the following organizational factors:

Organizational capabilities   Does the organization have the workload, resources, and technical capabilities to carry the program? Does the organization have the knowledge and experience to identify the required skills for performing the relevant business analysis?

Market trends and research   You, the program manager, must be aware of how different market conditions can influence the business strategy of your organization, and what kind of impact it will have on the program offerings from the organization. You should also know which market-research techniques can be applied to the proposed program.

Strategic analysis techniques   Even if you are not involved in the strategic business analysis of the organization, you must understand the strategic analysis and other techniques, such as cost-benefit analysis, that are relevant to verify the viability and justification for the proposed program.

You prepare the business plan and develop the case so that the program will be selected. But what are the selection criteria?

The selection criteria   Depending on the organization, the selection criteria may vary from being vague and informal to being specific and formal. Nevertheless, the following are the typical factors that are considered in selecting and approving a program:

Benefits analysis   Identification of benefits and a plan for achieving them.

Budget   Preliminary budget estimates for the program.

Resources   The total available resources for the program, such as equipment, funding, and personnel.

Risks   The risks inherent to the program.

Strategic fit   How well the program fits within the organization's business strategy. This is the most important factor.

Exam Spotlight

The selection criteria are supported by selection methods discussed later in this chapter. The selection methods are also called *assessment methods*.

The following are the possible results from the pre-program setup phase of a program:

1. The program is approved and therefore gets ready to move to the next phase, or the program is disapproved and everybody takes a deep breath. If the program is approved, the following happens.
    1. The program manager is appointed.
    2. A program charter is issued which contains the program vision, key objectives, expected benefits to be delivered by the program, and assumptions and constraints.
2. Key resources needed for the program planning are identified and committed.
3. A plan is developed for the next phase of the program: the program setup phase.

The high-level business plan discussed in this section may also include high-level milestones for the program, or you may have a separate high-level milestones plan.

Developing High-Level Program Milestones

High-level program milestones are an essential part of the high-level roadmap that you want to develop in the pre-program setup phase. A *milestone* is a significant point (or event) in the life of a program, marking the start or completion of an activity or a set of activities, and therefore has zero duration.

The phase gate reviews discussed in Chapter 2 are examples of program milestones. There could be more milestones that you can identify in each phase of the program. Here are some examples:

- Initiation of a new project in the program
- Closure of a project in the program
- Completion of important deliverables in the constituent projects

Here is the basic idea behind the high-level milestones. You have already determined the objectives and requirements of the program (in the high-level business plan), and determining high-level milestones is a starting point for working out the details of how to meet these objectives. More details will be worked out during the planning stage.

Program milestones are determined from the goals and objectives of the program and they must be aligned with them. The following tools and techniques can be used to develop high-level program milestones:

Decomposition   You can decompose objectives and goals into work- (or implementation-) oriented pieces called milestones. After all, each objective is achieved through implementation or work.

Organizational process assets   You can use the historical information from similar programs in your organization's knowledge base to determine how to break the objectives into milestones.

Negotiations   You may need to negotiate with the program sponsor and other stakeholders to finalize a realistic milestone plan.

Expert judgment   Expert judgment is among the tools and techniques common to several processes in program initiation and is discussed in "Common Tools and Techniques" later in this chapter. The experts relevant to the program can also be useful in determining the milestones from the program objectives.

Management information system   The automated information system can be used to facilitate feedback and incorporate changes as the milestone is being developed.

While preparing the milestone plan, you must take into account constraints such as those related to government regulations and industry standards. You should identify the constraints applicable to your program, quantify their impact, and integrate them to the plan.

The program schedule discussed in Chapter 5, "Planning the Program Schedule and Resources," establishes the timeline for the milestones. The program milestones and objectives must be aligned with the organization's strategic objectives. To ensure that, you need to perform what is called a *gap analysis*.

Performing the Gap Analysis

A gap analysis is performed to ensure that the program deliverables and objectives are aligned with the organization's strategic objectives. To be specific, the gap analysis begins with asking if there is any potential gap between:

- Program deliverables and program requirements
- Program benefits and program requirements
- Program deliverables and the appropriate parts of the strategic plan
- Program benefits and the appropriate parts of the strategic plan

If a gap is found, it is examined and analyzed further. While you're performing the gap analysis, factor in the performing organization's capabilities. You can learn about these capabilities by using the following tools and techniques:

- Consulting with the groups that are involved in delivering products and results for the organizations
- Studying the historical information in the organization's database
- Quantifying the experience, knowledge, and skills of different departments in the organization

The accompanying "Real-World Scenario" sidebar offers an example of the kinds of gaps that this analysis can find.

Like many other tasks and processes in program (and project) management, gap analysis is an iterative task. But it is performed first during the pre-program setup phase and before seeking the program approval. In this case, once you've performed the gap analysis and resolved any issues that turn up, the next phase is to get acceptance in the organization for the program. To do that, you will be conducting kickoff meetings at appropriate times, as discussed in the next section.

 Real World Scenario

Mind the Gap

You have just joined the company UnizonTunes as a program manager. You have taken charge of the Artist program that has already been initiated. The program sponsor has asked you to study the program documents created so far and perform the gap analysis. As a result of this analysis, you have found a few gaps, including the following.

Gap between Program Deliverables and Strategic Plan

The following is the UnizonTunes mission:

> *To facilitate the distribution of digital music online*

Obviously this mission is included in the company's strategic plan. One of the program deliverables, however, is to set up a CD on Demand system that accomplishes the following:

1. A customer selects songs on the company's website.

2. The customer requests a CD for these songs.

3. The selected songs are burned onto a CD.

4. The customer is charged online.

5. The CD is shipped to the customer.

You have argued that the CD on Demand deliverable of the Artist program is not properly aligned with the strategic plan of UnizonTunes. Here is your reason: The mission is to distribute digital music *online*, whereas the deliverable involves *shipping* CDs rather than downloading music. You have suggested to remove the gap by replacing the CD shipment element with the downloads element.

Gap between Program Deliverables and Program Requirements

The following is one of the program requirements:

Music copyrights must be honored.

One of the program deliverables is to set up a file-share system that will allow anybody to share music files with anybody else on your website. There is no mention of protecting the copyrights, for example, by implementing a digital rights management (DRM) system. Clearly there is a gap between the program requirement and the program deliverable.

To fix this problem, you have suggested that a committee of experts should determine which DRM system is suitable for the program and how it will be implemented.

Conducting Kickoff Meetings

To familiarize the organization with the program and get an organization-wide general acceptance for the program, you hold a series of kickoff meetings with the stakeholders at appropriate times. While planning and conducting these meetings, keep the following in mind:

- As stated earlier, the goal of these meetings is to familiarize the organization with the program and to gain general organization-wide acceptance.
- You need to identify and apply the appropriate tools and techniques to conduct these meetings.
- You need to understand the organizational culture to conduct these meetings effectively and successfully.

The program kickoff meetings can also be used to introduce program team members and other stakeholders. An ideal kickoff meeting will be a combination of serious business and fun.

In planning the kickoff meeting, you can assume that each team member or stakeholder has the following questions that need to be answered before the end of the meeting:

- Why am I here?
- Who are you and what are your expectations of me?
- What is this team going to do?
- How is the team going to do its work?
- How do I fit into all this?

Consider the following steps to make your kickoff meeting successful:

Agenda   Putting the meeting agenda in the hands of the team members and other stakeholders always helps in running the meeting more smoothly and effectively and in keeping it on track.

Welcome   Take charge of the meeting immediately by introducing yourself and welcoming the participants. Quickly walk through the agenda and set the stage for the rest of the meeting.

Program overview   Define the program, its goals, and its deliverables. Introduce the program team members and briefly describe their roles. The ultimate goal is to provide a big picture and to familiarize the attendees with the program.

Guest speakers   Depending upon the size and the visibility of the program, you may invite relevant guest speakers, such as the program sponsor, the customer, or an executive stakeholder. Before the meeting, spend some time to communicate with the guest speaker on the message to deliver.

Closure   Ask for feedback and hold a questions-and-answers session before closing the meeting.

Purpose   Remember that the main purpose of the kickoff meeting is to familiarize the attendees with the program and gain organization-wide acceptance for the program.

To perform gap analysis and many other tasks that I've mentioned so far in this chapter (such as preparing the business plan, performing feasibility analysis, and identifying stakeholders), you need to collect information.

Information-Gathering Techniques

Having the right information at the right time is crucial to the success of a program and its constituent projects. Therefore, information-gathering techniques are used for various purposes throughout the program life cycle. For example, to identify risks you need to gather risk-related information. The following are some of the information-gathering techniques:

Brainstorming   This is a creative technique used in a group environment to gather ideas as candidates for a solution to a problem or an issue without any immediate evaluation of these ideas. You can use brainstorming on issues such as how to gather information, plus other issues that arise in the information-gathering process. The goal here is to get a comprehensive list of potential solutions to the well-defined issues. The team, along with the relevant experts from different disciplines, can participate in the brainstorming session. Brainstorming is better performed under the guidance of a facilitator.

Delphi technique   This is an information-gathering technique used to reach consensus among experts who share their ideas and preferences anonymously. Here is how it works: A facilitator circulates a questionnaire among the experts to solicit ideas about the solution to a problem. The experts respond anonymously. The responses are compiled and circulated among the participating experts for further evaluation without a name attached to a response. It may take a few iterations before a general consensus is reached. The goal here is for the experts to reach consensus without biases toward each other. In other words, one expert should not be allowed to disproportionately influence the final decision. I'm sure you will have no problem recalling an example of a decision being made because somebody (usually higher in the management hierarchy) said so. The Delphi technique ensures that it is the quality of the information and the argument that is important—not who is saying it.

Interviews   This is one of the common methods used for information gathering. You interview the appropriate stakeholders and subject-matter experts to gather the required information.

Surveys and social maps   Surveys and social maps, which were discussed in Chapter 2, can also be used in information gathering.

SWOT analysis   *SWOT* refers to strengths, weaknesses, opportunities, and threats. For example, you can study these aspects of a choice in order to identify the risks and other issues related to that choice. In other words, if you examine the strengths, weaknesses, opportunities, and threats of a given program, you will be exposing the risks involved in it. A SWOT analysis may reveal that you need to gather more information in certain areas.

You will generally be using more than one of these tools and techniques to gather the required information.

Most of the tasks of initiating a program are accomplished by using the processes in the Initiating program process group. In the rest of this chapter, I will explore these processes in detail, starting with the Initiate Program process.

The Initiate Program Process

This is an unfortunate name for a process, because the Initiate Program process is only a part of initiating the program. As you have already seen, the program initiation actually starts with the activities of the pre-program setup phase. Often the starting point of a program is the need of the organization to change or advance in order to fulfill a vision as a matter of strategy. You know that you need a program (or programs) to materialize the vision or to fulfill the strategic objectives that will lead the organization to realize its vision. However, the concept of the program at this stage is not defined to adequate depth, and may even be poorly defined. So the main purpose of the Initiate Program process is to adequately define the program by clearly stating the scope and benefits expectations. Going through this process verifies and ensures that the program is properly linked to the organization's ongoing work and strategic priorities.

Practically speaking, there are two ways to design and organize programs. First, a program may be designed from scratch by working from the pure concept related to the strategic objectives: projects originate from the program. Second, a program may be organized by grouping the existing (or proposed) projects together. In this case, projects must be grouped and aligned to contribute to the program benefits, and the program benefits must be linked to the organization's strategic objectives.

The input and output items for the Initiate Program process are listed in Figure 3.2 and discussed in the following sections.

FIGURE 3.2   The Initiate Program process: input and output

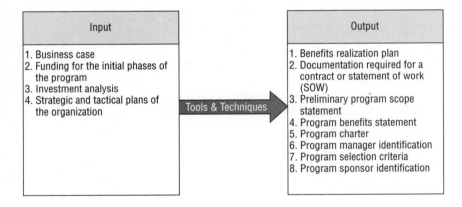

Input to Initiating a Program

One obvious input to the Initiate Program process is the strategic and tactical plans of the organization. Other input items are developed as part of the pre-program setup phase. The input items of the Initiate Program process are discussed in the following list.

Business case   The business case is developed by creating a high-level business plan (discussed earlier in this chapter). In short, the business case documents the business needs linked to the strategic plan that the program will fulfill, and the way in which these needs will be fulfilled.

Funding   Each phase of a program has a cost. Therefore, it is important that the funding for the initial phases of the program, such as pre-program setup and program setup, should be available. You must consider the funding sources and process while developing the benefits realization plan. The funding sources may be internal or external to the performing organization.

Investment analysis   Investment analysis generates results such as return on investment, relationships between costs and returns, and the time value of the money. Investment analysis is necessary to make a realistic business case for the program.

You perform the investment analysis to measure expected benefits from the program in order to develop the benefits realization plan. Some methods of benefit measurements use economic models to estimate the economic efficiency of a program, and may involve a set of calculations to provide overall financial data about the program. The common terms involved in economic models (or investment analysis) are explained in the following.

Benefit-cost ratio (BCR)   This is the value obtained by dividing the benefit by the cost. The greater the value, the more attractive the project is. For example, if the projected cost of producing a product is $20,000 and you expect to sell it for $60,000, then the BCR is equal to $60,000 ÷ $20,000 = 3. For the benefit to exceed the cost, the BCR must be greater than 1.

Cash flow (CF)   While *cash* refers to money, *cash flow* refers to both the money coming in and the money going out of an organization. Positive cash flow means more money coming in than going out. Cash inflow is a benefit (income) and cash outflow is a cost (expenses).

Discounted cash flow (DCF)   The discounted cash flow refers to the amount that someone is willing to pay today in anticipation of receiving the cash flow in the future. DCF is calculated by taking the amount that you anticipate to receive in the future and discounting (converting) it back to today on the time scale. This conversion factors in the interest rate and opportunity cost between now (when you are spending cash) and the time when you will receive the cash back.

Internal return rate (IRR)   This is an investment analysis method used to decide if a long-term investment should be made. The investment of capital in a project is a good investment proposition if its IRR is greater than the rate of interest that could be earned by alternative investments, such as investing in other projects, buying bonds, or depositing the money in a bank account. This is just another way of interpreting the benefit from the project. It looks at the cost of the project as the capital investment and translates the profit into the interest rate over the life of that investment. Calculations for IRR are beyond the scope of this book. Just understand that the bigger the IRR value, the more beneficial the project or program is.

Present value (PV) and net present value (NPV)   To understand these two concepts, understand that one dollar today can buy you more than what one dollar next year can buy (think of inflation and return). The issue arises because it takes time to complete a project, and even when a project is completed its benefits are reaped over a period rather than immediately. In other words, the project is costing you today but will benefit you tomorrow. So to make an accurate calculation of the profit, the cost and benefits must be converted to the same point in time. The PV is the present value of a future payment; that is, a future amount converted into the present time by taking into account the time value, such as predicted inflation and interest. The NPV of a project is the present value of the future cash inflows (benefits) minus the present value of the current and future cash outflows (cost). For a project to be worthwhile economically, the NPV must be positive.

As an example, assume you invest $300,000 today to build a house that will be completed and sold after three years for $500,000. Also assume that the real-estate property that is worth $400,000 today will be worth $500,000 after three years. So the present value of the cash inflow on your house is $400,000, and hence the NPV is the present value of the cash inflow minus the present value of the cash outflow: $400, 000 – $300,000 = $100, 000. That's a positive NPV.

Positive NPV means the investment in the program (or project) will add value to the organization. However, it does not necessarily mean that the project should be accepted, because you also need to consider opportunity cost.

Opportunity cost   This refers to selecting one project instead of another due to the scarcity of resources. In other words, by spending a dollar on this project we are passing on the opportunity to spend that dollar on another project. How big an opportunity are we missing? The smaller the opportunity cost, the better it is.

Return on investment (ROI)   The ROI is the percentage profit (or loss) from the investment in a project. For example, if you spend $400,000 on a project and the benefit for the first year is $500,000, then ROI = ($500,000 – $400,000) ÷ $200,000 = 50 percent.

The organization's strategic and tactical plans   As you know by now, the origin of any program is the strategic business plan of the performing organization. It's important to define the program objectives and align them with the strategic objectives that the program will meet. For this reason, the organization's strategic and tactical plans are mandatory input to preparing documents such as a program charter and a program benefits statement, the output items of the Initiate Program process.

You use some tools and techniques from the input of the process to generate the output.

Tools and Techniques for Initiating a Program

The key tools and techniques used for initiating a program are benefits analysis, expert judgment, and selection methods.

Benefits analysis   Benefits analysis helps iron out the benefits realization plan. It includes the following:

- Identify the required program benefits.
- Identify the relationship of the benefits to the organization's strategic plan and objectives.
- Determine how these benefits will be realized.

Expert judgment   Expert judgment refers to making a decision by relying on expert advice. This is one of the techniques used in program (and project) management to accomplish various tasks, including determining criteria for project selection, which is an output of the Initiate Program process. It's discussed in detail further on in this chapter.

Selection methods   To determine the project selection criteria for the constituent projects, an output of the Initiate Program process, you need to consider various selection methods. These methods are discussed in the section "Understanding Project Selection" later in this chapter.

You use these tools and techniques to generate the output shown in Figure 3.2.

Output of Initiating a Program

The output items of the Initiate Program process are discussed in the following list.

Benefits realization plan   A program is run for its benefits, which the organization uses to meet its strategic objectives. How will these benefits be realized? This is the question that the benefits realization plan answers. The benefits realization plan is maintained throughout the program. It includes the following:

- Communication plan for benefits management
- Definition of each benefit and a description of how it will be realized
- Mapping between program outcomes and benefits
- Metrics and procedures to measure benefits
- Roles and responsibilities for benefits management
- At the conclusion of the program, transition of responsibilities from program into ongoing operations for benefit sustainment

While developing the benefits realization plan, you need to deal with the organizational environment discussed in Chapter 1, "Overview of Project Management." You need to do the following:

- Identify the elements of the organizational environment that can affect the benefits realization plan.
- Factor in these elements and adapt the benefits realization plan to the organizational environment.
- Identify the potential funding sources for the program.
- Learn the funding process from a given resource.

To develop the benefits realization plan, you apply the financial investment-analysis techniques discussed earlier, which include NPV, ROI, and IRR.

The benefits realization plan is a very crucial output item of the Initiate Program process, as it is used in establishing the feasibility of the program and obtaining funding.

Documentation required for a contract or statement of work (SOW)   A program may include contracts or statements of work. This documentation will provide support for creating any contract or statement of work for a program component. It's not sufficient to figure out what is included in the program. You also need to state what is *not* included; that is, to draw boundaries around the program. This is called *scoping* the program.

Preliminary program scope statement   The preliminary program scope statement includes the objectives and high-level deliverables of the program. It draws program boundaries by stating what is included in the program and what is not. The scope estimates are in order of magnitude.

> Generally speaking, an order-of-magnitude estimate is an approximation rounded to the nearest power of 10. For example, with an accuracy of one order of magnitude, the exact value for the number 400 could be anywhere between 350 and 450, and that of 4,000 could be anywhere between 3,500 and 4,500. Remember that *A Guide to the Project Management Body of Knowledge, Third Edition* states that a rough order of magnitude is in the range of –50 percent to +100 percent.

Program benefits statement   The program benefits statement states the benefits that the program will deliver. This is the major output of any program. These benefits must be aligned with the organization's strategic plan.

Program charter   A program is typically chartered and the charter is authorized by an appropriate body such as an executive committee, a steering committee, or a portfolio management body. The program charter also properly links the program to the ongoing work of the organization. It documents the following:

- The mission statement.
- The vision statement that shows the end state of the organization as a result of the successful completion of the program. This statement is a pitch line that plays an important role in getting the authorization for the program.
- High-level key objectives of the program.
- Program requirements.
- Benefits expected from the program.
- Assumptions to be used in planning the program and the program constraints.

The program charter is used as a vehicle to get the program authorized. The accompanying "Real World Scenario" sidebar presents an example.

Program manager and program sponsor   The program manager and program sponsor for the program are identified in this step. These are two of several key stakeholders described in Chapter 2.

Project selection criteria   Selection criteria are determined for the constituent projects of the program. A general factor in these criteria is that the projects must contribute to the benefits that the program will deliver. The section "Understanding Project Selection" later in the chapter discusses these criteria in detail.

So, you have performed the Initiate Program process. Should I say congratulations? Before doing that, I must ask: Is your program actually approved?

 **Real World Scenario**

The MusicFlow Program

You have just joined the company UnizonTunes as a program manager. You have taken charge of the MusicFlow program. The program has a mission to let any artist publish songs online, and to let any customer purchase the songs. The program charter includes the following elements:

Program mission

To facilitate the selling and buying of digital music online.

Key objectives

The key objectives of the program include building the following software systems:

- A database system that will allow UnizonTunes to store and retrieve digital songs

- An interface to the database that will allow the artists to submit their songs

- An interface to the database that will allow the customers to buy the songs

- An online payment system that will charge the customers and will deposit the royalties for the artists into their bank accounts

Program requirements

- The music copyrights must be protected during the digital music distribution.

- The digital songs must have a near-CD quality.

- A genre must be assigned to each song.

Program assumptions

- Enough good and known artists will be interested in selling their music online.

- Enough customers will be interested in paying for the digital music downloads.

- The company has the expertise (or can arrange the expertise) to implement the digital rights management system.

Obtaining the Program Approval

Before you can proceed, you need to obtain senior management approval for your program. Who will approve the program? In other words, who will sign your program charter? The details of this process may vary from organization to organization. In general, a program is chartered (authorized) by an appropriate individual or a body in the organization, such as an executive management committee, a steering committee, or a project portfolio body. It's your job to identify the approval authority and the procedure, and to obtain the approval. You may need to make a presentation to the appropriate body. Keep the following points in mind:

- In your presentation, use terminology that the senior management will understand. For example, you may need to avoid technical jargon. It's always a good communication approach to know your audience and communicate accordingly.

- Use the appropriate presentation techniques. For example, a high-level PowerPoint presentation may be more suitable than presenting all the tiny details. However, keep the detailed information ready in case somebody asks for it.

- The skills that help in a successful presentation and in obtaining the approval include the following:

  - Effective verbal and written communication

  - Influencing

  - Negotiation

  - Selling the program vision and benefits

You use the Initiate Program process to initiate a program, which is composed of constituent projects. So, you need a project management framework within the program.

Establishing the Project Management Framework

A program consists of projects. Most of the program goals are achieved by running projects. Therefore you need to set up a project management framework integrated with your program. In other words, you need to establish project management standards regarding governance, tools, finance, and reporting. This framework should be based on best industry practices and standards to make your projects consistent and efficient. I discussed some crucial elements of this framework in Chapter 2, such as the program management office, the program governance structure, and the relationships between a program and its projects. While establishing the project management framework, you need to perform the following tasks:

- Identify regulations, standards, and best industry practices relevant to your program and constituent projects.

- Identify program office processes relevant to your program and constituent projects.

- Apply these practices, regulations, and standards to establish the project management framework within your program.

- Identify suitable measurement criteria, metrics, and techniques that will be used across the constituent projects to measure the projects and program performance.

As part of establishing project management framework, you will also need to identify standards for protecting intellectual property related to the program and its constituent projects.

It is this project management framework in which you initiate the projects as part of program initiation. A project is initiated by using a program management process called Authorize Projects.

Authorizing Projects

The Authorize Projects process is used to perform program management activities to initiate a constituent project within the program. The timing to initiate projects may differ from project to project and is usually controlled by the program management plan, which we will explore in the next chapter.

Although some projects will be initiated (authorized) during the early phases of a program, the Authorize Projects process can, in principle, be performed in any phase of the program except the closing phase. For example, think of a project whose need the program management team discovered toward the very end of the program (but before the closing phase, of course).

The Authorize Projects process includes the following program-level activities:

- Assign a project manager.
- Communicate the project-related information to the stakeholders.
- Develop a business case for the project by showing how it aligns with the benefits to be delivered by the program. This is important to secure funding for the project.
- Initiate a governance structure for the project that will monitor and track the project progress and benefit delivery from the perspective of the program.

Figure 3.3 lists the input and output items for the Authorize Projects process.

The input to the Authorize Projects process consists of the following:

- The program scope statement that was developed during the Initiate Program process
- The project selection criteria that was determined during the Initiate Program process
- The strategic plan of the performing organization

This process generates the following output:

- The project manager and project sponsor for the project are identified. In some cases it may make sense to assign the program manager as the project sponsor.

- The project charter is issued. Although the project management team may participate in developing the project charter, its approval and funding are handled external to the boundaries of the project management; that is, at the program or portfolio level.

- Program reporting requirements are determined.

- Project funding is approved.

 The use of a program scope statement as an input helps the project charter stay aligned with the program, and the use of the strategic plan as an input item helps the project charter to be aligned with the business objectives of the organization.

The Authorize Projects process triggers some project-level activities, such as developing a project charter. It may also trigger project activities that will be managed at the program level, such as redeployment of resources (human and other) from one project (or schedule activity) to another. To perform the program-level activities, you need some human resources assigned to the program. This is accomplished through the Initiate Team process.

FIGURE 3.3   The Authorize Projects process: input and output.

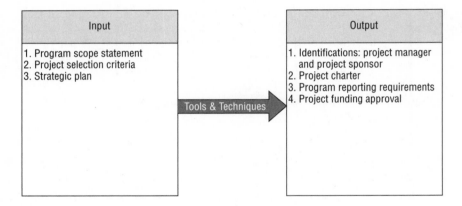

Initiating the Team

The Initiate Team process is used to obtain human resources required to work on the program. Figure 3.4 shows the input and output for the Initiate Team process.

FIGURE 3.4   The Initiate Team process: input and output

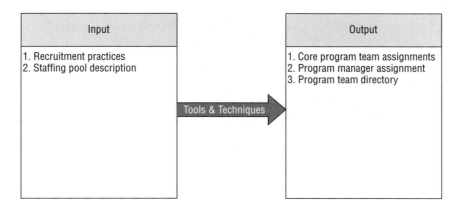

The key inputs to the Initiate Team process are recruitment practices and staffing pool description. It is the responsibility of the program manager to select the human resources that will be able to work effectively for achieving the program objectives and meeting the program requirements. This selection process typically involves designating individuals from within the organization. So, it's important to look carefully into the organization's staffing pool. However, if needed the human resources may be obtained by recruiting new employees or by using sub-contractors. All this should be accomplished according to the organization's recruitment practices and its human resources department.

Here are the main output items of the Initiate Team process:

Core program team assignments   This puts in place the key individuals who will comprise the core program team.

Program manager assignment   This formalizes the appointment of the program manager that was identified during the Initiate Program process.

Program team directory   This contains a list of program team members and information about them, such as roles, responsibilities, and communication (e.g., contact info).

The Initiate Program process and the Initiate Team process can be followed by a program kickoff meeting, described earlier in this chapter, where the appointments of the program manager by the program sponsor and the formation of the core program team should be formalized.

At this point in the program life cycle, the main role of the program manager and the program core team is to perform activities necessary to prepare the program for starting the planning processes.

> At this point in the program, some members of the core team may be assigned (temporarily only) to participate in the program initiating (or startup) activities. They may be replaced by more-permanent staff during the Resource Planning and Acquire Program Team processes.

Assembling the core team involves two tasks:

- Establishing roles and determining responsibilities for a given role
- Obtaining human resources to fill the roles

The tools and techniques used in accomplishing these and other tasks of the Initiate Team process are discussed in the following.

Organizational-process assets   You will need organizational-process assets such as employee databases and job descriptions to establish the roles and determine the responsibilities for each role.

Responsibility assignment matrix (RAM)   This is an accountability matrix used to specify the relationships between responsibilities, roles, and team members. Different matrices can be used to show these relationships at different levels. For example, you can also use a RAM to document the specific responsibilities assigned to specific team members for the schedule activities, as shown in Table 3.2.

A RAM is also called a *RACI chart* because it assigns four roles to team members for various activities: responsible (R), accountable (A), consult (C), and inform (I). For example, in Table 3.2 Mili has the responsibility to design the product, Barbara will be held accountable for the design, Susan and Maya will keep everybody informed of the design's status and progress, and Kiruba will play the role of a consultant for designing the product.

TABLE 3.2   An example of a responsibility assignment matrix (RAM) depicting the roles assigned to the team members for various activities

Activity	Mili	Barbara	Susan	Maya	Kiruba
Design	R	A	I	I	C
Develop	I	I	R	I	C
Test	C	R	A	I	C
Deploy	I	I	A	I	R

Negotiation Who you will negotiate with depends on the structure of your organization. For example, in a functional organization you will negotiate with the functional managers to obtain team members for specific roles. You may also need to negotiate with other program management teams within your organization. In these negotiations, you have a two-prong goal: to obtain the best available person for a role and to obtain the person for the required time frame. You must do your homework to get the best results from the negotiations. For example, you must know what the job requirements are and which staff members can meet those requirements.

Acquisition If the performing organization does not have in-house staff with the required skills, you may acquire the needed services from external sources, such as contractors. This is the area of procurement management, which we will explore in Chapter 5.

Virtual teams A virtual team is composed of geographically distributed members that do not have regular face-to-face meetings. In other words, the virtual teams are the teams composed of telecommuters, and are called *virtual* because the team works together on the same project (or program) without holding face-to-face meetings. The virtual-team format expands the team definition to offer the following benefits:

- People working for the same organization but living in different locations can join the same team.

- A needed expert can join a team even if the expert does not live in the same location as the rest of the team.

- The organization has the option to accommodate employees who can work only from their home offices for a certain period.

- Due to the availability of asynchronous communication, such as email and online bulletin boards, it is possible to form a team of members who have different work hours or shifts.

- Virtual teams eliminate or reduce the need to travel by using abundantly available means of communication such as video conferencing and the World Wide Web services such as email, web pages, and web bulletin boards. This enables the organizations to perform projects that were previously impossible due to travel expenses.

The Initiate Team process is often performed in conjunction with the Initiate Program process.

A program consists of projects, and selecting (and authorizing) projects is a part of program initiation. Therefore, it's important to know how the projects are selected.

Understanding Project Selection

The project selection criteria are an output of the Initiate Program process. A project can be selected by using one or more of the project selection methods, which fall into three categories: benefit measurement methods, constrained optimization methods, and expert judgment.

Benefit Measurement Methods

These methods compare the benefits obtained from the candidate projects so that the project with the maximum benefit will be selected. These methods fall into three categories: scoring models, benefit-contributions models, and economic models.

Scoring models

A scoring model evaluates projects by using a set of criteria with a weight (score) assigned to each criterion according to its degree of importance. That is, you can assign different weights to different criteria to represent the varied degree of importance given to various criteria. All projects are evaluated (scored) against this set of criteria, and the project with the maximum score is selected. The set of criteria may include both objective and subjective criteria, such as financial data, organizational expertise, market value, innovation, and fit with the corporate culture. The advantage of a scoring model is that you have the freedom to assign different weights to different criterion in order to select projects consistent with the goals, mission, and vision of your corporation. This freedom, however, is also a disadvantage because your selection is only as good as the criteria with larger weights. Furthermore, developing a good scoring model is a difficult task that requires unbiased cross-departmental feedback from different levels of the organization.

Benefit-contributions models

These methods are based on comparing the benefit contributions from different projects. These contributions can be estimated by calculating different metrics, such as performing the cost-benefit analysis, which typically calculates the projected cost, revenue, and savings of a project. This method favors the projects that create profit in the shortest time, and ignores the long-term benefits of projects, which may not be very tangible at the current time (such as innovation and strategic values).

Economic models

An economic model is used to estimate the economic efficiency of a project and it involves a set of calculations to provide overall financial data about the project. The common terms involved in economic models —benefit-cost ratio, internal rate of return, and similar concepts—were explained under "Investment analysis" earlier in this chapter.

So, as the name suggests, all the benefit-measurement methods are based on calculating some kind of benefit from the given project. However, the benefit will never be realized if the project fails. This concern has given rise to methods based on calculating the success of the projects; these methods are called *constrained optimization methods*.

Constrained Optimization Methods

The constrained optimization methods employ complex mathematical models that use formulae and algorithms to predict the success of a project. These models use the following kinds of algorithms:

- Linear
- Nonlinear

- Dynamic
- Integer
- Multiple objective programming

The details of these models are beyond the scope of this book but can be found in mathematical literature.

Exam Spotlight

For the exam, you need to know two things about the constrained optimization methods: the names of the algorithm types, and that these methods are used only for complex projects and therefore are not used for most projects.

Either in conjunction with other methods or in absence of them, organizations often rely on expert judgment in making selection decisions.

Expert Judgment

Expert judgment is one of the techniques used in project management to accomplish various tasks, including project selection. It refers to making a decision by relying on expert advice. Its details are discussed further on in this chapter.

An organization may use multiple selection methods to make a decision.

You have seen some examples of processes in this chapter. You now know that each process has three components: input, tools and techniques, and output. Some components are common to many program management and project management processes.

Common Process Component Items

You already know that a process is composed of three components: input, tools and techniques, and output. Each of these components consists of items: input items, tools and techniques items, and output items. Some of these items are unique to specific processes. In this section I discuss those that are common to several processes.

Common Input Items

Several input items appear as input to most of the program processes. Generally speaking, these input items can be considered to belong to a category called *common knowledge* within the performing organization. Assumptions and constraints are the most common input items. Some common input items to most of the program processes are discussed here.

Assumptions An assumption is a factor that you consider to be true without any proof or verification. For example, an assumption that you might make during planning for an in-house program could be the availability of the required skill set to perform the program. Assumptions affect all aspects of program planning, as they are part of *progressive elaboration*. This means that for the sake of moving ahead, you make some assumptions in the areas where full information is not yet available. At a later stage, when more information is available, the planning becomes more accurate and detailed, and assumptions are replaced with facts.

It's important to document the assumptions clearly and validate them at various phases of the program because assumptions, by definition, carry a degree of uncertainty, and uncertainty means risk. Assumptions may appear in both the input and the output of various processes.

 Assumptions can appear in both the input and the output of various processes.

Constraints A constraint is a restriction (or a limitation) that can affect the performance of the program. Constraints are factors external to the program, and will limit the flexibility available to the program manager. They can appear both in the input and the output of various processes. For example, there could be a schedule constraint that a certain phase of a program must be completed by a predetermined date. Similarly, a cost constraint would limit the budget available for the program. Constraints represent prefixed parameters, such as funds available and deadlines, that can also pose risks to the project. Constraints generally take the form of cost, time (schedule), resources, or specific deliverables.

Organizational process assets The organizational process assets are typically grouped into two categories: processes and procedures for conducting work, and a corporate knowledge base for storing and retrieving information. For example, the performing organization may have its own guidelines, policies, and procedures whose effect on the program must be considered while developing the program charter and other program documents that will follow. Another example of organizational process assets is the knowledge and learning base acquired from the previous programs. Here are some specific examples from the organizational process assets:

- Program closure guidelines and requirements.
- Templates to support some program management tasks.
- Procedures for executing some program-related tasks.

The organizational process assets can also be grouped into the following two categories:

- Those that can be used to the benefit of the program, such as templates and lessons learned
- Those that the program must comply with, such as guidelines and policies

Organizational process assets are also called a *process asset library (PAL)*.

Some process assets, such as policies and procedures, can also be used as tools and techniques for some processes. Historical information is an example of *organizational process assets*.

Historical information An intangible benefit of running a program is the lessons learned. The documentation on lessons learned, along with other useful information, should be produced and saved in the organization's knowledge or historical-information database so that future programs can benefit from it. For example, the current program can make use of historical information such as lessons learned from previous programs in the area of scope planning, resource types used for similar activities, actual duration and cost of similar activities, checklists, templates, and so on. Some other examples of historical information are artifacts, estimates, metrics, and risks relevant to the current program. The historical information on successes, failures, and lessons learned in integrating multiple projects into the programs is of particular importance.

Common Tools and Techniques

There is a set of common tools and techniques that are used for most of the program processes. Some of these are discussed here.

Expert judgment Expert judgment is one of the techniques used in program management to accomplish various tasks. It refers to making the decision by relying on the expert advice from one or more of the following sources:

- Functional- and technical-area specialists assigned to the program
- An appropriate unit within the organization
- The program stakeholders, including customers and sponsors
- Consultants
- Professional and technical associations
- Specialized governmental industry groups/bodies

As is clear from this list, the sources of expert judgment may exist internal or external to the organization. Keep in mind, however, that expert judgment can be very subjective and may include political influence. An excellent sales person or an executive with great influence can exploit this method successfully.

Meetings Meetings occur in some form in most of the processes before the output of the process is achieved. Depending upon the need of a given process, the meeting can be formal or informal, face-to-face or virtual, many-to-many (such as a gathering) or one-to-many (such as one person talking to many on a one-on-one basis), and so on. The meetings also help create harmony and synergy among different functional groups working for the program. Meetings, if not handled properly, can become useless and waste employees' valuable time. The following are some of the rules for holding successful meetings:

- Consider a meeting as real work with an intended purpose. Develop an agenda to stick to that purpose.

- Distribute the agenda well before the meeting, let the participants react to it and modify it before the meeting, and stick to the agenda during the meeting.

- Keep the information needed in the meeting readily available to avoid the postponement of issue resolutions.

- Take the meeting minutes, and make the minutes available after the meeting.

- Keep the meeting short. After a certain duration, typically two hours, individuals quit retaining information, and the active participation in the meeting starts diminishing. Look for the signs of this state in your meetings.

- The meeting must have an output: decision making and action items. The action items state who will do what by what deadline.

- All organizations and all individuals are different. Keep a record of what works and what does not, and improve your meeting style by lessons learned.

Policies and procedures   Policies and procedures are part of organizational process assets and can be used as tools and techniques in some processes. They serve to implement certain standards, procedures, and methods to complete the program work effectively and correctly. Policies and procedures may include the following:

- Classification (or confidentiality) of information

- Restriction on distribution

- Requirements for retention

- An organization policy to create a program management artifact, such as a plan.

- The content requirements for a specific artifact

- Specific methodology used to create an artifact

- The approval process for the artifact

Reviews   Reviews are performed to obtain lessons learned. They're also a control vehicle to ensure that that things are going the way they are planned and to recommend corrective actions if they are not. The following are some examples of the review forms:

- Management or peer reviews conducted before communicating with a set of stakeholders

- A project review to gain an insight and status of a given project in the program

- Program benefits review to ensure that the benefits process is being followed and each program benefit is being monitored and controlled properly

- Phase gate review to check that the criteria for an exit from the program phase just finished are met and to verify that the program is ready to enter the next phase

Common Output Items

Some output items, such as assumptions and lessons learned, are common to many program processes. I'll discuss these and some other common output items here.

Assumptions   I have already discussed assumptions as being input to processes. They can also become output of a process when, for example, some information cannot be verified during the execution of the process.

Information requests   Sometimes when you are performing a process, you realize that further information is needed. As a result an information request becomes an output of the process. Information requests can also be initiated by the stakeholders during appropriate program management processes and become output items of those processes. These requests can work as input to an information-distribution process, which will have the information as its output.

Lessons learned   Lessons learned are part of the historical information discussed earlier in this chapter. When you use the lessons learned from the previous programs, those lessons are an input item. However, when you actually learn the lessons from the current program, the lessons are an output of some process of the program. Here are some examples of lessons learned:

- Reasons for performance variances from the program management plan
- Corrective actions taken and their corresponding outcomes
- Risk mitigations and their effects

Supporting details   The program management documents, such as plans, procedures, and standards, are called *program artifacts*. Some artifacts will be produced by the program team as output of some processes, and the others will be produced by the program office. The *supporting details* consist of documents that contain the information required by the program but not included in the program artifacts.

The Three Big Takeaways

The following are the three most important takeaways from this chapter:

- A program originates from the strategic business plan of an organization to obtain some of its strategic objectives.

- The pre-program setup phase initiates the program and the Initiating process group is composed of three processes: Initiate Program, Authorize Projects, and Initiate Team.

- Some input items (such as assumptions and historical information), output items (such as information requests and lessons learned), and tools and technique items (such as meetings and reviews) are common to most of the program processes.

Summary

A program originates from an organization's strategic business plan to obtain the organization's strategic objectives. The pre-program setup phase initiates the program by performing the program selection process. The primary purpose of the pre-program setup phase is to establish a firm foundation of support and obtain approval for the program. As a part of the effort to accomplish this purpose, some important documents (such as a high-level business plan) are generated and some important tasks (such as appointing a program manager) are accomplished. Some of these tasks are accomplished by using the processes from the program Initiating process group, such as Initiate Program and Initiate Team. Business case and investment analysis are included in the input to the Initiate Program process, which generates a program charter, a preliminary program scope statement, and project selection criteria. The preliminary program scope statement and project selection criteria are input items to the Authorize Projects process, which generates project manager assignments and project funding approval.

Exam's-Eye View

Comprehend

- Programs originate from the strategic business plan of an organization to meet its strategic objectives.

- The high-level business plan and program charter are generated as part of the pre-program setup phase. The business case made by the high-level business plan is an input to the Initiate Program process, whereas the program charter is one of its output items.

- The preliminary program scope statement and project selection criteria are generated by the Initiate Program process as output and become input items to the Authorize Projects process.

- Each program has its mission, vision, and values, which must be integrated into the program scope statement.

- The Initiate Team process is often performed in conjunction with the Initiate Program process.

Look Out

- Programs are more strategic in nature than projects.

- The program manager is identified during the Initiate Program process and is assigned or appointed during the Initiate Team process.

- The Authorize Projects process can, in principle, be performed in any phase of the program except the closing phase.

- Some items, such as assumptions, can appear in both the input and output of various processes.

- While developing the benefits realization plan, consider the funding resources for the program.

- You must take into account the constraints such as those related to government regulations and industry standards while preparing the milestone plan.

- The program manager is identified during the Initiate Program process, but the Initiate Team process ensures that the program manager is assigned to the program.

Memorize

- The primary purpose of the pre-program setup phase is to establish a firm foundation of support and obtain approval for the program.

- The program charter is a result of the pre-program setup phase and is an output of the Initiate Program process. It contains the following:

  - The program vision

  - Key objectives

  - Expected benefits that the program will deliver

  - Assumptions and constraints

- The high-level business plan is delivered in the pre-program setup phase and contains a mission, vision, and values. It demonstrates the feasibility of the program and the justification and need for it.

- The program is chartered and authorized by an appropriate body in the organization, such as an organizational executive committee, steering committee, or portfolio management body.

Exam Essentials

Benefits realization plan   The benefits realization plan, developed during the Initiate Program process, is used to establish the program feasibility and obtain funding for it. The financial analysis techniques used to develop the benefits realization plan include return on investment (ROI), internal return rate (IRR), and net present value (NPV). The elements of the organizational environment that may affect the benefits realization plan must be considered and the plan must be adapted to the organizational environment.

Tools and techniques for assembling the core team   To assemble the core program team, you need to establish roles and determine responsibilities for each role. To accomplish this task you use organizational process assets such as employee databases, a responsibility assignment matrix (RAM), and job descriptions. You need to obtain human resources to fill these roles. To accomplish this task, you can use tools and techniques including negotiations, acquisitions, and virtual teams.

Program initiation documents   The Initiate Program process generates some important documents, such as a program charter, a preliminary program scope statement, and a benefits realization plan. The program charter includes the program vision and program benefits, and the preliminary program scope statement contains the high-level deliverables and objectives.

Tools and techniques   The main tools and techniques used in program initiation are program and project selection methods, scoring methods, investment-analysis techniques such as BCR, ROI, PV, and NPV, and expert judgment.

Program approval   The program charter is used as a vehicle to get the program authorized and it must be signed by an appropriate organizational body, such as an executive committee, a steering committee, or a portfolio management body.

Key Terms and Definitions

assumption   A factor that you consider to be true without any proof or verification.

Authorize Projects   A program initiating process used to authorize projects in the program; includes obtaining project approval, issuing a program charter, and assigning a project manager.

benefit-cost ratio (BCR)   The value obtained by dividing the benefit by the cost.

benefits realization plan   A document that contains a definition of each expected program benefit and other information about it, such as how the benefit maps to program outcome and how it will be realized.

brainstorming   A creative technique used in a group environment to gather ideas as candidates for a solution to a problem or an issue, without any immediate evaluation of these ideas.

cash flow (CF)   Refers to both the money coming in and the money going out of an organization. Positive cash flow means more money coming in than going out.

constraint   A restriction (or a limitation) of available options that can affect the performance of the project or a program.

Delphi technique   An information-gathering technique used to reach consensus among the experts, who share their ideas and preferences anonymously.

Initiate Program   A process used to begin the program initiation by generating important documents, such as the program charter and preliminary program scope statement, and by identifying a program manger.

Initiate Team   A program process used to put together a core program team.

internal return rate (IRR)   An investment-analysis method used to decide if a long-term investment should be made. It compares the expected benefit of investment in a project with benefits from other investment methods.

milestone   A significant point (or event) in the life of a program; refers to marking the start or completion of an activity or a set of activities, and therefore has zero duration.

net present value (NPV)   The present value of the future cash inflows (benefits) minus the present value of the current and future cash outflows (cost). For a project to be worthwhile economically, the NPV must be positive.

opportunity cost   Refers to selecting a project over another due to the scarcity of resources. Opportunity cost is the benefit missed by not selecting a project.

preliminary program scope statement   A document, generated as an output of the Initiate Program process, that defines the program scope at a high level. For example, it includes the program objectives and high-level deliverables.

present value (PV)   The present value of a future payment; that is, a future amount converted into the present time by taking into account the time value, such as inflation and interest.

program artifacts   Objects created for the program, such as program documents, which include plans, procedures, and standards.

program artifacts   The program management documents, such as plans, procedures, and standards.

program charter   A document generated by the Initiate Program process; states the key objectives, expected benefits, and assumptions and constraints of the program.

program team directory   A document that contains a list of program team members and information about them, such as roles, responsibilities, and communication (e.g., contact info).

RACI chart   A RAM that assigns four roles to team members for various responsibilities/activities: responsible (R), accountable (A), consult (C), and inform (I).

responsibility assignment matrix (RAM)   An accountability matrix used to specify the relationships between responsibilities, roles, and team members.

return on investment (ROI)   The percentage profit from the investment in the project or program.

SWOT analysis   An analysis used to gather information by examining the strengths, weaknesses, opportunities, and threats involved in an undertaking such as a program or a project.

virtual team   A team of members working on the same project (or program) with few or no face-to-face meetings. Various technologies, such video conferencing and the World Wide Web including email, web pages, and web bulletin boards are used to facilitate communication among team members.

Review Questions

1. To get the best results from its programs, an organization must ensure all of the following except:

   A. The programs are best aligned with the strategic goals of the organization.

   B. The programs make use of the existing expertise in the organization so that there will be no need to hire new employees.

   C. Programs are composed of the best mix of project investments.

   D. Programs make optimal use of resources.

2. The primary purpose of the pre-program setup phase is to:

   A. Establish a firm foundation of support and obtain approval for the program.

   B. Write a strategic business plan for the organization.

   C. Prepare a detailed program management plan.

   D. Write a detailed scope statement for each of the constituent projects.

3. Preparing for and going through the program selection process includes all of the following except:

   A. Define the program objectives.

   B. Develop a plan to initiate the program.

   C. Develop a detailed program management plan.

   D. Understand the strategic value of the program.

4. The program initiating process group includes all of the following processes except:

   A. Authorize Projects

   B. Initiate Projects

   C. Initiate Team

   D. Initiate Program

5. Which of the following is not an input to the Initiate Program process?

   A. Business case

   B. Investment analysis

   C. Program charter

   D. Funding for the initial phases of the program

6. All of the following are output items to the Initiate Program process except:

    A. Program charter

    B. Program benefits statement

    C. Project selection criteria

    D. Program management plan

7. All of the following are input items to the Authorize Projects process except:

    A. Program scope statement

    B. Project charter

    C. Project selection criteria

    D. Strategic plan of the organization

8. All of the following are output items of the initiate team except:

    A. Program team assignments

    B. Program manager assignment

    C. Program team directory

    D. Recruitment practices

9. Several program management processes have all the following items as input except

    A. Assumptions

    B. Constraints

    C. Meetings

    D. Historical information

10. The tools and techniques that are common to most of the program management processes include all of the following except:

    A. Probability and impact matrix

    B. Expert judgment

    C. Meetings

    D. Reviews

11. The main document, created by using the Initiate Program process, that establishes the feasibility of the program is called:

    A. Feasibility doc

    B. Benefits realization plan

    C. Statement of work

    D. Program charter

12. Which of the following is not an information-gathering tool or technique?

    A. Delphi

    B. ROI

    C. SWOT

    D. Social maps

13. The appointments made or identified during the Initiate Program process are:

    A. Program manager and core team members

    B. Sponsor and core team members

    C. Program manager, sponsor, and core team members

    D. Program manager and sponsor

14. A program is chartered and authorized by:

    A. The program management office

    B. The program manager

    C. The program core team

    D. An appropriate body, such as an executive committee, a steering committee, or a project portfolio body

15. You are planning to conduct kickoff meetings for your program. What is true about these meetings?

    A. There can be only one kickoff meeting.

    B. The main goal of a kickoff meeting is to raise money.

    C. The main goal of a kickoff meeting is to familiarize the organizations with the program.

    D. The main goal of a kickoff meeting is to introduce the core team members to each other.

16. Your manager has asked you to establish the selection criteria for projects in a program. What process will you perform?

    A. Initiate Program

    B. Initiate Team

    C. Authorize Projects

    D. Select Projects

Answers to Review Questions

1. B.

    B is the correct answer because a program's goal is to meet the strategic objectives of the organization, and it will have to use the expertise necessary to accomplish its goal regardless of whether that expertise already exists in the organization.

    A, C, and D are incorrect answers because an organization does need to ensure that a program meets all of these requirements.

2. A.

    A is the correct answer because the primary purpose of the pre-program setup phase is to establish a firm foundation of support and obtain approval for the program.

    B is an incorrect answer because the strategic business plan should be in place before you even talk about a program.

    C is an incorrect answer because a detailed program management plan is prepared during phase two: the program setup.

    D is an incorrect answer because the detailed scope statements for the constituent projects are written under project management, and will be the responsibilities of project managers.

3. C.

    C is the correct answer because during the selection process, you need to develop only a high-level business plan (case) for the program.

    A, B, and D are incorrect answers because all these are part of preparing for and going through the program selection process in phase one: the pre-program setup.

4. B.

    B is the correct answer because the process to initiate a constituent project within a program is called Authorize Projects.

    A, C, and D are incorrect answers because the program Initiating process group consists of three processes: Initiate Program, Authorize Projects, and Initiate Team.

5. C.

    C is the correct answer because program charter is an output of the Initiate Program process.

    A, B, and D are incorrect answers because the input items to the Initiate Program process are business case, investment analysis, funding for the initial phases of the program, and strategic plan of the performing organization.

6. D.

D is the correct answer because the program management plan is prepared during planning and not during initiating.

A, B, and C are incorrect answers because all these items are included in the output of the Initiate Program process.

7. B.

B is the correct answer because a project charter is the output of this process.

A, C, and D are incorrect answers because all these items are included in the input of the Authorize Projects process.

8. D.

D is the correct answer because recruitment practices are an input to the Initiate Team process.

A, B, and C are incorrect answers because all these items are included in the output of the Initiate Team process.

9. C.

C is the correct answer because meetings are generally considered as tools and techniques, not input.

A, B, and D are incorrect answers because the input items common to most of the program management processes include assumptions, constraints, historical information, and organizational process assets.

10. A.

A is the correct answer because a probability and impact matrix is not a common tool used in most of the program management processes.

A, B, and C are incorrect answers because tools and techniques common to most of the program management processes include expert judgment, meetings, reviews, and policies and procedures.

11. B.

B is the correct answer because the benefits realization plan is used to establish the feasibility of the program and to obtain funding for it.

A is incorrect because there is no standard program management document called a feasibility doc.

C is incorrect because a SOW describes the required work.

D is incorrect because the program charter is used to authorize the program.

12. B.

B is the correct answer because ROI refers to return on investment.

A is incorrect because Delphi is an information-gathering technique used to reach a consensus of experts without any one person having undue influence on the outcome.

C is incorrect because SWOT is an information-gathering technique that involves examining strengths, weaknesses, opportunities, and threats.

D is incorrect because social maps is a technique that can be used to gather information about, for example, the program stakeholders.

13. D.

D is the correct answer because program manager identification and sponsor identification are included in the output of the Initiate Program process.

A, B, and C are incorrect because core team members are assigned during the Initiate Team process.

14. D.

D is the correct answer because a program is chartered (authorized) by an appropriate individual or body in the organization at executive level, such as an executive committee, a steering committee, or a project portfolio body.

A, B, and C are incorrect because a program is chartered (authorized) at the executive level.

15. C.

C is the correct answer because the main goal of a kickoff meeting is to familiarize the organizations with the program and to gain organization-wide acceptance for the program.

A is incorrect because you typically conduct a series of kickoff meetings to familiarize the organization with the program.

B is incorrect because the purpose of the kickoff meeting is not to raise money.

D is incorrect because kickoff meetings do not include just the core team members.

16. A.

A is the correct answer because the projects-selection criteria are an output of the Initiate Program process.

B is incorrect because the projects-selection criteria are not an output of the Initiate Team process.

C is incorrect because the projects-selection criteria is an input to the Authorize Projects process.

D is incorrect because there is no standard program management process called Select Projects.

Chapter
4

Planning the Program

THE PGMP EXAM CONTENT FROM THE PLANNING THE PROGRAM PERFORMANCE DOMAIN COVERED IN THIS CHAPTER INCLUDES THE FOLLOWING OBJECTIVES:

- ✓ **3.1 Develop a detailed program scope statement by incorporating program vision, objectives, out of scope items, schedule, financial milestones, and legal/regulatory/safety concerns in order to aid in overall planning.**

- ✓ **3.2 Develop program scope definition using Work Breakdown Structure in order to determine the program deliverables and tasks.**

- ✓ **3.3 Establish the program management plan and baseline by integrating the plans for the constituent projects and creating the plans for the supporting program functions including management of scope, schedule, finance, benefits, quality, resource, procurement, risk response, change and communications in order to effectively forecast, monitor, and identify variances during program execution.**

- ✓ **3.6 Develop the transition plan by defining exit criteria, policies and processes to ensure all administrative, commercial, and contractual obligations are met upon program completion.**

After the program has been initiated, as discussed in the previous chapter, you need to develop a program management plan, which becomes the primary source of information for how the program will be planned, executed, monitored, controlled, and closed. Developing a program management plan belongs to the Integration Management knowledge area. So it should not come as a surprise that the program management plan is an integral document that contains several subsidiary plans, and some of those subsidiary plans also belong to the Integration Management knowledge area, such as the resource management plan and the interface management plan.

Another component of the program management plan is planning the program scope. The primary purpose of program scope management is to ensure that the required work and only the required work is performed to complete the program successfully. Before you start defining the scope, you need to know how to do so. In other words, you need to develop a scope management plan. Once you have defined the scope, you need to break it down into concrete manageable tasks that can be assigned and performed. This is accomplished through what is called the *program work breakdown structure (PWBS)*.

While developing all these plans, you are performing program setup from the perspective of the program life cycle, so the central issue in this chapter is planning for the program and its scope. To be able to put your arms around this issue, you will explore three avenues: the program setup phase, the program integration plans, and the program scope plans.

The Big Picture of Planning the Program

Before you actually start executing the program, you need to lay the foundations of the program for its successful execution; that is, you need to do some planning. The big picture of program planning includes program setup, integration plans, and scope plans. The exam objectives covered in this chapter include these topics.

The Exam Roadmap

The following table presents each PgMP exam objective covered in this chapter, along with its explanation:

Exam Objective	What It Really Means
3.1 Develop a detailed program scope statement by incorporating program vision, objectives, out of scope items, schedule, financial milestones, and legal/regulatory/safety concerns in order to aid in overall planning.	You must understand the Scope Definition process. You should also be able to distinguish between scope statement and scope management plan by knowing the elements of the two. You must also know the tools and techniques used in the Scope Definition process.
3.2 Develop program scope definition using Work Breakdown Structure in order to determine the program deliverables and tasks.	Understand the Create Program Work Breakdown Structure (PWBS) process. You must be able to identify the tools and techniques used for creating the PWBS. Also understand the relationship between the PWBS and WBS for each constituent project.
3.3 Establish the program management plan and baseline by integrating the plans for the constituent projects and creating the plans for the supporting program functions including management of scope, schedule, finance, benefits, quality, resource, procurement, risk response, change and communications in order to effectively forecast, monitor, and identify variances during program execution.	You should know how to perform the program setup and you should understand the Develop Program Management Plan process. You must be able to identify the components of the program management plan. You should also be able to identify the tools and techniques used in developing the program management plan. You must understand the Interface Planning and Resource Planning processes. Other aspects of this objective are covered in Chapter 5, "Planning the Program Schedule and Resources," and Chapter 6, "Planning for Quality, Risk, and Communication."

Exam Objective	What It Really Means
3.6 Develop the transition plan by defining exit criteria, policies and processes to ensure all administrative, commercial, and contractual obligations are met upon program completion.	You must understand the Transition Planning process. You should be able to identify the elements of the program transition plan. Also know the tools and techniques that can be used in the Transition Planning process.

Program Planning Processes

Most of the tasks in these exam objectives are performed by using the processes from the Program Planning process group. In Table 4.1 the processes included in the Program Planning process group are mapped to the knowledge areas; their major outputs are also listed.

TABLE 4.1   The Processes of the Program Planning Process Group Mapped to the Knowledge Areas

Knowledge Area	Program Planning Process	Major Output
Integration Management	1. Develop Program Management Plan 2. Interface Planning 3. Transition Planning 4. Resource Planning	1. Program Management Plan 2. Interface Management Plan 3. Transition Plan 4. Resource Management Plan
Scope Management	1. Scope Definition 2. Create Program Work Breakdown Structure (PWBS)	1. Program Scope Statement and Scope Management Plan 2. PWBS
Time Management	Schedule Development	Program Schedule
Cost Management	Cost Estimating and Budgeting	Program Budget and Cost Management Plan
Quality Management	Quality Planning	Quality Management Plan
Human Resource Management	Human Resource Planning	Staffing Management Plan
Communication Management	Communication Planning	Communication Management Plan

TABLE 4.1   The Processes of the Program Planning Process Group Mapped to the Knowledge Areas *(continued)*

Knowledge Area	Program Planning Process	Major Output
Risk Management	Risk Management Planning and Analysis	List of Identified Risks and Risk Response Plan
Procurement Management	1. Plan Program Purchases and Acquisitions 2. Plan Program Contracting	1. Procurement Management Plan 2. Contract Management Plan

In this chapter I discuss the planning processes that belong to the Integration Management and Scope Management knowledge areas. Other planning processes are explored in Chapters 5 and 6.

Planning is intimately related to the second phase of the program life cycle: program setup. So, before diving into program planning, let's take a close look at performing program setup.

Performing Program Setup

As you learned in the previous chapter, program setup is phase two of the program life cycle. Key tasks of and results from this phase are related to program planning. Recall that, before entering this phase, the program has passed the phase-one gate review. That means the program has been approved (in principle) and we have a program charter that defines the high-level program scope.

The main purpose of phase two (program setup) is twofold:

- Define the program's key deliverables.
- Develop a detailed roadmap that provides direction on and description of how the program will be managed.

This way, phase two continues building the foundation for the program, an activity that was started in phase one.

Main Tasks of Program Setup

Performing program setup may include the following:

Alignment of the program with the organization   Ensure that the mission, values, and vision of the program are in line with the organization's strategic objectives for which the program is being set up.

Alignment of the projects with the program   This consists of the following:

- Develop a program architecture that maps out how the projects in the program will contribute to developing capabilities that will result in benefits for which the program is being planned.
- Develop the business case for each project in the program, which includes addressing the investment, regulatory, and technical factors.

Feasibility study   Conduct any needed feasibility studies for the following:

- Economic and technical feasibility of the program
- Ethical feasibility and acceptability of the program

Planning   Perform planning for setting up the program, such as the following:

- Detailed cost and schedule plan
- Rules for make-or-buy decisions
- Rules for selecting subcontractors

Communication   Communicate with program stakeholders to gain support for the program.

Of course, these activities will generate some results, as detailed in the next section.

Results of Program Setup

The key results from performing program setup revolve around program planning and include the following:

Components   This includes identifying and defining the components that constitute the program.

Scope   This includes developing a scope definition and plan.

Schedule   The schedule is developed through the following steps:

- Define and identify activities
- Sequence the identified activities
- Make activity duration and resource requirement estimates
- Develop schedule from the information gathered from the first three steps

Risks   This includes risk-management consolidation, which refers to integrating and coordinating the plans for handling program risks, including the risks for the individual program components, such as projects. Handling risks means identifying and analyzing risks and determining the responses to these risks, should they occur.

Resources   This includes internal and external resource planning, such as the following:

- Cost estimating and budgeting

- Staffing allocation
- Identification of a preliminary program team

Approval   This includes getting the program management plan approved. The individual business cases and feasibility studies are used to gain the approval.

Ultimately, the desired output of the program setup phase is the approval that authorizes the execution of the program according to the program management plan. To gain this approval, the program management plan uses individual business cases and feasibility studies to address the following questions:

Deliverables   What are the program deliverables and when will the delivery be made?

Cost   How much will the program cost? A budget estimate with a timeline, called the *cost baseline*, is required.

Risks   What are the risks and issues involved in the program? How will these risks and issues be dealt with?

Assumptions and constraints   What assumptions and constraints does the program contain, and how will they impact the program?

Dependencies   What are the program dependencies, such as the dependencies among the constituent projects, dependencies between the program and its constituent projects, and dependencies of the program on factors external to the program? How will the program exploit some of these dependencies to optimize the use of resources?

Implementation   How will the program plan be implemented? In other words, how will the program be performed; for example, how will it be managed and executed?

To answer most of these questions, you perform the processes of the Program Planning process group.

Understanding Program Planning

Program planning lays the groundwork for the execution of the program. In other words, the Program Planning process group consists of the processes that are used to accomplish the following:

- Identify the deliverables that will meet the program's goal.
- Based on these deliverables, figure out exactly what work needs to be done; that is, develop the program scope.
- Plan how to do the required work.

The program deliverables created throughout the program consist of the final product, service, or results, as well as the documents created as a result of processes that are used for managing the program. For example, a key deliverable of program planning is the document that contains the program management plan, which defines the tactical means to carry out the program. This plan is so important and pervasive that executing the program is also called executing (or implementing) the program management plan.

The program management plan could be just one document that contains subsidiary plans as its components, or it could be a collection of documents and each document other than the main plan could contain a subsidiary plan.

The program management plan includes the following:

Scope   The program management plan contains the following scope-related items:

- What's included in the program and what's not: all aspects of the scope. See "Defining the Program Scope" further on in the chapter for details.
- The program work breakdown structure (PWBS), which presents the program scope in terms of deliverables and the work needed to generate those deliverables. See "Creating a Program Work Breakdown Structure (PWBS)" further on in the chapter for details.

Resources   The program management plan addresses the internal and external resources required to perform the work defined in the PWBS. These resources include the following:

- Program budget that defines the monetary plan for the program and all aspects of cost
- Human resources, including the organization of the program
- Procurement plans for using external resources to receive products or services needed to accomplish the program objectives

Schedule   The plan contains the program schedule for the milestones and deliverables. Chapter 5 covers scheduling in detail.

Quality   This describes the quality requirements of the deliverables and the means by which those requirements will be assured.

Risk   This includes all aspects of the risk, including the methodology to be used to manage those risks.

Communication   The program management plan includes the communication plans to be used for communicating with the program stakeholders.

Coordination   This involves plans for managing various relationships, including the relationship between project and non-project tasks within the program, relationship of the program to external factors, the relationship of the program to the projects, and so on.

Benefit delivery   The program management plan contains the plan to define metrics and systems in order to realize, track, and sustain benefits for which the program is to be performed.

> The Program Planning processes depend upon the information generated at the project level. These processes are *iterative*, which allows replanning during the program life cycle when, for example, a scope change is approved.

The program management plan is created early in the program, but it may be updated later due to the approved changes during the program life cycle. There are some milestones at which the plan must be revisited to ensure that it is still in line with the program goals. These milestones include the following:

- Initiation of a new project in the program

- Closure of a project in the program

- Beginning (or end) of the fiscal year of the performing organization, which affects the program's budgeting planning cycle

- Unplanned events at the organization level, such as acquisitions or mergers

- A change within the program, such as an output of the Risk Monitoring and Control process, that may require revisiting the plan and updating it

Some plans, such as the program management plan and the resource management plan, deal with the integration aspect of the program, and therefore are also called the *integration plans*.

Developing Integration Plans for the Program

Some program management tasks deal with the big picture of program management; for example, creating a program management plan that will describe how to manage and execute the program. These tasks require identifying, unifying, and coordinating various processes across process groups and knowledge areas. Therefore, these tasks are performed by using the processes in the Integration Management knowledge area. The following program planning processes fall into this knowledge area:

- Develop the program management plan.

- Develop the interface management plan.

- Develop the resource management plan.

- Develop the transition plan.

Developing the Program Management Plan

The program management plan defines the scope of the program and describes how the work within the scope will be performed to meet the program objectives. The program is executed according to this plan; that is, executing the program management plan is equivalent to executing the program. The program management plan is created by using the Develop Program Management Plan process, which consolidates the outputs of various planning processes. Figure 4.1 depicts this process, along with its input and output items.

FIGURE 4.1 The Develop Program Management Plan process: input and output

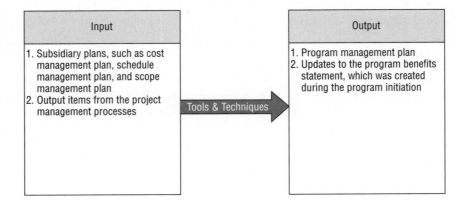

Input	Output
1. Subsidiary plans, such as cost management plan, schedule management plan, and scope management plan 2. Output items from the project management processes	1. Program management plan 2. Updates to the program benefits statement, which was created during the program initiation

Tools & Techniques

Input to the Develop Program Management Plan

The main purpose of the program management plan is to consolidate the output of different planning processes to guide the program execution. Therefore, the input to the Develop Program Management Plan consists of the subsidiary plans from the Program Planning processes and also some output items from the planning processes of the projects in the program.

Output items from the project planning processes Your program consists of individual projects. The projects are also planned by using the planning processes in project management. Obviously, the major output items (usually the plans) from the planning processes of the constituent projects are important input to the program management plan.

Subsidiary plans The subsidiary plans that are input to the Develop Program Management Plan process include the following:

- Benefits management plan
- Communication management plan
- Cost management plan
- Contracts management plan
- Interface management plan

- Procurement management plan
- Quality management plan
- Resource management plan
- Risk response plan
- Schedule management plan
- Scope management plan
- Staffing management plan

Benefits management is performed according to the benefits management plan, and was discussed in Chapter 2, "The Program Management Framework." Benefits management is one of the themes running through the life cycle of the program. In this chapter I will cover the interface management plan, resource management plan, and scope management plan. Other plans will be covered in Chapters 5 and 6. These subsidiary plans are consolidated into one master plan by using the tools and techniques discussed next.

Tools and Techniques for Developing the Program Management Plan

The following tools and techniques can be used in developing the program management plan.

The management information system   An automated information system can be helpful in developing the program management plan—for example, to collect suggestions, store and distribute the documents, and integrate the subsidiary plans into the program management plan.

The configuration management system   This system is used to process the changes to the program management plan; it includes the following:

- Submitting changes
- Tracking the reviews of the changes
- Defining approval levels for changes
- Validating the implementation of approved changes

In an integrated technical environment, the management information system, configuration management system, and change control system are components of the same system. The configuration management system can be a subsystem of the management information system, and the change control system can be a subsystem of the configuration management system.

The change control system   The change control system is a collection of formal procedures and tools to accomplish the following:

- Determine how the program deliverables and documents will be controlled.
- Control the change process to assure that only approved changes are implemented.

The plan describes how the change control system will be used to manage and control changes to the plan. This topic is discussed in detail in Chapter 8, "Monitoring and Controlling the Program."

Expert judgment   Expert judgment can be helpful in determining the technical and managerial details in the various components of the program management plan. It is also called *stakeholder skills and knowledge*.

With the help of these tools and techniques, the subsidiary plans from the input to the Develop Program Management Plan process are consolidated into one master plan, which is the major output of the Develop Program Management Plan process.

Output of the Develop Program Management Plan

The output of the Develop Program Management Plan process, obviously, includes the program management plan. But this process may also update the program benefits statement. Both output items are discussed here.

The program management plan   This is the major output of the Develop Program Management Plan process. This, along with other planning processes, is an iterative process; that is, the program management plan may be updated through the life cycle of the program. For example, the update may result from changes approved by the Integrated Change Control process (discussed in the previous section). The subplans may serve as subsidiary plans to the program management plan, or they may be incorporated into it.

Updates to the program benefits statement   Recall that the program benefits statement is generated by using the Initiate Program process. In developing (or updating) the program management plan, you may realize that the program benefits statement needs to be modified. After all, the program is to be executed to reap the benefits described in the program benefits statement. Because there is a direct relationship between the program benefits statement and the program management plan, they should stay consistent with each other.

A subsidiary plan of the program management plan that belongs to the Integration Management area is the interface management plan.

Developing the Interface Management Plan

A *program* consists of projects and other work, and an organization may be running multiple programs. Therefore, a program will be interacting with the world outside of the program, including other programs in the active portfolio of the performing organization, and other outside factors.

The interfaces of these interactions need to be managed, and that's where *interface planning* comes into the picture. The Interface Planning process is used to identify and map the relationships of a program with other programs in the organization's active portfolio, and with other external factors. The Interface Planning process, along with its input and output items, is depicted in Figure 4.2.

FIGURE 4.2   The Interface Planning process: input and output

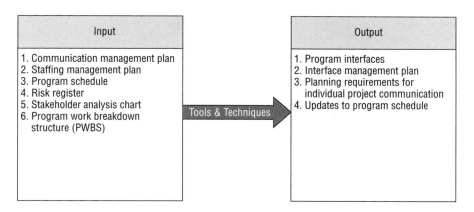

Input	Output
1. Communication management plan 2. Staffing management plan 3. Program schedule 4. Risk register 5. Stakeholder analysis chart 6. Program work breakdown structure (PWBS)	1. Program interfaces 2. Interface management plan 3. Planning requirements for individual project communication 4. Updates to program schedule

Tools & Techniques

Input to Interface Planning

The main purpose of the Interface Planning process is to identify and map the relationships of the program with other programs and with other external factors. To accomplish that the following input items are required.

Program Work Breakdown Structure (PWBS)   The PWBS represents the scope of the program in terms of deliverables. Therefore, the PWBS is an obvious input to identify the relationships of a program with other programs and other external factors.

Communication management plan   Communication and decision-making are two important elements of managing the interrelationships and interdependencies. The communication management plan helps set up formal communication channels and decision-making relationships. This plan is prepared by using the Communication Planning process, which belongs to the Communication Management knowledge area.

Staffing management plan   It is necessary to ensure that the staffing management plan supports the interfaces efficiently. A poorly developed staffing management plan, on one extreme, may leave the interfaces unattended; on the other extreme, it may expose the interfaces in an unorganized way to several people managing them and thereby mess them up. The staffing management plan is developed by using the Human Resource Planning process, which belongs to the Human Resource Management knowledge area.

Program schedule   The program schedule may reveal dependencies of the program on other programs and other external factors. It will also show exactly when certain dependencies and relationships need attention. The program schedule is developed by using the Schedule Development process, which belongs to the Time Management knowledge area. Chapter 5 covers scheduling in detail.

Risk register The *risk register* of a program contains a list of risks and information about those risks. Risk registers can reveal interdependencies. For example, a specific risk may be shared by multiple programs, or a risk response may create a risk for another program. The risk register is an output of the Risk Management Planning and Analysis process, which belongs to the Risk Management knowledge area.

Stakeholder analysis chart Stakeholder management is a theme that runs through the program life cycle. A stakeholder analysis chart will help you keep the interface management in line with the stakeholders' interests and expectations. The chart is produced by using a technique called stakeholder analysis, which you perform to accomplish the following:

- Identify the stakeholders: both positive stakeholders and negative stakeholders.
- Identify the influences and interests of the stakeholders.
- Identify the needs, wants, and expectations of various stakeholders, which may conflict with each other.
- Quantify and prioritize the needs, wants, and expectations of the stakeholders. This quantification and prioritization will create the requirements that will become part of the program requirements.

With these input items in place, you will need some tools and techniques to hammer out the output.

Tools and Techniques for Interface Planning

You can use the following tools and techniques in interface planning:

Human resource practices You will be dealing with human resources while planning interfaces. It is important that you use good human-resource practices during this interaction. Your organization may even have policies and procedures regarding human-resource practices. If it does, you must comply with those.

Organizational theory Managing interfaces involves dealing with different groups and departments in the organization, and possibly also dealing with the external organizations. Organizational theories attempt to model the individual and group dynamics in an organization. Understanding of different organizational theories will help you understand the ways the individuals and groups in an organization behave. This, in turn, will help you manage interfaces more effectively. Some examples of organizational theories are discussed in Chapter 5.

Stakeholder analysis The stakeholder analysis chart that is used as an input to interface planning is generated by using stakeholder analysis. This technique, discussed in Chapter 2, will also help you understand the stakeholder analysis chart.

Templates Some tasks in interface planning are repeated in the same interface over several interfaces, and over the interfaces in several programs. Your organization may already have some templates. Sometimes a standard (or required) way of doing something is also turned into a template. In such cases, you should make use of these templates for compliance with the Standards and for saving time.

By using these tools and techniques, you obtain output from the input to interface planning.

Output of Interface Planning

Program interfaces and the interface management plan are the obvious output items of the Interface Planning process. I'll discuss these and other output items next.

Program interfaces   This is a list and description of *program interfaces* (relationships and dependencies) identified during the process. These are the interfaces that need to be managed. For example, there will be an interface between two training programs in the same organization because they might be sharing resources such as instructors and classrooms.

Interface management plan   This is the plan that describes how the identified interfaces will be managed. This plan should take into account the existing structure of the performing organization. For example, such a plan will describe how the conflict of resources will be avoided or resolved and who will be the point person for certain kinds of interface issues.

Planning requirements for individual project communication   These are the requirements that need to be built into the communication plans for the individual projects in the program. For example, a project manager may be required to provide the status report of the project to the program manager each Friday.

Updates to the program schedule   In the process of identifying and mapping the interrelationships and interdependencies, you may realize that the program schedule needs to be updated to manage those elements. For example, task a_1 in program A is such that task b_1 in program B must be completed before task a_1 can start. This is a schedule constraint that must be accommodated.

Because the staffing management plan and communication management plan are input items to the Transition Planning process, the transition planning is often performed in conjunction with human resource planning and communication planning.

Another subsidiary plan of the program management plan that belongs to the Integration Management area is the resource management plan.

 Real World Scenario

Managing Interfaces

UnizonTunes, a company that facilitates the online distribution of digital music, has just started the email marketing program. The program includes the following work components:

- Build the database management system to store and retrieve email addresses.

- Build the automatic email sender system.

- Get ads from vendors to embed them in emails.

- Prepare ad copy for an email campaign.

- Pass the copy through the quality assurance (QA) team.

- Feed the copy to the email sender system and set the time to send the email.

- Monitor the responses of the email recipients.

The program manager, Srilata Moturi, has identified the following interfaces:

- The interface between the marketing manager of UnizonTunes, responsible for composing the email copy, and external vendors that will send the ad material such as text and graphics to the manager for inclusion in the email.

- The interface between the email marketing program and the artists program that facilitates bringing the works of popular artists to the website. The appearance of an artist's work on the website may trigger the need for an email campaign.

- The interface between the email marketing program and the sales department of UnizonTunes (because a sales deal can trigger an ad campaign).

- The interface between the email marketing program and the network operations team of UnizonTunes to ensure that the network will be up and running and that the appropriate bandwidth will be available at the time of the email campaign.

Interface Management Plan

Srilata developed the interface management plan by doing the following:

- Identifying the issues, dependencies, and relationships involved in an interface.

- Identifying the individuals with whom to discuss the interface in the groups involved in it. The marketing manager and sales manager were in the list to discuss the interface between the email marketing program and the sales department.

- Meeting with the relevant individuals to discuss the interface.

- Based on the feedback from the relevant individuals, preparing the interface management plan. Because UnizonTunes is based on the functional organizational structure, the plan mostly involved Srilata communicating with the functional manager of the group involved in the interface.

Developing a Resource Management Plan

A resource management plan is developed by using the Resource Planning process, which determines the type and quantity of resources needed for the program and determines the optimal use of these resources across the program. Resource planning is performed to accomplish the following:

- Determine the types of resources that will be needed to perform the program activities, such as people, equipment, material, financial resources, information resources, training resources, and so on
- Determine the required quantity of each type of resource
- Determine how to optimize the use of these resources across the program
- Determine how to ensure that the common program resources are allocated appropriately across the constituent projects and are not overcommitted

The results of this planning are recorded in two documents: the *resource requirements* and the *resource management plan*, which are the output of the Resource Planning process.

WARNING   Special attention should be given to any required resource that does not currently exist in the performing organization. For example, there could be a skill that is critical to the program but that no program team member has. In such a case, a position should be opened and the suitable candidate for the position must be identified efficiently with the help of the subject-matter experts (SMEs) and the operational teams.

Input to Resource Planning

The input items to this process, as depicted in Figure 4.3, are discussed in the following.

FIGURE 4.3   The Resource Planning process: input and output

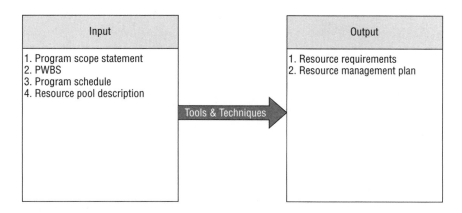

Program scope statement   To determine the required resources, you need to know the scope of the program, which is described in the program scope statement. The idea is to estimate resources for everything included in the scope of the program, and not to ask for the resources for anything that is outside the scope. The program scope statement is developed by using the Scope Definition process, which belongs to the Scope Management knowledge area.

Program Work Breakdown Structure (PWBS)   The PWBS describes the program scope in terms of deliverables. When it comes to quantifying the resources, the PWBS provides more concrete information than the scope statement. See "Creating the Program Work Breakdown Structure (PWBS)" later in this chapter for details.

Program schedule   The program schedule will help to determine when the resources are needed. It will also help you to optimize the use of resources across the program and to avoid the overcommitment of common resources across multiple projects. The program schedule is developed by using the Schedule Development process, which belongs to the Time Management knowledge area. Program scheduling is covered in Chapter 5.

Resource pool description   The resource pool description specifies what type and quantity of resources are available in the organization for the program. You need this information, for example, to determine if an external resource will need to be acquired. The human resource department or the program management office in your organization may be able to help you discover the resource pool description if you don't have one.

The following section covers the tools and techniques you'll use to produce output from this input.

Tools and Techniques for Resource Planning

Resource-planning tools and techniques, including optimization techniques and resource histograms, are discussed here.

Optimization techniques   An important task of resource planning is to ensure the optimal use of resources across the multiple projects within a program, which is accomplished by using optimization techniques. One such technique is called *load balancing*, which is used to distribute the workload from different projects across the resources in such a way that all the resources are busy all the time. For example, if four days' work were to be performed by resource A and resource B were unused during that time, load balancing would detect this situation and distribute the work between A and B. Another kind of optimization technique is *resource leveling*, discussed in Chapter 5. You can also use *alternative identification*, discussed later in this chapter, to optimize the use of resources.

Resource histogram   A resource histogram is a graph that displays resource requirements as a function of some parameter, such as time, and are useful in optimizing the use of resources. A resource histogram may also contain the following information:

- Number of hours that a person or a team will be needed each week or month in a project or nonproject work for the program
- Individual and cumulative resource levels
- Summary of resource requirements

For example, a resource histogram can display that a program (or a program component) needs two designers and five programmers in the month of January, and one programmer and three testers in the first week of February. Another resource histogram may display that 200 hours of work are required in the first week of January from the programming team, 100 hours of work are required from the QA team in the first week of February, and so on.

Management information system   The management information system includes the tools that can be used for resource planning, such as a software system to generate the resource histograms and to perform load balancing on these histograms to assign resources in an optimal way. It also includes the project management software.

Historical information   Historical information from the performing organization's knowledge base can be used to estimate the resource requirements. Some companies publish data on unit-production rates and unit cost of some resources. This data can be helpful in estimating the resource requirements, as well.

Expert judgment   Expert judgment can be used in estimating the resource requirements, an output of the Resource Planning process, for accomplishing the tasks of a program. These requirements can then be used to develop resource histograms.

You use these tools and techniques on the input to the Resource Planning process—the program scope statement, the program schedule, the PWBS, and the resource pool description—to generate the resource requirements and resource management plans discussed earlier.

Another planning process that belongs to the Integration Management knowledge area is called *Transition Planning*.

Developing a Transition Plan

Once the program is complete and benefits are realized, the benefits need to be sustained. For that purpose the control of the program's output (products, services, results, and benefits) are handed off to the group that manages ongoing activities. This transition is performed according to the transition plan, which is developed by using the Transition Planning process. Its purpose is to plan for transferring the program outcome from the program team to the appropriate group, such as the operations group in the performing organization. Figure 4.4 depicts the Transition Planning process, along with its input and output items.

Input to Transition Planning

To plan a transition for a program, you need to know the scope of the program whose output needs to be transferred, the time of transfer, and the stakeholders' list and expectations. Accordingly, the input items to the Transition Planning process are the program scope statement, the program schedule, and the stakeholder analysis chart.

Program scope statement   The scope statement defines the boundaries of the program scope. It is an important document for many activities, including transition. It will help you to determine the scope of the transition that must be stated in the transition plan. It is developed by using the Scope Definition process, which belongs to the Scope Management knowledge area.

FIGURE 4.4   The Transition Planning process: input and output

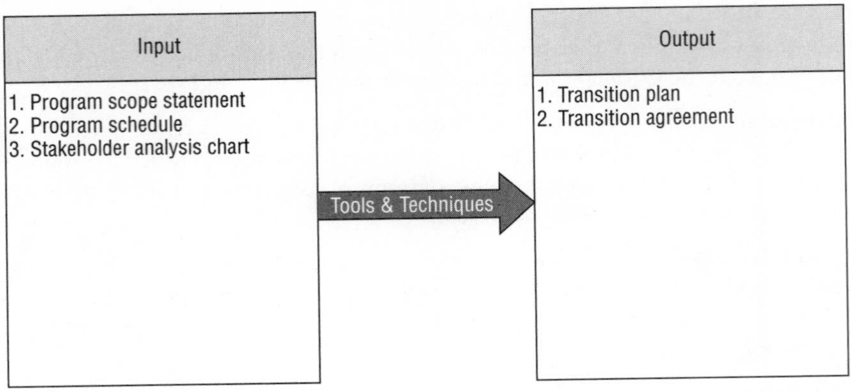

Input	Output
1. Program scope statement 2. Program schedule 3. Stakeholder analysis chart	1. Transition plan 2. Transition agreement

Tools & Techniques

Program schedule   The program schedule is a useful input to transition planning because it shows when something will be ready for transfer. The program schedule is developed by using the Schedule Development process, which belongs to the Time Management knowledge area.

Stakeholder analysis chart   Stakeholder management is a theme that runs through the program life cycle. A stakeholder analysis chart will help you keep the transition plan in line with the stakeholders' interests and expectations. Also, you will need to identify the stakeholders in the organization or group on the receiving end of the transition. The stakeholder analysis was discussed in the "Input to Interface Planning" section.

With this input in place, you need some tools and techniques to generate the output of this process, such as a transition plan.

Tools and Techniques for Transition Planning

The tools and techniques that can be used in transition planning are as follows.

Brainstorming   Brainstorming is a creative technique that is generally used in a group environment to gather ideas as candidates for a solution to a problem or an issue. The evaluation and analysis of these ideas happens later. It can be used in identifying the components of the transition plan and other kinds of planning, as you'll see throughout this chapter.

Standard contract forms   Your organization may have standard contract forms that will be used for ironing out a transition agreement. The contractual matters are usually handled by the organization's legal department. However, you must be involved to ensure that the needed tasks are accomplished in a timely fashion and in accordance with the program scope.

Enterprise environmental factors   The management information system can be used to develop the transition plan, to manage changes to it, and to ensure that the transition occurs at the right time. Additionally, the organizational culture and structure can impact the transition plan.

Organizational process assets   You need to check if the performing organization has a standard policy and procedure for the transition. If it does, it will impact the transition plan and the transition agreement.

Expert judgment   You may need technical expertise in developing the transition plan and legal expertise in developing the transition agreement.

By applying these tools and techniques to the input, you generate the output of transition planning.

Output from Transition Planning

The two output items of the Transition Planning process are the transition plan and the transition agreement.

Transition plan   The transition plan is a part of the program exit criteria, and it includes the following:

- Scope of the transition: what is included and what is not.
- Identification of stakeholders in the organization or group on the receiving end of the transition.
- Ensuring that the program benefits are measured and the benefits sustainment plan exists.
- Ensuring that the transition is executed at the right time.
- Resource release plan. For example, what will happen to the human resources? Will they move on to other assignments in the organization?
- Financial closure plan that includes requirements for the financial closures. For example, it might indicate that the savings from the program budget determined at the program closure time will be returned to the organization, and so on.
- Contract closure requirements. These requirements should be consistent with the terms in the contracts.
- Process to obtain deliverable acceptance.
- Communicating requirements for program closure. For example, who needs to be informed at what time, and whose approval is required to close a given component.
- Impact of closure, which describes how the organization and its structure will be impacted by the program closure. You may need a plan to deal with these impacts. For example, the program closure may include losing some experts.

The actual scope of the transition plan depends on the performing organization. In some organizations the transition plan may include all the points stated in the list—that is, the whole program closure plan. Other organizations may limit the transition plan to only tasks that literally include transition of some deliverables or resources, and make it part of the overall program-closure plan that will include program-exit criteria and other elements discussed in the list.

The transition does not have to wait until the completion of the program. The transition events can happen when necessary during the program life cycle, such as when a project or a nonproject work activity within the program is completed.

Transition agreement   If the transition is made to an organization external to the performing organization, the transition will probably be a contract-based activity. This is where the transition agreement comes into the picture.

In a nutshell, transition planning ensures that the benefits transferred by the program to the organization are sustained after program completion. For completing the program, you need resources, and thereby a resource management plan.

You've seen that most of the planning processes in the Integration Management knowledge area use the program scope as an input in the form of a program scope statement, a PWBS, or both. But, how do you determine and manage the program scope?

Defining the Program Scope

Determining the scope of a program means drawing program boundaries by stating what is included in the program and what is not. Defining the scope includes determining the scope and developing the scope management plan, which describes how to create PWBS and how to manage and control the scope.

The scope is defined by using the Scope Definition process, which generates the detailed program scope statement and the scope management plan. Figure 4.5 depicts the Scope Definition process with its input and output.

FIGURE 4.5   The Scope Definition process: input and output

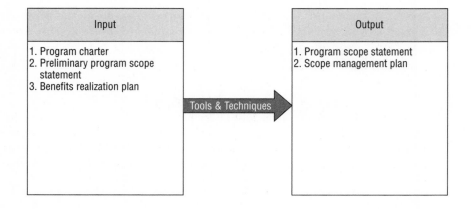

Input to Defining Scope

The Scope Definition process starts with the input items: program charter, preliminary program scope statement, and benefits realization plan.

Program charter   The program charter contains the program vision, key objectives, benefits expected from the program, assumptions, and constraints. All these elements help define the program scope.

Preliminary program scope statement   This is an obvious input to the Scope Definition process. The preliminary program scope statement defines the program scope at a high level: It includes the program's objectives and high-level deliverables. The scope estimates are in order of magnitude, that is, their accuracy is of the order of magnitude.

Benefits realization plan   The benefits realization plan includes a definition of each benefit and a description of how it will be realized, mapping of benefits to program outcomes, and metrics and procedures to realize benefits. This will help to determine the program scope.

All three input items are generated by the Initiate Program process, discussed in Chapter 3, "Initiating a Program."

You will need some tools and techniques, such as alternative identification, to generate output from this input. I'll discuss these next.

Tools and Techniques for Defining the Scope

The major tools and techniques used to define the program scope include identification of alternatives, stakeholder analysis, product analysis, and expert judgment. These and other tools and techniques are discussed in the following paragraphs.

Alternative Identification   This is a technique used to apply nonstandard approaches to perform program tasks, in this case to define the program scope. A host of general management techniques can be used in this category; the most common ones are brainstorming and lateral thinking. As discussed earlier in this chapter, brainstorming is a creative technique generally used in a group environment to gather ideas as candidates for a solution to a problem or an issue. The evaluation and analysis of these ideas happens later. Lateral thinking is synonymous with thinking outside the box. The idea is to think beyond the realm of your experience to search for new solutions and methods, not just better uses of the current ones.

Stakeholder analysis   This includes identifying the needs, wants, and expectations of the various stakeholders and prioritizing them according to the stakeholders' influence. The goal here is to quantify the interests of the stakeholders into concrete requirements. For example, what does customer satisfaction mean? Unless you quantify it into a feature, a benefit, or another deliverable, it is a vague and uncertain concept, and with uncertainty comes risk. This technique (discussed in detail in Chapter 2, "The Program Management Framework") helps determine program requirements. It involves elements such as interviews, questionnaires, surveys, and social maps.

Benefits/product analysis   Although the benefits realization plan is an input to the Scope Definition process, benefits analysis can help to understand the already-identified benefits and to identify new benefits during defining and planning the program scope. You also need to analyze other program deliverables, such as products, at the program level to iron out some parts of the program scope statement, such as product description.

Enterprise environmental factors   The environmental factors that impact the program scope definition include the following:

- Standards that the organization follows regarding scope planning and scope management. You can determine which of these standards apply to your program.

- Organizational policies and procedures that relate to program scope planning and management.

- Market conditions that could affect how the program scope will be managed. For example, the market conditions may demand that the scope be modified to maximize benefits.

Organizational process assets   The organizational process assets that can be used in defining scope include the following:

- Templates, such as scope management plan templates and PWBS templates.

- Program scope change-control forms. You can select which of the existing forms to use for the given program or you can develop new ones.

- Historical information from previous programs that might exist in the knowledge base of the performing organization.

Expert judgment   You can use help from relevant experts in the organization to develop parts of the detailed program scope. For example, expert judgment can help determine program requirements from the organization's strategic plan.

These tools and techniques are used to generate the program scope statement and other outputs of the Scope Definition process.

Output from Defining the Scope

The outputs of the Scope Definition process are the detailed program scope statement (which is also called the program scope statement, or just the scope statement) and the scope management plan.

Program scope statement   This document defines the program scope in detail by drawing boundaries around the program: what is included and what is not. This is a detailed version of the preliminary program scope statement, and becomes the basis for program decisions during the rest of the program life cycle. The following are the main elements of the program scope statement:

Business case   The business case for the program, described in Chapter 3, must be included in the scope statement. This will include the target market and customer needs and will identify benefits expected from the program.

Objectives   A program may include a variety of objectives, such as business, schedule, technical, and quality objectives. These objectives must be aligned with the organization's strategic objectives.

Program requirements   The requirements include the conditions that the program outcome must satisfy, the capabilities that the program items must possess, or both.

Program boundaries   This involves drawing boundaries around the program by specifying what is included and what is not, especially focusing on the gray areas where the stakeholders may make their own assumptions (which may be different from each other and different from what the program is offering).

Outcome description   The outcome of the program, such as benefits, must be described—including their scope and acceptance criteria. The scope statement can also describe the other program deliverables, such as products and results at a high level. The product description may be detailed at the project level.

Milestones   The milestones that accompany the imposed schedule (if any) should be included. Imposed schedule, for example, may come from a contract.

Program assumptions and constraints   Assumptions and constraints are initially included in the program charter. However, at this stage you have more information about the program and therefore you can revisit the initial assumptions and constraints and you may be able to identify additional ones. You should document the specific assumptions related to the program scope, and also analyze their impact should they turn out to be false. Due to the uncertainty built into them, the assumptions are potential sources of risks.

Standards and regulations   The standards and regulations included in the scope statement are contractual constraints, government regulations and standards applicable to the program, and standards necessary for the program, including the standards that are required for compliance in the creation of deliverables.

The scope statement must be reviewed with the relevant groups in the organization, such as media teams, marketing, and sales.

Program scope management plan   The scope management plan describes how the scope will be defined, managed, and controlled throughout the life cycle of the program. The management part includes documenting and verifying the scope. To be specific, the scope management plan includes the following elements:

- A procedure to create a detailed program scope statement (also simply called a scope statement) by using the preliminary scope statement
- A process to create the PWBS from the scope statement
- A description of how the PWBS will be approved and maintained
- A process for and description of how the requests for changes to the scope statement will be handled

In a nutshell, the Scope Definition process plans and defines the scope. The scope definition can be further elaborated upon in terms of work that needs to be done to produce program deliverables.

Creating the Program Work Breakdown Structure (PWBS)

What is the secret behind accomplishing seemingly impossible goals in any area? The breakdown of required work into smaller manageable pieces. This is also a very important process in program management and project management. To be able to execute the program and its constituent projects, we break the program scope down into manageable pieces by creating a program work breakdown structure (PWBS). The components in the PWBS that correspond to constituent projects can be further broken down by the corresponding project managers to create a work breakdown structure (WBS) for each project. In other words, a PWBS is a deliverable-oriented hierarchical decomposition of the work that must be performed to accomplish the objectives and create the program deliverables. Figure 4.6 depicts the Create PWBS process with its input and output.

Input to Creating the PWBS

The input items necessary to create the PWBS are as follows:

Program scope statement   The PWBS presents the scope of the program in terms of deliverables. Therefore, the program scope statement is the primary input to creating a PWBS. Also as a result of creating a PWBS, the scope statement may need to be updated.

Scope management plan   This plan provides guidelines on how to create a PWBS. Also as a result of creating a PWBS, the scope management plan may need to be updated.

Benefits realization plan   This plan maps expected program benefits to the program outcomes. It is a useful input to ensure no deliverable is left out, and that deliverables are aligned with the expected program benefits.

The next section covers the tools and techniques you'll use to create output from this input.

 The actual name of the process is Create Program Work Breakdown Structure. But in this book we call it *Create PWBS* for brevity.

Output from Creating the PWBS

An obvious output of the Create PWBS process is the PWBS. This and the other output items are discussed in the following paragraphs.

FIGURE 4.6   The Create PWBS process: input and output

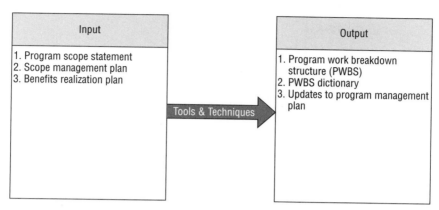

Program work breakdown structure (PWBS)   The PWBS is a deliverable-oriented hierarchical decomposition of the program work that represents the total scope of the program. In other words, if it is not included in the PWBS, it will not be delivered. A PWBS includes the following:

- Program management artifacts such as plans, procedures, processes, and standards
- The program deliverables
- The program office support deliverables

A PWBS presents, at a program level, the end products, services, or results of the program for which the work needs to be performed. A component at the lowest level of a PWBS is called a *program package.* A program package is a management interface between program management and project management. Technically speaking, a program package is a management control point where the program manager's control ends and a project manager's control starts. That means the program work decomposition should stop at the level of control required by the program manager. This will typically correspond to the first or the second level in the WBS of each constituent project.

WARNING   The PWBS does not eliminate the need for a WBS for each project. It may include the top few levels (though typically only one or two) of each constituent project to show where the control is transferred to a project manager.

Figure 4.7 presents a simple example of a PWBS for a project-management training program. This training program contains three projects: a Certified Associate Project Management (CAPM) exam course, a Project Management Professional (PMP) exam course, and a Program Management Professional (PgMP) course. The program packages are represented by dark boxes. Note that the program manager of this program wants a great deal of control on each project. Under a different situation or different requirements, the package level could be moved one level above the hierarchy; that is, the program packages could be CAPM course, PMP course, and PMOP course.

FIGURE 4.7 An example of a PWBS. The program packages are represented by the dark boxes at the end of each branch. If the program manager does not need this much control on the projects, the CAPM course, PMP course, and PMOP course can be considered as work packages instead.

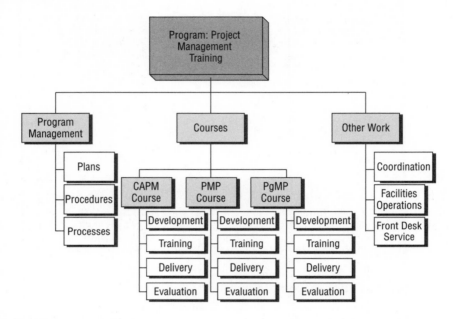

A PWBS contains the program work that is not part of any constituent project. It also includes the nonproject work of the program, such as the following:

- Program management artifacts, such as plans developed for the program
- Program-related external tasks, such as public relations or communication
- Operations related to facilities and infrastructure used by the program

In a nutshell, the following are the important characteristics of a PWBS:

- A deliverable not in the PWBS will be undelivered because it's outside the scope of the program.
- Different branches of the PWBS may have different number of levels—that is, different depth.
- A component at the lowest level of a branch in a PWBS, called a program package, represents the level of management control required by the program manager.

An integral part of PWBS is the PWBS dictionary.

PWBS dictionary This document contains detailed information about the PWBS components. Depending on the nature of a given PWBS component (that is, whether it is a program-level

Creating the Program Work Breakdown Structure (PWBS)   **161**

operation or a project), the PWBS dictionary may include some the following information about the component:

- A code identifying the component
- The individual or group responsible for the component (the name of the project manager if the component is a project)
- A statement of work for the component (contract statement of work if the component is being procured)
- A list of schedule milestones
- A list of quality requirements
- A list of resources required for completion
- A cost estimate

Updates to the program management plan   During the Create PWBS process, the program team might realize that something that is currently outside of the existing scope must be included to accomplish something inside the scope. This will give rise to a change request, which may also come from other stakeholders during or after the first creation of the PWBS. After the change request has been approved, not only the PWBS will be changed; the scope management plan (which is a part of project management plan), and the project management plan must be re-evaluated and updated accordingly.

This output is obtained by applying some tools and techniques to the input. I'll discuss those in the next section.

Tools and Techniques for Creating a PWBS

Decomposition of program deliverables is an obvious technique used in creating a PWBS. This and other tools and techniques used in creating the PWBS are discussed in the following paragraphs.

Decomposition   Decomposition is a technique for subdividing the program deliverables into smaller, manageable tasks called program packages. A work package corresponding to an individual project in the program is further decomposed into more levels of hierarchy, with the lowest level containing what are called *work packages* for the project. The hierarchical structure that contains work packages at the lowest level of each of its branches is called a work breakdown structure (WBS). Based on their complexity, different deliverables can have different levels of decomposition.

But what criteria do you use to subdivide (decompose) the deliverables? The multiple possible answers to this question give rise to multiple decomposition techniques. Some of them are listed here:

- Using the deliverables at the first level of a PWBS
- Using the projects and nonproject work at the first level of a PWBS

- Using the deliverables and projects at the first level of a PWBS
- Using the program phases at the first level of a PWBS
- Using different options for different branches of a PWBS
- Any combination of these options

During decomposition, the components are defined in terms of how the project work will actually be executed and controlled. You must verify the correctness of the decomposition at each level by requiring that the lower-level components are necessary and sufficient to the completion of the corresponding higher-level deliverables.

Brainstorming   This technique, described earlier in this chapter, can also be used to create work breakdown structures. Brainstorming is a group activity, and you perform it with the team.

Expert judgment   You do not create a PWBS and a WBS for each project by yourself. You identify the functional characteristics and needs of the program and assign appropriate subject-matter experts. You create work breakdown structures with these SMEs and also involve the project managers in creating the WBS for the projects.

Organizational process assets   Even though each program is unique, there are similarities among sets of programs in an organization. These similarities can be used to prepare templates that will be used as a starting point for the PWBS to avoid the duplication of work. With or without templates, you will need to go through breaking down the deliverables, a very important step in creating the PWBS and the WBS for each project in the program. The PWBS from previous programs that can be found in the organization's knowledge base can also be useful in creating a PWBS for the current program.

 Real World Scenario

A PWBS for an Email Marketing Program

UnizonTunes, a company that facilitates the online distribution of digital music, is developing an email marketing program that will need to accomplish the following:

- Build the database management system to store and retrieve email addresses
- Build the automatic email sender system
- Get ads from vendors that will be embedded into emails
- Prepare copy for an email campaign
- Pass the copy through a quality assurance (QA) team

- Feed the copy to the email sender system and set the time to send the email

- Monitor the responses of the email recipients

There were many ways to develop the PWBS, so Srilata had a brainstorm session with the program team and the subject-matter experts. After exploring different options, the PWBS was finalized. Its components include the following:

- The *program management* component at the first level, which will be further decomposed by the program team to make it easier to identify the team members who will be assigned to the lowest-level components.

- The *email database management system* at the first level. This component represents a project and will be further decomposed into a WBS with the help of the corresponding project manager.

- The *QA* component at the first level. The purpose of this component is to check and test the quality of the email copy. This component was further decomposed with the help of a subject-matter expert from the QA department.

- The *sign up ad vendors* component at the first level. The purpose of this component is to sign up the vendors who will buy ad space in the emails that will be sent out under this program.

- The *email generation* component at the first level. The purpose of this component is to generate an email and send it to the specified list of recipients.

It is important to understand the relationship of the PWBS with the WBS of each constituent project.

Linking PWBS to WBS

As you already know, the PWBS is the program-level WBS, and project-related components of the PWBS will be further decomposed to create a WBS for each constituent project. You will need to oversee the creation of a WBS for each project for many reasons, including consistency.

There are a few steps that you can take during the creation of PWBS to ensure that it is linked to each WBS underneath it. First, the PWBS that you developed should reveal interproject dependencies. Identify these dependencies to align milestones in projects to support the program milestones and phases. Obviously, this has implications in creating a WBS for projects.

Second, create guidelines to apply a common approach to create a WBS for each constituent project. This will help facilitate consistency across projects in many areas, such as scheduling, assigning, and using resources, and controlling cost.

Consistency among projects will also help in aligning the acceptance criteria for project deliverables with the program objectives.

Before and After the PWBS

From the Initiate Program process group until now, we have come across quite a few documents created in various processes. Some of these documents are input into another process, creating some other document. It is important to understand in which order the documents are created and which document is an input to creating which other document.

The PWBS is at the heart of program management. It affects—directly or indirectly—most of the processes that are performed after the creation of the PWBS. Figure 4.8 illustrates this point by showing that the PWBS is a direct input to several processes.

FIGURE 4.8   A number of documents created during the Initiating and Scope Planning processes. An arrow shows which document is an output from which process and an input to which other process or processes.

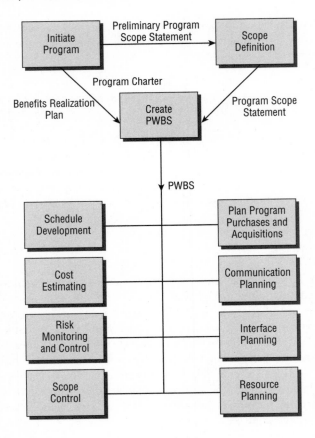

The Three Big Takeaways

The three most important takeaways from this chapter are the following:

- The program setup is phase two of the program life cycle and uses the processes from the Program Planning process group to generate most of its results.

- The program management plan is the master plan that contains other subsidiary plans and is used to run the program.

- The program scope statement describes the scope of the program in detail, whereas the PWBS presents the deliverable-oriented decomposition of the program scope.

Summary

After the program has been initiated in phase one (pre-program setup) of the program life cycle by using the processes of the Initiating process group, you need to lay the foundations for successful program execution. This is accomplished in phase two of the program life cycle: program setup. The major part of setting up the program is planning for the program by using the processes of the Planning process group. The program management plan is the master plan according to which the program is executed, and it is developed by using the Develop Program Management Plan process, which belongs to the Integration Management knowledge area. Other planning processes that belong to the Integration Management knowledge area are Interface Planning, which generates the interface management plan; Resource Planning, which generates the resource management plan; and Transition Planning, which generates the transition plan.

The planning processes that belong to the Scope Management knowledge area are Scope Definition and Create PWBS. The Scope Definition process takes the preliminary scope statement as an input and generates the program scope management plan and the program scope statement. The program scope statement is a document that defines the scope of the program in detail by stating what the program needs to accomplish. This is an input item to creating the program work breakdown structure (PWBS), which is a breakdown of program deliverables to manageable pieces (called program packages) that represent the level of management control required by the program manager. The PWBS is supported by another document, called the PWBS dictionary, which offers details for the PWBS components. The PWBS serves a twofold purpose: it presents the program scope in terms of deliverables and it serves as a management control framework between program manager and project managers.

Once you have a PWBS, you can use it to perform other planning, such as schedule development, cost estimating and budgeting, quality planning, and risk management planning. I will discuss these topics in the next chapter.

Exam's-Eye View

Comprehend

- The key results from the program setup are largely generated by using the processes of the Program Planning process group.

- Transition planning ensures that the benefits the program provides to the organization are sustained after the program completion.

- Program charter and preliminary project scope statement are input items to the Scope Definition process that is used to develop the detailed program scope statement and the program scope management plan.

- The detailed program scope statement and the program scope management plan are input items to creating the PWBS.

- The PWBS document is an input item to many other program management processes.

Look Out

- The program management plan may need an update due to milestones formally external to the program, such as project initiation or closure, end of the performing organization's fiscal year, or the buyout of the performing organization.

- The transition does not have to wait until the completion of the program. The transition events can happen when necessary during the program life cycle, such as when a project or a nonproject work activity within the program is completed.

- If the transition of the program output is made to an organization external to the performing organization, the transition will probably be a contract-based activity.

- The components at the lowest levels of the PWBS are called program packages, whereas the lowest components in a WBS for a project are called work packages.

Memorize

- The planning processes that belong to the Integration Management knowledge area are as follows:

  - The Develop Program Management Plan, which generates the program management plan

  - Interface Planning, which generates the interface management plan

  - Resource Planning, which generates the resource management plan

  - Transition Planning, which generates the transition management plan

- The planning processes that belong to the Scope Management knowledge area are as follows:

  - Scope Definition, which generates the program scope statement and program scope management plan

  - Create Program Work Breakdown Structure (PWBS), which generates the PWBS and the PWBS dictionary

Exam Essentials

Program setup   Program setup is phase two of the program. The main purpose of this phase is twofold:

- Define the key deliverables of the program.

- Develop a detailed roadmap that provides direction about and a description of how the program will be managed.

Program management plan   The program management plan is the key deliverable generated by the processes in the Planning process group. It contains the subsidiary plans produced by individual planning processes. The tools and techniques used in developing the program management plan include the following:

- The program management information system

- Stakeholder skills and knowledge

- The configuration management system

Scope definition   Program scope definition includes planning and defining the scope by generating the scope management plan and the scope statement. The Scope Definition process starts with three documents: the program charter, the preliminary program scope statement, and the benefits realization plan. The tools and techniques used in defining the scope include alternative identification, benefits/product analysis, expert judgment, and organizational process assets such as standards, templates, and historical information.

Program work breakdown structure (PWBS)   This is a deliverable-oriented hierarchical structure that represents the program scope, including the deliverables to be produced by the constituent projects. It is an input to many other planning and control processes.

Key Terms and Definitions

alternatives identification   A technique used to apply nonstandard approaches, such as brain-storming and lateral thinking, to perform program (or project) tasks.

brainstorming   A creative technique generally used in a group environment to gather ideas as candidates for a solution to a problem or an issue without any immediate evaluation of these ideas. The evaluation and analysis of these ideas happens later.

interface management plan   A document that is generated by the Interface Planning process and describes how to manage the interfaces of the program with other programs and with factors external to the program.

interface planning   A process used to identify and map the relationships of a program with other programs in the organization's active portfolio, and with other factors external to the program.

lateral thinking   Thinking outside the box, beyond the realm of your experience, to search for new solutions and methods rather than only better uses for the current solutions and methods.

program management plan   The grand program plan, generated by using the Develop Program Management Plan process, describes how to manage and execute the program to achieve its objectives. It consists of several subsidiary plans, such as the cost management plan, the schedule management plan, and the scope management plan.

program package   A component at the lowest level of a branch of the PWBS.

program scope management plan   A document that is generated by the Scope Definition process and describes how to manage the scope of the program (including how to create the PWBS and how to control the scope).

program scope statement   A document that is generated by the Scope Definition process and describes the scope of the program: what is included in the program and what is excluded.

program setup   Phase two of the program life cycle, which develops a detailed roadmap for the program by defining the deliverables and describing how to produce them. It uses the Program Planning processes to produce its key results.

program work breakdown structure (PWBS)   A deliverable-oriented hierarchical structure that represents the program scope, including the deliverables to be produced by the constituent projects.

PWBS dictionary   A document that is generated by the Create PWBS process and contains information about the PWBS components.

resource management plan   A document that is generated by the Resource Planning process and describes at the program level how to manage the program resources. This includes determining the resource requirements and allocating the resources.

Resource Planning   A process that determines the type and quantity of resources needed for the program, and the optimal use of these resources across the program.

Scope Definition   A process used to plan and define the program scope by creating the scope management plan and scope statement.

transition plan   A document that is generated by the Transition Planning process and describes how the program output after the program completion will be transferred to another organization or to a functional group within the performing organization.

Transition Planning   A process that plans for transferring the program outcome from the program team to the appropriate group, such as the operations group in the performing organization.

work breakdown structure (WBS)   A deliverable-oriented hierarchical decomposition of the work that must be performed to accomplish the objectives and create the project deliverables.

work package   A deliverable or a task at the lowest level of each branch of the WBS.

Review Questions

1. The program setup addresses all of the following issues except:

   A. How much will the program cost?

   B. How will the program be executed?

   C. What is the plan to initiate the program?

   D. What are the risks involved in the program?

2. Which of the following processes is not included in the Program Planning process group?

   A. Create PWBS

   B. Initiate Team

   C. Schedule Development

   D. Cost Estimating and Budgeting

3. Which of the following is not an input to the Develop Program Management Plan process?

   A. Benefits management plan

   B. Quality management plan

   C. Schedule management plan

   D. Program charter

4. Interface Planning belongs to which of the following knowledge areas?

   A. Integration Management

   B. Human Resource Management

   C. Procurement Management

   D. Communication Management

5. Resource requirements are an output of which of the following processes?

   A. Activity resource estimating

   B. Resource Planning

   C. Create PWBS

   D. Resource management

6. Which of the following is not an input item to the Scope Definition process?

   A. Program charter

   B. Preliminary program scope statement

   C. Benefits realization plan

   D. PWBS

7. Which of the following is not an output of the Create PWBS process?

   A. Program schedule

   B. Updates to the program management plan

   C. PWBS dictionary

   D. PWBS

8. A program package is:

   A. A component at the bottom of a PWBS branch

   B. A set of projects

   C. A set of benefits from a program

   D. The program scope

9. Which of the following is not a true statement about PWBS?

   A. PWBS facilitates effective control and communication between the program manager and the project managers.

   B. The description of PWBS components is documented in the PWBS dictionary.

   C. PWBS replaces WBS: once you have a PWBS for the whole program, you do not need a WBS for each individual project in the program.

   D. PWBS is a deliverable-oriented hierarchical decomposition of the program scope.

10. Transition Planning is the process of:

   A. Transferring the program output to an external organization or to a group within the performing organization

   B. Transitioning a program from one phase to another phase of its life cycle

   C. Transitioning from one project to another project within the program

   D. Transitioning procured items from the seller to the buyer

11. The Scope Definition process starts with:

   A. Program charter, preliminary scope statement, and WBS

   B. Program charter and scope management plan

   C. Program charter, preliminary scope statement, and benefits realization plan

   D. Preliminary scope statement and WBS

12. The components at the lowest level of a project WBS hierarchy are called:

   A. Program packages

   B. Work packages

   C. Schedule activities

   D. Program deliverables

13. You are performing the processes from the Planning process group for your program. What will be the key output delivered as a result of performing these processes?

   A. Benefits management plan

   B. Scope management plan

   C. Cost management plan

   D. Program management plan

14. You are performing the resource planning process for your program. Which of the following is not a tool or technique that can be used for this process?

   A. Alternative identification

   B. Pareto diagram

   C. Project-management software

   D. Expert judgment

15. Which of the following is not true about transition planning or transition?

   A. It maps to integration management.

   B. Transition planning is often performed in conjunction with human resource planning and communication planning.

   C. The transition agreement is an output of transition planning.

   D. The transition occurs once at the completion of the program.

Answers to Review Questions

1. C.

   C is the correct answer because a plan to initiate the program is developed in the pre-program setup phase: phase one of the program life cycle.

   A, B, and D are incorrect answers because all these are the issues addressed during the program setup phase: phase two of the program life cycle.

2. B.

   B is the correct answer because the Initiate Team process belongs to the Initiating process group.

   A, C, and D are incorrect answers because all these processes belong to the Program Planning process group.

3. D.

   D is the correct answer because program charter is not an input to the Develop Program Management Plan process.

   A, B, and C are incorrect answers because all these plans are subsidiary plans to the program management plan.

4. A.

   A is the correct answer because Integration Management contains the following planning processes: Develop Program Management Plan, Interface Planning, Resource Planning, and Transition Planning.

   B, C, and D are incorrect answers because Interface Planning belongs to Integration Management.

5. B.

   B is the correct answer because resource requirements (and the resource management plan) are an output item of the Resource Planning process.

   A and D are incorrect answers because activity resource estimating and resource management are not standard program management processes.

   C is an incorrect answer because resource requirements are not output from the Create PWBS process.

6. D.

   D is the correct answer because when you are performing the Scope Definition process for the first time, a PWBS may not even exist: the output of the Scope Definition process is an input to creating the PWBS.

   A, B, and C are incorrect answers because all of these are input items to the Scope Definition process.

7. A.

A is the correct answer because the program schedule is developed by using the Schedule Development process.

B, C, and D are incorrect answers because all of these are output items of the Create PWBS process.

8. A.

A is the correct answer because a program package is a bottom component of a branch of the PWBS hierarchy.

B, C, and D are incorrect answers because they do not describe a program package.

9. C.

C is the correct answer because PWBS does not replace WBS for individual projects. Roughly speaking, WBS begins where PWBS ends.

A, B, and D are incorrect answers because these are true statements about PWBS.

10. A.

A is the correct answer because transition planning is the process that is used to transfer the program output to a group other than the program team so that the program benefits can be sustained after the program is complete.

B, C, and D are incorrect answers because these are false statements about the Transition Planning process.

11. C.

C is the correct answer because the program charter, preliminary scope statement, and benefits realization plan are inputs to the Scope Definition process.

A and D are incorrect because the WBS is not an input to the Scope Definition process.

B is incorrect because the scope management plan is an output of the Scope Definition process.

12. B.

B is the correct answer because work packages are the components at the lowest level of a project WBS hierarchy.

A is incorrect because program packages are the components at the lowest level of a program WBS (PWBS) hierarchy.

C and D are incorrect because schedule activities and program deliverables can be created from work packages, but they themselves are not work packages.

13. D.

D is the correct answer because the program management plan is the key deliverable generated by the processes in the Planning process group.

A, B, and C are incorrect because none of these plans is a key deliverable from the Planning process group. They are the subsidiary plans that become part of the program management plan.

14. B.

B is the correct answer because a Pareto diagram is a quality-control tool.

A, C, and D are incorrect because these are valid tools and techniques used in developing the program management plan.

15. D.

D is the correct answer because the transition events can happen when necessary during the program life cycle, such as when a project of the program is completed or a nonproject work activity within the program is completed.

A, B, and C are incorrect because these are false statements about the Transition Planning process.

Chapter

5

Planning the Program Schedule and Resources

THE PGMP EXAM CONTENT FROM THE INITIATING THE PROGRAM AND PLANNING THE PROGRAM PERFORMANCE DOMAINS COVERED IN THIS CHAPTER INCLUDES THE OBJECTIVES LISTED IN THE FOLLOWING:

- ✓ **2.4 Develop an accountability matrix by identifying and assigning program roles and responsibilities in order to build the core team and to differentiate between the program and project resources.**

- ✓ **3.3 Establish the program management plan and baseline by integrating the plans for the constituent projects and creating the plans for the supporting program functions including management of scope, schedule, finance, benefits, quality, resource, procurement, risk response, change and communications in order to effectively forecast, monitor, and identify variances during program execution.**

- ✓ **3.4 Optimize the program plan by reviewing and leveling resource requirements (e.g., materials, equipment, facilities, finance, human capital) in order to gain efficiencies and synergies among projects.**

In the previous chapter you learned about the program scope and the program work breakdown structure (PWBS), which represents the program scope in terms of program deliverables. To produce the deliverables, some work needs to be scheduled and performed. Executing the schedule is going to cost money, and you will need human resources who will perform the work in the schedule. There will be elements in the PWBS for which your organization lacks the resources. You will need to get those elements produced by resources (a vendor) external to your organization. This practice is called *procurement*.

So, the core issue in this chapter is how to plan the program schedule and the resources needed to execute the schedule, such as cost and human resources. To enable you to put your arms around this issue, we will explore the following three avenues: developing a program schedule, planning cost and human resources, and planning procurement.

The Big Picture of Schedule and Resource Planning

Once you have ironed out the PWBS, you can start the process of developing the program schedule. Developing a schedule involves determining program components, assigning resources to the components, and determining in which order the components will be performed and when each component will start and finish. The resources include human resources, money, and external resources. By *external resources*, I mean procurement, which is the process of acquiring (procuring) some items for the program that the organization decides not to produce in-house. For example, if there are no resources available within the performing organization to perform a specific component of the program, you may decide that it is beneficial to procure the results of that component from outside the organization.

The program schedule partly depends upon the quantity of the available resources. For example, two qualified individuals can finish a task faster than a single individual.

These topics are included in the exam objectives covered in this chapter.

The Exam Roadmap

The following table presents each PgMP exam objective covered in this chapter, along with its explanation:

Exam Objective	What It Really Means
2.4 Develop an accountability matrix by identifying and assigning program roles and responsibilities in order to build the core team and to differentiate between the program and project resources.	This exam objective was largely covered in Chapter 3, "Initiating a Program." This chapter covers the resource element of this objective. You must know the general tools and techniques used to estimate the resource requirements.
3.3 Establish the program management plan and baseline by integrating the plans for the constituent projects and creating the plans for the supporting program functions including management of scope, schedule, finance, benefits, quality, resource, procurement, risk response, change and communications in order to effectively forecast, monitor, and identify variances during program execution.	This exam objective was partly covered in Chapter 4, "Planning the Program." In this chapter, I cover the schedule, finance, resource, and procurement elements of this objective. You must understand the program Schedule Development process. Know the several steps involved in developing the schedule, along with tools and techniques used at each of these steps. Also understand the following processes: • Cost Estimating and Budgeting • Human Resource Planning • Plan Program Purchases and Acquisitions • Plan Program Contracting
3.4 Optimize the program plan by reviewing and leveling resource requirements (e.g., materials, equipment, facilities, finance, human capital) in order to gain efficiencies and synergies among projects.	You must understand what *resource leveling* is and the different methods to implement it. Also understand the concept of *resource optimization* and how it can be achieved.

Understanding the Program Schedule and Resources

The schedule and resources need to be managed and you need to do some planning for this management. The relevant planning processes, along with their knowledge areas and major outputs, are presented in Table 5.1.

TABLE 5.1 Processes for Developing a Schedule and Planning Resource Management

Knowledge Area	Program Planning Process	Major Output
Time Management	Schedule Development	Program Schedule Schedule Management Plan
Cost Management	Cost Estimating and Budgeting	Program Budget Cost Management Plan
Human Resource Management	Human Resource Planning	Roles and Responsibilities Assignments Staffing Management Plan
Procurement Management	Plan Program Purchases and Acquisitions	Contract Statement of Work Procurement Management Plan
	Plan Program Contracting	Contracts Management Plan

Figure 5.1 shows the planning processes and their relationship to each other.

FIGURE 5.1 Planning processes for the program schedule and resources.

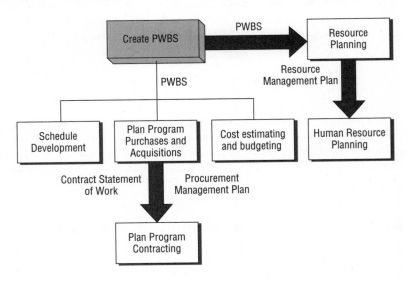

These processes belong to the following knowledge areas:

Time Management   Planning the program schedule is all about time management: when an activity will start, when it will be completed, how long it will take, and so on. The Schedule Development process, which belongs to Time Management, is discussed in this chapter.

Cost Management   Executing the program schedule will incur cost, and cost needs to be managed. Part of managing cost is planning the cost, which is accomplished through the Cost Estimating and Budgeting process discussed in this chapter.

Human Resource Management   You will need some individuals to perform the work that is scheduled. This is where human resource management comes into the picture. Planning for the human resources is performed by using the Human Resource Planning process discussed in this chapter.

Procurement Management   There will be situations when your organization does not have the expertise to perform certain schedule activities in-house. For this or other reasons, you might want to acquire some items or services from an outside vendor. This kind of acquisition is called procurement, which also needs to be managed. The planning part of procurement management is accomplished by performing the Plan Purchases and Acquisitions process discussed in this chapter.

Some of the work related to the program components will be performed at the program level, and the rest will be broken down to work breakdown structures (WBS) for individual projects and will be performed at each project level. In other words, program schedule does not replace the schedules of the individual projects. However, it does influence those schedules and get influenced by them.

Developing the Program Schedule

The program schedule is a roadmap to executing the program. The schedule is developed by using the Schedule Development process, which involves the following:

Component definition   Define the program components needed to produce the program deliverables.

Component sequencing   Determine in which order the components will be executed.

Component duration estimating   Estimate the time required to complete each component for given resources.

Component scheduling   Assign a timeline for completing the components. Some components will be broken into projects, and project activities will need to be scheduled. This schedule will be rolled up to determine the schedule of the program component.

During these steps in the scheduling process, you identify significant milestones in the program and document and unify your work into a *program schedule*. The Schedule Development process is depicted in Figure 5.2.

FIGURE 5.2   The Schedule Development process: input and output.

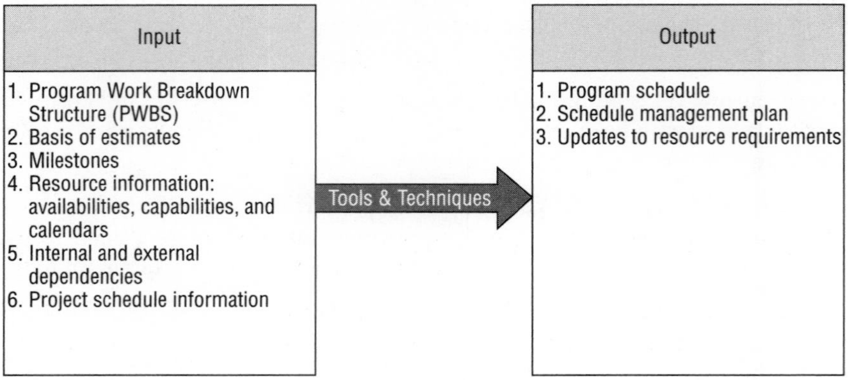

Input	Output
1. Program Work Breakdown Structure (PWBS) 2. Basis of estimates 3. Milestones 4. Resource information: availabilities, capabilities, and calendars 5. Internal and external dependencies 6. Project schedule information	1. Program schedule 2. Schedule management plan 3. Updates to resource requirements

Tools & Techniques

Input to Developing a Program Schedule

A program schedule is developed to produce the program deliverables that are represented by the PWBS. Therefore the PWBS itself is an obvious input to the Schedule Development process. This and other input items are discussed in the following:

Program work breakdown structure (PWBS)   The PWBS is typically used as a starting point for developing the program schedule. The schedule includes all of the program packages, the components at the lowest level of a PWBS that produce or contribute to producing the program deliverables. Chapter 4 discusses the PWBS in detail.

Basis of estimates   You will be making some estimates (assessments) to develop the schedule. For example, what quantity of a resource type will be needed to complete an activity, and for a given quantity of resource how long will it take to finish the activity? There must be some basis on which you will be making these estimates. For example, expert judgment can be used to make duration and resource estimates for an activity when enough information is not available. You can also use analogous estimating and parametric estimating techniques, discussed further on in this chapter.

Milestones   In addition to deliverables, a program may have predefined milestones. A schedule milestone (i.e., a milestone on the schedule) is a significant point (or event) in the life of a program, and it refers to marking the start or completion of an activity or a set of activities, and therefore has zero duration. Here are some examples:

- Initiation of a new project in the program
- Closure of a project in the program
- Completion of important deliverables in the constituent projects

These milestones must be considered during the Schedule Development process because they need to be scheduled.

The program schedule establishes the timeline for both program deliverables and program milestones.

Resource information   To develop the schedule, you need to know the following information about resources:

The capabilities of resources   This will help determine how long it will take to finish an activity. For example, an experienced person generally can finish a job faster than a newbie.

The availability of resources   This includes knowing the quantity of the available resources and when they are available.

Calendars   The performing organization may have various calendars, including resource calendars. These calendars must be consulted during the Schedule Development process because they specify when the work can be performed. They can affect all program (and project) activities because they, for example, can identify when no work can be performed on a site during certain periods of the year. Resource calendars can affect program (and project) activities that require a certain resource or a category of resources because they can identify when a resource or a category of resources is not available. It may take into account holidays, restrictions on contract workers, overtime issues, other commitments of a human resource within the organization, and the like.

Internal and external dependencies   The program components may depend on internal or external factors. It is necessary to determine these dependencies before you can develop a realistic schedule.

Internal dependencies   These are the dependencies inside the program. For example, consider two program packages in the PWBS: Develop Course and Test Course. The Test Course package depends on the Develop Course package because you cannot test a course before developing it.

External dependencies   When an activity in the program depends on a factor external to the program, the dependency is called an external dependency. For example, in a movie-production program, think of a program activity that involves shooting scenes with lots of tourists skiing. These scenes are planned to be shot at a ski resort during the skiing season. This is an example of external dependency because the skiing season, the presence of tourists, and the availability of the facility are the factors external to the organization.

Both internal and external dependencies can be grouped further into mandatory dependencies and discretionary dependencies, discussed in the following:

Mandatory dependencies   These are the dependencies that are inherent to the program components. For example, a course must be developed before it can be tested.

Discretionary dependencies   These are the dependencies that are at the discretion of the program management team. For example, it was possible to perform components A and B simultaneously or to perform A after B was finished, but the team decided, for whatever reason, to perform B after A is finished. Some of the guidelines for establishing discretionary dependencies can come from the knowledge of best practices within the given application area, and from the previous experience of performing a similar program.

> Mandatory dependencies are called hard logic, whereas discretionary dependencies are called soft logic.

Project schedule information   The program Schedule Development process typically starts with the program packages, which are the bottom-level components in the PWBS. Most of these packages are decomposed into WBSs for constituent projects by the project teams under the leadership of project managers. The individual project managers (with the help of their teams) develop the schedules for the projects and roll up the information into the program packages. This information is necessary to develop the program schedule.

> In accordance with the management control points set up by the program packages in the PWBS, there will be active interaction between the program manager and the project managers for the constituent projects in order to develop a realistic schedule that will be executed successfully.

Schedule development is a very involved process. Therefore, you can apply a multitude of tools and techniques on this input to crank out the output.

Tools and Techniques for Developing a Program Schedule

The tools and techniques that can be used in developing a program schedule are listed in Table 5.2. These tools and techniques can also be used to schedule project activities. A *project activity*, also called a *schedule activity*, is a component of work that is scheduled and performed for a project. The tools listed in Table 5.2 can also be used at the project level for activity definition, activity sequencing, activity duration estimates, and activity scheduling. In this chapter, I use the terms *activity* and *component* interchangeably. It should be clear from context whether I'm referring to the program level or the project level.

TABLE 5.2   Key Tools and Techniques Used in Developing a Program Schedule

Schedule Development Task	Key Tools and Techniques
Component definition	Decomposition Templates
Component sequencing	Precedence Diagramming Method (PDM) Arrow Diagramming Method (ADM) Conditional Diagramming Methods (CDM) Network Templates

TABLE 5.2   Key Tools and Techniques Used in Developing a Program Schedule *(continued)*

Schedule Development Task	Key Tools and Techniques
Component duration estimates	Analogous Estimating Parametric Estimating Expert Judgment Quantitative Analysis Reserve Analysis
Component scheduling	Mathematical Analysis Schedule compression Resource Leveling Program Management Software Coding Structure

These tools and techniques are explained here.

Decomposition   Recall from Chapter 4 that you use the decomposition technique to create the PWBS for the program and WBS for the projects. Decomposition is also used in the activity definition for subdividing the program packages (and work packages at the project level) into smaller, more manageable components, called *schedule activities* at the project level.

> You create the PWBS and WBS and decompose the program packages with the help of the program team and project managers. When decomposing a work package into activities, involve the individuals who either are familiar with the work packages or will be responsible for them.

Templates   As a time-saver and a guide, you can use a standard activity list or an activity list from a previous program (or project) similar to the program (or project) at hand as a template. The template can also contain information about the activities, such as required hours of effort. You can also use templates for other schedule-related tasks, such as network diagrams.

Arrow diagramming method (ADM)   This technique is used to draw a schedule network diagram in which an arrow represents an activity and also points to the successor activity through a junction represented by a node (box). This method is discussed in detail further on in this chapter.

Precedence diagramming method (PDM)   This technique is used to construct a project schedule network diagram in which a node (a box) represents an activity and an arrow represents the dependency relationship. This method is discussed in detail further on in this chapter.

The schedule network diagrams developed by using the ADM and the PDM are used in developing the program schedule.

Conditional diagramming methods (CDM)   There may be some conditional components (activities) or dependencies among program components (or activities) that cannot be handled by the PDM and the ADM. For example, a computer-code rewrite will occur only if the QA detects the existing code's performance is below a predetermined threshold. Also, there may be some activities depending on each other making a dependency loop with some check points (conditions) in the loop. For example, think of a software program going back and forth between QA and software development team until it passes the quality criteria.

Such situations are better handled by a category of diagrams called *conditional diagrams*, and the methods that use these diagrams to display dependencies are called conditional diagramming methods.

Analogous estimating   Analogous estimating techniques estimate the duration of an activity based on the duration of a similar activity in a previous program or in another project. The accuracy of the estimate depends upon how similar the activities are and whether the team member who will perform the activity has the same level of expertise and experience as the team member who performed the activity on which this estimate is based. This technique is useful when there is not enough detail about the activity available—for example, in the early stages of a program or a project. Note the following about the analogous estimation technique:

- It's generally less costly than other techniques, but it's also less accurate.
- Its accuracy and reliability improve if the person making the estimate is an expert and the components being compared are actually similar.

Parametric estimating   This is a quantitative technique used to calculate the activity duration when the productivity rate of the resource performing the activity is available. You use a formula such as the following to calculate the duration:

Activity duration = units of work in the activity ÷ productivity rate of the resources

For example, if you know that a team assigned to the activity of burying 40 miles of cable can bury 2 miles of cable in one day, the duration calculation can be performed as follows:

Activity duration = 40 miles ÷ (2 miles/day) = 20 days

Expert Judgment   Expert judgment can be used for accomplishing various tasks during schedule development such as estimating the activity durations. Expert judgment as a technique is discussed in detail in Chapter 3.

Reserve analysis   Reserve analysis is used to incorporate a time cushion into your schedule; this cushion is called a *contingency reserve*, a *time reserve*, or a *time buffer*. The whole idea is to accommodate the possibility of schedule risks. One method of calculating the contingency reserve is to take a percentage of the original activity duration estimate as the contingency reserve. Later, when more information about the program and its projects becomes available, the contingency reserve can be reduced or eliminated.

Quantitative and mathematical analyses   Quantitative analysis such as parametric estimating, described earlier in this chapter, can be used to estimate the activity duration. Mathematical analysis such as *Monte Carlo simulations* (a technique that uses randomly generated values as input) can be used to develop the program schedule. Another quantitative and mathematical technique is schedule network analysis.

Schedule network analysis   The most critical tool and technique for developing the program schedule is the schedule network analysis, including the critical path method. Because it is an involved method, it's discussed in the "Schedule Network Analysis" section further on in this chapter.

Resource leveling   This technique is applied to address the resource needs of activities that must be performed to meet specific delivery dates when there are limited resources. Resource leveling involves taking a part of resources from one component and assigning it to another. This technique is discussed in detail further on in this chapter.

Schedule-compression techniques   It is true that you, the program manager, build the schedule through hard, cold mathematical analysis and don't just accept whatever schedule goals come down the pipe from elsewhere, such as the customer or the program sponsor. However, once you have the schedule built through analysis, you can attempt to accommodate some critical stakeholder expectations or hard deadlines such as a predetermined program (or component) finish date. We already discussed one such method, resource leveling, to accommodate hard deadlines for components. In this section, we discuss two more methods for schedule compression:

Crashing   This is a program schedule-compression technique used to decrease the program (or one of its components') duration with minimum additional cost. A number of alternatives are analyzed, including the assignment of additional resources. In general, you analyze the tradeoff between the extra cost that will result from the compression and the benefit you will receive. Because it can result in increased cost, you must check the viability of this technique before applying it.

Crashing usually involves assigning more resources and hence increasing cost. However, guard yourself against the misconception that additional resources will improve the performance linearly. For example, if one software developer can develop an application in 14 days, it does not necessarily mean that two developers will develop the same application in 7 days. There will be overhead, such as the initial lag in productivity of the newly assigned resource, the time taken to reallocate the work, the interaction among the resources, and the like.

Fast-tracking   This is a program schedule-compression technique used to decrease the duration of a program (or a component) by performing in parallel program phases or schedule components that would normally be performed in sequence. For example, a programmer starts writing code for an application before the design is complete. An obvious risk in this technique is that the work may not meet all the requirements and reworking may be required at a later stage. However, this technique works well when applied to components that are relatively independent of each other.

Coding structure   A coding structure is used for program components and activities for tracking and accounting purposes. As mentioned in Chapter 4, for example, each component in a PWBS and a WBS has a unique identification code. Codes can be used for different purposes. The codes of scheduled components, also called *control accounts*, can be directly linked to the accounting system of the performing organization.

Program management software   Program management software includes tools that help draw schedule network diagrams and develop and maintain program and project schedules.

As you have seen, there is a variety of tools available for the schedule development. Depending on your specific program, you apply some or all of these tools on the input to develop the output of the Schedule Development process.

Output of Developing a Program Schedule

The obvious output of the Schedule Development process is the schedule. This and other output items are discussed in the following.

Program schedule   This is the major output of the Schedule Development process. It includes the following:

- Significant program milestones
- Timelines for program packages related to projects
- Timelines for program packages related to non-project program activities

This information helps determine the program finish date for a given begin date. This also determines the finish date for the milestones within the program.

> The milestones in a program may correspond to key deliverables within the constituent projects of the program.

Schedule management plan   Once the schedule is created and approved, it needs to be managed throughout the program life cycle. This plan basically determines how to control the schedule, and it becomes a part of the program management plan.

Update to resource requirements   During the schedule development, you might realize that you previously failed to identify a type of resource (or the right quantity of an identified type of resource). In this case, you will need to update the resource requirements accordingly.

A program consists of projects, so the program schedule obviously depends on the schedule of the constituent projects. This is why the project schedule information is an important input to developing the program schedule.

Information from Project Schedules

As stated earlier in this chapter, the program schedule development typically starts with the program packages, which are the bottom-level components in the PWBS. Most of these packages are decomposed into WBSs for constituent projects by the project teams under the leadership of project managers. The individual project managers (with the help of their teams) develop the schedules for the projects and roll up the information into the program packages. This information is necessary to develop the program schedule. In this section we explore some of the aspects of generating this information that answer the following questions:

- How do you determine the types of dependencies and display them in diagrams?

- How do you analyze the dependency diagrams to develop a schedule?

 The dependency determination, activity sequencing, and scheduling techniques discussed in this section in the context of projects are also applicable at the program level.

Dependency Determination

You learned earlier in this chapter that dependencies can be internal or external, and mandatory or discretionary. Dependencies can also be categorized from the schedule perspective. While developing network diagrams, you need to determine the type of dependencies (from the schedule perspective) among the activities and then display those dependencies in the form of network diagrams.

Types of Dependencies

To properly sequence the schedule activities, you need to determine the dependencies among them. As illustrated in Figure 5.3, a dependency relationship between two activities is defined by two terms: *predecessor* and *successor*. In other words, when two activities are in a dependency relationship with each other, one of them is a predecessor of the other, and the other one is the successor. In Figure 5.3, activity X is a predecessor of activity Y, and activity Y is the successor of activity X. By definition, the successor activity must start after the predecessor activity has already started. That means X must start before Y.

FIGURE 5.3   Predecessor/successor relationship between two activities

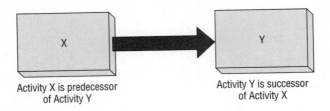

Activity X is predecessor   Activity Y is successor
    of Activity Y   of Activity X

But exactly when can the successor activity start after the predecessor activity? Well, both the predecessor and the successor have a start and a finish and there are at maximum four possible combinations between the start and finish points of the predecessor and the successor activities. Accordingly, there are four kinds of dependencies, also called *precedence relationships*, listed here:

Finish-to-start   The initiation of the successor activity depends upon the completion of the predecessor activity; that is, the successor activity cannot be started until the predecessor activity has already been completed. An example is that a programmer cannot start programming (the successor activity) until the application design (the predecessor activity) is complete.

Finish-to-finish   The completion of the successor activity depends upon the completion of the predecessor activity; that is, the successor activity cannot be completed until the predecessor activity has already been completed. For example, an instructor cannot finish grading all the courses (the successor activity) until the exams for all the courses she offers are conducted.

Start-to-start   The initiation of the successor activity depends upon the initiation of the predecessor activity; that is, the successor activity cannot be initiated until the predecessor activity has already been initiated. As an example, consider a software application with several components that need to be developed and tested. The application testing (the successor activity) cannot start until the application development (the predecessor activity) starts. For instance, when the first component of the application is developed, the testing can start.

Start-to-finish   The completion of the successor activity depends upon the initiation of the predecessor activity; that is, the successor activity cannot be completed until the predecessor activity has been initiated. Consider a scenario in which part of an application-development assignment is that the developer will train one member of the training team, who in turn will train the rest of the training team in using the application. In this case the relationship between the development (the predecessor activity) and training (the successor activity) is start-to-finish.

These types of dependencies describe the logical relationships between activities from the schedule perspective. The dependencies discussed in this section can be internal to the program or external, and can be mandatory or discretionary. These terms are already explained in this chapter.

The dependency between two schedule activities is an example of logical relationships. The logical relationships can be displayed in schematic diagrams called *project schedule network diagrams*, or just *network diagrams* for brevity. Two commonly used methods to construct these diagrams are the precedence diagramming method (PDM) and the arrow diagramming method (ADM), which were mentioned briefly earlier in the chapter.

Precedence Diagramming Method (PDM)

The precedence diagramming method is the method to construct a project schedule network diagram in which a box (for example, a rectangle) is used to represent an activity and an arrow is used to represent a dependency between two activities. The boxes representing activities are called nodes. Figure 5.4 is an example of a network diagram constructed by using the PDM, in which activity A is a predecessor of activity B, activity C is a predecessor of activities D and G, and so on.

In this diagram, only C, D, and I have more than one successor. In general, the PDM supports all four kinds of precedence relationships discussed earlier, but the most commonly used dependency relationship in the PDM is finish-to-start.

Although the PDM is the most commonly used method, if you are going to use only the finish-to-start dependencies, the arrow diagramming method is another option to consider.

FIGURE 5.4   A project schedule network diagram constructed using the precedence diagramming method (PDM).

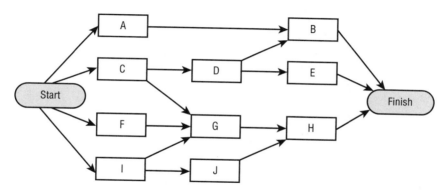

Arrow Diagramming Method (ADM)

The arrow diagramming method is the method to construct a project schedule network diagram in which a node (represented by a circle) acts as a junction between the predecessor activity and the successor activity, and the activity itself is represented by an arrow. The arrow representing an activity also points to the successor activity through a junction. Now, we have a problem inherent to this definition: An activity may have multiple successors, multiple predecessors, or both. In such cases, to show the dependencies we might need more arrows than the number of activities. But an arrow does not show just the relationship in the ADM; it also represent an activity. So, you cannot have more than one arrow for one activity. How would you then represent, for example, that an activity has more than one successor? This problem is solved by a dummy activity, represented by a broken arrow that shows the relationship but does not represent any real activity.

Figure 5.5 displays the set of dependencies identical to that shown in Figure 5.4. The only difference between the two diagrams is that Figure 5.5 uses the ADM instead of the PDM used in

Figure 5.4. Note the use of dummy activities in Figure 5.5 to show the dependency between C and G, between D and B, and between I and G.

 The ADM is used to represent only dependencies of the finish-to-start type.

Applying leads and lags   The finish-to-start dependency means that the successor activity starts where the predecessor activity finishes. *Applying a lead* means allowing the successor activity to start before the predecessor activity finishes, and *applying a lag* means starting the successor activity a few days after the predecessor activity finishes. Sometimes you may need to make such adjustments in the schedule.

So, finish-to-start is the most commonly used precedence relationship in the PDM diagramming method, although this method can also be used to represent the other three precedence relationships: finish-to-finish, start-to-start, and start-to-finish. The ADM method can be used only to show the finish-to-start relationship.

FIGURE 5.5   A project schedule network diagram constructed using the arrow diagramming method (ADM).

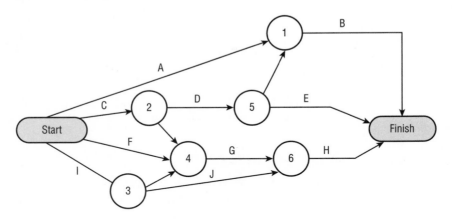

Schedule Network Analysis

The schedule network analysis is a set of techniques used to generate a program (or a project) schedule by identifying the early and late start dates and the early and late finish dates. It accomplishes this task by employing a schedule model and various analytical techniques, such as the critical path method, the critical chain method, what-if analysis, and resource leveling. These techniques are discussed in the following.

TABLE 5.3   Path Durations Calculated from the Network Diagram Shown in Figure 5.6

Path	Durations of Activities	Path duration
Start-A-B-Finish	6 + 5	11
Start-C-D-B-Finish	6 + 4 + 5	15
Start-C-D-E-Finish	6 + 4 + 1	11
Start-C-G-H-Finish	6 + 5 + 9	20
Start-F-G-H-Finish	8 + 5 + 9	22
Start-I-G-H-Finish	2 + 5 + 9	16
Start-I-J-H-Finish	2 + 2 + 9	13

The path Start-F-G-H-Finish is the critical path because it is the longest of all the paths.

TABLE 5.4   Early and Late Start and Finish Dates for Activities in the Network Diagram Shown in Figure 5.6

Activity	Early start	Early finish	Late start	Late finish	Float time
A	0	6	11	17	11
B	10	15	17	22	7
C	0	6	2	8 (C-G-H)	2
D	6	10	13	17 (C-D-B)	7
E	10	11	21	22	11
F	0	8	0	8	0
G	8	13	8	13	0
H	13	22	13	22	0

TABLE 5.4   Early and Late Start and Finish Dates for Activities in the Network Diagram Shown in Figure 5.6 *(continued)*

Activity	Early start	Early finish	Late start	Late finish	Float time
I	0	2	6	8 (I-G-H)	6
J	2	4	11	13	9

Early start and finish dates are calculated by using the forward pass method and late start and finish dates are calculated by using the backward pass method.

The schedule model   You know by now that the resource requirements and activity durations are the estimates based on assumptions such as "a typical programmer will take five days to write this program." However, we use this data to build the program schedule. Changing the assumptions will change the data and hence the schedule. So, a set of assumptions and the information based on those assumptions, such as activity durations resource requirements and available resources, is called a *schedule model*.

The critical path method   This is the schedule network analysis technique used to identify the schedule flexibility and the critical path of the project schedule network diagram. The *critical path* is the longest path (sequence of activities) in a project schedule network diagram. Because it is the longest path, it determines the duration of the project and hence the finish date of the project given the start date. As an example, consider the network diagram presented in Figure 5.6. The boxes in the figure represent activities such as activity A followed by activity B, and the number on top of a box represents the duration of the activity in time units (such as days).

FIGURE 5.6   An example of a project schedule network diagram. The duration of an activity is represented by the number on top of the box that represents the activity.

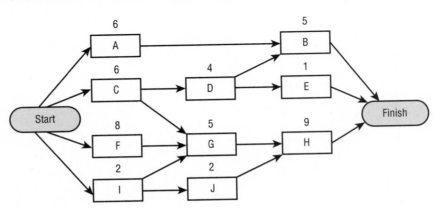

Table 5.3 shows the calculations for the duration of each path of the network diagram by adding the durations of the individual activities on the path. You can see from Table 5.3 that the path Start-F-G-H-Finish is the critical path because it is the longest path in the diagram—22 units of duration. This means if the project start date is March 2, the project finish date will be March 24 (2 + 22), given that the duration unit is calendar days.

The second important feature of the critical path method is to identify the flexibility in the project schedule by calculating the early start and finish dates and the late start and finish dates of each activity on each path. An activity's schedule flexibility is measured by the positive difference between the late start date and the early start date for the activity, which is called *float time*.

Table 5.4 shows calculations for the early start and finish dates, the late start and finish dates, and the float time for each activity in the network diagram being analyzed. The early start and finish dates of activities on a path are calculated by using the *forward pass method*, which means you start your calculations from the Start point (leftmost) and make your way forward. As an example, consider the path Start-A-B-Finish in the network diagram shown in Figure 5.6. Because A is the first activity on the path, its early start is day 0. The same is true about C. Because B depends on the completion of A, C, and D, and because C + D (that is, 10) is longer than A (that is, 6), the early start date for B is the early start date of C plus the duration of C + D (that is, 0 + 10 = 10. Because the duration of B is 5, the early finish date of B is 10 + 5 = 15.

The late start and finish dates are calculated by using the *backward pass method*, which means you start your calculations from the Finish point. The project finish date determined by the critical path is day 22 given that the project start date is day 0. Because activity B has a duration of 5 days, it must be started no later than the day 22 − 5 = 17. Therefore day 17 is the late start date of activity B and day 22 (17 + 5) is the late finish date of activity B. Activity A has a duration of 6 days, so given that B must start on day 17, A must not start later than day 17 − 5 = 12. Therefore the late start date for A is day 12. The float times are calculated as follows:

Float time for A = late start − early start = 11 − 0 = 11

Float time for B = late start − early start = 17 − 10 = 7

NOTE   Each activity on the critical path (F, G, and H) has a float time of zero. This obviously is a source of schedule risk.

Now that you have an idea of float time, you should know that there are two kinds of float times:

Free float (FF)   This is the maximum amount of time by which a given activity can be delayed without delaying the early start of any immediately following scheduling activities.

Total float (TF)   This is the maximum time by which a given activity can be delayed from its early start date without delaying the finish date of the project.

Each activity on a critical path has zero float time, and therefore poses a schedule risk. Therefore, you must monitor the activities on all critical paths very closely during the execution of the project.

The critical chain method   This is an alternative schedule network analysis technique that takes into account the uncertainties on activity durations caused by the uncertain availability of resources. It uses the schedule network diagrams to identify the critical paths and the schedule flexibility just like the critical path method. The only difference is that in this technique you work from more than one network diagram. For example, the durations in the first network are based on the planned scenario regarding the availability of the resources. You can draw another network diagram based on a pessimistic scenario regarding the availability of resources. The durations of some activities in the second diagram will be longer compared to the first diagram, and the second diagram may even have a different or an additional critical path. The extra durations in the second diagram are called *duration buffers*. So, the focus of the critical chain method is to manage the duration buffers and the uncertainties in the availability of resources applied to the planned schedule activities.

Resource leveling   Resource leveling is not an independent schedule network analysis method. It is applied to the schedule that has already been analyzed by using other methods, such as the critical path method or the critical chain method. The resource leveling technique is applied to address the resource needs of activities that must be performed to meet specific delivery dates. Resource leveling involves taking a part of resources from one activity and assigning it to another. This will change the activity durations and can also result in change of critical paths. This technique is discussed in detail further on in this chapter.

What-if scenario analysis   The purpose of the what-if scenario analysis is to calculate the effects of a specific scenario on the schedule—for example, how the schedule will be affected if a vendor does not make the delivery of a major component on the promised date. Because a what-if scenario by definition represents uncertainty, this analysis often leads to risk planning, which may include changing the schedule or changing the network diagram to get a few activities out of harm's way if possible.

So, the critical path method is used to develop a schedule for given resources, whereas the critical chain method factors in the uncertainty on the availability of the resources. The resource leveling technique is used to move the resources around to meet the resources need of the activities that must deliver on a specific date. In an ideal world where the required (or planned) resources are guaranteed, we would not need the critical chain method and resource leveling; just the critical path method would do.

Let's assume you have used the critical path method to determine the schedule for a project. You have also applied other techniques, such as the critical chain method and resource leveling. The final realistic schedule that you have come up with has an unacceptable project duration (the length of the critical path). What do you do? This is where the schedule-compression techniques discussed earlier in this chapter come to your rescue.

The word *free* is in abundant use these days (free lunches at companies and "buy one, get one free" deals in retail stores). However, at the end of the day there are no truly free lunches. Obviously, it's going to cost you to execute the program schedule, and even to develop it. Therefore, you need to do some planning for managing the program cost.

Real World Scenario

Analyzing a Precedence Diagram

Your program is in the planning stage. You are in the process of developing the program schedule. You have already finished breaking a program component down to activities. You have identified the activities, estimated the durations, and determined the dependencies among them. The
results are shown in the following diagram, in which the letters represent activities and the numbers represent durations in days.

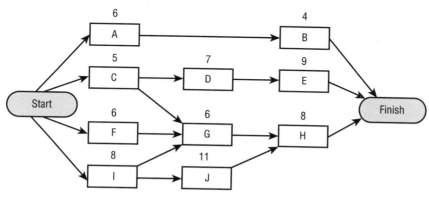

Critical path The critical path in this diagram is the following:

> Start-I-J-H-Finish

This is because the length of this path is as follows:

> 8 + 11 + 8 = 27

You can verify that the length of any other path is less than this.

Float time of activity H The float time of activity H is 0 because it's an activity that is on the
critical path.

Length of the critical path As already shown, the length of the critical path is 27.

The float time of C The float time of C is calculated as in the following.

> The early start day of C is 0 because it's the first activity in the path.

> Because the duration of C is 5, the early finish day of C is 5.

> The late finish day of C, considering the path C-D-E, is 27 − 9 − 7 = 11.

> The late finish day of C, considering the path C-G-H, is 27 – 8 – 6 = 13.
>
> So, the real finish day of C is 11 because you do need to finish all the activities on a path in the diagram on day 27 or before.
>
> The float time for activity C = late finish time of C – early finish time of C = 13 – 11 = 2.

Planning the Program Cost

First we need to distinguish between cost and budget. *Cost* is the value of the inputs that have been used up to perform a task or to produce an item: a product, service, or result. This value is usually measured in units of money. For example, you paid two programmers $500 each for developing a software program, and you paid $100 to a tester to test the program. The cost for the task of developing and testing the software program is $1,100. You can add the costs of components of a system, and the sum will represent the cost of the system, but it's still a cost and not a budget. *Budget* is an aggregated cost with a timeline. For example, in a program you aggregate the costs of all the resources needed to perform the program, and you put a timeline on it: the availability of funds over time is the budget.

Cost estimating for a program is a process of aggregating all costs at the program level, which includes the costs of the following elements:

- All activity at the program level
- Project activities
- Program-related non-project activities

The program team (under the leadership of the program manager) makes the cost estimates for the activities that happen only at the program level. Who makes the estimates for the cost that will be incurred at the project level? Depending upon the nature of the program and the organization, one of the following three methods can be used to make these program cost estimates:

- The estimates are entirely made by the program manager and the program team.
- The estimates are made by aggregating the cost estimates from the individual project teams.
- The estimates are made by using the hybrid approach: estimates for some projects will be made by the program team and for other projects they'll be made by the corresponding project teams.

NOTE   Generally speaking, a budget refers to a list of all planned expenses and revenues. However, with a project there is availability of funds that is relevant instead of revenues. With a program, the revenues are part of the benefits for which the program is being executed.

The program costs are estimated and the program budgets are established by performing the Cost Estimating and Budgeting process depicted in Figure 5.7.

FIGURE 5.7   The Cost Estimating and Budgeting process: input and output

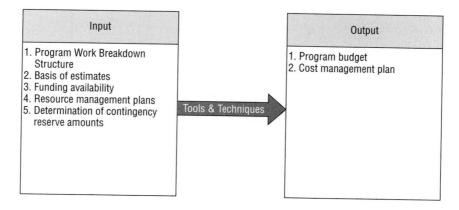

Input	Output
1. Program Work Breakdown Structure 2. Basis of estimates 3. Funding availability 4. Resource management plans 5. Determination of contingency reserve amounts	1. Program budget 2. Cost management plan

Tools & Techniques

Input to Cost Estimating and Budgeting

The cost is estimated for the PWBS components and there must be some basis for estimates. So, the PWBS and basis of estimates are the obvious inputs to the Cost Estimating and Budgeting process. These and other input items are discussed in the following.

PWBS   You use the program packages of the PWBS to estimate the program cost because these packages encompass the scope of the program. Therefore the PWBS is an obvious input to the Cost Estimating and Budgeting process.

Basis of estimates   An estimation is an approximation made because of the lack of precise and complete data. However, it is a calculated approximation that will be usable even if the input to this calculation is incomplete and uncertain. To assess the accuracy and integrity of these estimates, you need to consider what the basis for each estimate is. The following are some examples of estimate bases:

- Expert judgment

- Aggregation of costs of the constituent projects

- Analogous estimate based on historical information (discussed earlier under "Tools and Techniques for Developing a Program Schedule")

- Parametric estimate (discussed earlier under "Tools and Techniques for Developing a Program Schedule")

Funding availability   To establish the program budget it is important to know when the funds are available; for example, the amount x is available in the beginning, amount y after the first milestone, and so on.

Resource management plan   To estimate the cost you need to know the required resources. The resource management plan describes how to manage the resources, including the optimal use of these resources across the program. Therefore, it's a useful input to the Cost Estimating and Budgeting process. The resource management plan in generated by using the Resource Planning process and becomes part of the program management plan.

Contingency reserve   There are two issues associated with the estimates:

- Estimates are approximations, and approximations imply uncertainty, which means risk.
- Some stakeholders will always be pushing the envelope on the program scope, and each organization has some tolerance for overrunning the objectives; that is, how much more you can offer than what is planned.

You will need some funds to deal with both of these situations. The contingency reserve comes to your rescue here. The *contingency reserve*, in general, is an amount of resource (funds or time) allocated in addition to the calculated estimates to reduce the risk arising from various sources—for example, from the overruns of program (or the constituent project) objectives to a level acceptable to the performing organization. In other words, the contingency reserves are the funds reserved to deal with the events that are anticipated but not certain. Contingency reserves may be allocated at the program level and at the levels of the constituent projects, and can be used at the discretion of the program manager (at the program level) and the project managers (at the constituent projects' levels). The overall cost estimate should include the contingency reserves.

So, starting with the PWBS and the resource management plan, you collect all the input items necessary to begin estimating the cost using several available techniques.

Tools and Techniques for Cost Estimating and Budgeting

There are several techniques available to estimate the cost for performing the program work and then aggregating that cost to create a budget. These tools and techniques are discussed in the following.

Analogous estimation   Analogous cost estimation is a technique that uses costs from other program components in the same or the previous programs to estimate the cost of a given program component. This technique is useful when very limited cost information about the component is available, especially in the beginning of a program. This technique is discussed in detail earlier in this chapter in the context of schedule development.

Exam Spotlight

Analogous estimation is sometimes also called *top-down estimation*. Do not confuse it with *bottom-up estimation*. Analogous estimation can also be used in duration estimates and in estimating resource requirements.

Bottom-up estimation   This technique involves estimating the cost of the parts of a component and then aggregating the cost of those parts to calculate the cost of the whole component. This technique can generate accurate results when you can generally make a better estimate of a part than of the whole, which is usually the case.

Cost aggregation   Cost aggregation is the technique used to calculate the cost of a whole by summing up the costs of the parts that comprise the whole. Bottom-up estimation uses cost aggregation. You can aggregate the costs of all the program components to calculate the total cost of the program.

Funding-limit reconciliation   The key issue that this technique addresses is the large variations in expenditures over different periods, which are undesirable for organizational operations because organizations usually have a well-defined smooth budget. The large variations in expected spending will run into a limitation on available funds over certain periods. So the expenditure will need to be reconciled with these funding limitations by regulating or smoothing the expenditures. This will impact allocation of resources, resulting in schedule constraints on some program components or milestones. The reconciliation method can be iterated by using different options to create an acceptable cost baseline: a time-phased budget against which all the cost-performance measurements will be made.

Parametric estimation   This is a technique that uses some parameters (statistical relationships among them) to make the estimate. For example, if the unit cost is known, the cost of the whole package containing a number of units can be calculated. This technique can generate quite accurate results depending on the accuracy of the quantity of resources and other data that goes into the estimation. Historical information can also be used in parametric estimation. The accuracy and reliability of this technique depends on the following:

- How accurate the historical information used in this technique is
- How precise (or quantified) the parameters used are
- How scalable the model is; for example, its ability to work for both small and large projects and programs

Quantitative estimation   In certain situations some costs can be estimated quantitatively to great accuracy. For example, if you know the costs of different parts of one item, you can add those up and multiply them by x to calculate the cost of x items. Similarly, if you know the cost rates for a certain type of resource, you can calculate the cost of the required resources of that type by multiplying the rate with the quantity required.

Reserve analysis   The reserve analysis in cost estimation is the cost analysis that includes extra cost (called *reserves*) for some schedule activities or components. These reserves are usually needed to compensate for the uncertainty in estimates or an anticipated (but not certain) risk. Such risks are called *known unknowns*. Note that contingency reserve is determined through reserve analysis.

Table 5.5 shows which of these techniques are typically used for cost estimating and which ones are used for cost budgeting.

TABLE 5.5   The Typical Uses of Cost Estimating and Budgeting Techniques

Tool or Technique	Cost Estimating	Cost Budgeting
Analogous estimation	X	
Bottom-up estimation	X	
Cost aggregation		X
Funding-limit reconciliation		X
Parametric estimation	X	X
Quantitative estimation	X	
Reserve analysis		X

Note that some of these techniques are used just for cost estimating, some just for cost budgeting, and others for both. Nevertheless, all these techniques contribute to generating the output of the Cost Estimating and Budgeting process.

Output of Cost Estimating and Budgeting

The program budget is an obvious output of Cost Estimating and Budgeting. A less obvious output is the cost management plan. Both are discussed in the following.

Program budget   A program budget is created by aggregating the following elements:

- Budget for non-project program activities
- Budget for constituent projects
- Financial constraints on the budget, such as the fiscal-year budgetary planning cycles and funding limits for particular periods of the year

Programs usually span multiple budgetary-planning periods. In this case, the program team can use different budget techniques for different periods over the program life cycle.

Cost management plan   The cost management plan describes how to manage the cost, including controlling it. The cost management plan can also specify the following:

Control thresholds   This refers to the tolerance of the organization to the variations in the cost with respect to the planned cost and budget. If the cost exceeds this threshold, it is called *out of control*.

Precision level   This refers to how precise the cost estimates are. For example, it may specify the precision level to which the estimation number will be rounded off—e.g., $100 or $1,000.

At the precision level of $100, an estimate of $3,675 is reported as $3,700, whereas in the precision level $1,000, it will be reported as $4,000.

Units of measurements   This refers to the units of measurements for the resources—for example, work in hours and cost in U.S. dollars.

The cost of a program is mostly the cost of resources required to execute the program. The general planning for the resources is performed by using the Resource Planning process, which generates the resource management plan, an input to the Cost Estimating and Budgeting process. Out of all the resources, the human resources are critical and therefore we have a whole knowledge area called Human Resource Management. Like all resources, human resources need to be managed.

Planning Human Resources

Program roles, the responsibilities of the roles, and the reporting relationships among the roles need to be defined to perform a program effectively. A role is a defined function to be performed by a team member. The other issue that needs to be addressed before the program can be executed is how and when the program team members (who will perform the program work) will be acquired. The Human Resource Planning process is used to address these issues.

The following are the two main goals of the Human Resource Planning process:

- Identify and document program roles, responsibilities for each role, and reporting relationships among the roles.
- Create the staff management plan.

The Human Resource Planning process is shown in Figure 5.8.

FIGURE 5.8   The Human Resource Planning process: input and output

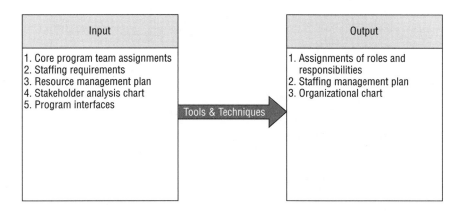

Input to Human Resource Planning

Staffing requirements and the resource management plan are the obvious inputs to the Human Resource Planning process. These and other input items are discussed here.

Core program team assignments   Before you define new roles and responsibilities, you need to consider the roles that have already been defined and are being performed by the existing program team members. The core program team members were selected for specific roles and assignments were made to those roles during the Initiate Team process.

Staffing requirements   This refers to the needed roles and their responsibilities. The resource requirements are an output of the Resource Planning process. Staffing requirements are a subset of the resource requirements. Obviously, you need to know what the staffing requirements are before you can obtain the staff members.

The resource management plan   The resource management plan describes how to manage the resources, including the optimal use of these resources across the program. Therefore, it's a useful input to the Human Resource Planning process. The resource management plan is generated by using the Resource Planning process, and becomes part of the program management plan.

The stakeholder analysis chart   Stakeholder management is a theme that runs through the program life cycle. A stakeholder analysis chart will help you keep the interface management in line with the stakeholders' interests and expectations. A stakeholder analysis chart is produced by using a technique called stakeholder analysis. You perform this analysis to accomplish the following:

- Identify the stakeholders: positive and negative.
- Identify the influences and interests of the stakeholders.
- Identify the needs, wants, and expectations of various stakeholders, which may conflict with each other.
- Quantify and prioritize the needs, wants, and expectations of the stakeholders. This quantification and prioritization will create the requirements that will become part of the program requirements.

You want to identify the human roles and responsibilities in line with the expectations, needs, and wants of the stakeholders.

Program interfaces   Program interfaces are identified by using the Interface Planning process, whose main purpose is to identify and map the relationships of the program with other programs and with other external factors. Understanding these interfaces is important to get the right human resources and make the right assignments.

You use some tools and technologies on the input to create the output of the Human Resource Planning process.

Tools and Techniques for Human Resource Planning

You need resources to complete the program components, and some of these resources will be human resources. For example, consider marketing personnel who are marketing the product of your program. Before you even know the name of a marketing person, you can work with this need as a role and assign a real individual to fill this role later. You will also need to develop a plan to manage the human resources: the staffing management plan. The tools and techniques used to accomplish these tasks are discussed in the following.

Networking   Write it on your heart: Networking is one of the golden secrets you have for succeeding as a program (or project) manager, especially in an organization in which functional managers hold all the powers (hiring, firing, bonuses) and the program (and project) managers are running around with nothing in their hands other than the program (and project) schedules and status reports. To network effectively, you should understand the influence of political and interpersonal factors in your organization that might impact various staffing-management options. Some of the essential networking happens at the beginning of each program, and you must make full use of it. However, networking is a regular practice and you should be using all the human resource network activities, such as proactive correspondence, informal conversations, luncheon meetings, and trade conferences.

Organizational theories   Various organizational theories provide information on and insight into how people behave in a team or an organization, what motivates team members, and the like. If you have knowledge of these theories, it will help you plan human resources quickly and use them more effectively.

Templates   You can use templates to document team members' roles and responsibilities. There are different kinds of templates (and formats) that you can use to produce different kinds of organizational charts discussed in the output of the Human Resource Planning process.

Human resource practices   You, the program manager, should be aware of standard human resource practices. While planning for human resources, you should follow the standard policy and procedures of the performing organization regarding human resources.

To summarize, networking, organizational theories, and templates for (creating organizational charts) are the main tools and techniques used to determine roles and develop the staff management plan, which are the major output items of the Human Resource Planning process.

Output of Human Resource Planning

The output of the Human Resource Planning process includes roles and responsibilities and the staffing management plan. These and other output items are discussed here.

Assignments of roles and responsibilities   The program activities will be completed by individuals working in certain roles and performing responsibilities that come with the roles. So, roles and responsibilities are an important output of human Resource Planning. While determining roles and responsibilities, you must be clear about the following concepts:

Role   In real life, most of our activities are performed while playing certain roles, such as a parent, a teacher, or a student. Similarly, in program management a role is essentially a set of responsibilities, and its examples include the program, researcher, or an accountant. A role is assigned to a team member who will perform the responsibilities included in the role to complete one or more program activities.

Responsibility   A responsibility is a piece of work (task) that must be performed as a part of completing a program activity. Responsibilities can be grouped together as a role.

Competency   Competency is the ability of a team member to play a certain role; that is, to perform the responsibilities assigned to the role. While assigning a role to a team member, you should know if the team member possesses the skills required to perform the responsibilities of the role. A mismatch may need to be addressed with training, hiring, schedule changes, or scope changes.

Authority   The authority is a right assigned to a role that enables the person playing the role to apply program resources, make certain decisions, or sign approvals.

> The roles must be clarified by specifying the responsibilities and the authorities assigned to each role. A good match between the levels of responsibilities and authority for each team member generally produces the best results. This gives the team members a sense of ownership.

The roles are assigned to individuals from both inside and outside the performing organization. The internal assignments usually include program management team members, representatives from the relevant functional departments of the performing organization, and the key members from the project management teams for the constituent projects. External assignments may include end users and program stakeholders from other organizations.

Staffing management plan   Once you have determined the roles to perform the activities, you need to identify individuals (humans) to fill those roles. The staffing management plan describes when and how human resource requirements for a program will be met. While preparing the staffing management plan for your program, you must consider the following items:

Staff acquisition   While planning staff acquisition, you may need to struggle with a set of questions including:

What are the levels of expertise needed for the program and what are the assigned costs?

Will the human resources come from within the organization, outside the organization, or both?

Will the team members be required to work in a central location or can they work from distant locations?

Will you need the assistance of the human resources department of your organization to acquire the staff?

Timetable and release criteria   You need to have a timetable for the human resource requirements describing when and for how long a staff member is needed. The program schedule will help you in determining that. You should also determine the release criteria and time to release each team member from the program. Planning of release criteria is very important for smooth transition of team members from one program to another, and for the optimal use of the resources in the organization.

Training needs   If some team members lack the adequate level of skills needed for the project, a training plan can be developed as a part of the program.

Compliance and safety   The staff management plan can also include strategies for complying with relevant government regulations, union contracts, and human resource policies. Your organization may have some policies and procedures that protect the team members from safety hazards. These policies and procedures must be included in the staff management plan.

Recognition and rewards   Recognitions and rewards are good tools to promote and reinforce desired behaviors. However, to use this tool effectively you must have a clear criteria based on activities and performance of team members. The potential candidate for a reward must have an appropriate level of control over the activity for which the reward will be offered. For example, if a team member is to be rewarded for completing the project within the budget, the team member must have an adequate level of control over decision making that affects spending.

Remember that each project of the program has its own staffing management plan, but all will have similar elements. Some of these items may be more important at a project level than at a program level. The interaction between the project staffing management plans and program staffing plans depends on the management control interface between the program manager and the project managers.

Organizational charts   These charts are used to identify and document the roles of the program team members, the responsibilities assigned to the roles, and the reporting relationships among the roles. Most of the chart formats fall into three categories: hierarchical, matrix, and text-oriented.

Hierarchical   The hierarchical charts are the traditional ways to represent the reporting relationships in an organization, in a top-down format. Such a chart is also called an *organizational breakdown structure (OBS)* and is arranged according to the organization's existing departments, units, or teams. An OBS will help you to identify team members for the program. After you have the team members, if needed you can develop an OBS for your program organization.

Matrix   A matrix is used to specify the relationships between schedule activities, roles, and team members. Such a matrix is generally called a *responsibility assignment matrix (RAM)*. Different matrices can be used to show these relationships at different levels. For example, you can use a RAM to document resource requirements for each activity. You can also use a RAM to document the responsibilities assigned to specific team members for the program activities, as shown in Table 5.6.

Text-oriented   When the team member responsibilities need to be described in detail, text-based documents may be more useful. These documents may be known by various names in different organizations, such as *responsibilities forms, position descriptions,* and *role-responsibility-authority forms.* These documents, once established, can act as templates for other programs.

TABLE 5.6   A Responsibility Assignment Matrix (RAM) Depicting the Roles Assigned to the Team Members for Various Activities

Activity	Nancy	Linda	Ram	Bholi	Pablo
Budget	R	A	I	I	C
Coordination	I	I	R	I	C
Research	C	R	A	I	C
Legal	I	I	A	I	R

Letters are used as symbols to represent roles: R for responsible, A for accountable, C for consult, and I for inform.

Assessing Human Resource Competence

The competence of a human resource such as program team member (including project managers and program managers) has three main components:

Knowledge competence   This refers to the requirement that the resource has the knowledge needed to perform the assigned role. For example, a project manager and a program manager must know the project management and program management processes in detail.

Performance competence   This refers to how well the resource applies the knowledge to do the work. For example, this competency requires that a project manager or a program manager must be able to apply project management and program management knowledge to meet most of the requirements most of the time.

Personal competence   This refers to the personal behavior and style of the resource. This competence determines how the resource behaves while operating within the program (and project) environment.

The competence of human resources should be assessed at the time of role assignments and also afterwards. For example, a team member may be found quite competent at the time of hiring. Because the competence is measured for the work you do, it can change depending on what you do. In other words, a team member who was competent to do assignments in the past may not be competent for a new assignment. So, competency assessment is an iterative task. You can use a number of tools and techniques to assess competence:

Exams and certifications   This technique is useful in testing knowledge competence. For example, a program manager's knowledge competence can be assessed with the PgMP exam, and a project manager's knowledge competence can be assessed with the PMP exam.

Interviews   Knowledge competence can also be assessed during interviews with the candidates. The assessment may involve verbal questions, written tests, or both.

Performance appraisals   This refers to the formal annual reviews of the employees by their supervisors. These reviews may assess all three components of competence: knowledge, performance, and personal.

Peer reviews   Peer reviews are performed by the employees at the same hierarchical level as the employee who is under review. Another review closely related to the peer review is called *360-degree feedback*. As the name suggests, it's a multirating feedback or review. It comes from various individuals who have interacted with the employee (human resource). These reviews can also shed light on the knowledge, performance, and personal elements of resource competence.

Human resources are only one of several kinds of resources you will need to complete your program.

Estimating and Managing Resources

The program will need many types of resources. Some of those types are listed here:

- Human resources
- Materials and equipment
- Facilities
- Finances
- Services

All these resource requirements need to be estimated and the resources need to be managed. I have already covered two resource-related processes: Resource Planning (in Chapter 4) and Human Resource Planning in this chapter. This section explores three common aspects of resources: tools and techniques for estimating resource requirements, resource management, and resource leveling.

Tools and Techniques for Estimating Resource Requirements

Once you have determined the components (or activities) that need to be performed to complete the program, you can estimate the resources needed to perform those components. Estimating the resource requirements involves estimating the types of resources and the quantity for each type. Table 5.7 presents some of the general tools and techniques that can be used in estimating the resource requirements. These techniques have already been discussed in detail elsewhere in this chapter and in previous chapters.

These are very general techniques that can be used to estimate several quantities. For example, analogous estimation and parametric estimation can be used to estimate activity duration, cost, and resource requirements. Similarly, historical information and the Delphi technique can be used to collect relevant information in order to make an estimate of some quantity.

TABLE 5.7   Tools and Techniques for Estimating Resource Requirements

Tool or Technique	Description
Analogous estimation	A technique that is used to make an estimate of some quantities such as cost or duration for a current activity based on the actual values of these quantities for similar activities in a previous project or program
Parametric estimation	A quantitative technique used to calculate some quantities by using rates, historical information, and statistical relationships between some parameters
Historical information	The information from the knowledge base about similar activities in previous projects and programs
Delphi technique	An information-gathering technique used for experts to reach a consensus while sharing their ideas and preferences anonymously

Estimating resource requirements and obtaining the required resources is critical to the success of the program. Equally important is managing those resources well.

Resource Management

The program resources are managed at the program and project levels. You must keep track of what resources are allocated to projects and what resources are allocated to program-level activities. The resources that are allocated to program-level activities will obviously be managed at the program level. Form the management perspective, the resources that are allocated to projects fall into the following three categories:

- Resources that are owned and managed by a project manager
- Resources that are owned and managed by the program manager
- Resources that are managed by the project managers but overseen by the program manager

The program manager manages some of the project resources, such as the shared resources, so that they could be optimally used across multiple projects.

Resource Leveling

Resource leveling is a technique used to resolve conflicts and over-allocation in resource assignments. An example of a conflict is a person being scheduled to conduct two meetings at different locations at the same time, or a room being booked for two meetings at the same time. An example of over-allocation is a person being scheduled to work full time to finish three tasks on Friday, with each task taking 10 hours to finish. To have 30 hours in a day is impossible. The resource usage needs to be leveled.

There are different methods used in resource leveling. Some of them are listed in the following:

Schedule dilation   Delaying a task until the resource is available may result in *schedule dilation* as opposed to *schedule compression.*

Crashing   An example of crashing, a technique covered earlier in this chapter, is working on the weekends to stay on schedule.

Ranking   The tasks/activities can be ranked in order of priorities, and the resource time is allocated according to this ranking. For example, an activity on a critical path will have a higher rank than an activity with a reasonable float time.

The whole idea of different resource-leveling methods is to resolve the over-allocation and conflicts in resource assignments with minimum impact on the overall schedule. In this effort you can also use resource optimization. A common method for resource optimization involves the following three steps:

1. Identify unused work time of resources
2. Identify activities that can be scheduled into that time
3. Match the resources with the activities and make the assignments

So, resource leveling supports a smooth resource-usage pattern over the duration of a program component, such as a project. It also helps balance the workload of the main resources in a program (or project) over a time period.

In some situations, you will not find the resources in the organization to complete a PWBS component or parts of a component. This is when a concept called procurement comes into the picture.

Exam Spotlight

Resource leveling and resource optimization are not identical. Even if a plan has used resource leveling—that is, no resource is over-allocated—it does not necessarily mean that the resources are being used optimally.

Planning Procurement

Procurement refers to obtaining some PWBS components (or some parts of them) from outside the program team to complete the program. Obtaining the components means obtaining what would be produced by completing the PWBS component. Procurement management is an execution of a set of processes used to obtain (procure) the PWBS elements from outside the program team to complete the program. There are two main roles involved in procurement management:

Buyer   The party purchasing (procuring) the product, service, or result of the PWBS component

Seller   The party delivering the product, service, or result to the buyer

Program procurement management includes the following processes:

Plan Program Purchases and Acquisitions   The process used to determine what needs to be obtained, and when and how it will be obtained

Plan Program Contracting   The process used to determine the type and details of documentation required to obtain the elements from the sellers

Request Seller Responses   The process used to solicit information, quotations, bids, offers, or proposals from the potential sellers

Select Sellers   The process of selecting sellers by reviewing offers, choosing from the candidate sellers, and negotiating a written contract with the sellers

Program Contract Administration   The process used to manage the contract and the relationship between the buyer and the seller at the program level

Contract Closure   The process of resolving any open issues to complete and close a contract that was executed at the program level

In the following, I discuss two of these processes: Plan Program Purchases and Acquisitions, and Plan Program Contracting.

Planning Program Purchases and Acquisitions

Planning program purchases and acquisitions is the process of determining what needs to be procured, when it will be procured, and how. This includes validating product requirements and developing procurement strategies. The process is depicted in Figure 5.9.

FIGURE 5.9   The Plan Program Purchases and Acquisitions process: input and output

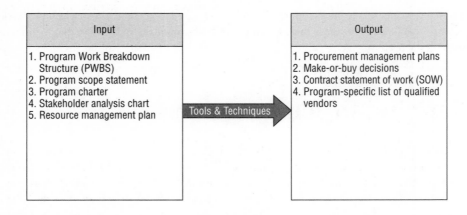

Input to Planning Purchases and Acquisitions

The program deliverables are represented by the PWBS. Therefore the PWBS is used to decide which component will be procured. You need to know exactly what you are going to procure; for example, the scope and the requirements of the item to be procured. The scope and the requirements of each component can be looked up in the program charter and program scope statement. These and other input items are discussed in the following.

PWBS   This is the basic document that is used to determine which element (a PWBS component or a part of it) will be obtained (procured) from external vendors (sellers).

Program scope statement   The program scope statement is necessary to find out the details of the element that is to be procured. It may also play a role in a make-or-buy decision (see the discussion of this topic further on). For example, the scope statement may contain constraints that can limit both the buyer's and seller's options, such as availability of funds. The requirements are another important element in the program scope statement relevant to the Plan Purchases and Acquisitions process.

Program charter   A program charter contains key objectives, program benefits, assumptions, and constraints that will be useful in make-or-buy decisions and for planning purchases and acquisitions.

Stakeholder analysis chart   Stakeholder management is a theme that runs through the program life cycle. A stakeholder analysis chart will help you keep the planning for purchases and acquisitions in line with the stakeholders' interests and expectations.

Resource management plan   A resource management plan describes how to manage the resources, including the optimal use of these resources across the program. This is useful information for make-or-buy decisions. Therefore, a resource management plan is a useful input to Plan Purchases and Acquisitions. The resource management plan is generated by using the Resource Planning process and becomes part of the program management plan.

These input items tell you what the program needs to accomplish. You need some tools and techniques to determine which of these input items can be produced in-house and which need to be procured.

Tools and Techniques for Planning Purchases and Acquisitions

Tools and techniques used in planning purchases and acquisitions are discussed in the following.

Make-or-buy analysis   Obviously *procurement* refers to buying as compared to making in-house. But you need to analyze the situation to make a decision about buying. The decision to buy or make can be based on one or more of the reasons listed in Table 5.8. Note that *buy* may mean purchase or rent. The decision to purchase or rent should be based on the effective cost in the long term. For example, if you're considering a piece of hardware that will be used only in this program (or in only one project of the program), you do not anticipate its use in any future program (or in multiple projects of the same program), and renting is significantly cheaper than buying, you will probably rent it. You may decide to buy it if the hardware is of common use in the kind of work your organization does and therefore it will be used outside of your program as well.

Contract types Different types of contracts are suitable for different types of purchases. To identify the correct type of documentation for contracting, you need to be aware of different contract types so you can select the most appropriate contract type for your program procurement. The common contract types are discussed further on in this chapter.

Expert judgment Expert judgment plays a very important role in planning for purchases and acquisitions. It can be used to assess both the input and the output of the Plan Purchases and Acquisitions process. It could be crucial in performing make-or-buy analysis. The expertise may be needed in multiple areas, including business, technical, and legal.

The first step in the use of these tools and techniques is to determine what needs to be procured; that is, the make-or-buy decision, an important output of this process.

TABLE 5.8 Reasons to Make or Buy

Factor	Reason to Make In-house	Reason to Buy
Cost	Less cost	Less cost
Skills availability	Use in-house skills	In-house skills don't exist or are not available
Skills acquisition	Learn new skills that will be used even after this project	These skills are not important to the organization
Risks	Deal with the risk in-house	Transfer the risk
Work	Core project work	Not core project work
Human resource availability	Staff available	Vendor available

Output of Planning Purchases and Acquisitions

To say you want to procure an item, you need to make a make-or-buy decision. Once you decide to procure a few items, you need a statement of work to spell out what exactly the supplier is going to supply, and you need to draft a procurement management plan. These and other output items are discussed in the following.

Procurement management plan This plan specifies how the procurement processes will be performed and managed, from preparing the procurement documents through closing contracts. The procurement management plan includes the following:

- Types of contracts to be used and the format for the contract statement of work

- Identifying any prequalified selected sellers
- Procurement metrics to be used to manage contracts and evaluate sellers
- Coordination of program procurement with the other program aspects, such as schedule and performance reporting
- Assumptions and constraints that could affect planned purchases and acquisitions
- Scheduled dates for the contract deliverables
- Directions to be provided to the seller on developing and maintaining a contract work break down structure

Make-or-buy decisions   Obviously procurement refers to buying as compared to making in-house. The make-or-buy analysis discussed earlier generates the make-or-buy decisions. Decisions about which program items (product, service, or result) will be acquired and which items will be developed in-house need to be documented. The document should also contain the reasons for each decision. Some of these decisions can also be made iteratively; that is, they can be revisited and reviewed at a later stage of the program.

Another output item of the procurement planning process is the *statement of work (SOW)*, which is a document that may be written by the buyer or the seller to specify what products will be delivered or what services will be performed. It is also called the *contract statement of work*.

Contract statement of work (SOW)   The contract statement of work for the items being procured describes the scope of the program related to those items that will be included in the contract. The SOW for a contract is developed from the PWBS and program scope statement. It describes the procurement item (or element) in sufficient detail. The definition of sufficient detail depends upon the nature of the item and needs of the buyer. The details may include performance data, quality levels, quantity, specifications, and other requirements. The SOW should be clear, complete, and concise.

List of qualified vendors   Your organization may already have a list of sellers it has used in the past. Based on the items that you need to procure, you may make a short list of sellers who qualify to provide these items. You may also prepare this list from various sources, such as the Web, library directories, and trade associations.

So, a procurement management plan and a contract statement of work are the two major output items of the Plan Program Purchases and Acquisitions process, and these two items are also a major input to the Plan Program Contracting process.

Planning Program Contracting

Plan Program Contracting is the process used to identify the type and determine the detail of documentation required to contract with the vendors who will supply the PWBS components that need to be acquired. The suppliers can be internal or external to the performing organization.

Figure 5.10 shows the input and output of the plan program contracting process.

FIGURE 5.10   The plan program contracting process: input and output

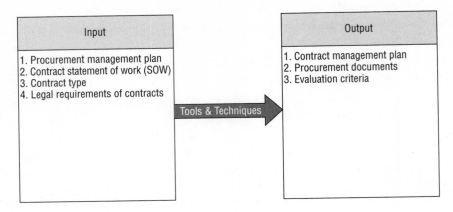

Input	Output
1. Procurement management plan 2. Contract statement of work (SOW) 3. Contract type 4. Legal requirements of contracts	1. Contract management plan 2. Procurement documents 3. Evaluation criteria

Tools & Techniques

WARNING   The range and complexity of documents for contracting at the program level tends to be greater than that at the project level. Part of the reason is that the component being acquired at the program level is usually more complex and has more dimensions to it than at the project level.

Input to Planning Program Contracting

To plan a contract for procurement, you obviously need to know what exactly is being procured and how you are going to manage the procurement. Therefore the contract statement of work and procurement management plan are the obvious inputs to planning program contracting. These and other input items are discussed here.

Procurement management plan   The procurement management plan, discussed in the previous section, describes how the procurement will be managed, and therefore is an essential input to the Plan Program Contracting process.

Contract statement of work   Before identifying the documents for procurement contracts, you need to know the details of what is being procured. Those details are in the contract statement of work, which is prepared by using the Plan Program Purchases and Acquisitions process.

Contract type   To identify the correct type of documentation for contracting, you need to be aware of different contract types so you can select the most appropriate contract type for your program procurement. The common contract types are discussed in the next section.

Legal requirements of a contract   A contract usually involves a document that is a legally binding agreement between the buyer and the seller. The legal requirements of the contract are determined by the Plan Program Contracting process.

Once you have these input items in place, you will need some tools and techniques to iron out the output.

Tools and Techniques for Planning Program Contracting

The most important tools and techniques used in planning program contracting are standard contract forms and expert judgment:

Standard contract forms   Your organization may have standard contract forms that will be used for procurement purposes. The contractual matters are usually handled by the organization's legal department. However, you must know what standard forms the organization uses and ensure that they are available. These forms may include the following:

- Standard contracts
- Non-disclosure agreements (NDAs)
- Checklists for proposal evaluation criteria
- Parts of the bid documents

Expert judgment   Expert judgment will be needed to assess the input to the Plan Program Contracting process and also the output of the process. The expertise may be needed in multiple areas including business, technical, and legal.

Expert judgment is frequently used in generating the output of this process.

Output of Planning Program Contracting

Planning for contracting obviously involves preparing the procurement documents and the contract management plan. These and other output items are discussed in the following.

Contract management plan   This is the document that specifies how a specific contract will be administered. This may include items such as delivery of certain documents and performance requirements. Depending upon the size and complexity of the procurement, a contract may be administered through its life cycle by a contract management plan, which becomes a subset of the project management plan.

Procurement documents   Procurement documents are used to seek bids or proposals from the potential sellers. The buyer structures these documents with two goals in mind:

- To facilitate an accurate and complete response from each prospective seller
- To facilitate easy evaluation of the responses

The procurement documents include the following:

- A description of the desired form of the response
- Relevant contract statement of work
- Any required contractual provisions, such as a copy of a model contract and non-disclosure provisions

In government contracting, some or all of the content and structure of a procurement document may be already defined by regulation.

Different terms are used for these documents for various purposes:

- A term such as *bid*, *tender*, or *quotation* is used when the seller-selection decision will be based on the price, when buying commercial or standard items.
- A term such as *proposal* is used when multiple factors are considered, such as cost, technical skills, and technical approach.
- Common names for the different kinds of documents include *invitation for bid*, *request for quotation*, *tender notice*, *request for proposal*, and *contractor initial response*.

The procurement documents should be rigorous enough to ensure consistent responses from different sellers that could be fairly compared with one another, and flexible enough to allow the sellers to offer suggestions on better ways to satisfy the requirements. How are the requests sent to the potential sellers? It is done according to the policies of the buyer's organization; for example, publication of the request in the public media: newspapers, magazines, and the Internet.

Exam Spotlight

Remember that bids and quotations are typically used to ask for prices, whereas proposals are used to ask for solutions. Invitations for bid, requests for quotation, and requests for proposal travel from buyer to seller, whereas bids, quotations, and proposals travel from seller to buyer.

Evaluation criteria   The buyer develops the evaluation criteria to rate the responses from the sellers. The evaluation criteria could be as simple as price for off-the-shelf standard items or a combination of factors for a more complex proposal. The following is a list of some possible factors in the evaluation criteria:

Cost   To evaluate the overall cost, you should consider all the cost-related factors, such as purchase price, delivery cost, and operating cost.

Business size and type   Does the business size or type meet a condition set forward in the contract, such as small business or disadvantaged small business?

Financial capacity   Does the seller have or is the seller in a position to obtain the necessary financial resources required to do the job?

Production capacity and interest   Does the seller have the capacity and the interest to meet potential future requirements?

References   Can the seller provide reliable references (such as from previous customers) verifying the seller's work experience and history of compliance with contractual requirements?

Management approach   If the procurement itself involves a project, does the seller have the capability of executing management processes and procedures to run a successful project?

Intellectual property rights   Will the seller own the intellectual property rights for the work processes or services that will be used to produce the deliverables?

Proprietary rights   Will the seller have the proprietary rights for the work processes or services that will be used to produce the deliverables?

Technical approach   Will the technical methodologies, techniques, solutions, or services proposed by the seller meet the procurement requirements, or will they provide more than the expected results?

Technical capability   Does the seller have or is the seller capable of acquiring the technical skills and knowledge required to produce the deliverables?

So, the Plan Program Contracting process lays the foundation and spells out the guidelines for an effective program-level contract administration. To perform this process effectively, you need to understand the contract types.

Understanding Contract Types

A contract is a mutually binding agreement between a buyer and a seller that obligates the seller to provide the specified product, service, or result and obligates the buyer to make the payment for it. Contracts generally fall into the three categories discussed here.

Fixed-price (lump-sum) contracts   A *fixed-price contract*, also called a *lump-sum contract* or a *firm fixed-price contract*, is an agreement that specifies the fixed total price for the product, service, or result to be procured. An example of a fixed-price contract is a purchase order for the specified item to be delivered by a specified date for a specified price. This category of contracts is generally used for products and services that are well-defined and have good historical information. A fixed price for a poorly defined product or a service with very little historical record is a source of high risk for both the seller and the buyer.

Cost-reimbursable contracts   A contract in this category includes two kinds of costs:

Actual cost   This is the payment (reimbursement) to the seller for the actual cost of the item, which includes the direct cost and the indirect cost (overhead). The actual cost, such as the salary of the project staff working on the item, is incurred directly from the work on the item, whereas indirect cost, such as cost of utilities and equipment for the office of the staff member, is the cost of doing business. Indirect cost is generally calculated as a percentage of the actual cost. The actual cost is also called the *project cost*. The *project* here refers to the project of the seller to produce the items for the buyer.

Fee   This typically represents the seller's profit.

As discussed in the following sections, there are three types of cost-reimbursable contracts:

Cost plus fee (CPF) or cost plus percentage of cost (CPPC)   The payment to the seller includes the actual cost and the fee, which is a percentage of the actual cost. Note that the fee is not fixed: it varies with the actual cost.

Cost plus fixed fee (CPFF)   The payment to the seller includes the actual cost and a fixed fee, which may be calculated as a percentage of the estimated project cost. Note that the fee is fixed and does not vary with the actual project cost.

Cost plus incentive fee (CPIF)   The payment to the seller includes the actual cost and a predetermined incentive bonus based on achieving certain objectives.

> Both fixed-price contracts and cost-reimbursable contracts can include incentives; for example, a bonus from the buyer to the seller if the seller meets certain target schedule dates or exceeds some other predetermined expectations.

Because cost overrun can occur in any type of cost-reimbursable contract, and the cost overrun will be paid by the buyer; this category of contracts poses risk to the buyer.

Time-and-material (T&M) contracts   This category of contracts is a hybrid that contains some aspects from both the fixed-price category and the cost-reimbursable category. The contracts in this category resemble cost-reimbursable contracts because the total cost and the exact quantity of the items is not fixed at the time of the agreement, and they resemble fixed-price contracts because the unit rates can be fixed in the contract. These types of contracts are useful when you do not know the quantity of the procured items. For example, you do not know how much time a contract programmer will take to develop a software program, so you determine the hourly rate in the contract but not the total cost for writing the program. In this category of contracts the risk is high for the buyer because the buyer agreed to pay for all the time the seller takes to produce the deliverable.

The Three Big Takeaways

The three most important takeaways from this chapter are the following:

- The Schedule Development process generates the program schedule and the schedule management plan.

- The Human Resource Planning process generates roles and responsibilities, assignments, and a staffing management plan, whereas the Cost Estimating and Budgeting process is used to generate a program budget and a cost management plan.

- The Plan Program Purchases and Acquisitions process generates a contract SOW and a procurement management plan, which become inputs to the Plan Program Contracting process.

Summary

Once you have ironed out the program breakdown structure (PWBS), you can plan the completion dates for the PWBS components by using the Schedule Development process. Furthermore, you can estimate the cost of the PWBS components and aggregate the cost to establish the budget. This is accomplished by using the Cost Estimating and Budgeting process, which generates the program budget and also the cost management plan. Human resources will be needed to complete the PWBS components. You can perform the Human Resource Planning process to make the roles and responsibilities assignments, and to prepare the staffing management plan.

You also need PWBS to make the make-or-buy decisions about the PWBS components by using the Plan Program Purchases and Acquisitions process. This process also generates the procurement management plan and contract statement of work, which can be used to perform the Plan Program Contracting process, which in turn generates the procurement documents and contract management plan.

By now, you have realized how important the program planning is. One advantage of planning is that it identifies the uncertainties in the program. It is important because uncertainties give rise to risks which, if gone unidentified and unmanaged, can potentially kill the program. Risk management, along with quality management, is discussed in the next chapter.

Exam's-Eye View

Comprehend

- The create PWBS process generates PWBS, which becomes an input item to the Resource Planning process, which in turn generates the resource management plan.

- The two major output items of the Schedule Development process are the schedule and the schedule management plan, whereas the two output items of the Cost Estimating and Budgeting process are the program budget and the cost management plan.

- The procurement management plan and contract statementare generated by the plan program purchases and acquisition process and become input to the program contracting process.

- Neither ADM nor PDM allow loops or conditional branches in showing the dependencies among program (or project) activities.

Look Out

- The pre-defined milestones become an input to the Schedule Development process.

- Core program team assignments that are already in place before the Human Resource Planning process is performed are input to this process.

- Each activity (or a program component) on a critical path has zero float time, and therefore poses a schedule risk. Therefore, you must monitor the activities (or components) on all critical paths very closely during the execution.

- Legal requirements of contracts are input to the Plan Program Contracting process.

Memorize

- The PWBS is an input item to these processes: Resource Planning, Schedule Development, Cost Estimating and Budgeting, and Plan Program Purchases and Acquisitions.

- The resource management plan is an input to theses processes: Cost Estimating and Budgeting, Human Resource Planning, and Plan Program Purchases and Acquisitions.

- In a PDM, finish-to-start is the most commonly used dependency relationship, whereas the ADM uses only the finish-to-start dependency.

Exam Essentials

Program schedule development   The process of program schedule development contains these steps: identifying components (or activities), determining the dependencies among the components used to sequence them, estimating the component durations for given resources, and scheduling the components. An important input to the Schedule Development process is the project schedule information that is created at the project level and rolled up to the program level. The key tool used in component sequencing is the schedule network diagramming methods: the precedence diagramming method (PDM), the arrow diagramming method (ADM), and the conditional diagramming method (CDM).

Schedule-compression techniques   The crashing compression technique typically uses more resources to compress the schedule, whereas the fast-tracking compression technique compresses the schedule by performing activities (or phases) in parallel when they will normally be performed in sequence.

Program cost estimating and budgeting   The program cost estimates include the project activities, program-related non-project activities, and program-level activities (or components). These costs are aggregated and a timeline is assigned; this time-phased budget is called the *cost baseline*. The key tools and techniques for cost estimating are analogous estimation, parametric estimation, and bottom-up estimation, whereas the key tools and techniques for budgeting are cost aggregation, funding-limit reconciliation, reserve analysis, and parametric estimation.

Human resource planning   The two key output items of the Human Resource Planning process are the identification of roles and responsibilities and the staffing management plan. Networking, organizational theories, and templates are key tools and techniques in human resource planning. The program manager should also be aware of the standard human resource practices.

Key Terms and Definitions

analogous estimation   A technique that is used to make an estimate of some quantities for an activity, such as activity based on the actual values of these quantities for similar activities in a previous project or program. The quantities that can be estimated using this technique include activity duration, cost, and resource requirements.

arrow diagramming method (ADM)   A technique used to draw a network diagram in which an arrow represents an activity and also points to the successor activity through a junction represented by a node (box).

budget   An approved aggregated cost with a timeline.

conditional diagramming methods (CDM)   Network diagramming methods used to display dependency relationships among program components or activities when conditions, loops, or both are involved in these relationships.

contract   A mutually binding agreement between a buyer and a seller that obligates the seller to provide the specified product, service, or result and obligates the buyer to make the payment for it.

contract management plan   A document that specifies how a given contract will be administered. This may include items such as performance requirements and delivery of certain documents.

contract statement of work (SOW)   A document that describes the procurement item in sufficient detail. This describes the scope of what will be delivered by the seller and becomes part of the contract.

cost   The value of the inputs that have been used up to perform a task or to produce an item: product, service, or result.

cost baseline   A time-phased budget against which cost performance is measured, monitored, and controlled.

Cost Estimating and Budgeting   A process used to aggregate all cost at the program level and to put a timeline on it. The process is used to generate a program budget and a cost management plan.

cost management plan   A plan used to manage and control the program cost.

crashing   A schedule-compression technique used to decrease the project duration with minimum additional cost. A number of alternatives are analyzed, including the assignment of additional resources.

critical path   The longest path (sequence of activities) in a project schedule network diagram. Because it is the longest path, it determines the duration of the project.

fast-tracking   A schedule-compression technique used to decrease the project duration by performing project phases or some schedule activities within a phase simultaneously when they would normally be performed in sequence.

float time   The positive difference between the late start date and the early start date of a schedule activity.

free float (FF)   The maximum amount of time by which a given activity can be delayed without delaying the early start of any of the immediately following scheduling activities.

Human Resource Planning   A process used to perform roles and responsibilities assignments and to generate a staffing management plan.

milestone   A significant event happening at a specific point in the life cycle of a program. Some examples of program milestones are initiation of a project in the program, closure of a project in the program, and completion of a key deliverable.

network diagram   A schematic display of logical relationships among the program (or project) activities. The time flow in these diagrams is from left to right. Also called *schedule network diagram*.

parametric estimation   A quantitative technique used to calculate some quantities by using rates, historical information, and statistical relationships between some parameters. The quantities that can be calculated by using this technique include activity duration, cost, and resource requirements.

Plan Program Contracting   A process used to identify the type and determine the detail of documentation required to contract with the vendors who will supply the PWBS components that need to be acquired (procured). This process generates procurement documents and a contract management plan.

Plan Program Purchases and Acquisitions   A process used to determine what will be procured, when it will be procured, and how it will be procured. This process generates a procurement management plan and a contract statement of work.

precedence diagramming method (PDM)   A technique used to construct a network diagram in which a node (a box) represents an activity and an arrow represents the dependency relationship.

procurement   The process of acquiring products, services, and results from outside the program team (and the constituent project teams) to complete the program.

procurement documents   The documents used to seek bids or proposals from potential sellers.

procurement management   Execution of a set of processes used to obtain products, services, or results from outside the program team to complete the program.

procurement management plan   A document that specifies how the procurement processes will be performed and managed, from preparing the procurement documents through closing contracts.

program schedule   The planned dates for completing the PWBS components and the program milestones.

resource leveling   A technique used to resolve over-allocation and conflicts in resource assignments.

Schedule Development   A process used to generate the program schedule and the schedule management plan.

schedule management plan   A plan used to manage and control the program schedule.

staffing management plan   A document that describes when and how human resource requirements for a program will be met.

total float (TF)   The maximum time by which a given activity can be delayed from its early start date without delaying the finish date of the project.

Review Questions

1. You are going to perform each of the following processes for the first time for your program. Which of these processes will you perform first?
   - **A.** Schedule Development
   - **B.** Resource Planning
   - **C.** Create PWBS
   - **D.** Cost Estimating and Budgeting

2. The program schedule management plan is generated by:
   - **A.** The planning effort that is part of developing the program management plan
   - **B.** Using the Schedule Development process
   - **C.** Using the schedule planning process
   - **D.** The project managers; it's integrated by the program manager

3. All of the following are inputs to the Cost Estimating and Budgeting process except:
   - **A.** PWBS
   - **B.** Funding availability
   - **C.** Program schedule
   - **D.** Resource management plan

4. An organization chart is an:
   - **A.** Input to the Human Resource Planning process
   - **B.** Output of the Human Resource Planning process
   - **C.** Input to the Plan Program Purchases and Acquisitions process
   - **D.** Output of the Schedule Development process

5. All of the following items are the output of the Plan Purchases and Acquisitions process except:
   - **A.** Make-or-buy decisions
   - **B.** Procurement management plan
   - **C.** Contract statement of work
   - **D.** Stakeholder analysis chart

6. All of the following items are inputs to the Plan Program Contracting process except:
   - **A.** Procurement documents
   - **B.** Procurement management plan
   - **C.** Contract statement of work
   - **D.** Contract type

7. Which of the following processes does not have a PWBS as an input?

   A. Plan Program Purchases and Acquisitions

   B. Schedule Development

   C. Cost Estimating and Budgeting

   D. Develop Program Management Plan

8. Which of the following is not an element of Schedule Development?

   A. Determine the completion dates for the program components.

   B. Forecast the program finish date.

   C. Create a PWBS.

   D. Determine the finish dates for the milestones within the program.

9. The Plan Program Purchases and Acquisitions process is used to accomplish all of the following except:

   A. Determine what to procure, when to procure it, and how to procure it

   B. Validate product requirements

   C. Develop procurement strategies

   D. Develop a contract management plan

10. Which of the following is not true about the Human Resource Planning process?

   A. It identifies the roles and the responsibilities of the roles.

   B. It assigns individuals to the roles.

   C. The individuals assigned to the roles must be from inside the performing organization.

   D. It generates the program organizational chart.

11. You are in the process of defining the components of your program and the dependencies among them. You have figured out that some components will be needed only if some conditions are true. Which network diagramming method will you use to display these components?

   A. Arrow diagramming method (ADM)

   B. Precedence diagramming method (PDM)

   C. Conditional diagramming method (CDM)

   D. Logical diagramming method (LDM)

12. You are in the process of developing the program schedule. Which of the following tools and techniques will you generally not use?

   A. Crashing and fast-tracking

   B. Resource leveling and the earned value technique

   C. Coding structure and mathematical analysis

   D. Program management software

13. You have determined the dependencies among the schedule activities. All the dependencies are of the type finish-to-finish. Which network diagramming method will you use to display these dependencies?

A. Arrow diagramming method (ADM)

B. Precedence diagramming method (PDM)

C. ADM or PDM

D. Finish-to-finish diagramming method (FFDM)

14. You overheard Rita, a program manager, saying she was using the coding structure technique in performing a process. Which process Rita was most likely referring to?

A. Program Schedule Development

B. Human Resource Planning

C. Program Cost Estimating and Budgeting

D. Decomposition

15. You are making a list of tools and techniques that you could use to perform the Human Resource Planning process. Which of the following are the standard tools and techniques you can use in Human Resource Planning?

A. Human resource practices, networking, and coding structure

B. Organizational theories, templates, and organizational charts

C. Human resource practices, networking, and organizational theories

D. Human resource practices, networking, and program interfaces

Answers to Review Questions

1. C.

   C is the correct answer because the Schedule Development, Resource Planning, and Cost Estimating and Budgeting processes use the PWBS as an input item and the PWBS is generated by the Create PWBS process.

   A, B, and D are incorrect answers because all these processes use PWBS as an input item, which is generated by the Create PWBS process.

2. B.

   B is the correct answer because the Schedule Development process generates the schedule and the schedule management plan.

   A, C, and D are incorrect answers because these are false statements about the schedule management plan.

3. C.

   C is the correct answer because you don't need the program schedule as an input to the Cost Estimating and Budgeting process.

   A, B, and D are incorrect answers because all these items are input to the Cost Estimating and Budgeting process.

4. B.

   B is the correct answer because an organization chart is an output of the Human Resource Planning process.

   A, C, and D are incorrect answers because all these are false statements about the organization chart.

5. D.

   D is the correct answer because the stakeholder analysis chart is an input to the Plan Purchases and Acquisitions process.

   A, B, and C are incorrect answers because these are major output items of the Plan Purchases and Acquisitions process.

6. A.

   A is the correct answer because procurement documents are an output of the Plan Program Contracting process.

   B, C, and D are incorrect answers because all these items are input to the Plan Program Contracting process.

7. D.

D is the correct answer because a PWBS may not even exist when you are performing the Develop Program Management Plan process for the first time.

A, B, and C are incorrect answers because all these processes take a PWBS as an input.

8. C.

C is the correct answer because PWBS is used to develop the schedule; it should be there before the Schedule Development starts.

A, B, and D are incorrect answers because all these are essential elements of program schedule development.

9. D.

D is the correct answer because a contract management plan is developed by using the Plan Program Contracting process.

A, B, and C are incorrect answers because all these are parts of the Plan Program Purchases and Acquisitions process.

10. C.

C is the correct answer because the individuals assigned to the roles may be from inside or outside of the performing organization.

A, B, and D are incorrect answers because all these are true statements about the Human Resource Planning process.

11. C.

C is the correct answer because conditional diagramming methods are designed to handle conditional existence and dependencies of activities.

A and B are incorrect because the ADM and the PDM cannot handle conditions and loops.

D is incorrect because there is no network diagramming method called the logical diagramming method.

12. B.

B is the correct answer because earned value technique is not a tool used in schedule development.

A is incorrect because crashing and fast tracking are schedule-compression techniques.

C is incorrect because coding structure can be used for the scheduled components for tracking and accounting purposes.

D is incorrect because the scheduling tools provided by the program management software can be used in schedule development.

13. B.

B is the correct answer because the PDM can be used to display any of the four types of dependencies: start-to-start, finish-to-finish, start-to-finish, and finish-to-start.

A and C are incorrect because the ADM can be used only to display finish-to-start dependencies.

D is incorrect because there is no standard network diagramming method called FFDM.

14. A.

A is the correct answer because coding structure, used for program components for accounting and tracking purposes, is a technique used in the Schedule Development process.

B and C are incorrect because these processes do not use coding structure.

D is incorrect because decomposition is a technique and not a process.

15. C.

C is the correct answer because the key tools and techniques used in Human Resource Planning are networking, organizational theories, templates, and human resource practices.

A is incorrect because coding structure is generally used in Schedule Development and not in Human Resource Planning.

B is incorrect because organizational charts are an output of Human Resource Planning.

D is incorrect because program interfaces are an input to Human Resource Planning.

Chapter

6

Planning for Quality, Risk, and Communication

THE PGMP EXAM CONTENT FROM THE PLANNING THE PROGRAM PERFORMANCE DOMAIN COVERED IN THIS CHAPTER INCLUDES THE OBJECTIVES LISTED IN THE FOLLOWING:

✓ **3.3 Establish the program management plan and baseline by integrating the plans for the constituent projects and creating the plans for the supporting program functions including management of scope, schedule, finance, benefits, quality, resource, procurement, risk response, change and communications in order to effectively forecast, monitor, and identify variances during program execution.**

✓ **3.5 Define project management information system (PMIS) by selecting tools and processes to share knowledge, intellectual property and documentation across constituent projects in order to maximize synergies and savings.**

Once you know the program scope—that is, you have the program scope statement—it's time to start planning for the program quality, which is a measure of the degree to which the completed program objectives and deliverables meet the program requirements. Once you have ironed out the program work breakdown structure (PWBS) from the program scope statement and developed the program schedule from the PWBS, it's time to start planning for risk management because risks can impact the program objectives. Risk tolerance and threshold level are important in optimizing risk management, and they—along with program requirements—largely come from the program stakeholders. So, communication with the program stakeholders is the key to successful quality and risk management. You need to plan for all three kinds of management: quality, risk, and communication.

So, the core question in this chapter is: How do we plan quality, risk management, and communication management? In search of an answer, we will explore three avenues: planning for quality, planning for risk management, and planning for communication management.

The Big Picture of Planning for Quality, Risk, and Communication

Quality, risk, and communication are defined in the following:

Quality   Program quality is the degree to which a set of characteristics of a program deliverables and program objectives fulfill the requirements.

Risk   Risk is an uncertain event or condition that, if it occurs, has a positive or negative effect on meeting the objectives of a program or its constituent projects.

Communication   Communication is an exchange of information between persons and groups by using an effectively common system of signs, symbols, and behavior. I've used the term *effectively common* to take into account the fact that even if two communicating entities are using two different systems, the "translators" between the communicating entities produce the results as if the two entities are using a common system.

These topics are included in the exam objectives covered in this chapter.

The Exam Roadmap

The following table presents each PgMP exam objective covered in this chapter, along with its explanation:

Exam Objective	What It Really Means
3.3 Establish the program management plan and baseline by integrating the plans for the constituent projects and creating the plans for the supporting program functions including management of scope, schedule, finance, benefits, quality, resource, procurement, risk response, change and communications in order to effectively forecast, monitor, and identify variances during program execution.	This exam objective has partly been covered in Chapter 4 ("Planning the Program") and Chapter 5 ("Planning the Program Schedule and Resources"). This chapter covers the quality, risk, and communication elements of this objective. You must understand the significance of quality, risk, and communication management in the context of a program. Also understand the following processes: • Quality Planning • Risk Management Planning and Analysis • Communication Planning
3.5 Define project management information system (PMIS) by selecting tools and processes to share knowledge, intellectual property, and documents across constituent projects in order to maximize synergies and savings.	You must know what a project information system (PMIS) is and how it can be used in a program. You must also know what services it offers and what factors you should consider in designing it.

The topics from these exam objectives covered in this chapter fall into three knowledge management areas: quality management, risk management, and communication management.

Planning for Quality, Risk, and Communication

It will not take much thinking to realize that these three concepts are highly correlated. While *quality* refers to the degree to which a set of characteristics of deliverables and objectives fulfill the requirements, *risk* refers to an uncertain event or condition that, if it occurs, has a positive or negative effect on meeting the objectives. Communication is necessary to effectively manage quality and risk. You need to plan for quality management, risk management, and communication management. The processes used for this planning and their main outputs are shown in Table 6.1.

TABLE 6.1   The Processes Used for Planning Communication, Quality, and Risk Management

Knowledge Area	Program Planning Process	Major Output
Quality management	Quality Planning	Quality management plan
Risk management	Risk Management Planning and Analysis	List of identified risks and risk response plan
Communication management	Communication Planning	Communication management plan

Before we dive into these planning processes, let's take a bird's-eye view of quality, risk, and communication.

Understanding Quality, Risk, and Communication

Now that you've been introduced to the concepts of quality management, risk management, and communication management, it's time to look at the big picture of each of these concepts. Quality management, risk management, and communication management are three of nine knowledge areas used in program and project management.

Understanding Quality Management

When you plan to produce a deliverable, the deliverable has some requirements that it is expected to meet when it's complete. After the deliverable has actually been produced, it has some characteristics—for example, features. The question is to what degree the characteristics fulfill the requirements. Also, recall that a program is started to meet some objectives that align with the strategic objectives of the organization. The question is to what degree do the objectives met by the finished program satisfy the required objectives planned for the program? *Program quality* refers to the degree to which a set of characteristics of program deliverables and program objectives fulfill the requirements. In other words, it is the sum of program characteristics and the deliverable characteristics that help fulfill the requirements. For example, "a program milestone was completed in time" is a program characteristic (or objective), whereas "a program product had all the features it was required to have" is a deliverable characteristic.

 WARNING   The performing organization may have its own quality policy and procedures in addition to the three standard quality management processes discussed in this book.

The broader goal of quality management is to ensure that a given program will satisfy the needs and requirements for which it was undertaken. The program has two components: how it performs (for example, in the areas of schedule and cost) and what it delivers. Accordingly, quality management has two components: program quality management (quality of its performance) and the quality management of the deliverables. The deliverables' quality largely comes from the quality of the products at the constituent project level because it is the products of the constituent projects that provide capabilities that are integrated at the program level to deliver benefits. While product quality management techniques depend upon the specific product that the program (through its constituent projects) is going to produce, the program quality management applies to all programs, independent of the nature of their products.

Quality management offers three processes: Quality Planning, Perform Quality Assurance, and Perform Quality Control. The performing organization may have its own quality policy and procedures in addition to these three quality management processes. These three processes are shown in Figure 6.1 and explained in the following:

Quality Planning A process used to identify which quality standards are relevant to the program at hand and to determine how to meet them.

Perform Quality Assurance A process used for applying the planned systematic quality activities to ensure that the program employs all the planned processes needed to meet all the program requirements.

Perform Quality Control A process to monitor a specific set of program deliverables and results to ensure they meet the agreed-upon quality standards.

The Perform Quality Assurance and Perform Quality Control processes are used during the program execution and program monitoring and controlling and are therefore discussed in Chapter 7 ("Executing the Program") and Chapter 8 ("Monitoring and Controlling the Program"), respectively. The Quality Planning process is used during program planning and therefore is discussed in this chapter.

FIGURE 6.1 The interaction among Quality Management and some other processes

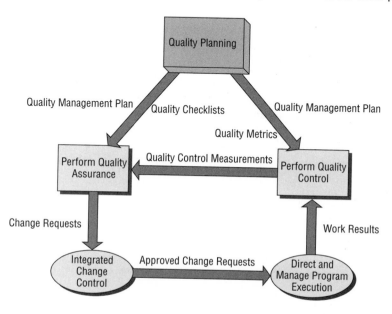

So quality management is about optimizing the degree to which a set of characteristics of deliverables and objectives fulfill the requirements. However, an uncertain event or condition can have a positive or negative effect on meeting the objectives. Such events are called risks and need to be managed.

Understanding Risk Management

To most of us, risk means danger—something that, if it happens, will result in negative undesired consequences. However, as stated earlier in this chapter, in the discipline of program (and project) management, risk arises from uncertainty and it can have positive or negative effect on the program (or project) objectives related to elements such as schedule (time), cost, scope, or quality, or to the ultimate program objective: program benefits. For example, one of the obvious schedule objectives for a program is to complete the program (or its milestones) by the scheduled deadlines. A risk related to the schedule can delay the completion of the program or can make it possible to finish it earlier. Another example is an expected benefit from the program—say, revenue. A positive risk on revenue means the program may yield more revenue than expected, and a negative risk means it may yield less revenue than expected. So, the two characteristics of a risk as used in program (and project) management are the following:

- It stems from the elements of uncertainty.
- It may have a negative or positive effect on meeting the program objectives and realizing its benefits.

The Risk Management processes, along with their context, are shown in Figure 6.2 and described in the following.

Risk Management Planning and Analysis   Used to determine the *how* of the risk management: how to plan and execute the risk management activities for the given program. It includes identifying risks, analyzing risks, and planning responses for the risks.

Risk Monitoring and Control   Used for tracking identified program risks, identifying new risks to the program, executing risk response plans, and evaluating the effectiveness of executing response plans throughout the life cycle of the program.

The Risk Monitoring and Control process is used during program control and is therefore discussed in Chapter 8. The Risk Management Planning and Analysis process is used during program planning and therefore is discussed in this chapter.

Risk management is performed both at program level and at the project level. Program management should support the risk management activities being performed at the project level. The risk management activities at the program level include the following:

- Identify and analyze interproject risks and determine their root causes.
- Review the risk response plans from the constituent projects. Look for the responses to a project risk that may affect another project.
- Propose responses for the risks that have been escalated by the project managers of the constituent projects.

Communication is necessary to effectively manage quality and risk.

FIGURE 6.2   The interaction among Risk Management and some other processes

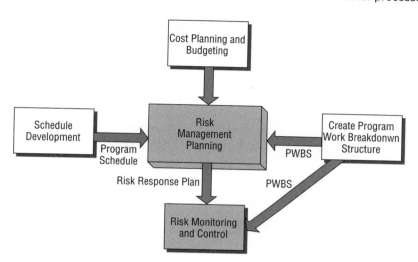

Understanding Communication Management

The importance of communication in program management cannot be overemphasized. Even a well-scheduled and well-funded program in the hands of a hard-working team of experts can fail due to the lack of proper communication. As a program manager, you may be dealing with a wide functional variety of individuals ranging from executives to marketing personnel to sales folks to technologists. You should be able to wear different communication hats depending upon who you are communicating with. For example, you will not be talking in technical jargon to executives or marketing folks, and you will not speak the marketing lingo to the software developers. You will be speaking to different stakeholders in their own languages while filling the language gap between different functional groups and eliminating misunderstandings due to miscommunication. The key point is that you put on the appropriate communication hat depending on which individual you are communicating with. Be able to switch the communication hats quickly and avoid the technical jargon and acronyms that are not understood by the person or the group you are communicating with. The goal is the clarity of the language to convey the message accurately. When we are talking about what to communicate, how to communicate, and to whom to communicate, we are talking about communication management.

Communication Management is a knowledge area that offers four processes. These processes are shown in Figure 6.3 and explained in the following:

Communication Planning   This is the process of determining the communication needs of the program stakeholders and planning to satisfy those needs. This includes determining what information needs to be communicated and when, who will communicate it and to whom, and how it will be communicated. This process is covered in this chapter.

Information Distribution   This is the process of providing needed and accurate information to the program stakeholders in a timely fashion. This process is performed as part of program execution and therefore is covered in Chapter 7.

Communication Control   This is the process of managing communication to ensure that the information needs of the program stakeholders are satisfied and resolve the issues that are of interest to the stakeholders. This process is performed as part of program monitoring and control and therefore is covered in Chapter 8.

Performance Reporting   This is the process of consolidating the program performance data collected from project and non-project activities and providing the information based on this data to the program stakeholders. This process is performed as part of program monitoring and control and therefore is covered in Chapter 8.

Now that you have an overall view of quality, risk, and communication, let's explore how you plan for managing these three important aspects of a program.

FIGURE 6.3   The interaction among Communication Management processes

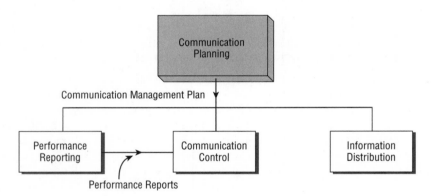

Planning the Program Quality

Before you can perform quality assurance or quality control, you need a quality management plan, which is developed by using the Quality Planning process. Planning the program quality involves the following two major elements:

- Identify the standards that are relevant to the program.
- Specify how to meet these standards.

Because these quality standards will have their impact on planning critical activities of the program, quality must be planned early in the program. Figure 6.4 shows the input and output elements of the Quality Planning process.

FIGURE 6.4   The Quality Planning process: input and output

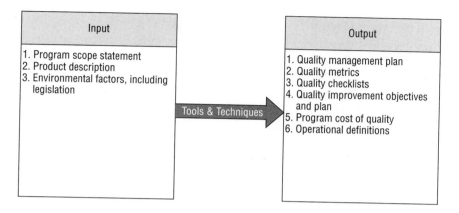

Input to Quality Planning

Quality planning can start right after the scope definition process, which generates the program scope statement, an input to Quality Planning. This and other input items are discussed in the following:

Program scope statement   The program scope statement is the major input into Quality Planning. Before you can plan quality for a program, you need to define quality for that specific program. Therefore, the following components of the program scope statement are especially relevant to Quality Planning:

- Program deliverables
- Program objectives
- Program requirements

Product description   As you already know by now, the major purpose of a program is to deliver a set of benefits. This is accomplished by creating some products (by *products* I mean products, services, or results), usually at the project level. As described previously, quality has two components: program quality and product quality. To plan product quality, you must understand the product description, especially its following two components:

- The product scope description, which may contain the details of technical issues and other quality-related concerns.
- The product acceptance criteria, which impact the quality cost.

Most of the product-related quality will be implemented at the project level, but it should be supported and monitored from the program level.

Environmental factors, including legislation   Guidelines, legislation, regulations from a government agency, rules, and standards relevant to the program at hand are examples of enterprise environmental factors that must be considered during quality planning.

In a nutshell, the program scope statement, product description, and environmental factors are the main inputs to the Quality Planning process. These inputs are necessary to plan for the quality. While planning for quality, you must consider the cost of quality, which is one of several tools and techniques you apply on the input to the Quality Planning process to generate the output.

Tools and Techniques for Quality Planning

The tools and techniques used for quality planning include benchmarking, cost-benefit analysis, experiment design, flowcharting, and program cost of quality.

Benchmarking   Benchmarking involves comparing practices, products, or services of a program (or one of its components) with those of some reference programs (or components) for the purpose of learning, improving, and creating the basis for measuring quality and performance. These references might be the previous programs or program components performed inside or outside of the performing organization. Improvement and performance are, of course, quality-related factors. For example, you might have a similar program performed in the past that accepted no more than two defects in each of its product features. You might use that as a quality criterion—a *benchmark*—for your program components.

Cost-benefit analysis   This analysis is performed to determine the cost of quality and to optimize the quality benefits and cost. The *cost of quality* is the total cost incurred in the following elements:

- Implementing conformance to the requirements included in the plan
- Reworking due to the defects resulting from failure to meet the requirement
- Updating the product or service in the future to meet the requirements in case those requirements are not included in the quality plan now

During quality planning you must consider the tradeoff between the cost and the benefit of quality and strike the appropriate balance for a given program or program component. Implementing quality has its costs, including quality management and fulfilling quality requirements. The benefits of meeting quality requirements include less rework, resulting in overall higher productivity; lower costs of maintaining the product or service; and higher customer satisfaction.

Experiment design   This is a statistical method that can be used to identify the factors that might influence a set of specific variables for a product or a process under development or in production. You can change all of the factors simultaneously to see the effect of the change. This is convenient because you don't need to decouple the factors from each other—that is, change them one at a time. By using the results from these experiments, you can optimize the products and processes.

Flowcharting   A flowchart is a diagram that depicts inputs, actions, and outputs of one or more processes in a system. Flowcharts, used in many disciplines, show the activities, decision points, and order of processing. They help to understand how a problem occurs. You, the program manager with your team, can use flowcharts to anticipate what quality problems might be, where they might occur, and how you might deal with them.

Program cost of quality   The program cost of quality is the total cost incurred in implementing the required quality for the program and the cost incurred in the rework that results from not implementing the quality. To be specific, the cost of quality includes the following:

Failure cost   These are the costs of poor quality; for example, the cost incurred in rework such as fixing defects, taking the product off the shelf, and launching it again after fixing the problems. These costs result from not properly or fully implementing the required quality. This is also called *nonconformance cost* or *rework cost*. The failure cost can be internal to the performing organization or external to it; e.g., the product can fail before shipment or it can fail after being purchased by a customer. If the product fails after a customer purchases it, the organization pays in the areas of customer satisfaction and customer (or public) relations.

Appraisal cost   This is the cost incurred in appraising the program outcome, such as product or service, to verify the conformance to quality requirements. This is part of the conformance quality cost because you are incurring it while verifying the conformance.

Implementation cost   This is the cost incurred in implementing the quality requirements, part of the conformance cost. If you try to save on the conformance cost, you usually end up paying more in terms of nonconformance cost.

Cost-benefit analysis is an important technique used to prepare the quality plans, a major output of the Quality Planning process.

Output of Quality Planning

The quality management plan is an obvious output of the Quality Planning process. This and other output items are discussed in the following.

Quality plans   The Quality Planning process generates two plans:

- An overall quality management plan
- A quality improvement plan

The quality management plan describes how the quality policy for this program will be implemented by the program management team. It also addresses quality assurance and quality control, explained in the previous section. This plan becomes a component of the overall program management plan.

Whether the quality management plan is informal and high-level or formal and detailed depends upon the program's size, complexity, and needs. It also depends upon how much detail will be covered at the project level.

The quality improvement plan, which contains the quality improvement objectives, describes how to improve some quality aspects of the program—for example, some of the processes to be used in the program. The purpose of the process improvement is to prevent activities in the processes that are not needed for this particular program. This is accomplished by describing the purpose, start, and end of a given process, the input to the process, and the output of the process.

Operational definitions   An operational definition is a description of an entity or a property of an entity in terms of measurable specifics. Such variables or measurables should be verifiable; that is, the people other than the definer should be able to measure and confirm them independently. Operational definitions are necessary to establish a set of metrics for the program quality.

Quality metrics   This is an operational criterion that defines in specific terms what something (such as a characteristic or a feature) is and how the quality control process measures it. For example, it will not be specific enough to say the defects in the product will be minimized. Rather, specifying something like "no feature will have more than two defects" is a measurable criterion and hence a metric. The metrics that you set during quality planning will be used in quality assurance.

Quality checklists   A checklist is a structured tool used to verify that a predetermined set of required quality-related steps has been performed. The checklists may come in imperative form (the *do* lists), or in interrogative forms (the *have you done this* lists). Checklists are prepared (or identified if they already exist in the organization) in the Quality Planning process and used during the Perform Quality Control process.

Program cost of quality   As a part of quality planning, you should estimate the cost of program quality. The cost of quality is the total cost incurred in implementing conformance to the requirements and quality standards set for the program, the rework due to the defects resulting from failure to meet the requirements, and updating the product or service to meet requirements later if they are not met during the development. During quality planning, you must consider the tradeoff between the cost and benefit of quality and strike the appropriate balance for a given program. Implementing the quality has its cost, including the quality management and fulfilling quality requirements. As mentioned earlier, the benefits of meeting quality requirements include less rework, resulting in overall higher productivity, lower costs of maintaining the product or service, and higher customer satisfaction.

So, the program scope statement is a major input to the Quality Planning process and the quality management plan, quality metrics, and quality checklist are its major output items. Quality planning is about identifying the standards (based on requirements) that the program must meet and specifying how the program will meet these standards. The quality standards are related to the program deliverable and objectives meeting certain requirements. However, the risks lurking in the program can have a big impact on meeting the program objectives. So the risks need to be managed and the risk management needs to be planned.

Planning Risk Management

Risk management planning is performed by using the rather involved Risk Management Planning and Analysis process, which includes the following components:

Risk identification   This involves identifying the risks that, if they occur, will affect the program, and identifying their characteristics on a regular basis throughout the program life cycle.

Qualitative risk analysis   This involves analyzing the risks to estimate the probability of their occurrence and the impact on the delivery of program benefits if they do occur. Based on this analysis the risks can be prioritized for quantitative analysis.

Quantitative risk analysis   This involves using numerical techniques to analyze the effects of the risks on the program deliverables (such as benefits) and to determine the probabilities for the successful delivery of the benefits. Based on this analysis, you prioritize the risk responses.

Risk-response planning   This involves determining the procedures and techniques to maximize the probability of occurrence and impact of a positive risk (opportunity) and minimize the same for a negative risk (threat).

The Risk Management Planning and Analysis process is depicted in Figure 6.5.

FIGURE 6.5   The Risk Management Planning and Analysis process: input and output

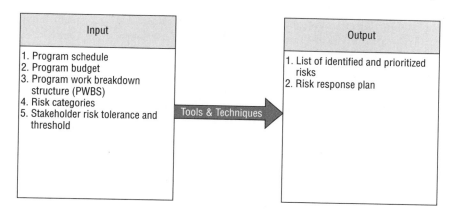

Input to Risk Management Planning and Analysis

The common risks can arise from (and affect) the program schedule and cost. Therefore the program schedule, the PWBS used to develop the schedule, and program budget are the obvious input items to the Risk Management Planning and Analysis process. These and other input items are discussed in the following.

Program schedule   The program schedule is an input to the Risk Management Planning and Analysis process for the following reasons:

- It may help to identify some risks, such as dependencies among different tasks in the schedule.

- It can indicate when a certain risk can occur.

- It can help to design schedule-related responses to certain risks. For example, there could be a risk that can be avoided by simply modifying a part of the schedule.

- You need the program schedule to analyze the effects of some risks on the program objectives.

Risks can arise from a program schedule and affect it. They can also arise from and affect the program budget.

Program budget   You need the program budget to identify cost-related risks and to analyze the effects of some risks on the program objectives. The cost for risk management will need to be estimated and included in the budget.

Program work breakdown structure (PWBS)   The PWBS is an input because you want to identify which PWBS elements will be affected by the identified risks.

Risk categories   Maybe your organization has defined specific categories of typical risks that you are required to use. Depending upon the size and complexity of the program, you may need to develop a risk breakdown structure (RBS), which is a hierarchical structure that breaks the identified risk categories into subcategories. You can also take a look at RBSs from previous programs. The risk categories typically correspond to the sources of risks. In developing this structure, you will end up identifying various areas and causes of potential risks. However, you need to examine this input categorization for each program and tailor it according to the needs of the program at hand. In addition to finding the root causes of the risks, the risk categorization also helps identify the risks.

Stakeholder risk tolerance and threshold   How much risk is acceptable to the stakeholders? The answer to this question helps determine the risk responses. For example, if a risk is below the threshold of stakeholders' tolerance, we can simply put it on the watch list. In other words, you need to know the stakeholder risk tolerance and threshold to estimate the optimal funds, time, or both needed to respond to the risks. Note that *tolerance* is the ability and *threshold* is the limit.

You need to use some tools and techniques on these input items to generate the output of Risk Management Planning and Analysis.

Tools and Techniques for Risk Management Planning and Analysis

During Risk Management Planning and Analysis you need to identify risks, analyze the identified risks, and plan the response for each risk. Accordingly you need tools and techniques corresponding to each of these three tasks.

Risk identification techniques   These techniques are used to identify the risks.

Risk analysis techniques   The risk analysis techniques are used to prioritize the risks based on the probabilities of their occurrence and the impact they will have on the program objectives should they occur.

Risk response planning techniques   These techniques are used to plan a response for each identified risk.

These techniques are discussed in detail further on in this chapter. You use these tools and techniques on the input items to generate the output of Risk Management Planning and Analysis.

Output of Risk Management Planning and Analysis

The ultimate purpose of the Risk Management Planning and Analysis process is to identify the risks and develop the risk response plan. These output items are discussed in the following:

List of identified and prioritized risks   As a part of Risk Management Planning and Analysis process, you identify risks and make a list of them. Subsequently, you analyze those risks to prioritize them, and thereby prepare the list of prioritized risks. The risks are prioritized according to the probability and impact matrix. A separate list can be created for each program (or project) objective, such as cost, quality, scope, and time. These lists help prioritize efforts in preparing and executing risk responses.

A document that contains the list of all risks with information about each risk, such as priority and a response plan, is called the *risk register*.

Risk response plan   The risk response plan consists of the appropriate risk responses planned and agreed upon by the risk management team. The responses to high and moderate risks are entered in detail, while the low-priority risks can be put on a watch list for monitoring. The risk response plan includes the following main elements:

- Roles and responsibilities in managing the risks; that is, risk owners and the responsibilities assigned to them

- Symptoms and warning signs of risk occurrences, contingency plans, and triggers for contingency risks

- Planned and agreed-upon risk response strategies and specific actions to implement each strategy

- Budget and schedule requirements to implement the planned responses, including the *contingency reserve* (the amount of funds, time, or both needed in addition to the estimates to meet the organization's and stakeholders' risk tolerances and thresholds)

- Fallback plans in case the planned responses prove to be inadequate

- A list of risks to remain, which include the passive accepted risks; the residual risks that will remain after planned responses have been performed; and a list of secondary risks that will arise as a result of implementing the responses. You must plan for the secondary risks like any other risk.

The goal of risk response planning is not to eliminate all the risks; it is to maximize the opportunities offered by the positive risks and minimize the threats posed by the negative risks.

So the Risk Management Planning and Analysis process has the program budget, program schedule, and PWBS as main input items and identified and prioritized risks and risk response plan as outputs.

Techniques and Strategies for Risk Management Planning

First you identify the program risks by using the risk identification techniques. Then you use the risk analysis techniques to prioritize the risks based on the probabilities of their occurrence and the impact they will have on the program objectives should they occur. Based on the risk priorities, you use different strategies to design the risk response plans. These techniques and strategies are discussed in the following.

Risk Identification Tools and Techniques

Risk identification is crucial to risk management: if you fail to identify a risk, you will not be able to manage it. There is a multitude of tools and techniques available to aid you in identifying risks.

Assumptions analysis   Assumptions in the program charter, program scope statement, or any other program document represent uncertainty. You analyze these assumptions to identify the risks. *Assumptions analysis* is the technique used to examine the validity of the assumptions and thereby to identify the risks resulting from the inaccuracies, inconsistencies, or incompleteness of each assumption. For example, assume that there is only one person in the organization who has a rare skill needed for the program component. An obvious assumption would be that the person will not quit the organization before completing the assignment. The inaccuracy of this assumption amounts to the risk.

Checklists analysis   The carefully prepared checklists in any process are great no-brainer time-savers. The projects in the same program will, more often than not, have similarities. As a result, you can develop a risk identification checklist based on the information gathered from similar projects in a program or from previous similar programs. Also, if you developed the risk breakdown structure (RBS) in risk planning, the lowest level of RBS can be used as a checklist.

Risk identification checklists are rarely exhaustive. Always explore what is left out of the checklist you are using. Also, improve the checklist when you close a project in the program to enhance its value for other projects or programs.

Documentation reviews   A structured review of the relevant parts of input documents, such as the program scope statement and the program management plan, will certainly help in identifying risks. Furthermore, the knowledge base related to risk management from the previous programs can also be reviewed.

Diagramming techniques   These techniques use diagrams to identify risks by exposing and exploring the risks' causes. Here are a few examples:

Cause-and-effect diagram   A cause-and-effect diagram illustrates how various factors (causes) can be linked to potential problems (effects).

Flowchart   A flowchart depicts how the elements of a system are related to each other and shows the logical flow of a process. By examining a process's flowchart, the risk management team can identify the points of potential problems in the flowchart.

Influence diagram   An influence diagram is a graphical representation of situations that shows relationships among variables and outcomes, such as causal influences and time-ordering of events. By examining these diagrams, the risk management team can recognize the potential problem areas and thereby identify risks.

Information-gathering techniques   To identify risks, you need to gather risk-related information. The following are some of the information-gathering techniques used in risk identification:

Brainstorming   The goal here is to get a comprehensive list of potential risks so that no risk goes unidentified. The program team, along with the relevant experts from different disciplines, can participate in the brainstorming session. Brainstorming is better performed under the guidance of a facilitator. You can use the categories of risks or the RBS as a framework to keep the session focused on the issue.

Delphi technique   The goal here is for the experts to reach a consensus without biases toward each other. I'm sure you will have no problem recalling a time when a decision was made because somebody (usually higher in the management hierarchy) said so. Contrary to this, the Delphi technique is used to ensure that it is the quality of the information and the argument that are important, not who is saying them. A facilitator circulates a questionnaire among the experts to solicit ideas about the risks of the given program or a program component. The experts respond anonymously. The responses are compiled and circulated among the participating experts for further evaluation without attaching a name to a response. It might take a few iterations before a general consensus is reached.

Interviewing   This is one of the common methods used for information-gathering for risk identification. You interview the appropriate stakeholders and subject-matter experts to gather information that will help identify risks for the program (or program component) at hand.

Root-cause identification   A powerful way to identify risk is to look for anything in the program that might generate a risk. In other words, if you can spot a potential cause for risks, it's simple to identify the risks resulting from that cause. Furthermore, if you know the cause of a risk, it helps to plan an effective response. You can also look for risks at the opposite side of causes—that is, impacts.

SWOT analysis   While root-cause identification techniques look into the causes of risks to identify the risks, a SWOT analysis looks at the potential impacts of risks to identify the risks. If you examine the strengths, weaknesses, opportunities, and threats (SWOT) of a given program (or a program component), you will be exposing the risks involved. Remember that a strength is an opportunity, a weakness is a threat, and opportunities and threats are posed by risks. This helps broaden the spectrum of risks considered. For example, a strength of your program might be that most of its components are well understood from previously executed similar programs. Therefore, the risks involved in those components will be easy to identify. A weakness of your program might be that one of the components involves new technology that is not well-tested. So this is a source of unknown risks. An opportunity might be that your organization will be the first one to take the product from this component to the market. An example of a threat might be that the government is considering a bill that, if it becomes a law, will have profound implications for your program.

You will generally be using more than one of these tools and techniques to identify risks. During risk identification, you might discover the causes of the risks and you might even think of some potential risk responses. However, some risks will require analysis before you plan responses for them.

Risk Analysis Techniques

The main purpose of risk analysis is twofold: determine the probability that a risk will occur, and determine its impact if it does occur. The following are some common risk analysis techniques.

Risk probability and impact assessment   Risk probability refers to the likelihood that a risk will occur, and impact refers to the effect the risk will have on a program objective if it occurs. The probability for each risk and the impact of each risk on program objectives such as cost, quality, scope, and time must be assessed. Note that probability and impacts are assessed for each identified risk.

Methods used in making the probability and impact assessment include holding meetings, interviewing, using expert judgment, and drawing from the information base from previous programs. A risk with a high probability may have a very low impact, and a risk with a low probability may have a very high impact. So, to prioritize the risks we need to look at both probability and impact.

Probability and impact matrix   Risks need to be prioritized for the quantitative analysis, response planning, or both. The prioritization can be performed by using the probability and impact matrix: a lookup table that can be used to rate a risk based on where it falls both on the probability scale and the impact scale. Table 6.2 is an example of a probability and impact matrix that shows both the probability scale and the impact scale. Here is an example of how to read this matrix: risk R_{45} has a probability of 0.75 (that is 75 out of 100 chances) for occurrence and it has an impact of 0.40 on the program (or project) objective for which this matrix is prepared. How to calculate the numerical scales for probability and matrix and what they mean depends upon the program and the organization. However, remember the relative meaning: a higher value on the probability scale means greater likelihood of the risk occurrence, and a higher value on the impact scale means a greater effect on the program objective. The higher the values for a risk, the higher its priority is. For example, risk R_{38} has higher priority than risk R_{26}.

So, each risk is rated (prioritized) according to the probability and the impact value assigned to it separately for each objective. Generally speaking, you can divide the matrix in Table 6.2 into three areas: high-priority risks represented by higher numbers such as R_{59}, medium-priority risks represented by moderate number such as R_{23}, and low-priority risks represented by lower numbers such as R_{12}. However, each organization has to design its own risk score and risk threshold to guide its risk response plan.

Note that impact can be a threat (negative effect) or an opportunity (a positive effect). You will have separate matrices for threats and opportunities. Threats in the high-priority area may require priority actions and aggressive responses. Also, you will like to capitalize on any high-priority opportunities that you can act on with relatively less effort. Low-priority risks that pose threats may not need any response but must be kept on the watch list.

Sensitivity analysis   This is a technique used to determine which risk has the greatest impact on the program. You study the impact of one uncertain element on a program objective by keeping all other uncertain elements fixed at their baseline value. You can repeat this analysis for several objectives, one at a time. You can also repeat this study for several uncertain elements (creating risks), one element at a time. This way you can see the overall program impact of each element (or risk) separate from other elements (or risks).

Expected monetary value analysis   The expected monetary value (EMV) analysis is used to calculate the expected value of an outcome when different possible scenarios exist for different values of the outcome, with some probabilities assigned to them. The goal here is to calculate the expected final result of a probabilistic situation. EMV is calculated by multiplying the value of each possible outcome by the probability of its occurrence and adding the results. When you are using opportunities and threats in the same calculation, you should express EMV for an opportunity as a positive value, and that for a threat as a negative value.

EMV can be used in a decision-making technique such as decision tree analysis.

TABLE 6.2   An example of risk probability and impact matrix for an objective

Probability					Impact				
0.00	0.05	0.10	0.25	0.35	0.40	0.50	0.60	0.75	0.90
0.15	R_{11}	R_{12}	R_{13}	R_{14}	R_{15}	R_{16}	R_{17}	R_{18}	R_{19}
0.35	R_{21}	R_{22}	R_{23}	R_{24}	R_{25}	R_{26}	R_{27}	R_{28}	R_{29}
0.55	R_{31}	R_{32}	R_{33}	R_{34}	R_{35}	R_{36}	R_{37}	R_{38}	R_{39}
0.75	R_{41}	R_{42}	R_{43}	R_{44}	R_{45}	R_{46}	R_{47}	R_{48}	R_{49}
0.95	R_{51}	R_{52}	R_{53}	R_{54}	R_{55}	R_{56}	R_{57}	R_{58}	R_{59}

R_{ij}, where i and j are integers, represent risks in the two-dimensional (probability and impact) space.

Real World Scenario

Expected Monetary Value

MySuccess is a training company and is considering offering courses in emerging technologies. The program manager, Delon Dotson, has identified two possible scenarios for revenues. In scenario A the company will earn $200,000 from these courses, and in scenario B it will earn only $100,000.

There is 70 percent probability that scenario A will be true and 30 percent probability that scenario B will be true. Delon's manager asked Delon to calculate EMV. This is how Delon calculated it:

$$EMV = (0.70 \times 200000) + (0.30 \times 100000) = 140000 + 30000 = 170,000$$

So the EMV in this case is $170,000.

There is a course in this program that Delon is not sure whether to offer. The problem is that there is 40 percent probability that the course will bring in an earning of $10,000, but there is 60 percent probability that it will result in a loss of $8,000. So Delon calculated the EMV as follows:

$$EMV = (0.40 \times 10000) - (0.60 \times 8000) = 4000 - 4800 = -800$$

Therefore the EMV for the course in question is −$800.

Delon decided not to offer this course.

Decision tree analysis   This is a technique that uses the decision tree diagram to choose from different options available; each option is represented by a branch of the tree. This technique is used when there are multiple possible outcomes with different threats or opportunities that have certain probabilities assigned to them. EMV analysis is done along each branch, which helps to decide which option to choose.

Modeling and simulation   In general, a model is a set of rules to describe how something works; it takes input and makes predictions as output. The rules may include formulas and functions based on assumptions, facts, or both. A simulation is any analytical method used to imitate a real-life system. For example, simulations in risk analysis are created by using the Monte Carlo technique (named after Monte Carlo, France, known for its casinos presenting games of chance based on random behavior). Monte Carlo simulation models take random input iteratively to generate output for certain quantities as predictions. This technique is used in several disciplines such as physics and biology in addition to program management. In risk analysis, the input is generated randomly from a probability distribution, and the output for impact on program objectives is predicted. The name Monte Carlo refers to the random behavior of the input (in that spirit, it could easily be called Las Vegas).

Real World Scenario

Decision Tree Analysis

Rajinder Kaur Sandhu is the project manager of a software development project. She needs to make a decision about one component of the software system the project is supposed to build: to update an existing version of it or to build it from scratch. The following diagram presents a decision tree that depicts these two options: update the existing product or build the new product from scratch. The initial cost for the update option is $60,000, whereas the initial cost for the build-from-scratch option is $100,000. However, the probability for failure is 50 percent for the update option as compared to 20 percent for the build-from-scratch option, and the impact for failure in both cases is a loss of $300,000. As the accompanying table shows, even though the initial cost for the update option is less than that for the build-from-scratch option, the decision will be made in favor of the build-from-scratch option. This is because when we combine the initial cost with the EMV that results from the probability of failure, the build-from-scratch option turns out to be a better deal.

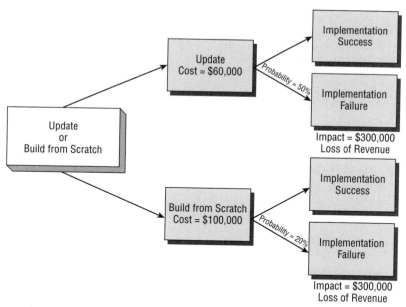

Option	Initial cost	Risk cost	Probability	EMV for risk cost	Total cost
Update	$60,000	$300,000	50%	0.50 × $300,000 = $150,000	$60,000 + $150,000 = $210,000
Build from Scratch	$100,000	$300,000	20%	0.20 × $300,000 = $60,000	$100,000 + $60,000 = $160,000

Risk management techniques and strategies discussed here can be applied at both the program level and the constituent-projects level.

Interviewing   The interviewing technique is used to collect the data for assessing the probabilities of achieving specific program objectives. We collect the data to look for results, such as "there is 80 percent probability of finishing the program within the schedule desired by the customer" or "we have 70 percent probability of finishing the program within the budget of $500,000." The goal is to determine the scale of probabilities for a given objective: for example, 30 percent probability the program will cost $60,000, 50 percent probability that it will cost $100,000, and 20 percent probability that it will cost $175,000.

The data is collected by interviewing relevant stakeholders and subject-matter experts. Most commonly you will be exploring three points: the optimistic (best case), pessimistic (worst case), and most likely scenarios for a given objective. For example, for the program cost, the optimistic estimate may be $20 million, the pessimistic $50 million, and the most likely $30 million.

Expert judgment   In quantitative risk analysis, expert judgment can be used to validate the collected risk data and the analysis used for the program at hand.

Risk Response Techniques

Risk, as you have already learned, can come in two categories: negative risks (which pose threats to meeting the program objective) and positive risks (which offer opportunities). The goal is to minimize the threats and maximize the opportunities. In program management, there are three kinds of possible responses toward risks: take an action, take no action, and take a conditional action. When you want to take an action, different response strategies for negative and positive risks need to be planned. Accordingly, there are three strategies to handle three kinds of scenarios:

- Strategies to respond to negative risks (threats) when action is required
- Strategies to respond to positive risks (opportunities) when action is required
- Strategies that can be used to respond to both negative and positive risks when no action or a conditional action is taken

There are only three common-sense ways to take an action against a potential problem: get out of harm's way, pass the problem to someone else, or confront it to minimize the damage. In program management, these three strategies are called *avoid*, *transfer*, and *mitigate*, the *ATM approach*.

Avoid   You avoid the risk by changing your program management plan in such a way so that the risk is eliminated. Depending upon the situations, this can be accomplished in various ways including the following:

Obtaining information and clarifying requirements for risks based on misunderstanding or miscommunication. This is to answer two questions: do we really have this risk, and if yes, how can we avoid it?

- Acquiring expertise for risks that exist due to the lack of expertise
- Isolating the program objectives from the risk whenever possible
- Relaxing the objective that is under threat, such as extending the program schedule

Transfer   Risk transfer means you shift the responsibility for responding to the risk (ownership of the risk), the negative impact of the risk, or both, to another party. Note that transferring the risk transfers the responsibility for risk management; it does not necessarily eliminate the risk. Risk transfer almost always involves making payment of a risk premium to the party to which the risk has been transferred. Some examples are buying an insurance policy and contracting out the tasks involving risk.

Mitigate   Mitigation in general means taking action to reduce or prevent the impact of a disaster that is expected to occur. Risk mitigation means reduction in the probability of risk occurrence, reduction in the impact of the risk if it does occur, or both. A good mitigation strategy is to take action early on to first reduce the probability of the risk happening, and then plan for reducing its impact if it does occur rather than letting it occur and then trying to reduce the impact or repair the damage. The following are some examples of mitigation:

- Adopting less-complex processes
- Conducting more tests on the product or service of the program
- Choosing a more stable supplier for the program supplies
- Designing redundancy into a system so that if one part fails the redundant part takes over and the system keeps working

Each of these three strategies has a counter strategy to deal with the opportunities.

Response Strategies for Opportunities

Just like in the case of threats, you have three strategies to deal with opportunities. Not surprisingly, each response strategy to deal with an opportunity is a counterpart of a response strategy to deal with a threat; there's a one-to-one correspondence:

- Exploit (corresponds to avoiding a threat)
- Share (corresponds to transferring a threat)
- Enhance (corresponds to mitigating a threat)

So you use the SEE (share, exploit, enhance) approach to dealing with the opportunities presented by the positive risks.

Exploit   Exploiting an opportunity means ensuring that the opportunity is realized; that is, the positive risk that presents the opportunity does occur. This is accomplished by eliminating or minimizing the uncertainty associated with the risk occurrence. An example of exploiting is to assign more talented resources to the program to reduce the completion time and therefore to be the first to market. Another example is to provide better quality than planned to beat a competitor.

Share   Sharing a positive risk that presents an opportunity means transferring the ownership of the risk to another party that is better equipped to capitalize on the opportunity. Transferring the ownership here means transferring the responsibility to manage the risk. The benefits will, of course, be shared. Some examples of sharing are as follows:

- Forming risk-sharing partnerships
- Starting a joint venture with the purpose of capitalizing on an opportunity
- Forming teams or special-purpose companies to exploit opportunities presented by positive risks

Enhance   While *exploit* refers to ensuring that the positive risk occurs, *enhance* refers to increasing the impact of the risk once it occurs. This strategy means increasing the size of the opportunity by increasing the probability, the impact, or both. You can increase the probability by maximizing the key drivers of the positive risks or strengthening the causes of the risks. Similarly, you can increase the impact by increasing the program's susceptibility to the positive risk.

You have just learned the different strategies that you need to plan for negative and positive risks if you intend to take an action. If, on the other hand, you intend to take no action or to take a conditional action, then the response planning strategies for both negative and positive risks are the same.

Response Strategies for Both Threats and Opportunities

There are two response strategies available when you need to take either a conditional action or no action.

Acceptance   Acceptance of a risk means letting it be. Generally, it is not possible to take action against all the risks. Depending upon their probabilities and impacts, some risks will simply be accepted. There are two kinds of acceptance:

- Passive acceptance that requires no action
- Active acceptance that requires a conditional action, called a *contingent response*

Contingency   Generally speaking, contingency means a future event or condition that is possible but cannot be predicted with certainty. So, your action will be contingent upon the condition; that is, it will be executed only if the condition happens. In risk management, a contingent response is a response that is executed only if certain predefined conditions (or events) happen. These events trigger the contingency response. Examples of such triggers include missing a milestone or a customer escalating the priority of a feature. The events that can trigger contingency response must be clearly defined and tracked.

The program requirements that set the quality standards for the program and the risk threshold and tolerance (which are inputs to the Risk Management Planning and Analysis process) largely come from the program stakeholders. Communication is the key to keeping all the stakeholders on the same page regarding these crucial program factors.

Planning Communication Management

Communication Planning is the process of determining the following:

- The communication and information needs of the program stakeholders
- The four Ws: what information is needed, when it is needed, who needs it, and who will deliver it
- How the information will be delivered; for example, email, phone call, or presentation

The Communication Planning process is depicted in Figure 6.6.

FIGURE 6.6   The Communication Planning process: input and output

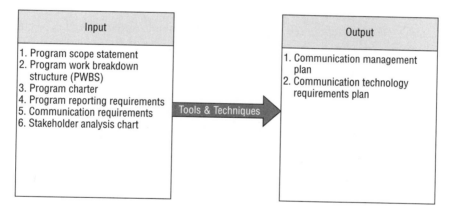

Input	Output
1. Program scope statement 2. Program work breakdown structure (PWBS) 3. Program charter 4. Program reporting requirements 5. Communication requirements 6. Stakeholder analysis chart	1. Communication management plan 2. Communication technology requirements plan

Tools & Techniques

The communication requirements are an input to the Communication Planning process.

Input to Communication Planning

Communication planning and requirements basically stem from the program scope. Therefore the obvious input to the Communication Planning process is the program scope statement and PWBS. These and other input items are discussed in the following.

Program scope statement and PWBS   One important purpose of communication is to ensure that all the stakeholders are on the same page regarding the program scope. The program scope statement, discussed in Chapter 4, is a documented reference for the scope. The PWBS is a representation of the scope in terms of deliverables. As discussed in Chapter 4, if it's not in the PWBS, it will not be delivered.

Program charter   Also introduced in Chapter 2, "The Program Management Framework," the program charter is the first document of the program and contains the program's key objectives and the expected benefits. It will be helpful to include it as an input in addition to the program scope statement and the PWBS in case you need to refer back to the beginning of the program.

Program reporting and communication requirements   In order to plan communication, you do need to gather the reporting and communication requirements for the program.

Stakeholder analysis chart   This chart, in part, will help determine the communication and reporting requirements because most of these requirements will come form the stakeholders.

In a nutshell, you must know the program scope and the reporting and communication requirements to plan communication. To gather the communication requirements, you need to perform the stakeholder analysis, which is one of several tools you can apply on the input discussed in this section to generate output.

Tools and Techniques for Communication Planning

Communication is transferring information from one point to another. It expends resources. To optimize the use of resources and the benefits of communication you need to analyze the communication requirements and determine the communication technology to be used.

Communication requirements analysis for stakeholders   Communication requirements analysis, a part of stakeholder analysis, is a technique that you can use in communication planning. Communication requirements, an input to the Communication Planning process, needs to be analyzed. This analysis will generate the communication needs of the program stakeholders. For example, a communication requirement may specify the type of information and the format in which this information should be delivered. The analysis of this requirement will estimate the value of this communication requirement; e.g., the fulfillment of this requirement will significantly contribute to the success of the program, or the lack of it will result in the failure of the program or one of its components. So, one of the purposes of communication requirements analysis is to optimize the use of resources in communication.

Complexity of communication can be appreciated by realizing that there are $n(n-1) \div 2$ communication channels among n stakeholders. For example, if there are 20 stakeholders, the possible number of communication channels are $20 \times 19 \div 2 = 190$. These channels are managed by determining who will communicate with whom and what will be communicated at which time. You need to gather the following information to determine the communication requirements:

- Departments and experts involved in the program
- External information needs, such as communicating with the media or other communications for public-relations
- Internal information needs; that is, communication within the organization

- Information about stakeholders, such as the influence level of a stakeholder
- Logistics of the program, such as how many individuals will be involved at what locations, etc.
- Organizational charts
- Reporting relationships among roles and the responsibilities assigned to the roles

Stakeholder analysis in general is covered in Chapters 2, 3, and 5.

Communication-technology determination   Depending on the communication needs and nature of the information, a communication technology may vary from a conversation in a hallway to a sophisticated information system. The following factors can contribute to determining the communication technology to be used for your program:

Availability   If you are considering a number of options, obviously the technology that's already in place is more likely to be chosen.

Program environment   The program environment can also affect the choice of communication technology. For example, the communication-technology requirements for a program team that meets face-to-face will be different from that of a virtual team.

Program length   The length of the program affects the communication-technology requirements in two ways. First, is it worth it to spend on a technology for the given length of the program? Second, will the technology under consideration change during the course of the program? If yes, will that mean extra cost for the new technology and for training the team members to use it?

Urgency of the information need   How frequently the information needs to be updated will also play a role in determining the communication technology. For example, the information that does not need to change frequently can be delivered in written reports, whereas the information that can change very frequently can be delivered through web pages.

Preparation level   Another factor that can be considered in making the communication-technology decision is the users' (program team and other stakeholders) level of preparation for using a given technology. Are the users already fluent in this technology or will they need to be trained?

You use these tools and techniques to generate the output of the Communication Planning process.

Output of Communication Planning

What would be an obvious output of the Communication Planning process? Yes, you are right; it's a communication management plan. This and other output items are discussed in the following.

Communication management plan   This is the document that describes the communication expectations, needs, and plans for the program. It specifies what information will be communicated, when and how it will be communicated, and who will communicate it to whom. It includes the following:

- Communication requirements of the program stakeholders
- Information to be communicated: content, format, and level of detail
- Who will communicate the information and who will receive it
- Methods of communication that will be used, such as email, presentation, and press release
- Frequency of communication, such as daily or weekly
- Method and procedure for escalating the issues that cannot be resolved at a lower staff level, such as the project level
- Glossary of common communication terminology
- Methods and procedures for updating and refining the communication management plan if needed as the program progresses

Communication-technology requirements plan   When executing a program in this information age, you will likely need multiple communication technologies, such as email, web calendars, and video conferencing. Therefore, it is important that you plan for the communication-technology requirements. This planning has two components: the tools that are needed and the usage of those tools. To determine which tools are needed, ask questions such as the following:

- How frequently do you need to update the information?
- Will the team hold face-to-face or virtual meetings?

For the information that does not change often, the written reports will be sufficient, whereas the information that needs to be updated frequently and on a moment's notice needs web communication tools. To plan the effective usage of the tools, ask the following questions:

- Are the tools (communication systems) already in place and ready to be used?
- Will the available communication tools change before the program ends?
- Are the team members familiar with the tools or do they need training to use them?

 The program manager should covey the communication requirements as an input to the projects in the program to facilitate the information capture from the projects into the program in an effective manner.

So, the program charter, the program scope statement, and the PWBS are the main input items to the Communication Planning process, which generates a communication management plan as a main output item.

For communication and many other program tasks, you will need the project (or program) management information system.

The Project Management Information System

The project management information system (PMIS) is an information system that consists of tools and techniques used to collect, integrate, store, and retrieve (to disseminate) the outputs of project management processes. The PMIS is also used to control changes to the documents. It's an integrated system of mostly automated tools (and possibly some manual tools) and is used throughout the project, from initiating to closing.

In a program, you put together a PMIS by selecting tools, techniques, and processes with the purpose of sharing documentation, information, and intellectual property across the constituent projects to achieve optimization for cost and benefits.

An effective PMIS is capable of serving the following purposes:

Program-wise information Your PMIS must be capable of collecting information and status across the constituent projects, integrating it, and reporting it to the program stakeholders.

Knowledge management The PMIS must support knowledge management, such as a knowledge base to store and retrieve lessons learned and other historical information.

Measurement and analysis tools Your PMI must support measurements and analysis. For example, it should support the metrics system that you are going to use for your program, and it should also support analysis such as statistical analysis by offering statistical analysis techniques.

Communication It must have communication tools to support the communication needs of the program.

Support for intellectual property As a program manager, you must be able to identify the intellectual property as the program progresses. The PMIS system must be able to support the development of intellectual property and to protect it.

You must consider the following aspects of PMIS in your planning:

Needs A PMIS must be planned and designed to the needs and requirements of the program. If there already is a PMIS, you should adapt it to these needs and requirements.

Organizational characteristics Identify the relevant characteristics of the performing organization, including the following:

> **Capabilities** Does the organization have the capabilities to support and use the PMIS being designed? For example, implementing a high-tech PMIS in a low-tech organization will create the need for training.

> **Culture** Is the PMIS being proposed compatible with the culture of the organization? For example, you will not create communication blocks or hierarchies in the PMIS that do not exist in the actual organization.

Policies and procedures The PMIS must conform to the policies and procedures of the organization.

Implementation constraints You should plan a PMIS that can actually be implemented. For example, consider the factors such as budget and time.

The Three Big Takeaways

The three most important takeaways from this chapter are the following:

- Program Quality Planning takes a program scope statement as an input and generates a quality management plan, checklists, and a quality metrics as major output items.

- There is only one risk planning process, called Risk Management Planning and Analysis, and it includes risk identification, qualitative risk analysis, quantitative risk analysis, and risk response planning.

- Program Communication Planning takes the program charter, the program scope statement, and the PWBS as main input items and generates a communication management plan as the major output item.

Summary

Program quality, risk management, and communication management are highly correlated concepts. While quality refers to the degree to which a set of characteristics of deliverables and objectives fulfill the requirements, risk refers to an uncertain event or condition that, if it occurs, has a positive or negative effect on meeting the objectives. Program requirements and risk threshold and tolerance levels largely come from the program stakeholders. Therefore communication with the stakeholder is the key to the success of the quality and risk management.

Once you have the program scope statement generated by the Scope Definition process, you can perform the Quality Planning process, which generates the quality management plan, quality checklists, and quality metrics. After generating a PWBS from the program scope statement and generating a program schedule from the PWBS, you can perform the quality Risk Management Planning and Analysis process, which generates a list of program risks and a risk response plan. You also need the PWBS as an input to perform communication planning, which generates a communication management plan as an output.

After you have performed planning for your program it's time to begin the program execution, which is covered in the next chapter.

Exam's-Eye View

Comprehend

- Quality management is about optimizing the degree to which a set of characteristics of deliverables and objectives fulfill the requirements, whereas risk management is about maximizing the impact of positive risks and minimizing the impact of negative risks on meeting the program objectives.

- Risk categorization is a part of the risk management plan, and it helps in identifying the risks and finding their root causes.

- Program scope statement is a major input to Quality Planning; the quality management plan, quality metrics, and the quality checklist are its major output items.

- The Risk Management Planning and Analysis process has the program budget, the program schedule, and the PWBS as main input items, and the identified and prioritized risks and the risk response plan as output items.

Look Out

- Quality checklists and metrics are input (and not output) to Quality Planning.

- Risk stems from elements of uncertainty and may have a negative or positive effect on meeting the program objectives.

- Risk identification, qualitative risk analysis, quantitative risk analysis, and risk response planning are part of the same program process, called Risk Management Planning and Analysis.

Memorize

- Program Risk Management consists of only two processes:

  - Risk Management Planning and Analysis

  - Risk Monitoring and Control

- You must perform the scope definition before you can perform Quality Planning, Risk Management Planning and Analysis, or Communication Planning because the program scope statement is directly or indirectly an input to these processes.

Exam Essentials

Outputs of Quality Planning, Risk Management Planning, and Communication Planning
The major outputs from Quality Planning, Risk Management Planning, and Communication Planning are quality management, the risk identification and response plan, and the communication management plan.

Input from stakeholders   The stakeholders' risk tolerance and threshold is an important factor to consider while performing Risk Management Planning and Analysis. Also in Communication Planning, the communication needs of the stakeholders must be determined through stakeholder analysis.

Risk management planning   Risk Management Planning and Analysis is a rather involved process that includes the following steps:

- Identify risks.
- Analyze risks qualitatively to prioritize them according to their estimated probability of occurrence and their impact on the program in the event of their occurrence.
- Analyze selected risks quantitatively.
- Based on the risk analysis, prepare a response for each risk should it occur.

Project Management Information System   A project management information system (PMIS) in a program, also called a *program management information system*, is an integrated system of tools and processes used to generate (e.g., through analysis), maintain, and share information across the constituent projects of the program. In designing and planning this system the program needs and the organization's capabilities and culture must be considered.

Key Terms and Definitions

benchmarking   A technique that involves comparing practices, products, or services of a program (or program component) with those of some reference programs (or program components) for the purposes of learning, improving, and creating the basis for measuring performance.

brainstorming   A creative technique generally used in a group environment to gather ideas as candidates for a solution to a problem or an issue without any immediate evaluation of these ideas. The evaluation and analysis of these ideas happen later.

communication   An exchange of information between persons or groups by using an effectively common system of signs, symbols, and behavior.

communication control   The process of managing communication to ensure that the information needs of the program stakeholders are satisfied and resolve the issues that are of interest to the stakeholders.

communication planning   The process of determining the communication needs of the program stakeholders and planning to satisfy those needs. This includes determining what information needs to be communicated and when, who will communicate it and to whom, and how it will be communicated.

decision tree analysis   A technique that uses the decision tree diagram to choose from different options available; each option is represented by a branch of the tree.

Delphi technique   An information-gathering technique used for experts to reach a consensus while sharing their ideas and preferences anonymously.

expected monetary value (EMV) analysis   A statistical technique used to calculate the expected outcome when there are multiple possible outcome values with probabilities assigned to them.

information distribution   The process of providing needed accurate information to the program stakeholders in a timely fashion.

mitigation   The process of taking actions to reduce or prevent the impact of a disaster that is expected to occur.

operational definition   A description of an entity or a property of an entity in terms of measurable specifics which can be verified.

Perform Quality Assurance   A process used for applying the planned systematic quality activities to ensure that the project employs all the planned processes needed to meet all the project requirements.

performance reporting   The process of consolidating the program performance data collected from project and non-project activities and providing the information based on this data to the program stakeholders.

program cost of quality   The total cost incurred in implementing conformance to the requirements and quality standards set for the program, the rework due to the defects resulting from the failure to meet the requirements, and updating the product or service to meet the requirements.

project management information system (PMIS)   An information system, also called program management information system, that consists of tools and techniques used to collect, integrate, store, and retrieve (to disseminate) the outputs of project management processes.

quality   The degree to which a set of characteristics of program deliverables and program objectives fulfill the requirements.

quality control   A process to monitor a specific set of program deliverables and results to ensure they meet the agreed-upon quality standards.

quality metrics   An operational criterion that defines in specific terms what something (such as a characteristic or a feature) is and how the quality-control process measures it.

Quality Planning   A process used to identify which quality standards are relevant to the project at hand and determines how to meet them.

residual risk   A risk that remains after the risk response has been performed.

risk   An uncertain event or condition that, if it occurs, has a positive or negative effect on meeting the objectives of a program or its constituent projects.

Risk Management Planning and Analysis   The process used to determine the *how* of the risk management: how to plan and execute the risk management activities for the given program. It includes identifying risks, analyzing risks, and planning responses for the risks.

Risk Monitoring and Control   The process used for tracking identified program risks, identifying new risks to the program, executing risk response plans, and evaluating the effectiveness of executing response plans throughout the life cycle of the program.

secondary risk   A risk that arises as a result of implementing a risk response.

strengths, weaknesses, opportunities, and threats (SWOT) analysis   A technique used to gather information for risk identification by examining a given project from the perspectives of its strengths, weaknesses, opportunities, and threats.

Review Questions

1. Quality is the degree to which:

   A. Customer satisfaction is achieved.

   B. The needs, wants, and expectations of the program stakeholders are met.

   C. A set of characteristics of program deliverables and program objectives fulfill the requirements.

   D. A product can be used without encountering its failure.

2. All of the following statements about risk are true except:

   A. All risks pose threats to a program.

   B. Risks stem from uncertainty.

   C. Risks have impact on meeting the program objectives.

   D. Risks must be managed both at the program level and at the project level.

3. All of the following are included in communication planning except:

   A. Determine the information needs of the program stakeholders.

   B. Determine who needs what information and when.

   C. Provide the needed information to the stakeholders in a timely fashion.

   D. Determine how information will be distributed.

4. Which of the following is not an input to the Quality Planning process?

   A. Regulations and legislation

   B. Product description

   C. Program scope statement

   D. Program cost of quality

5. Quality checklists are:

   A. Input to Quality Planning

   B. Output of Quality Planning

   C. Input to quality assurance

   D. Output of quality control

6. All of the following items are input to the Risk Management Planning and Analysis process except:

   A. Program schedule

   B. Program budget

   C. PWBS

   D. Risk response plan

7. Program Risk Management includes which of the following processes? (Choose one.)

   A. Risk Management Planning, Risk Identification, and Risk Analysis

   B. Risk Management Planning and Analysis and Risk Monitoring and Control

   C. Risk Management Planning and Analysis, Risk Response Planning, and Risk Monitoring and Control

   D. Risk Management Planning, Risk Identification, Qualitative Risk Analysis, Quantitative Risk Analysis, Risk Response Planning, and Risk Monitoring And Control

8. All of the following items are included in the input of the Communication Planning process except:

   A. Program charter

   B. Program scope statement

   C. PWBS

   D. Communication management plan

9. Which of the following processes will you perform first?

   A. Scope Definition

   B. Quality Planning

   C. Communication Planning

   D. Risk Management Planning and Analysis

10. Regulations and legislation are input to which of the following program processes?

   A. Quality Planning

   B. Communication Planning

   C. Risk Response Planning and Analysis

   D. Risk Identification

11. For many program management and project management processes, the project management information system (PMIS) acts as:

   A. Input

   B. Output

   C. Tool and technique

   D. QA

12. You overheard a senior program manager telling a junior program manager to use the experiment design technique. Which process the senior program manager was most likely referring to?

   A. Quality Planning

   B. Risk Management Planning

   C. Communication Planning

   D. Procurement Planning

13. You are in the process of planning risk management for your program. Which of the following statements about risk analyses is false?

   A. Qualitative risk analysis is usually performed before the quantitative risk analysis.

   B. An updated risk register is the output of both qualitative risk analysis and quantitative risk analysis.

   C. A risk register is an input to both qualitative risk analysis and quantitative risk analysis.

   D. Quantitative risk analysis can be performed only on the risks on which the qualitative risk analysis has already been performed.

14. Which of the following is the correct statement about the secondary risks?

   A. These are the risks that have been mitigated.

   B. These are the risks which have medium or low priority.

   C. These are the residual risks.

   D. These are the risks that result from responses to the originally identified risks.

15. Which of the following are tools and techniques for Communication Planning?

   A. Stakeholder analysis and communication technology determination

   B. Program communication requirements and stakeholder analysis

   C. Communication technology determination and communication management plan

   D. Flowcharting and sensitivity analysis

Answers to Review Questions

1. C.

C is the correct answer because quality is the degree to which a set of characteristics of program deliverables and program objectives fulfill the requirements.

A is incorrect because satisfaction does not necessarily mean the quality requirements are met and vice versa.

B is incorrect because needs, wants, and expectations of the program stakeholders include more than just quality.

D is incorrect because if a product does not fail, it does not necessarily mean that it meets all the quality requirements.

2. A.

A is the correct answer because only negative risks pose threats, whereas positive risks offer opportunities.

B, C, and D are incorrect answers because all these are true statements about risks.

3. C.

C is the correct answer because providing information is part of the Information Distribution process.

A, B, and D are incorrect answers because all these are parts of communication planning.

4. D.

D is the correct answer because program cost of quality is an output of Quality Planning.

A, B, and C are incorrect answers because all these items are valid input to Quality Planning.

5. B.

B is the correct answer because quality checklists are an output of Quality Planning.

A is incorrect because quality checklists are an output of Quality Planning.

C is incorrect because it's quality metrics and not quality checklists that are input to quality assurance.

D is incorrect because quality checklists are an input to quality control.

6. D.

D is the correct answer because a risk response plan is an output of Risk Management Planning and Analysis process.

A, B, and C are incorrect answers because these items are valid input to the Risk Management Planning and Analysis process.

7. B.

B is the correct answer because program Risk Management contains only two processes: Risk Management Planning and Analysis and Risk Monitoring and Control.

A, C, and D are incorrect answers because program Risk Management contains only two processes: Risk Management Planning and Analysis and Risk Monitoring and Control.

8. D.

D is the correct answer because the communication management plan is an output of Communication Planning.

A, B, and C are incorrect answers because these items are valid input to the Communication Planning process.

9. A.

A is the correct answer because the Scope Definition process generates the program scope statement, which is directly or indirectly an input to Quality Planning, Communication Planning, and Risk Management Planning and Analysis.

B and C are incorrect answers because these processes need a program scope statement as an input, and this document is generated by the Scope Definition process.

D is an incorrect answer because the Risk Management Planning and Analysis process uses a PWBS, which is generated by the Create PWBS process, which in turn uses the program scope statement as an input. The program scope statement is generated by the Scope Definition process.

10. A.

A is the correct answer because regulations and standards are included in the input to the Quality Planning process.

B and C are incorrect answers because these processes don't take regulations and legislation as input.

D is incorrect because there is no standard program process called Risk Identification. It's part of the Risk Management Planning and Analysis process.

11. C.

C is the correct answer because the PMIS is used as a tool and technique from initiation to closing of a program and each of its constituent projects.

A and B are incorrect because the PMIS can support input and can help to generate output, but it is not an input or an output; it's a tool.

D is incorrect because the PMIS may be used for QA-related tasks, but it itself is not QA.

12. A.

A is the correct answer because experiment design is a statistical method that can be used to determine the impact of some factors on some characteristics of a product or service related to quality.

B and C are incorrect because experiment design is not a tool used for these processes.

D is incorrect because there is no standard process called Procurement Planning.

13. D.

D is the correct answer because depending upon the experience of the team, a risk can be moved directly after the identification process to the quantitative process without performing the qualitative analysis.

A, B, and C are incorrect answers because these are true statements about risk analyses.

14. D.

D is correct because secondary risks are those risks which arise as a result of risk responses.

A is incorrect because the risk response will depend upon the analysis results of the risk.

B incorrect because depending upon the nature of the secondary risk it may have any priority.

C is incorrect because a residual risk is a risk that remains after a response has been performed.

15. A.

A is the correct answer because stakeholder analysis will determine the communication needs of the stakeholders and the communication technology determination is used to determine which technology will be used for communication.

B is incorrect because program communication requirements are an input to Communication Planning.

C is incorrect because the communication management plan is an output of Communication Planning.

D is incorrect because flowcharting and sensitivity analysis are tools and techniques for Quality Planning and Risk Management Planning and Analysis, respectively.

Executing the Program

THE PGMP EXAM CONTENT FROM THE INITIATING, PLANNING, AND EXECUTING THE PROGRAM PERFORMANCE DOMAINS COVERED IN THIS CHAPTER INCLUDES THE OBJECTIVES LISTED IN THE FOLLOWING:

- ✓ **2.8** Conduct program kick-offs with stakeholders by holding a series of meetings in order to familiarize the organization with the program.

- ✓ **3.2** Develop program scope definition using Work Breakdown Structure in order to determine the program deliverables and tasks.

- ✓ **4.2** Charter constituent projects by assigning project managers and allocating appropriate resources in order to meet program objectives.

- ✓ **4.3** Motivate the team using appropriate tools and techniques in order to increase commitment to the program objectives.

- ✓ **4.4** Establish program consistency by deploying uniform standards, resources, infrastructure, tools and processes in order to enable informed program decision making.

- ✓ **4.5** Capture program status and data by ensuring the population of the program management information system in order to maintain accurate and current program information for the use of stakeholders.

- ✓ **4.6** Execute the appropriate program plans (quality, risk, communication, staffing, etc.) by using the tools identified in the planning phase and by auditing the results of the use of these tools in order to ensure the program outcomes meet the stakeholder expectations and standards.

After you have performed the program planning by using the processes in the Planning process group, you need to manage the program execution by using the processes in the Executing process group. The program team determines which of the processes in the Executing process group are relevant to the program at hand. The goal of the execution stage is to complete the program work specified in the program management plan to meet the program requirements. To accomplish that you will need to acquire and develop the program team. Furthermore, your organization may not have the resources to finish certain parts of this work. Therefore, you will need to use procurement (such as outsourcing) for those parts of the work. You also need to ensure that all the planned quality activities are performed because the program work and the results of the work must meet the planned quality standards. This is accomplished by using the Perform Quality Assurance process.

So the core question in this chapter is how to execute a program as planned. In search of an answer, we will explore three avenues: performing the program work by acquiring and developing the program team, implementing procurement, and performing quality assurance.

Program Execution: The Big Picture

Executing the program means implementing the program management plan. The topics related to the program execution are included in the exam objectives covered in this chapter.

The Exam Roadmap

The following table presents each PgMP exam objective covered in this chapter, along with its explanation:

Exam Objective	What It Really Means
3.2 Develop program scope definition using Work Breakdown Structure in order to determine the program deliverables and tasks. 2.8 Conduct program kick-offs with stakeholders by holding a series of meetings in order to familiarize the organization with the program.	These exam objectives have been largely covered in Chapters 3 and 4, "Initiating a Program" and "Planning a Program." This chapter covers the following elements of these exam objectives: • Acquire Program Team • Develop Program Team

4.2 Charter constituent projects by assigning project managers and allocating appropriate resources in order to meet program objectives.	Understand the Authorize Projects process covered in Chapter 3, "Initiating a Program." This chapter briefly revisits this topic to emphasize some important points. You must understand what a project charter is.
4.3 Motivate the team using appropriate tools and techniques in order to increase commitment to the program objectives.	You must understand the Develop Program Team process along with its tools and techniques. You should also know different conflict-resolution techniques.
4.4 Establish program consistency by deploying uniform standards, resources, infrastructure, tools, and processes in order to enable informed program decision making. 4.5 Capture program status and data by ensuring the population of the program management information system in order to maintain accurate and current program information for the use of stakeholders.	Understand phase three of the program life cycle, which establishes the infrastructure for the program execution. You must understand the Information Distribution process. Know the tools and techniques used for storing, consolidating, retrieving, and distributing information.
4.6 Execute the appropriate program plans (quality, communication, staffing, etc.) by using the tools identified in the planning phase and by auditing the results of the use of these tools in order to ensure the program outcomes meet the stakeholder expectations and standards.	Understand the following processes: • Direct and Manage Program Execution • Perform Quality Assurance • Acquire Program Team • Develop Program Team • Information Distribution • Request Seller Responses • Select Sellers

The topics from these exam objectives covered in this chapter fall into five knowledge management areas: Integration Management, Quality Management, Human Resource Management, Communication Management, and Procurement Management.

Understanding Program Execution

The program is executed by using the processes of the Executing process group shown in Table 7.1 along with their main outputs and the knowledge areas to which they belong. These processes will be discussed one by one in detail further on in this chapter.

TABLE 7.1   Processes for Executing a Program

Knowledge Area	Program Execution Process	Major Output
Integration management	Direct and Manage Program Execution	Work results
Quality management	Perform Quality Assurance	Quality-related findings and results
Human resource management	1. Acquire Program Team 2. Develop Program Team	1. Staff assignments 2. Performance assessments
Communication management	Information Distribution	Formal and informal communication of information
Procurement management	1. Request Seller Responses 2. Select Sellers	1. Requests for information, proposal, and quotation 2. List of selected sellers and contracts

Figure 7.1 shows the relationships among the processes of the Executing process group. It demonstrates that the processes may be related to each other in several ways, including the following:

- Two processes are obviously related to each other when the output of one process is an input to the other process; for example, the Direct and Manage Program Execution process and the Perform Quality Assurance process.

- Two processes are related to each other when one process must be performed before the other process can begin. For example, you must acquire the program team before you can develop the team.

- A process may be logically related to several other processes. For example, you cannot effectively perform any process in the Executing process group if you are not directing and managing the program execution. In other words, all the processes in the Executing process group are directly or indirectly related to the Direct and Manage Program Execution process.

These processes are defined in the following:

Direct and Manage Program Execution   Used to manage various interfaces in the project to execute the program work smoothly with the goal of delivering the planned benefits.

Acquire Program Team   Used to obtain the program team members needed to perform the program work.

Develop Program Team   Used to improve individual and group competencies to enhance the program performance.

Perform Quality Assurance   Used to regularly evaluate the program performance to assure that the program complies with the planned quality standards.

Information Distribution   Used to provide the needed accurate information to the program stakeholders in a timely fashion.

Request Seller Responses   Used to obtain quotations, bids, offers, and proposals from sellers outside the program team for their product or services needed for the program.

Select Seller Responses   Used to select sellers based on their responses and negotiate written contracts with the selected sellers.

FIGURE 7.1   Processes of the Executing process group

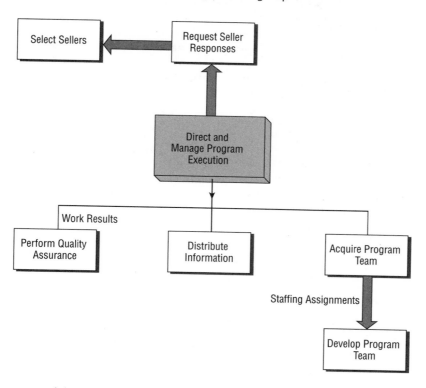

The processes of the Executing process group drive the program work according to the program management plan: the full plan including the subsidiary plans. In other words, executing the program is equivalent to executing the program management plan. The big picture of the Executing process group includes the following:

- Using these processes the program team acquires the resources including the program staff, contractors, and suppliers needed to meet the program objectives and deliver the program benefits.

- The program Executing process group involves acquiring the program team, developing the program team, and ensuring the planned quality standards are implemented.

- The program Executing process group ensures that all the program stakeholders receive the necessary information in a timely fashion.

The program work defined in the program management plan is executed by using the processes in the Executing process group. The program is executed in an infrastructure established as phase three of the program life cycle. Let's take a closer look at this execution-related program phase before discussing the program execution processes.

Establishing Program Management and Technical Infrastructure

Once the program setup (phase two) has been completed and the program has passed the phase-two gate review, you are, in principle, ready to begin the program execution. However, you need an infrastructure in which the program execution will occur. In other words, you need to establish an infrastructure to facilitate the execution of the program. This infrastructure has two dimensions: management and technical.

Management infrastructure As the program manager, you are part of the management infrastructure. However, your focus is on the program, and it could be just one program. The organization may have more than one program, and the programs are executed to support the strategic business plan of the organization. So, there is a management infrastructure bigger than you that connects all the programs to the business strategic goals of the organization. This infrastructure includes the following:

Program board This body is empowered to make decisions regarding important program aspects such as scope, budget, and schedule. It is also responsible for resolving the program issues that are escalated to it from lower management levels. The program-related roles in the program board include executive sponsor and program director.

The executive sponsor is a member of the program board who is responsible for creating an environment for the program to succeed; that is, bears the primary responsibility for the delivery of program benefits.

The program director is a member of the program board who is the executive owner of the program policies.

Program Management Office A program board is generally supported by the program management office (PMO), which is responsible for managing cross-program governance for the organization that runs multiple programs. The PMO is responsible for defining and managing the program-related governance procedures, processes, and templates.

Program office A given program may have its own office called a program office that provides administrative support for the program team and the program manager.

Program team This team is responsible for developing the planned benefits at the program level. The two main roles of the program team are team members and program manager:

Program team members are the individuals who perform the program activities.

Program manager is the individual who is responsible for the overall management of the program, including the program team, the project managers, and the cross-project activities.

> The same individual can perform both the executive sponsor and program director roles. This can reduce the managerial overhead and improve efficiency.

In addition to the managerial infrastructure, you also need the technical infrastructure to execute the program.

Technical Infrastructure   The technical infrastructure refers to the tools and procedures that will facilitate the program execution, and includes the following:

Program facilities   This refers to the space and equipment needed to execute the program, such as building, office space, operational rooms, computer system, and so on.

Program tools   This refers to the tools to facilitate different aspects of program management, such as tools to track the program progress, performance measurement tools, tools to measure, monitor, and track program benefits, and enterprise resource planning (ERP), which is a software system that integrates data and processes from different parts of an organization to facilitate planning for the effective utilization of enterprise-wide resources

Program-specific governance guidelines   This refers to the program-specific processes, procedures, and templates.

> In general, the term *technical* does not necessarily refer to technology, but rather to the specifics of a discipline. For example, technical terminology means the terminology of a specific discipline, and the discipline may be any discipline: program management, software engineering, music, and so on.

In a nutshell, this program phase produces the following key items to support the program:

- Program team
- Program office
- Governance structure
- Processes, procedures, and tools for monitoring and controlling the program and measuring the results
- Program facilities, IT systems, and communication tools and technologies

---

Exam Spotlight

One of the important purposes of deploying uniform standards, resources, infrastructure, tools, and processes is to establish program consistency that enables informed program decision making.

Once the infrastructure is in place, you are ready to begin the program execution. The process that focuses on the program packages currently in progress and integrates all other execution processes is called Direct and Manage Program Execution.

Directing and Managing Program Execution

The granddaddy of all the processes in the Executing process group is the Direct and Manage Program Execution process. In other words, the program work defined in the program management plan is performed by using this process. While executing this process, you will be interacting with other processes and departments in your organization. A program team, in general, includes people from different departments. Usually the reporting relationships within the same department are very well defined and structured. However, the relationships between different departments (especially between individuals from different departments at the same level of authority) are not well defined. So, managing such program interfaces is a crucial function of a program manager during the program execution. Generally speaking, program interfaces are the formal and informal boundaries and relationships among team members, departments, organizations, or functions; for example, how the engineering department and the marketing department interact with each other while working on the same program. Directing and managing program execution is the process used to manage various technical and organizational interfaces in the program to facilitate the smooth execution of the program work.

The main purposes of directing and managing program execution are as follows:

- Produce the program deliverables by executing the program management plan.
- Implement the approved change requests and recommendations for corrective and preventive actions.
- Implement the planned methods, processes, and standards.
- Ensure that all the transition plans are executed.
- Produce and distribute the status information. The work progress is tracked regularly and reported through updates on individual projects. This information is passed on to the Performance Reporting process.
- Resolve interproject issues, risks, and constraints.

The key words during execution are *implement*, *manage*, and *inform* (status). Figure 7.2 shows the Direct and Manage Program Execution process with its high-level input and output.

Input to Directing and Managing Program Execution

Recall that directing and managing program execution involves implementing the program management plan according to the program schedule. Therefore, the program management plan and the program schedule are the obvious input items to this process, and are discussed in the following.

Program management plan   The program execution is the implementation of the program management plan. Therefore this plan is an obvious input to this process. Recall that the program management plan contains all the subsidiary plans and it describes how the work will be executed to meet the program objectives and deliver benefits. In other words, once the program execution has begun, the program management plan execution becomes the primary responsibility of the program manager and the program team.

WARNING   Approved changes and recommendations for corrective actions and preventive actions are implicit input to the Direct and Manage Program Execution process, even though it's not explicitly mentioned. These input items, after approval, become parts of the corresponding subsidiary plans, which are part of the program management plan.

Program schedule   The program must be executed according to the planned schedule. So the program schedule is another obvious input to directing and managing the program execution.

You use some tools and techniques such as program/project management information systems to generate output from the input.

FIGURE 7.2   The Direct and Manage Program Execution process: input and output

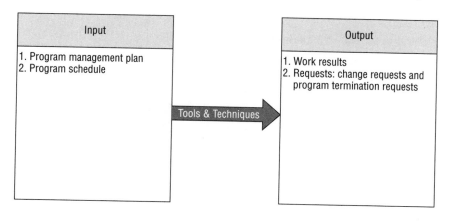

Tools and Techniques for Directing and Managing Program Execution

General management skills and a management information system are the main tools used to generate the output of the Direct and Manage Program Execution process. These and other tools are discussed here.

General management skills   When you are directing and managing the program execution, your general management skills are in full demand. These skills include the following:

- Ability to grasp the big picture and how the different pieces relate to the big picture
- Communication and motivation abilities
- An eye for detail
- Analytical thinking
- Ability to negotiate and resolve conflicts
- Ability to solve problems
- Ability to influence people and processes in order to get things done

Management information system   The program management information system (PMIS), discussed in the previous chapter, facilitates managing the execution of the program components according to the program management plan. It may also contain a change-control system.

Work authorization system   This is a subsystem of the overall program management system that determines how the program work will be properly authorized in order to ensure that the work is performed in the right sequence by the right individuals or groups at the right time. This system consists of the following:

- Approval levels required for work authorization
- Tracking system to track the work authorization–related actions and progress
- Documents that explain steps and procedures

Status-review meetings   Program status reviews are necessary to properly direct and manage program execution. A review is better performed in a meeting where all relevant parties are represented. It keeps everyone on the same page. Timely review meetings facilitate timely change requests to keep the program and its components on track.

Product skills and knowledge   The program team needs to have the skills and knowledge about the product (or outcome) that is being produced by the program. These skills and knowledge are used in directing and managing the program execution. This will help determine if the program is generating the correct results and if change requests are needed.

Organizational process assets   One of the tasks of the Direct and Manage Program Execution process is to ensure that the planned methods, processes, and standards are implemented. You should also make sure that the organizational procedures are followed.

You use these tools to generate the output from the input to the Direct and Manage Program Execution process.

Output of Directing and Managing Program Execution

The program execution generates some results and during the execution some change requests will arise. Therefore work results and change requests are the obvious output of the Direct and Manage Program Execution process, and are discussed in the following.

Work results   The purpose of directing and managing program execution is to produce cumulative deliverables and other work products of the program. Implementation of approved changes and recommendations is also included in the work results. Implementation of transition plans is also part of the work results.

Requests   While directing and managing the program execution, you will receive some requests, which fall into two major categories: program termination request and other requests. When the program ends by achieving the planned benefits, it's called program completion. The program can also be terminated due to reasons such as a change in the organization's strategic plan or the realization that it's not possible to achieve the planned benefits. Other changes are mostly related to the program execution, and they may arise from the execution itself or they may come from the stakeholders. For example, the change requests may be in the areas of program scope, program cost, program schedule, and program policies and procedures. These requests are passed to the Integrated Change Control process for review, and only requests that are approved by this process will be implemented.

Exam Spotlight

The planned benefits of the program are delivered by the Direct and Manage Program Execution process. Therefore, a large portion of the program budget is expended on this process.

The program work is performed by the program team that you need to acquire and develop.

Managing the Program Team

Managing the program team includes acquiring and developing the team. The program work will be executed by the program team, and therefore the role of the team in the success of the program is crucial. This is how important it is to acquire and develop the right program team for your program.

Acquiring a Program Team

The roles and the responsibilities of those roles required to complete the program are defined during the Human Resource Planning process discussed in Chapter 5, "Planning the Program Schedule and Resources." Before the work can start, the roles need to be assigned to real individuals who will become the members of the program team. These team members need to be acquired through the Acquire Program Team process shown in Figure 7.3.

FIGURE 7.3 The Acquire Program Team process: input and output

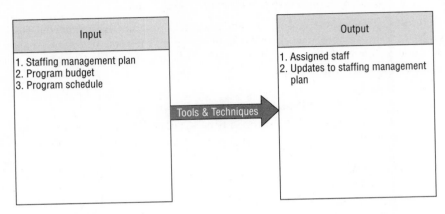

The input to this process comes from several planning processes: Human Resource Planning, Cost Estimating and Budgeting, and Schedule Development.

Input to Acquiring the Program Team

As discussed in Chapter 5, the Human Resource Planning process generates the staffing management plan, the Cost Estimating and Budgeting process generates the program budget, and the Schedule Development process generates the program schedule. These three items are the input to the Acquire Program Team process.

Staffing management plan   The staffing management plan is an important input item to acquiring the program team because it provides the detailed information about the roles that need to be filled, such as start and finish date for a role and the responsibilities assigned to the role. This information is necessary to match the candidates with the roles. The roles are explained in Chapter 5.

Program budget   The team members will cost the program because they will need to be paid. That's why the program budget is an input to the Acquire Program Team process. It will also play a role in determining if you want to hire internally or externally.

Program schedule   The program schedule will tell what particular skill sets and roles are needed and when.

With this input in place, you need some tools and techniques to generate the output of the Acquire Program Team process.

Tools and Techniques for Acquiring the Program Team

You will either negotiate within your organization for a team member to fill a role, or you will acquire the team member from outside your organization, such as by hiring a contractor. Negotiation and acquisition are discussed in the following list, along with other tools and techniques.

Acquisition or procurement   If the performing organization does not have the human resources to fill one or more roles needed to run the program, the required team member can be obtained from outside the organization as contractor or as a regular employee, or the corresponding work can be given to the source outside the performing organization. This is also called *procurement*, and we will talk more about this area of procurement management later in this chapter.

Negotiations   You may need to negotiate within your organization for the staff assignments for your program. In these negotiations, you have a two-prong goal—to obtain the best available person for a program responsibility and to obtain the person for the required time frame. You must do your homework to get the best results from the negotiations.

> While negotiating with, for example, a functional manager, sometimes it's important to understand the functional manager's perspective in light of the politics of the organization. For example, a functional manager will weigh the benefits (for example, visibility of your program compared to that of a competing program) in determining where to assign the best performers. In this case, it is to your advantage to explain the importance of your program and the role and responsibility for which you are asking for the best performer.

Pre-assignment   In some cases, there will be some staff members already assigned to the program. This can happen, for example, due to the following situations:

- You already have a core program team that was acquired through the Initiate Team process during the program initiation.

- A staff member was promised as part of a specific proposal to compete with another proposal. Acceptance of this proposal automatically affirms that staff-member assignment.

- There is only one person in the organization who has the expertise to perform a specific responsibility.

- A staff assignment was specified in the program charter.

The team (assigned staff) itself is the major output of the Acquire Team process—no surprise there.

Output of Acquiring the Program Team

The major output of the Acquire Program Team process is the staff assignments to fill the roles defined during human resource planning. This and other output items are discussed here.

Program staff assignments   This document contains the list of individuals assigned to the program, along with their roles. These individuals can be obtained from inside or outside the performing organization as described in the following:

Internal human resources   Obtaining internal human resources for open positions involves identifying the individuals qualified for the open positions, negotiating for obtaining the services of the identified individuals with their current management, and transitioning the selected individuals from their current positions to the open positions.

External human resources   The decision whether to use internal or external human resources depends on factors such as availability of the internal candidates with the needed skills, timing of the need and the duration for which the skill set for the open position is needed, and the cost of external resources, including the hiring cost.

Even if you decide that you need external human resources, you will need to decide if it will be a permanent or a contract position. In making this decision consideration should be given to a permanent hire's long-term value to the organization.

For internal appointments, consideration must be given to the needs of the candidate's current assignments, the candidate's fit for the open position, and the candidate's career path.

Updates to the staffing management plan   The program team is acquired by matching the staffing requirements specified in the staffing management plan to the candidate members. Hardly ever there is a perfect match between the two. So, during the process of acquiring the program team, you may realize that the staffing management plan needs to be updated. The other updates to the staffing management plan may come from the following sources:

- Promotions
- Retirements
- Illnesses
- Performance issues
- Changing workloads

After the staff assignments have been made, you have the raw material out of which you need to develop that special team for your program.

Developing the Program Team

Developing the program team consists of developing competencies of the team as a group and the team members with one main goal in mind: improve the program performance. These competencies enable the team to perform the current program tasks more effectively and prepare the team to successfully perform the program tasks in the future. Furthermore, the development also prepares a team member for the following:

- Expand the existing role
- Taking on a new assignment in the same program
- Getting a role in another program when this program concludes

A successful development plan strikes a balance between the program needs and the needs of the team member's career path.

Development of the program team is performed by using the Develop Program Team process shown in Figure 7.4.

FIGURE 7.4   The Develop Program Team process: input and output

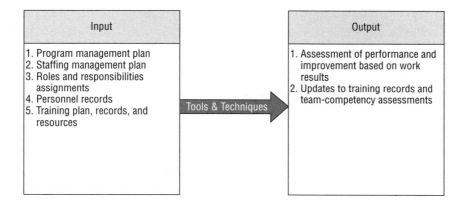

Input	Output
1. Program management plan 2. Staffing management plan 3. Roles and responsibilities assignments 4. Personnel records 5. Training plan, records, and resources	1. Assessment of performance and improvement based on work results 2. Updates to training records and team-competency assessments

Tools & Techniques

Input to Developing the Program Team

The program management plan and staffing management plan are the obvious input to developing the program team. These and other input items are discussed in the following.

Program management plan   The program management plan contains the resource management plan that will be useful for developing the program team. The resource management plan can answer the following questions:

- What types of resources are needed to perform the program activities, including the human resources?

- How many people are needed?

- How can you optimize the use of the human resources across the program?

- How can you ensure that the common resources are allocated appropriately across the constituent projects and are not overcommitted?

Staffing management plan   The staffing management plan describes when and how human-resource requirements for a program will be met. It can also have training needs and plans for the program.

Roles and responsibilities assignments   It's important to know what role and responsibilities have been assigned to a team member. This will provide a context for the development of the team member. Collectively, roles and responsibilities assignments will help determine what kind of training is needed to prepare the team members for future assignments.

Training plan, records, and resources   The following pieces of information are important to perform effective and efficient team development:

- Training plan for the program
- Personnel records including records of training conducted in the past
- A list of available training resources and methods (explained further in the output of this process)

With this input in place, you use tools and techniques such as management skills and training to generate the output of the Develop Program Team process.

Tools and Techniques for Developing the Program Team

As discussed in the following list, there are some standard tools and techniques that you can use to develop a winning team.

General management skills   You (the program manager) and the program management team can minimize problems and maximize cooperation by understanding the sentiments of each team member, anticipating their actions, acknowledging their concerns, and following up on their issues. To accomplish this, the following general management skills are necessary:

Effective communication   This is needed to facilitate the smooth flow of necessary information among the team members.

Ability to influence the organization   This is needed to get things done.

Leadership   This is needed for developing a vision and strategy and for motivating people to achieve that vision. During the time of possible uncertainty, such as changes in upper management, you should clarify the situation and help the team stay focused on the program.

Motivation   This is needed for energizing team members to achieve high levels of performance and to overcome barriers to change. When the team is in a low-morale mode, you should be able to lift the team morale and thereby contribute to team development.

Negotiation and conflict management   This is needed to work with the team members to resolve their conflicts and facilitate negotiations when necessary in resolving conflicts or in task assignments. Depending on the nature of the conflict, you can take it as a team-development opportunity. An effective resolution of a conflict contributes to team building.

Problem-solving   This ability is needed to define, analyze, and solve problems.

Ground-rules setting   A very important management technique is to establish clear expectations at the very beginning of a program component. The expectations can be established by laying some ground rules. Early commitment to these guidelines will increase cooperation and productivity by decreasing misunderstandings.

Team-building activities   Team-building activities can range from indirect ones such as participating in constructing the PWBS to direct ones such as social gatherings where the team members can get to know each other and start feeling comfortable with each other. While planning such activities, you should keep in mind that the team members might have different interests and different levels of tolerance for games and different icebreakers.

Training   The goal of training is to improve the competencies of the program team members, which in turn helps in meeting the program objectives. It might be aimed at the individual members or at the team as a whole, depending upon the needs. The training might be scheduled in the staff management plan or it might result from the observations, conversations, and performance appraisals as the program progresses. The following are examples of some training methods:

- Coaching
- Mentoring
- On-the-job training of a team member by another team member
- Online training
- Instructor-led classroom training

Co-location   This technique keeps all (or most) of the program team members in the same physical location to improve communication and to create a sense of community among the team members. In this age of virtual teams, this technique is losing popularity, but when most of the team members are in the same location, this technique is a default choice. It can include a war room, which is a meeting room used for regular face-to-face meetings.

Recognition and reward system   The recognition and rewards strategy set up during the Human Resource Planning process can be used to develop the program team. Remember the following rules in setting up a fair reward system:

- Only desirable behavior should be rewarded.
- Any member should be able to win the reward.
- Win-lose rewards, such as team member of the month, can hurt the team cohesiveness.
- The cultural diversity of the team should be considered and respected.

The effects of the team-development efforts are measured by the team-performance assessment, which includes the following indicators:

- Improvement in individual skills that enables a team member to perform project activities more efficiently
- Improvement in team skills that help the team to improve overall performance and work more effectively as a group
- Reduced staff turnover rate

These tools and techniques can be used to generate the output of the Develop Program Team process.

Output of Developing the Program Team

The results of the Develop Program Team process can be measured only by assessing the team performance. This and other output items are discussed in the following.

Team performance assessment How would you know that the team (or a team member) has improved as a result of team development activities? You determine that by measuring the improvement in performance based on the work results. In general, the effects of the team-development efforts are measured by the team-performance assessment, which includes the following indicators:

- Improvement in individual skills that enables a team member to perform program activities more efficiently
- Improvement in team skills that help the team to improve overall performance and work more effectively as a group
- Reduced staff turnover rate

Updates The team-development process will keep updating the following:

- Training records.
- Team competency assessment; it's supposed to improve. This topic is discussed in detail in Chapter 5.

Program team development is ongoing; it continues throughout the program. The team works not only to produce the deliverables but also to ensure that the work and the deliverables meet the planned quality standards.

 Real World Scenario

Training Methods Used in Team Development

You are the program manager of New Horizons, Inc., which offers services in implementing radio frequency identification (RFID) technology. You hired Anita Wong to manage an RFID-related project. Anita is a beginner in project management, but she has a very strong background in technology. She is a networking expert but is new to RFID. You collected this competency information about Anita by various methods, including the following:

- Interviewing
- Observation
- Performance assessment

You applied various training methods to get Anita up to speed, including the following:

- You paired Anita with Linda Syal, a senior project manager in the RFID field. Linda provided on-the-job training and some coaching.

- You asked Anita to pass the Certified Associate in Project Management (CAPM) exam offered by the Project Management Institute (PMI) within the next three months. This way, she would become familiar with the project management terminology and processes.

- You asked Linda to pass the RFID+ exam offered by CompTIA within the next six months. This would introduce her to the RFID application area.

You were happy to see that this training helped Linda to become one of your best project managers by the end of her first year at the job.

Performing Quality Assurance

Quality planning, discussed in Chapter 6, "Planning for Quality, Risk, and Communication," is used to identify which quality standards are relevant to the program at hand and to determine how to meet them. *Quality assurance (QA)* is the application of the planned systematic quality activities. It involves evaluating overall program performance to ensure that the planned quality standards are implemented. This process is continually used during the execution of the program.

Performing organizations typically have a QA department that oversees the quality assurance activities and fosters continuous process improvement, which is an iterative method for improving the quality of all processes.

Continuous process improvement enhances the efficiency and effectiveness of the processes by minimizing waste (unnecessary activities) and duplication of efforts. It includes identifying and reviewing the business processes inside the organization, such as coding of modules within software programs, and the process of program and project approval.

Figure 7.5 depicts the Perform Quality Assurance process.

FIGURE 7.5   The Perform Quality Assurance process: input and output.

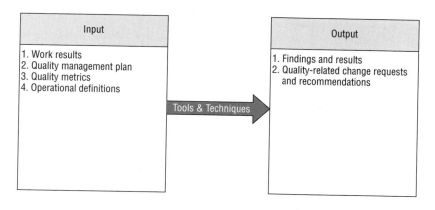

The input for the Perform Quality Assurance process comes from the Direct and Manage Program Execution process and the Quality Planning process.

Input to Performing Quality Assurance

Quality assurance involves evaluating overall program performance to ensure that the planned quality standards are implemented. Therefore, the work results and the quality management plan are the obvious input items to quality assurance. These and other input items are discussed here.

Work results The work results generated by the Direct and Manage Program Execution process are the targets on which the quality assurance is performed. The results are examined to ensure that they meet the agreed-upon quality standards. The work results consist of implemented items such as change requests and recommendations for corrective and preventive actions, deliverables, and work-performance information.

Quality management plan A quality management plan, generated by the Quality Planning process, is an input because it describes how QA will be performed for this specific program.

Quality metrics Quality metrics, generated by the Quality Planning process, are input to the Perform Quality Assurance process because they provide the stick to measure if the quality standards are being met. A quality metric is an operational criterion that defines in specific terms what something (such as a characteristic or a feature) is and how the Quality Control process measures it. The quality metrics such as defect density, failure rates, reliability, and test coverage developed during quality planning must be employed during QA.

Operational definitions Operational definitions, generated by the Quality Planning process, help define quality metrics and make measurements to determine if the quality standards are being met by the program execution.

On this input, you apply tools and techniques such as quality audits and process analysis to generate the output of the Perform Quality Assurance process.

Tools and Techniques for Performing Quality Assurance

Quality audits and process analysis, along with the tools and techniques used in quality planning and the quality control processes, can be used in the QA process.

Quality audits A quality audit is a structured and independent review to determine whether the execution of a program or one of its components complies with the policies, processes, and procedures of the program and the performing organization. It verifies the implementation of approved change requests, corrective actions, defect repairs, and preventive actions. The audits can occur as scheduled or at random, and can be conducted by a third party or by the properly trained in-house auditors of the performing organization. These audits accomplish the following:

- Because one of the objectives of a quality audit is to identify inefficient and ineffective policies, processes, and procedures being used for the program, audits reduce the cost of quality on the subsequent program execution.

- Audits increase customer satisfaction and acceptance of the product or service delivered by the program.

Process analysis   This is a technique used to identify the needed improvements in a process by following the steps outlined in the process improvement plan. It examines the problems, constraints, and unnecessary (non-value-added) activities identified during the implementation of the process. Process analysis typically includes the following steps:

1. Identify a technique to analyze the problem.
2. Identify the underlying causes that led to the problem.
3. Examine the root cause of the problem.
4. Create preventive actions for this and similar problems.

Other tools and techniques   The tools and techniques used in the following processes can also be used in the QA process:

- Quality planning, discussed in Chapter 6
- Quality control, discussed in the next chapter, "Monitoring and Controlling the Program"

The Quality Assurance process recommends corrective actions and other change requests as an output item.

Output of Performing Quality Assurance

The findings and results of quality audits are the obvious output of the Quality Assurance process. This and other output items are discussed in the following.

Findings and results   You record the findings and results of the Perform Quality Assurance process. In doing that, you may find that a certain aspect of quality is not being met. For example, some defect repair has not been implemented, the program is behind schedule, or the program is overrunning costs. You use the findings and results to make the quality-related change requests.

Quality-related change requests and recommendations   To fix the problems in meeting the quality requirements, you make change requests and recommendations for corrective and preventive actions. These requests and recommendations must go through the approval process (the Integrated Change Control process) before they can be implemented.

Recall that there is a quality assurance process at the project level as well. The quality assurance at the program level is not a replacement for the quality assurance efforts being made at the constituent projects level. Quality assurance for a project is performed for that specific project, whereas quality assurance at the program level focuses on the following:

- Cross-program quality activities
- Cross-project quality activities
- Quality activities for the non-project program work including service management
- Activities to address the overarching quality needs of the customers, which would generally be outside the boundaries of a specific project

So, quality assurance is performed to ensure that both the program work and the deliverables meet the planned quality standards. As you learned in Chapter 5, sometimes you may decide to procure some of the program deliverables. For those you will need to plan and implement procurement.

Implementing Procurement

As you learned in Chapter 5, the major tasks of procurement planning are making make-or-buy decisions, preparing the procurement management plan, preparing the statement of work, determining the suitable type of contract, and preparing or acquiring the procurement documents. Once you have these elements in place, you are ready to implement the procurement plan. The Plan Program Purchases and Acquisitions and Plan Program Contracting processes are used to plan the procurement, whereas the Request Seller Responses and Select Sellers processes are used to implement the procurement.

Requesting Seller Responses

Seller responses are requested and received by using the Request Seller Responses process. The responses may be solicited in various forms, such as bids, quotations, proposals, or offers. Accordingly the requests have different names such as request for information (RFI), request for proposal (RFP), and request for quotations (RFQ). The Request Seller Responses process is depicted in Figure 7.6, along with its input and output.

FIGURE 7.6   The Request Seller Responses process: input and output

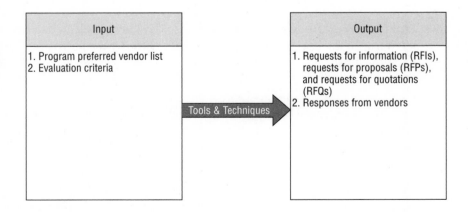

Input	Output
1. Program preferred vendor list 2. Evaluation criteria	1. Requests for information (RFIs), requests for proposals (RFPs), and requests for quotations (RFQs) 2. Responses from vendors

Tools & Techniques

Input to Requesting Seller Responses

The input items should provide the answer to the question: to whom should I send the requests? Accordingly, the input items to this process are the program preferred vendor list and evaluation criteria.

Program preferred vendor list   If your program is going to procure items, you will need to develop a vendors list relevant to the program. To develop this list, you can use the organizational assets and other sources, such as the World Wide Web, library directories, relevant professional associations, and trade catalogs. This list is an output of the Plan Program Purchases and Acquisitions process discussed in Chapter 5.

Evaluation criteria   Usually the evaluation criteria developed by using the Plan Program Contracting process is used in evaluating the responses from the vendors. However, some evaluation criteria based on the available information can also be used to determine the vendors that will receive the requests.

  With the availability of this input, responses can be sought by using various techniques.

Tools and Techniques for Requesting Seller Responses

The goal for the tools and techniques here is to find the sellers and provide them with the information about the requests for responses. Main techniques used in requesting seller responses are advertising and bidder conferences. These techniques are discussed in the following.

Advertising   The request for seller responses can be advertised in the public media or in relevant professional journals. Whether to use advertising depends on the organization's policy. However, some government jurisdictions require public advertising of pending government contracts.

Bidder conferences   This refers to meetings with prospective sellers prior to preparation of a response to ensure that the sellers have a clear understanding of the procurement, such as the technical and contractual requirements. These meetings can generate amendments to the documents. All potential sellers should be given the same amount of information (or help) during this interaction so that each seller has an equal opportunity to produce the best response. These conferences are also called *contractor conferences*, *vendor conferences*, or *pre-bid conferences*.

  By using these techniques, you can generate the output of the Request Seller Responses process.

Output of Requesting Seller Responses

Output of the Request Seller Responses process consists of the following two types of documents:

- Requests (RFI, RFP, or RFQ) sent to the vendors
- Responses received from the vendors

  Based on the responses you receive, you can begin the process of selecting the sellers.

Selecting Sellers

Responses such as proposals received from the sellers during the Request Seller Responses process are evaluated in the Select Sellers process, which is used to select one or more sellers for procurement. The following are the main tasks performed during the Select Sellers process:

- Review the seller responses to the buyer requests
- Select one or more sellers based on their responses by using the evaluation criteria
- Negotiate written contracts with the selected sellers, which will include the following:
  - Technical terms and conditions
  - Roles and responsibilities
  - Deliverables
  - Overall cost

Figure 7.7 shows the Select Sellers process.

FIGURE 7.7 The Select Sellers process: input and output

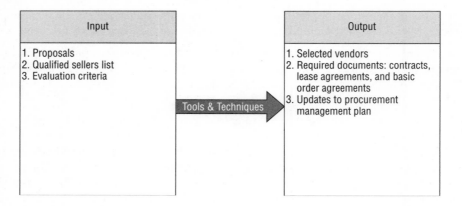

Input	Output
1. Proposals 2. Qualified sellers list 3. Evaluation criteria	1. Selected vendors 2. Required documents: contracts, lease agreements, and basic order agreements 3. Updates to procurement management plan

Tools & Techniques

Input to Selecting Sellers

The main task in selecting sellers is to evaluate the proposals. Therefore, the proposals and the evaluation criteria are the obvious input items. These and other input items are discussed in the following.

Proposals   These are the responses received from the vendors in response to the requests for seller responses, an output of the Request Seller Responses process.

Qualified sellers list   This is the list of sellers who were asked to submit the proposals. It is used to determine if a given proposal has actually been submitted by a qualified seller.

Evaluation criteria   The buyer develops the evaluation criteria to rate the responses from the sellers. The evaluation criteria could be as simple as price for off-the-shelf standard items or a combination of factors for a more complex proposal. The evaluation criteria are an output of the Plan Program Contracting process discussed in Chapter 5.

Once these input items are in place, you can apply some tools and techniques to hammer out the output of the Select Sellers process.

Tools and Techniques for Selecting Sellers

The tools and techniques used to select the sellers are discussed in the following.

Independent estimates   The purpose of independent estimates is to have a check on the proposed pricing by the seller. The procuring organization prepares the independent estimate in-house or has it done by a third party. Significant differences between the proposed price and the independent estimate mean that either the market has changed or the seller has failed to offer reasonable pricing due to reasons such as failure to understand the contract statement of work. The independent estimates are also called *should-cost estimates*.

Seller rating system   A seller's rating does not depend on a specific response that you are evaluating. Rather, the seller's rating comes from the seller's rating system, which is developed by multiple organizations based on multiple factors related to seller's past performance, such as delivery performance, contractual compliance, and quality rating.

Weighting system   The purpose of putting a weighting system in place is to have an objective evaluation as opposed to a subjective evaluation influenced by personal prejudice. The weighting system uses a method to quantify the qualitative data and typically involves the following steps:

1. Assign a numerical weight to each of the evaluation criteria according to its importance, such as w1, w2, and w3 for three criteria, and make these weights the same for each seller.

2. Rate the seller on each criterion, such as r1, r2, and r3. These ratings depend upon the seller.

3. Multiply the weight by the rate for each criterion.

4. Add the results in the previous step to compute an overall score, such as s1 for seller 1: s1 = r1 $\times$ w1 + r2 $\times$ w2 + r3 $\times$ w3.

Expert judgment   The expert judgment is made by an expert committee that consists of experts from each of the disciplines covered by the procurement documents and the proposed contract. The committee can include experts from functional disciplines, such as accounting, contracts, engineering, finance, legal, manufacturing, and research and development.

Proposal-evaluation techniques   Different techniques can be used to evaluate responses from sellers. All these techniques can use expert judgment and evaluation criteria. The factors that can be considered in the evaluation include the following:

Price   This can play a primary role in the selection of off-the-shelf standard items. However, you should consider that the lower price does not mean lower cost if the seller does not deliver in time.

Multiple aspects   Proposals are usually evaluated for different aspects, such as technical and commercial. Technical refers to the overall approach, whereas commercial refers to the cost.

Multiple sources   For products critical to the program, multiple sources (sellers) might be required. This redundancy will help mitigate such risks as failure to meet the delivery schedule or failure to meet the quality requirements.

In the context of procurement, sellers are sometimes also called *sources*.

Screening system   A screening system consists of minimum requirements as a threshold that must be met if the seller has to stay in the list of candidate sellers. It might, for example, consist of one or more evaluation criteria. The screening system can also use the weighting system and independent estimates.

Contract negotiations   The contract negotiations have the following goals:

- Clarify the structure and requirements of the contract
- Reach an agreement

The subjects covered during the negotiations might include the following:

- Applicable terms and laws
- Authorities, rights, and responsibilities
- Business management and technical approaches
- Contract financing
- Payments and price
- Proprietary rights
- Schedule
- Technical solutions

The conclusion of contract negotiations is a document, the contract, which can be signed by both the buyer and the seller. The final contract signed by both parties can be an offer by the seller or a counteroffer by the buyer. Sometimes for simple procurement items the contract is non-negotiable.

A contract is a mutually binding legal relationship subject to remedy in the court. The program (or project) manager might not be the lead negotiator on the contract. However, the program (or project) manager might be required to be present during negotiations to provide any necessary clarification on the requirements.

In the Select Sellers process, you basically evaluate, screen, and negotiate. In general, multiple tools and techniques are used to evaluate responses and make a selection.

Output of Selecting Sellers

An obvious output of the Select Sellers process is a list of selected sellers (vendors). This and other output items are discussed in the following.

Selected vendors   This is the list of the sellers that you have selected as a result of response evaluations.

Required documents   The documents resulting from this process include the following:

- Contracts. A contract is a legal agreement signed by the buyer and the seller. It may contain details of the work, including cost, roles, responsibilities, and technical terms and conditions.

- Lease agreements. A lease agreement is a type of contract that allows the owner to rent a resource such as building or equipment to some individual or organization for a certain period of time. This is an alternative to buying resources.

- Basic order agreements. This refers to basic buying and selling agreements, such as a purchase order, that specifies the type, quantity, and agreed-upon price for the product or service that will be provided by the seller to the buyer.

Updates to the procurement management plan   You may need to update the procurement management plan to reflect the developments and changes that may occur due to the Select Sellers process. For example, you may need to enter the final agreed-upon scheduled dates for contract deliverables into the procurement management plan.

The main program-level responsibilities regarding selecting sellers include negotiating and finalizing program-wide policies and agreements such as basic order agreements and integrated volume discounts. A contract ironed out with a seller needs to be administered. This is accomplished by using the Program Contract Administration process discussed in the next chapter. The high-level relationships among the procurement processes discussed so far and the Program Contract Administration process are depicted in Figure 7.8.

FIGURE 7.8   The relationship among some procurement management processes

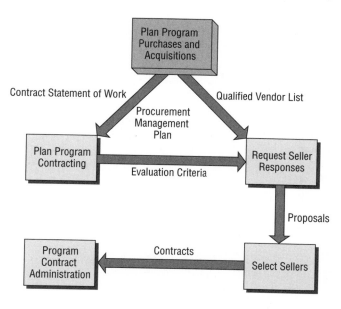

Regardless whether it's the procurement part of the work or the in-house program work, you need to communicate important information to the stakeholders on a regular basis.

Communicating the Program Execution

Communication during the program execution is performed by using the Information Distribution process, shown in Figure 7.9. This process is used to provide needed accurate information to the program stakeholders in a timely manner. It includes managing the three main communication channels with the following stakeholders:

- Clients
- Project managers of the constituent projects
- Sponsors

Input to Information Distribution

The Information Distribution process is used to distribute the information according to the communication management plan. Therefore, the information to be distributed and the communication management plan are the obvious input items to the Information Distribution process. These and other input items are discussed here.

FIGURE 7.9   The Information Distribution process: input and output

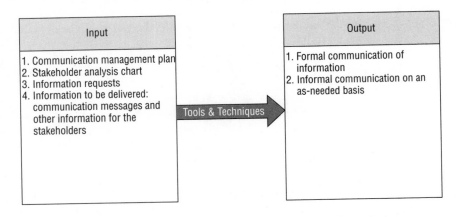

Communication management plan   You distribute the information according to the communication management plan that was generated as an output of the Communication Planning process.

Stakeholder analysis chart   The information is distributed to satisfy the information needs of the program stakeholders, which are determined during the stakeholder analysis. Therefore, the stakeholder analysis chart is an important input to the Information Distribution process. In order to meet the information needs of the stakeholders, you need to collect the right data by taking the following steps:

1. Determine what data is needed to satisfy the stakeholders' information needs.

2. Identify the sources of the needed data.

3. Gather data from the identified sources.

4. Verify the relevance and accuracy of the gathered data.

5. Demonstrate that you can calculate the planned metrics, such as performance and quality metrics, from the gathered data.

This data is used to produce the needed information.

Information requests   You distribute the information as planned. However, during the program execution you may get unplanned and unexpected requests for information. You will need to respond to these requests as well.

Information to be delivered   This is the actual information that you will deliver to the stakeholders. It can include the following:

- Information about the status and progress of the program and the constituent projects. This information can include performance information in such areas as cost and schedule, results from risk analysis and risk monitoring, and any other useful information

- Notification of the change requests and responses to the change requests

- Budgetary information

- External filings with government and other regulatory bodies to meet the legal requirements

- Public announcements to communicate the program information that is of interest to the public

Information is generated from the gathered data, which comes from multiple sources such as projects. To make sense of this data and to generate the needed program information from this data, you will need to consolidate this data pouring in from different sources. You accomplish this by taking the following steps:

1. Think through the consolidation process in terms of the benefits of consolidation and the information you need to generate.

2. Develop the data consolidation process.

3. Implement the data consolidation process.

For storing and consolidating the data you will need some tools, such as data storage and retrieval tools.

Tools and Techniques for Information Distribution

Communication skills are necessary for successful information distribution. This and other tools and techniques for information distribution are discussed in the following.

Communication skills   As communication is an exchange of information, communication skills are the necessary requirement for information distribution. Communication skills, an essential part of general management skills, are used to ensure the following:

- The right stakeholders get the right information at the right time
- The communication requirements and expectations of stakeholders are properly managed

The communication line has two ends. There is a sender on one end and the receiver on the other. Both the sender and the receiver need to have communication skills. The sender has the following responsibilities:

- Ensure that the information is clear and complete
- Confirm that the information is received and properly understood

The receiver has the following responsibilities:

- Ensure that the information is received in its entirety
- Ensure that the information is correctly understood

So, the success of information distribution depends on both the sender and the receiver. The communication has two flavors in each of the following dimensions:

Media   Written and speaking on the sender end, and reading and listening on the receiver end.

Place   Internal to the program (that is, within the program) and external (that is, communicating to the entities external to the program such as customer, media, and public).

Format   Formal (such as reports and briefings) and informal (such as memos and ad hoc conversation).

Hierarchy   Horizontal means communication among the peers; vertical means communication between different levels of organizational hierarchy—for example, a manager communicating with the team that reports to the manager.

The information that needs to be communicated also needs to be gathered, stored, and retrieved.

Information storage and retrieval systems   The information that is distributed is generated from the data that needs to be gathered, consolidated, stored, and retrieved when needed. To be specific, you need the tools that will allow you to do the following:

- Set up the program database
- Add the data to the database
- Manipulate the data in the database, such as by consolidating it
- Retrieve the data
- Retrieve the information created from the data

To accomplish these tasks, you need a database management system such as Oracle, MySQL, or Microsoft SQL Server.

> A database management system (DBMS) is a set of software programs that allows a user to manage a database; that is, to store, manipulate, and retrieve the data in a database. A *database* is an information system that contains a structured collection of records, such as student identification with the student's name and the student's grades in different courses attached to the identification. The identification may be represented by some suitable field in the record with a unique value such as a social security number. *Data* is a raw fact or figure, such as cost equal to one million dollars.

Information distribution methods   The information can be distributed in a number of ways that fall into the following two broad categories:

Synchronous   Both the sender and the receiver have to be present at the same time, such as in face-to-face meetings and in teleconferences.

Asynchronous   The sender and receiver don't have to be present at the same time, such as in written papers or electronic documents, online bulletin boards, email, and the Web in general.

The following are some specific examples of information distribution methods:

Documents   There are two kinds of documents:

- Electronic documents, such as Microsoft Word files
- Paper documents, also called hard copies

Meetings   Examples are face-to-face meetings and teleconferences.

World Wide Web tools   Websites, email, electronic bulletin (or discussion) boards, and collaborative work-management tools fall into this category.

You use these tools and techniques to generate the output of the Information Distribution process.

Output of Information Distribution

The output of the Information Distribution process is, well, the distribution of information. This distribution (or communication) of information falls into two categories:

Formal communication   This refers to communicating the information as planned, such as via regular status and progress information at scheduled times, such as every Wednesday.

Informal communication   This refers to the communication of information on an as-needed basis. For example, the program sponsor can ask you for information that is not part of the regular schedule of distributing information.

So, information distribution is critical to successful program execution. The program execution is the execution of its components, and some of the components will be managed and executed as projects.

Chartering Constituent Projects

Recall that a program consists of projects and non-project tasks. The projects need to be initiated and for that they need to be chartered. A project charter authorizes a project by assigning a project manager to it and allocating resources such as funding. This task is part of initiating the project, and is performed by using the Authorize Projects process covered in Chapter 3. This section summarizes important points related to this topic.

Initiation   The initiation of a constituent project begins by accomplishing the following:

- Assign the project manager.
- Develop and approve the project charter.
- Identify a project sponsor. Depending on the performing organization and the project, the program manager is a possible project sponsor.
- Approve project funding.

All these items are included in the output of the Authorize Projects process. The projects can be initiated during any of the program phases except the closing phase. The project manager is named in the project charter.

Project charter   The project charter is a high-level document that summarizes the business need, understanding of customer requirements, and how the new product or service will satisfy these requirements. To be specific, the project charter should include the following information items:

- Project justification, which includes the purpose of the project and the business case for the project, which in turn may include return on investment
- Project description that includes the business need that the project addresses and the high-level product requirements
- Project requirements based on the needs of customer, sponsor, and other stakeholders
- Description of how the project contributes to the program objectives and benefits
- List of participating functional departments of the organization and their roles in the project
- Organizational, environmental, and external assumptions and constraints
- Summary of high-level project schedule, including milestones
- Summary of project budget
- Assignment of a project manager, specifying the authority level of the project manager and defining stakeholder influences

The project charter authorizes the project manager to use the allocated resources to complete the project work. This is just one element of the governance structure.

Exam Spotlight

Remember that formally speaking, the project charters are prepared external to project management. Therefore, the project approval and funding is external to the project management boundaries. However, practically speaking, the would-be project manager may actually be involved in writing the project charter or a part of it.

Governance   The Authorize Projects process also specifies the reporting requirements. Project managers generally report to the program managers, and you need to determine the reporting requirements up front. You also need to determine the following:

- Management control points where your (program) control ends and the project manager takes over.
- The level of authority, including control and influence to be given to the project manager.
- Priorities and roadmaps for all the projects.
- The appropriate timesheet management, including time-reporting procedure. If your organization has a PMO, it may already have this procedure in place.

The governance structure also depends on the organizational structure discussed in Chapter 1, "Project, Portfolio, and Program: Mind the Gap." Depending on the organizational structure, you may need to use one or more of the following techniques in overseeing and coordinating projects:

- Negotiations with executives, project managers, and functional managers for various things, such as resources
- Networking
- Matrix management, discussed in Chapter 1, in a cross-functional environment
- Training for project managers and project team members to improve performance
- Conflict resolution
- Career development that includes identifying individual aspirations and career goals, identifying the career path relevant to available roles, and mentoring and coaching

All these techniques are described at different places in this book. The Authorize Projects process approves project funding, which is needed to secure resources needed for performing the project work. The project governance structure is further discussed in Chapter 8, "Monitoring and Controlling the Program."

Resources   For each project, you need to do the following:

- Identify the required resources
- Obtain the identified resources

- Assemble the project team
- Define roles and responsibilities of human resources in the team
- Establish the ground rules for the team

Some of these tasks will be performed by the project manager or in conjunction with the project manager, depending on the management control points. You also need to define procedures for budget allocation and a method for processing the change requests related to the budget.

You, the program manager, will need to optimize the use of resources across the constituent projects by using techniques such as resource leveling, discussed in Chapter 5.

 Real World Scenario

Starting Projects in a Program

The Excelsior, Inc., a nonprofit organization, is about to start a program named Mind the Digital Gap. The goal of the program is to provide computers and Internet connections in selected underprivileged communities all over the country at affordable costs. The program was split into multiple projects, including the following:

- Feasibility project. This project conducts the feasibility study to justify the program by verifying that it will reap the intended benefits and will meet the strategic goals of the organization.

- Building project. The goal of this project is to gather (build from parts or acquire) a given number of computers in a predetermined time period.

- Marketing project. The goal of the project is two-prong: to sign up the Internet service providers (ISPs) and the computer vendors to help the program, and to sell the program to the community members by raising awareness for the need of getting connected.

- Sales project. This project's goal is to handle all the purchases and sales in the program.

The feasibility project will be performed in phase one (called pre-program setup) of the program life cycle, before the program is chartered. The building project will be initiated in phase four (called deliver the benefits).

Marketing and sales projects will be initiated in phase three (called establishing program infrastructure).

As said earlier in this section, conflict resolution is one of the techniques that you use while coordinating the constituent projects. Conflict management is a general management skill that is used in many program management processes, such as Direct and Manage Program Execution and Develop Program Team.

Understanding Conflict Management

The purpose of conflict management is to nourish positive working relationships among team members, which results in increased productivity. The common sources for conflicts include the following:

- Scarce resources resulting in unsatisfied needs
- Scheduling priorities
- Personal work styles
- Perceptions, values, feelings, and emotions
- Power struggle

You can reduce the number of conflicts by setting the ground rules, clearly defining the roles and goals, and implementing solid project/program management practices.

> Generally speaking, differences of opinion should not be considered as sources of conflict. If managed properly, differences can be very healthy and can lead to better solutions and therefore increase productivity.

Initially, the parties to a conflict should be given the opportunity to resolve it themselves. If they fail to resolve the conflict and it begins to become a negative factor for the program (or the project), the program manager or the project manager should facilitate the conflict resolution, usually in private and using a direct and collaborative approach. If the conflict continues, you may have no option other than using the formal procedures, including disciplinary actions as a last resort.

The first step in conflict management is to find the origin of the conflict by analyzing its nature and type, which may involve asking questions. You can meet with or interview the parties involved in the conflict. The next step is to determine the management strategy for the conflict at hand. Different management strategies to deal with the conflicts are summarized here:

Accommodating   The accommodating, also called *smoothing*, strategy is opposite of the competition strategy. In this strategy, one party attempts to meet other party's needs at the expense of its own. This may be a justifiable strategy when the concerns of the accommodating party are less significant than the concerns of the other party in the context of the program. Sometimes it's used as a goodwill gesture. However, it is a lose-win (accommodating party loses and the accommodated party wins) approach, and the accommodating party runs the risk of losing credibility and influence in the future.

Avoiding   This is the strategy in which at least one party to the conflict ignores (or withdraws) from the conflict and decides not to deal with the problem. This strategy can be used by the program (or project) manager to provide a cooling-off period, to collect more information, or when the issue is not critical. However, if the issue is critical, this is the worst resolution strategy and can gives rise to a lose-lose situation if both parties withdraw, or a yield-lose situation if one party withdraws. This strategy is also called the *withdrawal* strategy.

Collaborating   This strategy is based on reaching consensus among the parties in the conflict. Both parties work together to explore several solutions and agree on the one that satisfies the needs and concerns of both parties. This is a win-win strategy and is generally considered the best of all the strategies, as it helps build commitment and promotes good will for each other. This approach is also known by other names, such as *confronting*, *problem solving*, and *negotiating*.

Competing   In this approach, one party uses any available means to get its way, often at the expense of the other party. This is a win-lose situation. It can be justified under some situations, such as when the basic rights of a party in conflict are at stake or to set a precedent. However, if used unfairly from a power position, for example, using this approach as a part of management style, it can be destructive for team development. This strategy can cause the conflict to escalate and the losing party may attempt to retaliate.

Compromising   In the compromising strategy both parties gain something as well as give up something. So this is a lose-win/lose-win strategy. You can use this strategy to achieve temporary solutions and to avoid a damaging power struggle when there is a time pressure. But be aware of the downside of this approach, which is that both parties can look at the solution as a lose-lose situation and can be distracted from the merits of the issues involved. This way, this short-term solution can hurt the long-term objectives of the project and the program.

Forcing   This technique uses the power of someone's position to resolve a conflict: "I'm right because I'm your boss." It involves imposing one party's viewpoint on another, and the solution is a win-lose. It is often used by managers in emergency or urgent situations when time is of the essence and quick decisions and actions are required. It can also be used to deal with unpopular issues such as reorganization, staff cutbacks, budget cuts, and schedule-compression techniques such as fast-tracking. Its upside is that it takes less time than many other techniques. However, its downside is that the party on which the decision is imposed may live with hard feelings, and the problem may reappear at a later time. Therefore, this technique should be used as only a last resort.

 Real World Scenario

Conflict-Resolution Techniques

Monica is a project manager who reports to Rick, the program manager. Email is one of the communication method that Monica uses. Monica has decided that the recipient of an email message does not need to know who else has received the same email, so she types the email addresses of all the recipients in the Bcc field of the email header.

Rick calls Monica to his office and asks why she is doing that. Rick does not like this approach. Rick and Monica discuss this issue for about half an hour but fail to agree. At the end, Rick says, "Do me a favor, Monica; please write the email addresses of all the recipients in the Cc field and no address in the Bcc field. I want to know who exactly received the email. Now, excuse me; I have to go to this meeting."

What conflict resolution technique did Rick use? Forcing, of course!

Monica was left with hard feelings. After a few weeks, she adopted her previous policy again. Some other project managers followed. This time Rick called a meeting of all the project managers and started the meeting with discussing all the problems that he has noticed so far in the email communication within the program. The issue was discussed in an open way and a collective decision was made in order to improve the overall email communication. Everybody agreed with the decision.

What approach was this? The collaborating approach.

All the conflict-resolution approaches or techniques are summarized in Table 7.2.

TABLE 7.2   Conflict-Resolution Strategies

Technique	Description	Used ...	Results
Accommodating/ smoothing	One party retreats and attempts to meet other party's needs at the expense of its own.	... when the concerns of the accommodating party are less significant than the concerns of the accommodated party.	Lose-win
Avoiding/withdrawing	At least one party tries to ignore the problem.	... when a cooling-off period is needed or when the issue involved is not critical.	Lose-lose if both parties withdraw
Collaborating/ confronting/ negotiating/ problem solving	Both parties work together to explore several solutions and agree on the one that satisfies the needs and concerns of both parties.	... whenever you can. This is generally the best approach.	Win-win
Competing	At least one party uses any available means to get its way, often at the expense of the other party.	... when the basic rights of a party in conflict are at stake.	Lose-win or lose-lose

TABLE 7.2   Conflict-Resolution Strategies *(continued)*

Technique	Description	Used ...	Results
Compromising	Strategy both parties gain something as well as give up something.	... to achieve temporary solutions under time pressure.	Lose-win, but can be looked upon as lose-lose
Forcing	Uses the power of the position to resolve a conflict.	... in emergency or urgent situations when time is of the essence.	Lose-win

The purpose of conflict management is to nourish positive working relationships among the team members, which results in increased productivity. So resolving a conflict can also be looked upon as a team-development activity.

The Three Big Takeaways

The three most important takeaways from this chapter are the following:

- Direct and Manage Program Execution is a high-level process to produce the program deliverables. To accomplish that you need to do two things:

    - Acquire a program team and develop it to perform the program activities.

    - Procure the items that cannot be produced by the program or the constituent projects.

- You implement the procurement plan by requesting seller responses, evaluating the seller responses, selecting the sellers based on the evaluation criteria, and negotiating and signing a contract with the selected sellers.

- You use the Perform Quality Assurance process for applying the planned systematic quality activities to ensure that the program complies with the agreed-upon quality policies and standards.

Summary

The program management plan is executed by using the processes in the Executing process group. The high-level process in this group is the Direct and Manage Project Execution process, whose main goal is to produce the program deliverables. To make that happen, you need to put together a program team, and then you and the team need to perform multiple actions, such as performing schedule activities, training and managing the program team members, and obtaining proposals from the seller for the program items that need to be procured. These actions are performed by using processes of the Executing process group. For example, you put together a program team by using the Acquire Program Team process. The main output of this process is the program staff assignments, which become the input to the Develop Program Team process. This process uses training and other team-building techniques to develop a coherent and efficient team with high performance.

If the performing organization lacks the required resources, you may need to obtain the corresponding products, services, or results from outside the program team and the constituent projects' teams to complete the program scope. The procurement plan is implemented by using the Request Seller Responses and Select Sellers processes, which involve obtaining seller responses, selecting the sellers based on the responses, and reaching an agreement with the selected sellers, such as a contract to obtain (procure) the products, services, or results.

In addition to performing the program work to produce the program deliverables, a significant task to perform during the program execution is quality assurance. The goal of quality assurance is to ensure that the program meets the planned quality policies and standards. All these processes are coordinated by a glue called *communication*. The communication process in the Executing process group is called the Information Distribution process, which is used to provide the stakeholders with needed accurate information in a timely manner.

Execution, along with other aspects of the program, needs to be monitored and controlled. This is the topic of the next chapter.

Exam's-Eye View

Comprehend

- A program is executed within the managerial and technical infrastructure established during phase three of the program life cycle.

- Program execution is the implementation of the program management plan according to the program schedule. Therefore, the Direct and Manage Program Execution process has the program management plan and the program schedule as its input, and work results such as deliverables as its output.

- Contracts are negotiated and signed as part of the Select Sellers process.

Look Out

- Approved change requests and recommendations for corrective and preventive actions are also input items to the Direct and Manage Program Execution process. These items are integrated with the program management plan before their implementation.

- The Direct and Manage Program Execution process is responsible for ensuring that all transition plans are executed at both the program and project level.

- Both the Acquire Program Team and Develop Program Team processes belong to the Executing process group.

- Continuous process improvement through process analysis is part of quality assurance.

- The projects can be initiated during any of the program phases except the closing phase.

Memorize

- Direct and Manage Program Execution belongs to the Integration Management knowledge area.

- The Request Seller Responses and Select Sellers processes belong to the Procurement Management knowledge area.

- The managerial and technical infrastructure in which the program will be executed is established in phase three of the program life cycle.

Exam Essentials

Program management and technical infrastructure   Phase three of the program life cycle establishes the infrastructure, including the management and the technical components. This is the infrastructure in which the program is executed. Deploying uniform standards, infrastructure, resources, tools, and processes establishes program-wide consistency that helps in making informed program decisions.

Direct and Manage Program Execution   The program work defined in the program management plan is performed by using the Direct and Manage Program Execution process. While executing this process, you will be interacting with other processes and departments in your organization. The planned benefits of the program are delivered by the Direct and Manage Program Execution process. Therefore, a large portion of the program budget is expended on this process.

Information distribution   Data is collected from multiple sources, such as projects, and consolidated to generate information needed by the program stakeholders. To accomplish this data storage, manipulation, and retrieval, tools such as database management systems (DBMS) can be used. To satisfy the varied needs of different stakeholders, multiple information distribution methods can be used.

Chartering constituent projects   The charters for the constituent projects are issued at the program level by using the Authorize Projects process. For each project, you need to determine the appropriate level for the project manager's authority, and you need to define a procedure for budget allocations and for processing budget-related change requests.

Key Terms and Definitions

Acquire Program Team   A process used to obtain the program team members needed to perform the program work.

asynchronous communication   A communication method in which the two communicating entities do not have to be present on both ends of the communication line at the same time. Email is an example of asynchronous communication because when the sender of the email pushes the Send button, the intended recipient of the e-mail message does not have to be logged on to the email server.

communication   An exchange of information between persons and groups by using an effectively common system of signs, symbols, and behavior.

continuous process improvement   An iterative method for improving the quality of all processes.

contract   A mutually binding legal agreement between a buyer and a seller that obligates the seller to provide the specified product, service, or result and obligates the buyer to make the payment for it.

data   A raw fact or figure, such as cost equal to one million dollars.

database   An information system that contains a structured collection of records, such as student ID with the student name and the grades in different courses attached to the identification.

database management system (DBMS)   A set of software programs that allows a user to manage a database—that is, to store, manipulate, and retrieve the data in a database.

Develop Program Team   A process used to improve individual and group competencies to enhance the program performance.

Direct and Manage Program Execution   A process used to manage various interfaces in the project to execute the program work smoothly with the goal of delivering the planned benefits.

Information Distribution   A process used to provide the needed accurate information to the program stakeholders in a timely fashion.

Perform Quality Assurance A process used to regularly evaluate the program performance to assure that the program complies with the planned quality standards.

project charter A document issued by the project initiator or the project sponsor that, when signed by an appropriate person in the performing organization, authorizes the project by naming the project manager and specifying the authority level of the project manager.

quality assurance The application of the planned systematic quality activities.

quality audit A structured and independent review to determine whether program-execution activities comply with the policies, processes, and procedures determined in the program management plan. It verifies the implementation of approved change requests, corrective actions, defect repairs, and preventive actions.

Request Seller Responses A process used to obtain responses in terms of quotations, bids, offers, and proposals from sellers outside the program team for their product or services needed for the program.

Select Sellers A process used to select sellers based on their responses and negotiate written contracts with the selected sellers.

synchronous communication A communication method in which the two communicating entities have to be present on both ends of the communication line at the same time. An example is a phone conversation.

work authorization system A subsystem of the overall program management system that determines how the program work will be properly authorized in order to ensure that the work is performed in the right sequence by the right individuals or groups at the right time.

Review Questions

1. The infrastructure for a program is established in which phase of the program life cycle?
    A. One
    B. Two
    C. Three
    D. Four

2. All of the following items are input to the Direct and Manage Program Execution process except:
    A. Approved change requests
    B. Program management plan
    C. Program schedule
    D. Implemented change requests

3. All of the following items are input to the Acquire Program Team process except:
    A. Staffing management plan
    B. Staffing assignments
    C. Program schedule
    D. Program budget

4. The output of the Develop Program Team process includes:
    A. Performance assessment and personnel records
    B. Updates to training records and staffing management plan
    C. Performance assessment and updates to team competency assessments
    D. Staffing management plan and personnel records

5. Quality assurance at the program level includes all of the following except:
    A. Cross-program quality activities
    B. Cross-project quality activities
    C. Quality activities for the non-project but program-related work
    D. Quality activities for some selected projects at the project level

6. The input to the Request Seller Responses process includes:
    A. Program vendors list and request for quotations (RFQ)
    B. Program preferred vendors list and evaluation criteria
    C. Evaluation criteria and request for information (RFI)
    D. RFI and RFQ

7. The input to the Select Sellers process includes all of the following except:

   A. Proposals from vendors

   B. Selected sellers list

   C. Evaluation criteria

   D. Qualified sellers list

8. The output of the Information Distribution process includes:

   A. Formal and informal communication of information

   B. Information requests

   C. Stakeholder analysis chart

   D. Communication messages to be delivered

9. Which of the following processes will be performed first?

   A. Acquire Program Team

   B. Develop Program Team

   C. Program Schedule Development

   D. Create PWBS

10. The Information Distribution process is part of the:

    A. Initiating process group

    B. Planning process group

    C. Executing process group

    D. Communication process group

11. You are in the middle of managing a program execution. You want to initiate a project within the program. Which document will you use to authorize the project?

    A. Program charter

    B. Project charter

    C. Authorize Projects

    D. Project management plan

12. You heard a program manager saying that she needed data storage and retrieval tools to perform a process. Which process was she most likely referring to?

    A. Information Distribution

    B. Database Management

    C. Communication Management

    D. Human Resource Management

13. A work authorization system is used to perform which process?

    A. Information Distribution

    B. Perform Quality Assurance

    C. Direct and Manage Program Execution

    D. Human Resource Management

14. You are in the process of developing the program team. Which of the following tools and techniques will you usually *not* use to accomplish this?

    A. Procurement

    B. Training

    C. Mentoring

    D. Co-location

15. You are in the process of performing quality assurance. Which of the following is included in the tools and techniques that you will use to accomplish this?

    A. Procurement

    B. Training

    C. Process analysis

    D. Work authorization system

Answers to Review Questions

1.   C.

C is the correct answer because establishing program management and technical infrastructure is phase three.

A is an incorrect answer because phase one is the pre-program setup phase.

B is an incorrect answer because phase two is the program setup phase.

D is an incorrect answer because phase four is the phase to deliver the program benefits.

2.   D.

D is the correct answer because implemented change requests are a work result and therefore an output of the Direct and Manage Program Execution process.

A is an incorrect answer because approved change requests are integrated with the program management plan and therefore are input to the Direct and Manage Program Execution process.

B and C are incorrect answers because the program management plan and the program schedule are input to the Direct and Manage Program Execution process.

3.   B.

B is the correct answer because staffing assignments are an output of the Acquire Program Team process.

A, C, and D are incorrect answers because the staffing management plan, program schedule, and program budget are the input items to the Acquire Program Team process.

4.   C.

C is the correct answer because the output items of the Develop Program Team process are team assessment, updates to training records, and updates to team competency assessments.

A and D are incorrect answers because the staffing management plan and personnel records are input to the Develop Program Team process.

B is an incorrect answer because the staffing management plan is an input to the Develop Program Team process.

5.   D.

D is the correct answer because quality activities at the project level are the responsibility of project managers.

A, B, and C are incorrect answers because all these are included in program-level quality assurance.

6. B.

B is the correct answer because a program preferred vendors list and evaluation criteria are input to the Request Seller Responses process.

A, C, and D are incorrect answers because the RFI and the RFQ are the output of the Request Seller Responses process.

7. B.

B is the correct answer because the selected sellers list is an output of the Select Sellers process.

A, C, and D are incorrect answers because all these items are input to the Select Sellers process.

8. A.

A is the correct answer because formal and informal communication of information is the output of the Information Distribution process.

B, C, and D are incorrect answers because all these items are input to the Information Distribution process.

9. D.

D is the correct answer because PWBS is an output of the Create PWBS process and is an input to the Schedule Development process. The schedule is an input to the Acquire Program Team process, which generates the team assignments that are necessary to make before you could develop the team.

A is an incorrect answer because the Acquire Program Team process takes the program schedule as an input, and the program schedule is generated by using the Schedule Development process.

B is an incorrect answer because the Develop Program Team process takes staffing assignments as an input, and the staffing assignments are generated by using the Acquire Program Team process.

C is an incorrect answer because the Schedule Development process takes a PWBS as an input, and the PWBS is generated by using the Create PWBS process.

10. C.

C is the correct answer because the Information Distribution process belongs to the Executing process group.

A and B are incorrect answers because the Information Distribution process belongs to the Executing process group.

D is an incorrect answer because there is no process group called Communication.

11. B.

B is the correct answer because the project charter, created during the Authorize Projects process, initiates a project by naming the project manager.

A is incorrect because the program charter is used to initiate a program.

C is incorrect because Authorize Projects is a process that generates a project charter.

D is incorrect because a project management plan is created after the project is initiated.

12. A.

A is the correct answer because data storage and retrieval tools are used in storing and retrieving data needed to generate information that is distributed to the stakeholders.

B is incorrect because database management is not a standard program management process.

C and D are incorrect because Communication Management and Human Resource Management are knowledge areas and not processes.

13. C.

C is the correct answer because the program work defined in the program management plan is performed by using the Direct and Manage Program Execution process. Therefore this process needs the work authorization system.

A and B are incorrect because these processes do not generally need to use a work authorization system.

D is incorrect because Human Resource Management is a knowledge area and not a process.

14. A.

A is the correct answer because procurement is a technique used to acquire the program team.

B, C, and D are incorrect because all of these are valid tools and techniques used in the Develop Program Team process.

15. C.

C is the correct answer because process analysis is one of the tools used in performing quality assurance.

A is incorrect because procurement is used in the Acquire Program Team process and not in Perform Quality Assurance.

B is incorrect because training is used in the Develop Program Team process and not in Perform Quality Assurance.

D is incorrect because a work authorization system is used in the Direct and Manage Program Execution process and not in Perform Quality Assurance.

hapter

8

Monitoring and Controlling the Program

THE PGMP EXAM CONTENT FROM THE INI-
TIATING, EXECUTING, AND CONTROLLING
THE PROGRAM PERFORMANCE DOMAIN
COVERED IN THIS CHAPTER INCLUDES THE
FOLLOWING OBJECTIVES:

- ✓ **2.6 Define meaningful measurement criteria for success by analyzing stakeholder expectations and requirements across the constituent projects in order to accurately control program performance.**

- ✓ **4.1 Consolidate project/program data (documented issues, status reviews, risks, financial reports, resources, etc.), using predefined reporting tools and methods to monitor program performance.**

- ✓ **4.5 Capture program status and data by ensuring the population of the program management information system in order to maintain accurate and current program information for the use of stakeholders.**

- ✓ **5.1 Analyze variance of costs, schedule, quality and risks by comparing actual values to planned values from the program plan, trends, and extrapolation in order to identify corrective actions necessary.**

- ✓ **5.2 Identify potential corrective actions by forecasting program outcomes using simulations, what-if scenarios and causal analysis in order to incorporate corrective actions into the program management plan.**

✓ **5.3 Manage change in accordance with the change management plan to control scope, quality, schedule, co[st] and contracts.**

✓ **5.4 Address program level issues by identifying and selecting a course of action by taking into account the program constraints and objectives in order to enable continued program progress.**

You need to monitor and control your program continually. Executing a program means executing the program work according to the program management plan based on approved budget, schedule, and scope. *Monitoring*, in general, means watching the course, and *controlling* means taking action to either stay the course or to change the wrong course. You monitor the program by generating, collecting, and distributing information about the program performance against the planned performance. The deviations of the performance results from the plan may indicate that some changes to the original program plan are required. Other change requests may come from stakeholders, such as expanding the program scope by adding new requirements. You control all these changes by influencing the factors that generate them, processing them through a system called Integrated Change Control (which contains the Integrated Change Control process), evaluating their impact across the program, and ensuring the implementation of the approved change requests. Also based on the past performance, you make a forecast.

So, the core question in this chapter is how to monitor and control a program. In search of an answer, we will explore three avenues in the area of Monitoring and Controlling: performance, changes, and forecasts.

Monitoring and Controlling the Program: The Big Picture

You monitor and control your program by monitoring and controlling the program performance, changes, and risks. This monitoring and controlling includes enabling the monitoring, and controlling the projects by establishing the project governance structure and initiating the projects in the program as part of program phase four.

These topics are included in the exam objectives covered in this chapter.

The Exam Roadmap

The following table presents each PgMP exam objective covered in this chapter, along with its explanation:

Exam Objective	What It Really Means
4.1 Consolidate project/program data (documented issues, status reviews, risks, financial reports, resources, etc.), using predefined reporting tools and methods to monitor program performance. 4.5 Capture program status and data by ensuring the population of the program management information system in order to maintain accurate and current program information for the use of stakeholders.	Understand the Performance Reporting process. You must understand how the data from different projects is consolidated to prepare the performance reports. Data storage, consolidation, and retrieval are discussed in Chapter 7, "Executing the Program." You must understand the tools and techniques used in performance reporting.

Exam Objective	What It Really Means
5.1 Analyze variance of costs, schedule, quality and risks by comparing actual values to planned values from the program plan, trends, and extrapolation in order to identify corrective actions necessary. 2.6 Define meaningful measurement criteria for success by analyzing stakeholder expectations and requirements across the constituent projects in order to accurately control program performance.	You must know how to monitor the program cost, schedule, quality, and risks by using the following processes: • Cost Control • Schedule Control • Quality Control • Risk Monitoring and Control Understand the metrics, tools, and techniques used to measure the performance of the program, including the performance across the constituent projects.
5.2 Identify potential corrective actions by forecasting program outcomes using simulations, what-if scenarios and causal analysis in order to incorporate corrective actions into the program management plan.	You must understand the Monitor and Control Program Work process. Understand tools and techniques used in the following: • Quality Control • Cost Control • Risk Monitoring and Control • Schedule Control You should also understand the parameters in the earned value technique used for forecasting.
5.3 Manage change in accordance with the change management plan to control scope, quality, schedule, cost, and contracts.	You must understand the Integrated Change Control process. You should also know how the Program Contract Administration process works.
5.4 Address program level issues by identifying and selecting a course of action by taking into account the program constraints and objectives in order to enable continued program progress.	You must understand the Issue Management and Control process. You should know what tools and techniques you can use in performing issue management.

The topics covered in these exam objectives apply to all the processes used in monitoring and controlling the program.

Understanding Monitoring and Controlling

Monitoring and controlling are related concepts: monitoring refers to watching the course, whereas controlling means taking action to either stay the course or to change the wrong course. Accordingly, program monitoring involves performance measurements and recommendations for corrective and preventive actions based on the variance of the measured performance from the planned performance, and controlling involves implementing the approved preventive and corrective actions.

A program is largely executed through executing the constituent projects, but it also involves executing non-project program-related work. Program Monitoring and Controlling involves monitoring and controlling the work on program packages, which includes the following:

- Obtaining the progress and status information about the program-related non-project work
- Obtaining and consolidating data on the progress and status of the constituent projects
- Monitoring interfaces of the program with the program governance structure to ensure that the organization has clear and accurate information about the following:
  - Current status of the program benefits delivery
  - Benefits expected to be delivered in the future

The processes performed to accomplish these tasks are listed in Table 8.1 along with their major output items and the knowledge areas to which they belong.

TABLE 8.1   Processes for Executing a Program

Knowledge Area	Program Execution Process	Major Output
Integration management	1. Integrated Change Control 2. Resource Control 3. Monitor and Control Program Work 4. Issue Management and Control	1. Approvals and rejections of change requests 2. Expenditure and utilization reports 3. Change requests and forecasts 4. Proposed resolutions
Scope management	Scope Control	Approvals and rejections of the scope-related changes
Time management	Schedule Control	Change requests and updates to the program schedule
Cost management	Cost Control	Change requests and updates to program budget
Quality management	Perform Quality Control	Inspection reports
Communication management	1. Communication Control 2. Performance Reporting	1. Change requests and updates to the communication management plan 2. Performance reports and communication messages
Risk management	Risk Monitoring and Control	Risk-related change requests and updates to the risk register
Procurement management	Program Contract Administration	Change requests and approved payment requests

Figure 8.1 presents some examples of interaction between various processes of the Monitoring and Controlling process group.

FIGURE 8.1   The main interactions among the processes in the Monitoring and Controlling process group

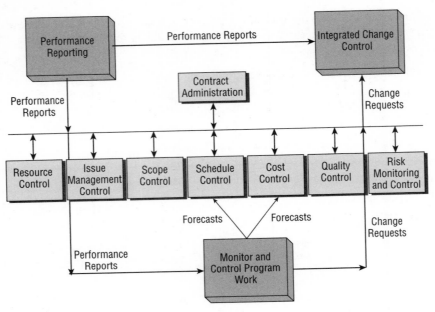

Constituent projects are important components of any program. To perform the Monitoring and Controlling tasks effectively, you need each project's governance structure, which is established in phase four of the program life cycle.

Delivering the Program Benefits: Phase Four

Once the program infrastructure (phase three) has been established and the program has passed the phase-three gate review, the core work of the program through its constituent projects can begin. The purpose of phase four of the program life cycle is to establish the project governance structure for monitoring and controlling the projects, initiate the projects in the program, and coordinate the deliverables to create the incremental benefits for the program. Therefore, this phase is also called the benefits delivery phase. The program management team is responsible for coordinating the constituent project activities to achieve these incremental benefits, which could not be achieved by managing each of these projects as a stand-alone effort. The following activities are performed during phase four of the program life cycle:

Project oversight   This includes the following:

- Establish the project governance structure to monitor and control the projects.
- Initiate constituent projects to achieve the program objectives.
- Ensure that the project managers adhere to the established project management methodologies.
- Ensure that the project deliverables meet their business and technical requirements.

Communication and coordination   This includes the following activities:

- Coordinate the cross-project activities and manage the dependencies among the constituent projects and dependencies of the program on other programs in the portfolio.
- Coordinate efficient use of resources across the program and project activities.
- Perform effective communication with the program stakeholders and the program governance board.

Changes and actions   This category includes the following activities:

- Identify the changes in the program environment that may impact the program management plan or the planned program benefits.
- Review change requests and authorize the needed additional work required to implement the approved change requests.
- Identify issues and ensure the required approved corrective actions are taken.
- Identify, monitor, and track risks and ensure that the planned risk responses are implemented.

Performance measurements   Phase four includes the following performance-related activities:

- Analyze the program performance and monitor how to measure up to the program management plan.
- Set thresholds for the variation of the actual benefit delivery from the planned benefit delivery, and apply corrective actions if the threshold is not met; that is, if the variation exceeds a predetermined limit.

You, the program manager, review the efforts of the constituent project teams. You will also be determining and managing the critical interfaces between the projects in your program and between the program and its projects. In a large program you may share this responsibility with the program management office (PMO).

Most of the activities in phase four are of iterative nature and can be repeated as often as necessary. This phase continues until the program benefits have been realized by completing the program or until the program is terminated for some reason.

A general task during the benefits delivery phase is to continually manage the transition from the as-is state to the to-be state; that is, from the actual performance to the expected performance. This and most of the other activities in this phase are performed as part of the Monitoring and Controlling processes discussed in this chapter.

Certain activities in monitoring and controlling a program need to be integrated.

Integrating Program Monitoring and Controlling

Activities for monitoring and controlling a program need to be integrated. This integration is accomplished through the following four processes:

- Integrated Change Control
- Resource Control
- Monitor and Control Program Work
- Issue Management and Control

Performing Integrated Change Control

Changes in a program are bound to occur. They can come from various sources, such as the following:

- Changes (and corrective and preventive actions) needed to bring the program back on the track when the actual performance is not in line with the planned expectations.
- Change requests made by the stakeholders.
- Changes that could originate from interfaces internal and external to the program. An example of an internal interface is the interface of the program with the non-project work or the interface between two constituent projects. An example of an external interface is a government regulation related to the program work.
- Other changes that have crept into the program without approval. These changes need to be identified and controlled.

Part of controlling a change is to put it through a process of approval or disapproval. In other words, the requests for changes and recommendations for corrective and preventive actions must be reviewed before implementation by using the Integrated Change Control process, which manages the changes across the program in a coordinated way. These changes may belong to various aspects of the program, including cost, scope, schedule, and quality.

The Integrated Change Control process, along with its input and output, is depicted in Figure 8.2.

FIGURE 8.2   The Integrated Change Control process: input and output

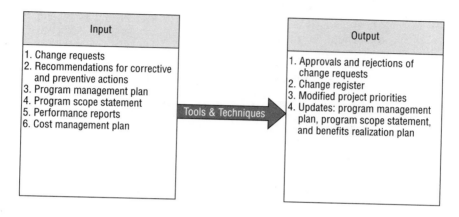

Input	Output
1. Change requests 2. Recommendations for corrective and preventive actions 3. Program management plan 4. Program scope statement 5. Performance reports 6. Cost management plan	1. Approvals and rejections of change requests 2. Change register 3. Modified project priorities 4. Updates: program management plan, program scope statement, and benefits realization plan

Tools & Techniques

Input to Integrated Change Control

A major task of the Integrated Change Control process is to review change requests and recommendations for corrective and preventive actions for approval or disapproval. Therefore, change requests and recommendations for corrective and preventive actions are the obvious input to the Integrated Change Control process. These and other input items are discussed in the following.

Change requests   These are the requests that will be evaluated for approval or disapproval. These change requests largely come from various monitoring processes, such as Monitor and Control Program Work, Resource Control, Schedule Control, Issue Management and Control, and Cost Control.

Recommendations for corrective and preventive actions   These are the recommendations that will be evaluated for approval or disapproval. These recommendations largely come from monitoring the program performance. Corrective actions are proposed to bring the program back in line with the program management plan, and preventive actions are suggested to reduce the probability of negative consequences associated with risks.

The program management plan   The program management plan is used to review the change requests and recommendations for preventive and corrective actions. It will also need to be updated after a change request or a recommendation is approved.

The program scope statement The program scope statement is used to review the change requests and recommendations for preventive and corrective actions. It will also need to be updated after a scope-related change request or a recommendation is approved.

Performance reports Performance reports are important in the review of change requests and recommendations for corrective and preventive actions. These are input to most of the monitoring and controlling processes and are generated by using the Performance Reporting process.

The cost management plan The cost management plan is used during the review of the change requests and recommendations for corrective and preventive actions for reasons such as how they affect the cost management plan.

   With these input items in place, you apply some tools and techniques to generate the output.

Tools and Techniques for Integrated Change Control

You can use a program (or project) management information system and a configuration management system to implement the Integrated Change Control process. You can also use the expertise of the stakeholders to approve and reject change requests. The following are the tools and techniques available for the Integrated Change Control process.

The management information system This is a collection of tools and techniques (manual and automated) used to gather, integrate, and disseminate the output of program (and project) management processes. This system is used to facilitate processes from the initiating stage all the way to the closing stage. A simple example is a software tool that lets you create a schedule. Another example of the components of the program/project management information system could be a document management system to create, review, change, and approve the documents to facilitate the change control procedure.

Such a management information system might also have tools that can help the program management team implement the Integrated Change Control process.

The configuration management system This system is used to process the changes, which includes the following:

- Submitting changes
- Tracking the reviews of the changes
- Defining approval levels for changes
- Validating the implementation of approved changes

A configuration management system may be a part of the program management information system.

The change control system This system controls the change process to assure that only approved changes are implemented. This system may be an integrated part of the configuration management system.

Performance measurements You will need to analyze the program performance and monitor how to measure up to the program management plan. Also, you will need to set thresholds for the variation of the actual benefit delivery from the planned benefit delivery, and apply corrective actions if the threshold is not met; that is, if the variation exceeds a predetermined limit. Performance measurements will be discussed throughout this chapter.

Expert judgment   The program management team can use the experts on the change control board to make approval or rejection decisions about change requests.

The rejection or approval of the change request is an obvious output of the Integrated Change Control process, but there are others, as you'll see next.

Output of Integrated Change Control

The main output of the Integrated Change Control process is the approval or disapproval of a given change request. This and other output items are discussed in the following.

Approvals and rejections of change requests   Each request for change and each recommendation for corrective or preventive action is reviewed and is either approved or rejected. Upon approval a change or a recommendation will be implemented.

The change register   This document contains the record of change requests; for example, the information about where the change request originated from, the status of the request, etc.

Modified project priorities   During coordinating changes across the program, the priorities among the constituent projects may need to be modified. For example, a low-priority project may be escalated to be a high-priority project to deal with a changed situation.

Updates   As a result of monitoring and controlling program changes, the following documents may need modifications:

- The program management plan
- The program scope statement
- The benefits realization plan

The updates may include modifying the baselines, such as cost, schedule, and scope baselines, which will mean modifying the performance measurement baseline. As an example, a change in scope will mean you need to modify the scope statement, which in turn will mean you need to modify the program management plan. With the change of scope, the benefits may also change and thereby the benefits realization plan will need to be modified.

Other Integrated Change Control Tasks

The discussion so far has focused on approving or rejecting the change requests (and recommendations for corrective and preventive actions). In addition to approval and refusal of change requests, the Integrated Change Control process includes the following tasks:

- Escalate the change requests; that is, move a change request from lower priority to higher priority.
- Determine if a change has occurred.
- Influence factors that create changes.
- Determine how and when the changes will be applied.

Exam Spotlight

You must adapt the change processing system for approving and rejecting change requests to the culture and structure of the performing organization. For effective change management, you must have skills in communication, brainstorming, negotiating, and identifying and analyzing the factors that are driving the change.

In determining which changes and recommendations for corrective and preventive actions should be approved, program goals and objectives should be included in the approval criteria.

The change requests that are input to the Integrated Change Control process are generated by most of the Monitoring and Controlling processes, including the Resource Control process that I'll discuss next.

Controlling Resources

As you already know, the program execution is the implementation of the program management plan. A part of the program management plan is the resource management plan. You manage the program resources according to the program management plan in general, and the resource management plan in particular, by using the Resource Control process depicted in Figure 8.3.

FIGURE 8.3   The Resource Control process: input and output

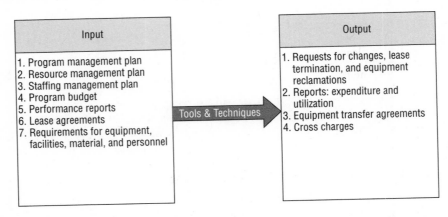

So, Resource Control is the process used to manage all the program resources (human and material) and the cost associated with them according to the resource management plan and the program management plan.

Input to Controlling Resources

Resources are monitored and controlled according to the management plans. Therefore, the program management plan, resource management plan, and staffing management plan are obvious input items to the Resource Control process. These and other input items are discussed in the following.

Management plans   Resources are managed and controlled according to the resource management plan, which is part of the program management plan. Controlling resources includes allocating and releasing them according to the plan. The resources also include human resources, which are managed and controlled according to the staffing management plan. So, the following plans are included in the input to the Resource Control process:

- Program management plan
- Resource management plan
- Staffing management plan

The program budget   Controlling resources includes tracking and controlling the cost related to the resources. Therefore, the program budget is a useful input to the Resource Control process.

Performance reports   Performance reports are an output of the Performance Reporting process, discussed further on in this chapter, which takes work results as an input. Performance reports help you determine a few things about the resources, including the following:

- Are the resources being used optimally?
- Do we need to shift some resources from one task to another?
- Do we need more resources?

Lease agreements   Some resources that need to be controlled; for example, office space may include real estate leases.

Requirements   The program has requirements in the area of equipment, facilities, material, and personnel, such as software, vehicles, and office supplies. These expenditures must be managed as a part of program expense.

You apply some tools and techniques on these input items to generate the output of the Resource Control process.

Tools and Techniques for Controlling Resources

The tools and techniques used by you, the program manager, in controlling resources can be influenced by the following factors:

- Type of resources; for example, human resources or material resources
- Reporting relation of the human resource to the program manager
- Program manager's authority, which partly depends on the organizational structure of the performing organization (discussed in Chapter 1, "Project, Portfolio, and Program: Mind the Gap")

In general, the tools and techniques used in controlling the resources (especially the human resources) include observation and conversation, conflict management, an issue log, and project performance appraisals. These and other tools and techniques are discussed in the following.

Observation and conversation Observations and conversations are both means to stay in touch with the work and attitudes of the team members. The indicators to monitor these include the following:

- Progress toward completion of assigned work and therefore deliverables
- Distinguished accomplishments contributing to the program performance
- Interpersonal issues

This technique also helps monitor and control the resources other than human resources.

Conflict management Conflicts may arise among the human resources for various reasons, including over the distribution of resources. The purpose of conflict management is to nourish positive working relationships among the team members, which results in increased productivity and optimal use of resources. Conflict management is discussed in detail in Chapter 7.

Issue log Issues generally involve obstacles that can stop the program team from achieving the program objectives. Resources-related issues make up a large percentage of all the issues that may arise during the program cycle. A written log should be maintained that contains the list of team members responsible for resolving the issues by target dates. The purpose of the issue log is to monitor the issues until they are closed. The importance of issue management is underlined by the fact that there is a whole process to manage issues in program management, which I'll discuss further on in this chapter.

Performance appraisals Conducting performance appraisals includes evaluating the performance of the team members and providing them with feedback based on the evaluation. The evaluation is based on information collected from several people interacting with the team member. This method of collecting information is called the *360-degree feedback principle* because the information comes from several sources.

The objectives for conducting performance appraisals include the following:

- Providing positive feedback to team members in a possibly hectic environment
- Clarifying roles and responsibilities
- Discovering new issues and reminding of unresolved issues
- Discovering the needs of individual training plans
- Setting specific goals for the future

Resource-leveling techniques You will use resource-leveling techniques to level resources across the program, ensuring that the resources are used where they are needed in an optimal way. These techniques are discussed in detail in Chapter 5, "Planning the Program Schedule and Resources."

Program Management Information System (PMIS) The PMIS can help you in various Resource Control tasks, such as integrating the resource utilization data and conducting resource expense analysis. The PMIS may also have resource-tracking tools.

Brainstorming   Depending on the size and complexity of the program, you may need quite a bit of brainstorming with your team to balance the competing resource requirements across the program for their optimal use.

Policies and procedures   While monitoring and controlling the resources, you must follow the organizational and program policies and procedures related to them, such as resource allocation, equipment reclamation, and equipment transfers.

While you are controlling the resources by using these techniques, you might recommend some actions as an output of the Resource Control process.

Output of Controlling Resources

The main output items that the Resource Control process generates are change requests, reports, and equipment transfer agreements.

Requests   As a result of controlling resources, the following requests may arise:

Change requests   These requests may include resource-related changes, such as allocating more or fewer resources, or switching the resources around.

Requests for lease termination   There will be situations in which you want to terminate the lease before its expiration date for some reasons, such as if the resource is not needed any more.

Requests for equipment reclamation   Equipment reclamation means reclaiming the equipment from loss or from a less useful condition. Some examples are repairing malfunctioning equipment, replacing a stolen item, and replacing any irreparably broken equipment. This will obviously add to the program expenses.

Reports   As part of Resource Control, you need to keep track of the resource utilization and the program expenditures. This generates the following two reports:

- Expenditure reports
- Utilization reports

Equipment transfer agreements   You need these agreements to transfer some resources after they have been used for the program. For example, software programs and office equipment can be transferred during the program transition. Leased resources should also be appropriately returned at the expiration of the lease or when they are no longer needed. This will help avoid penalties and hidden expenses.

Cross-charges   Cross charging means one entity charging another entity within the same organization. The bigger issue here is how the expenses are allocated. This includes the authorized cross-charging in addition to other forms of allocation. For example, cross-charging may include charging between the program and its constituent projects, or between different functional departments involved in the program. For instance a department used a facility that belongs to another department and therefore will be charged (that is cross charged) for this use.

The change requests generated by the Resource Control process (or by any process, for that matter) become input to the Integrated Change Control process. Another important Monitoring and Controlling process in the Integration Management knowledge area is Monitor and Control Program Work.

Real World Scenario

Controlling Resources

You are the program manager for the Fill the Gap program, launched to decrease the high-school dropout rate in underprivileged communities in your county. The program includes offering training courses to high-school students in math and science. You have just started two new projects in the program corresponding to two new courses that will be offered.

The latest performance reports from these projects have revealed the following:

- The curriculum-development task that is on the critical path is behind schedule.

- The task of hiring instructors for these courses is also behind schedule. Interviews were conducted and offers were made, but it turned out that the selected instructors did not have much interest in the job and they declined the offers.

Your further investigation of these matters revealed the following facts:

- Monica Jain, who is developing the curriculum, has some teaching experience but not any solid experience in curriculum and course development. She was assigned to the current responsibility just because she volunteered for it from within the organization. However, Monica does have a track record of hiring successful employees in the area of education.

- Surge Sandhu, who is leading the efforts of hiring the instructors, has considerable teaching and curriculum-development experience. However, Surge has no interviewing or team-development experience.

To solve this problem, you have switched the roles of Monica Jain and Surge Sandhu.

However, by looking at the class schedule and the requirements for the facilities, you have discovered another problem. The classes for one of the two news courses are scheduled on weekends at the building for which your organization has a lease for one year. However, the requirements state that the facility cannot be used on weekends and national holidays. So, you have moved these classes to the main headquarters of the organization after consulting with the program sponsor.

Monitoring and Controlling Program Work

Monitor and Control Program Work is the process used to generate, gather, and consolidate performance information, and to measure performance and trends to make improvements. To be specific, Monitor and Control Program Work includes the following:

- Measuring the program performance against the program management plan in terms of parameters in different aspects of the program, such as cost, schedule, and scope

- Collecting performance information—for example, from the constituent projects

- Consolidating the performance information coming from various components of the program
- Evaluating performance measurements and determining trends to make improvements

In general, Monitor and Control Program Work includes the following two aspects:

- Understand each constituent project's performance as it contributes to the overall program.
- Monitor and control the non-project work being performed at the program level.

The program work is monitored and controlled by using the Monitor and Control Program Work process depicted in Figure 8.4.

FIGURE 8.4   The Monitor and Control Program Work process: input and output

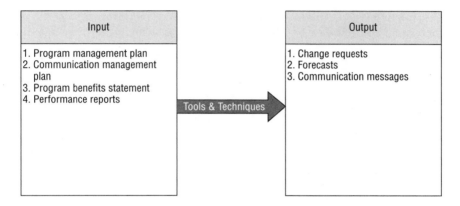

Input	Output
1. Program management plan 2. Communication management plan 3. Program benefits statement 4. Performance reports	1. Change requests 2. Forecasts 3. Communication messages

Tools & Techniques

Input to Monitoring and Controlling Program Work

The program work is monitored and controlled to keep the performance in line with the program management plan. Therefore the program management plan and performance reports are the obvious input items to this process. These and other input items are discussed in the following.

Program management plan   Monitoring and controlling program work includes understanding the program performance, and the performance is always measured against the baseline in the program management plan. This is why the program management plan is an essential input to monitoring and controlling program work.

Communication management plan   Monitoring and controlling program work involves communication, and therefore a communication management plan is an input item to this process.

Program benefits statement   The ultimate goal of the program is to deliver the planned program benefits. Therefore, the program benefits statement is an essential input to monitoring and controlling program work.

Performance reports   Work results from the Direct and Manage Program Execution process are evaluated to produce performance reports by using the Performance Reporting process. These performance reports are useful input to monitoring and controlling program work.

These input items are used to generate the output of the Monitor and Control Program Work process.

Tools and Techniques for Monitoring and Controlling Program Work

Tools and techniques used to monitor and control the program work include the following.

Management information system   As mentioned earlier, this is a collection of tools and techniques (manual and automated) used to gather, integrate, and disseminate the output of program (and project) management processes. These tools can be used to monitor and control program work. The management information system can also be used to create forecasts based on the past performance.

Earned value technique   This technique is used to measure the performance of the program and its components. You will learn about some aspects of this technique further on in this chapter.

Expert judgment   The program management team can use the experts in making judgments on issues related to coordinating the program work across its multiple components.

These tools and techniques are used to generate the output of monitoring and controlling program work, as listed in Figure 8.4.

Output of Monitoring and Controlling Program Work

An important task of monitoring and controlling the program work is to make forecasts based on the past performance. This and other output items are discussed in the following.

Change requests   Change requests may be made to bring the future performance in line with the program management plan. The change requests arising from monitoring and controlling the program work or originating from any other source, such as the stakeholders, must be processed through the Integrated Change Control process.

Forecasts   Monitoring and controlling program work includes making forecasts based on the past performance. These forecasts include estimates such as cost and predictions of conditions and events. These forecasts can be updated as more performance information comes in.

Communication messages   The consolidated performance information needs to be communicated to the program stakeholders. For this purpose, this information is organized into communication messages, which become input to the Information Distribution process.

Communication messages to be delivered to the stakeholders are an important output of monitoring and controlling program work. You also need to manage the stakeholders' issues.

Performing Issue Management and Control

Issue Management and Control is the process that is used to identify, track, review, resolve, and close issues in order to keep the stakeholders' expectations aligned with the program activities and deliverables. This process is depicted in Figure 8.5 with its input and output.

FIGURE 8.5   The Issue Management and Control process: input and output

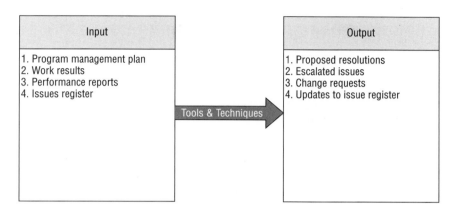

Input	Output
1. Program management plan 2. Work results 3. Performance reports 4. Issues register	1. Proposed resolutions 2. Escalated issues 3. Change requests 4. Updates to issue register

Tools & Techniques

Input to Issue Management and Control

The issues are recorded in the issue register and are managed according to the program management plan. Therefore the issue register and the program management plan are the obvious input items to the Issue Management and Control process. These and other input items are discussed in the following.

Program management plan   The issues will be prioritized, reviewed, and resolved. You will also need to communicate with the stakeholders regarding the issues. Furthermore, the goal of the Issue Management and Control process is to keep the stakeholders' expectations aligned with the program activities and deliverables. All these tasks should be performed according to the program management plan.

Work results   Work results are the raw data for identifying issues. For example, an unexpected result may give rise to an issue.

Performance reports   These can be used to identify, prioritize, and resolve issues.

Issue register   When you identify an issue, you record it in a document called the issue register. Because this document contains issues, it is a basic input to the Issue Management and Control process.

You will apply some tools and techniques to these input items to generate the output of the Issue Management and Control process.

Tools and Techniques for Issue Management and Control

Tools and techniques that can be used to support Issue Management and Control include those discussed in the following.

Communication methods   Communication is needed to manage and control the issues. If possible, face-to-face meetings are most effective in identifying, monitoring, controlling, and resolving the issues. However, in some situations face-to-face meeting may not be an option. In such cases other appropriate communication methods can be used, such as teleconferencing or email.

Status-review meetings   The status of the issues can be reported and reviewed in the general program-status review meetings. Some issues may need separate status-review meetings.

General management skills   General management skills, discussed in Chapter 7, are needed to identify, track, and resolve issues.

Management information system   Such a system can be used to make progress on an issue visible within a group. To that end, you use the management information system to accomplish the following tasks:

- Log the issue
- Change the escalation level of the issue
- Change the status of the issue, such as resolved or closed

You apply these tools and techniques to the input items to generate the output of the Issue Management and Control process, as listed in Figure 8.5.

Output of Issue Management and Control

The issue resolution proposals and the corresponding updates to the issue register are obvious outputs of the Issue Management and Control process. These and other output items are discussed in the following.

Proposed resolutions   You may need to go through several steps before the resolution of an issue can be proposed. After an issue is recorded in the issue register, it is reviewed and analyzed by an appropriate body or individual that has the authority to do so. In other words, each issue has an owner who has the authority and means to resolve and close the issue. All the open issues should be tracked by reviews conducted on a regular basis. An issue that cannot be resolved at its present level should be progressively escalated higher on the authority scale until it is resolved.

Escalated issues   Issue control at the program level also includes issues from the constituent projects which could not be resolved at the project level and have been escalated to the program level. Because these issues can affect the program progress, they must be reviewed, tracked, and resolved. The program governance infrastructure must have processes and procedures that provide appropriate visibility for issues because they may have impact across the portfolio of the organization.

There is a very close relationship between risks and issues. Therefore, the Issue Management and Control process is often performed in parallel with the Risk Monitoring and Control process.

Change requests   Resolving the issues may involve some changes, such as modification of the program requirements or scope, or adjusting organizational policies. This will result in change requests.

Updates to the issue register   As the issues are tracked, escalated, and resolved, the issue register will need to be updated accordingly.

Issues will arise both at the program level and at the project level. Some project-level issues will impact the program that you will need to assess. While resolving the issues, you should do the following:

- Consider different project scenarios and select those that help achieve program goals and objectives.

- Identify and resolve the key issues that prevent continued program progress.

The work results and performance reports, which are the main input to the Issue Management and Control process, indicate how well the program is being executed in areas such as cost, schedule, and scope. These three areas are correlated and are collectively called the triple constraint.

Controlling the Triple Constraint

The program scope, schedule (time), and cost are controlled by using the Scope Control, Schedule Control, and Cost Control processes, respectively. These three parameters compose a *triple constraint*, which is a framework for evaluating competing demands. As shown in Figure 8.6, the triple constraint is often depicted in a triangle with the length of each side of the triangle representing one of the three parameters. It means if one of these parameters change, at least one of the other two must change as well.

FIGURE 8.6   The triple constraint: scope, time, and cost

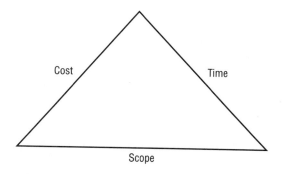

Therefore, scope, cost, and schedule should be monitored and controlled closely. Any change in one of these should be analyzed for its effects on the other two parameters.

> Theoretically speaking, the three elements of the triple constraint are: cost, scope, and time. Practically speaking time appears in form of schedule. So, we use time and schedule interchangeably in this context.

Controlling Scope

The program scope is controlled by using the Scope Control process shown in Figure 8.7. It includes performing the following tasks:

- Capture a change request and move it through evaluation and approval process.

- Make sure each change request is handled; that is, evaluated and approved or disapproved through the Integrated Change Control process.

- If a change request is approved, ensure its inclusion in the program management plan and its implementation.

- Archive the change requests and the associated details.

- Watch out for scope creep; that is, capture the unapproved changes in progress and correct the situation.

FIGURE 8.7   The Scope Control process: input and output

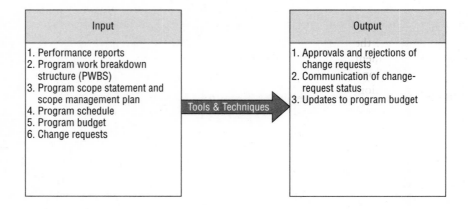

Input to Scope Control

The obvious input items to the Scope Control process are the elements that define the scope, such as the program scope statement and the program work breakdown structure (PWBS), and the scope management plan that describes how to manage the scope. These and other input items are described in the following.

Performance reports   These reports provide information on the program work performance. Therefore, they may help to detect a scope change; some change requests in other areas reflecting from the performance reports can result in scope change, as well.

Program work breakdown structure (PWBS)   This structure represents the program scope in the form of deliverables or program packages.

Program scope statement and scope management plan   The program scope statement describes the program scope, and the scope management plan describes how to manage the program scope. Therefore both of these documents are important input to the Scope Control process.

Program schedule and budget   Remember the triple constraint? If there is a change in scope, time, cost, or both (that is, schedule and budget) must change. This is why schedule and budget are input items to the Scope Control process. If there is a scope change request, always evaluate its potential effect on schedule and budget.

Change requests   These are the requests for change that are evaluated for their impact on the program scope.

You apply some tools and techniques to these input items to generate the output of the Scope Control process.

Tools and Techniques for Scope Control

The main tools used in the Scope Control process are the change control system and the performance analysis, as discussed in the following.

Performance measurements and analysis   Performance analysis that involves measuring quantities such as scope variance and schedule variance is necessary to monitor the scope. The goal here is to estimate the magnitude of variance from the expected performance stated in the program scope statement. The schedule variance is important because schedule variance can have an effect on the scope if you want to finish the program (or one of its components) on time and there are no additional resources available.

Scope change control system   The scope change control system, documented in the program scope management plan, is a collection of formal documented procedures that specify how the program deliverables and documents will be changed, controlled, and approved. It can include the documentation, the tracking system, and the approval levels to facilitate the authorization of changes.

Configuration management system   This system can be used to ensure that the requested changes to the program scope are thoroughly considered and documented before being processed through the Integrated Change Control process.

Both the change control system and the configuration management system may be part of the organization's management information system.

You use these tools and techniques to generate the output of the Scope Control process, listed in Figure 8.7.

Output of Scope Control

The output items of the Scope Control process are the following:

Approvals and rejections of change requests   The change requests are processed through the Integrated Change Control process and are ultimately approved or disapproved.

Communication of change requests status   The status of the change request is communicated to the stakeholders.

Updates   Approval and implementation of change requests will require some updates, such as updates to the program budget, schedule, or scope.

Any change in scope will create a change in schedule, scope, or both.

Controlling the Schedule

Schedule Control has a two-pronged goal: ensure that the program (along with its projects) is progressing in time as planned, and monitor and control any change to this progress. As a program manager, you should be out in front of the program performing the following tasks on a regular basis:

- Track the actual start and finish dates for activities and milestones and compare them with the planned timeline.

- Influence the factors that generate schedule changes.

- Determine if the program schedule has changed—for example, as a result of an approved change—and update the plan accordingly.

- Manage the changes as they occur.

Schedule Control works closely with other program control processes. For example, a change in scope or cost can cause a change in schedule. The schedule control involves identifying the following two kinds of changes:

Slippage   This is a change that delays the finish date for an activity or milestone.

Opportunity   This is a change that enables you to finish an activity or reach a milestone earlier than planned.

So you should be watching out for slippage and looking for opportunities. The schedule is controlled by using the Schedule Control process shown in Figure 8.8.

Input to Schedule Control

You detect a schedule change by comparing the actual start and finish dates with the planned dates in the program schedule, which is a major input to the Schedule Control process. The schedule is controlled according to the schedule management plan. So, the program schedule and the schedule management plan are obvious inputs to the Schedule Control process. These and other input items are discussed in the following.

FIGURE 8.8   The Schedule Control process: input and output

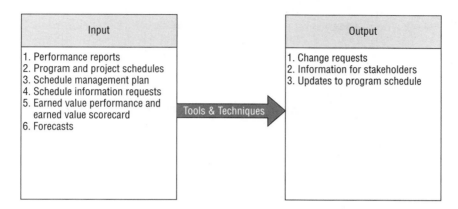

Performance reports   These reports contain information on schedule performance of the project, such as the missed and met planned dates for completing activities.

Program and project schedules   These are the approved versions of the program schedule and the schedules for the constituent projects against which the schedule performance of the program (and the constituent projects) will be measured.

Schedule management plan   This plan specifies how to monitor and control the program.

Schedule information requests   These requests may come from the program stakeholders. As a result you will need to communicate the required information to the stakeholders.

Earned value performance and earned value scorecard   The earned value performance is the program (and projects) performance measured by using the *earned value technique*, which is a commonly used method for measuring performance. This technique integrates the three correlated elements of the triple constraint (schedule, scope, and cost) in making the performance measurements. The scorecard refers to the values of a set of parameters (or metrics) measured in the earned value technique.

Forecasts   Forecasts include the estimates or predictions about the program's future, such as the remaining cost or the completion dates for the remaining activities based on the current work-performance information. These forecasts are updated as the program progresses. Note that the cost forecast can also affect the schedule. These forecasts are discussed in detail further on in this chapter. This is an important item of information to monitor and control the program schedule.

With these input items in place, you need some tools and techniques to generate the output.

Tools and Techniques for Schedule Control

The schedule is monitored by progress reporting and performance measurements and is controlled using the schedule change control system. These and other tools and techniques are discussed in this section.

Schedule change control system   This is the system you use to receive, evaluate, and process schedule changes. It can include forms, procedures, approval committees, and tracking systems.

Progress reporting   Progress reports and current schedule status are key items to monitor the schedule. They can include the finished component activities, the percent of in-progress components or activities that have been completed, and the remaining durations for unfinished (but started) components or activities.

Performance measurement and analysis   The following tools and techniques can be used to measure and analyze the schedule performance of the program or one of its components:

Performance measurement techniques   These techniques are used to calculate the schedule variance and schedule performance index and are discussed further on in this chapter. The schedule variance discussed there is in terms of cost, but you can also perform a barebones schedule variance analysis based on the start and end dates of the schedule activities.

Variance analysis   Performing a barebones schedule variance analysis is crucial to schedule monitoring because it reveals the deviation of the actual start and finish dates from the planned start and finish dates of schedule activities. It might suggest corrective actions to be taken to keep the program on track.

Schedule comparison bar charts   Bar charts can be used to facilitate the schedule variance analysis. You can draw two bars corresponding to one schedule activity—one bar shows the actual progress, and the other bar shows the expected progress according to the baseline. This is a great tool to visually display where the schedule has progressed as planned, and where it has slipped.

A schedule variance does not necessarily mean that a schedule change is required. For example, a delay on a schedule activity that is not on the critical path might not trigger any schedule change.

Program management software   You can use some program management software tools for scheduling to track planned start/finish dates versus actual dates for schedule activities. These kinds of software tools usually also enable you to predict the effects of schedule changes. These are important pieces of information for monitoring and controlling the schedule.

By using these tools and techniques, you generate the output of the Schedule Control process.

Output of Schedule Control

The output of the Schedule Control process includes change requests, information for stakeholders, and updates to the program schedule.

Change requests   The schedule performance analysis and progress report review may result in requests for changes to the program or project schedules. These changes must be processed through the Integrated Change Control process for approval. Like any other change, you must think through if a change to the schedule has any other effect across the program. If it does, you may need to update the corresponding component of the program management plan accordingly.

Information for stakeholders   The information requests may come from the program stakeholders. As a result you will need to communicate the required information to the stakeholders.

Updates to program schedule   Schedule changes may happen at the activity level (the start/finish date of an activity is changed) or at the program/project level (the start/finish date of the program or a constituent project is changed). The schedule change at the project level is called the *project schedule revision*. For example, when the schedule scope is expanded, the project finish date may have to be changed to allow the extra work. The schedule change at the program level is called the *program schedule revision*. All significant schedule changes must be reported to the stakeholders.

Any change in the program schedule will generate a change in cost, scope, or both.

Controlling Cost

The program cost is monitored and controlled by using the Cost Control process, which includes the following:

- Monitor and control changes to the program budget.
- Generate information from these changes.

Monitoring and controlling the changes includes both proactive and reactive approaches:

Proactive approach   Analyze actual cost incurred against the planned cost to determine the performance variance from the plan. From the variance over time, perform the trend analysis to predict the problems in the future.

Reactive approach   Deal with the unanticipated problems and opportunities that crop up. Problems have a negative effect on the cost (cost overrun), whereas opportunities have a positive effect on the cost (cost underrun).

The program budget is monitored and controlled by using the Cost Control process shown in Figure 8.9.

FIGURE 8.9   The Cost Control process: input and output

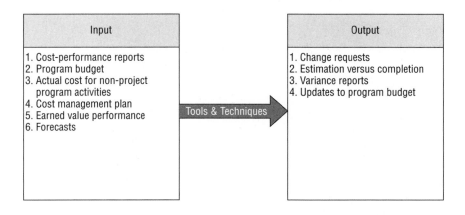

Input	Output
1. Cost-performance reports 2. Program budget 3. Actual cost for non-project program activities 4. Cost management plan 5. Earned value performance 6. Forecasts	1. Change requests 2. Estimation versus completion 3. Variance reports 4. Updates to program budget

Tools & Techniques

The conventional wisdom of cost control is to keep the program on budget; that is, to hold down the cost to keep the program on budget or to apply corrective actions to bring the program back in line with the planned budget in case of an overrun. However, in addition to watching out for cost-overrun problems, you should be looking for *underrun* opportunities where you can save money and return it to the organization. Won't that be nice?

Input to Cost Control

The Cost Control process is the process of monitoring and controlling the program budget, and the cost management plan describes how to do it. Therefore the program budget and the cost management plan are the obvious inputs to the Cost Control process. These and other input items are discussed in the following.

Cost-performance reports   These reports provide information about the cost performance and the resource usage performance. This information is necessary to control the cost.

Program budget   The goal for monitoring and controlling the cost is to keep the program within budget. So, the cost is monitored and controlled with respect to the program budget.

Actual cost for non-project program activities   The cost for the non-project activities that are part of the programs can be controlled only at the program level.

Cost management plan   This describes how to monitor and control the cost. This may also need to be updated due to the approved changes.

Earned value performance   The earned value technique used in the performance analysis is also used to calculate some cost-related metrics. The performance represented by these metrics is called *earned value performance*. This is a useful input to the Cost Control process.

Forecasts   Forecasts include the estimates or predictions about the program's future, such as the remaining cost or the completion dates for the remaining activities based on the current work-performance information. These forecasts are updated as the program progresses. This is an important piece of information for monitoring and controlling the program cost and schedule.

You apply some tools and techniques to these input items to generate the output.

Tools and Techniques for Cost Control

The tools and techniques used in controlling cost are discussed in the following.

Cost change control system   The cost change control system, documented in the program cost management plan, is a collection of formal documented procedures that specify how the cost baseline will be changed, controlled, and approved. It can include the documentation, tracking system, and approval levels to facilitate the authorization of changes.

Earned value management   Earned value management involves calculating and tracking some performance metrics using earned value techniques. This analysis helps to estimate the magnitude of performance variance from the expected performance. Performance analysis, including earned value management, is described in detail further on in this chapter.

Forecasting   Earned value management also allows forecasting. Based on the performance of the program (or its components) in the past, you can forecast its performance in the future. These performance variables (metrics) are discussed further on in this chapter.

Management software and computerized tools   The program/project management software, including computerized analysis tools, can be used to monitor the performance variables.

You use these tools and techniques to generate the output of the Cost Control process.

Output of Cost Control

Almost any monitoring and controlling process can generally generate change requests. Due to the cost-related changes, you may need to update the program budget. Therefore, the change requests and updates to the program budget are the obvious output items of the Cost Control process. These and other output items are discussed in the following.

Change requests   The program performance analysis can generate requests for changes to certain aspects of the program. Those change requests if approved can have an impact on the cost and therefore the budget. The resulting change request for the budget will need to be processed through the Integrated Change Control process like any other change request.

Estimation versus completion   One important task included in the Cost Control process is to keep track of estimated (predicted) cost versus actual cost at the completion of an activity, milestone, or program. At a given point in the program (or a constituent project), you can estimate how much the remaining program (or project) will cost; that estimate is called the *estimate to complete (ETC)*. You can also estimate the total cost that will be incurred in completing the whole program (or project), and this is called *estimate at completion (EAC)*. These estimates can also be made at the activity level.

Variance reports   Variance reports show how the actual cost incurred varies from the planned cost.

Updates to program budget   The approved changes regarding the cost will require updating the program budget.

While monitoring and controlling cost and budget, you should also do the following:

- Identify the issues that are posing challenges to the budget of the program or a project.
- Analyze the cost of non-project program activities and compare the cost to the impact that these activities have on the program benefits.
- Identify any threats of project cost overruns and opportunities of cost savings from the projects. Use these threats and opportunities to keep the program budget on track.
- Identify the opportunities to save from the program and return funding to the organization.

Performance measurement analysis is a technique used in controlling the schedule and the cost. Performance measurements include a number of variables (or metrics) that are measured as disused in the next section.

Measuring Performance

You would not know if the program succeeded if you did not define success. So, during the program initiation and planning, you define meaningful measurement criteria for the program success. This is accomplished by analyzing stakeholder expectations and requirements. The criteria for program success across the constituent projects allow you to accurately control program performance. The goal here is two-pronged: to determine the metrics that will measure the performance and to determine the acceptable values for these metrics. Measuring performance includes the following tasks:

- Determine metrics (or variables) that will be measured.
- Determine the acceptable values for these variables.
- Review the defined metrics and the criteria with the stakeholders and get their acceptance.
- Determine tools and techniques to measure and track these metrics.

In general, program performance is measured by comparing the execution (that is, the actual performance) against the performance measurement baseline, which is an approved integrated plan for scope, schedule, and cost for the program, as explained here:

Cost baseline   This is the planned budget for the program over a time period, used as a basis against which to measure, monitor, and control the cost performance of the program. The cost performance is measured by comparing the actual cost with the planned cost over a time period.

Schedule baseline   This is a specific version of the program schedule developed from the schedule network analysis and the schedule model data, discussed in Chapter 5. This is the approved version of the schedule with a start date and a finish date, and is used as a basis against which the program schedule performance is measured.

Scope baseline   This is the approved program scope that includes the approved program scope statement, the PWBS based on the approved program scope statement, and the corresponding PWBS dictionary.

The performance measurements discussed in this section can be applied to measure the progress of the program or one of its components, such as a project. The elaborative nature of the performance measurement analysis can be seen in the Cost Control process.

Performance Measurement Analysis for Cost Control

Cost control includes influencing the factors that can create changes to the cost baseline. But to detect the arising changes, you need to detect and understand variances from the cost baseline by monitoring cost performance.

In general, variance is a measurable deviation in the value of a variable (or parameter), such as cost or schedule, from a known baseline or expected value. Variance analysis is a technique used to assess the magnitude of variation in the value of a variable, such as cost, from the baseline or expected value, to determine the cause of the variance, and to decide whether a corrective action is required. A common technique to assess the cost variance is called the *earned value technique* (EVT), in which you calculate the cumulative value of the budgeted cost of work performed in terms of the originally allocated budgeted amount and compare it to the following:

- Budgeted cost of work scheduled; that is, planned
- Actual cost of work performed

Don't worry if these terms sound confusing right now, as we will go through an example soon. However, as you will see, the greatest difficulty in understanding the EVT stems from the coupling of cost and schedule. So, you must realize that the cost and the schedule are inherently related to each other. Schedule relates to performing certain work over a certain time period, whereas cost refers to the money spent in performing the work on a program (or a program component) over a certain period of time. The relationship between cost and schedule can be realized by understanding that it costs money to perform a schedule activity. The "time is money" principle is at work here. For example, a program activity can be looked upon in terms of an amount of work that will be needed to complete it, or in terms of its monetary value, which will include the cost of the work that needs to be performed to complete the activity.

The EVT involves calculating some variables where you will see the interplay of schedule (or work in the schedule) and cost to perform the scheduled work. I will work through an example to help you understand the upcoming variables. Consider a program component: Construction of a 12-mile-long road. Assume that the work required for this construction is uniformly distributed over 18 weeks. The total approved budget for this component is $500,000. At the end of the first three weeks of work, $125,000 has been spent, and 3 miles of road have been completed.

We will use this example to perform the cost-performance analysis and the schedule-performance analysis in terms of cost.

Cost Performance

Cost performance refers to how efficiently you are spending the money on the program work as measured against the expectations set in the program management plan; that is, the cost baselines. The total cost approved in the baseline is called *budget at completion (BAC)*.

 The variables discussed here, such as BAC, EV, and AC, can be calculated for the whole program, for a component of the program (such as a project), or for a part of the component (such as a project activity).

Budget at completion (BAC)   This is the total budget authorized for performing the work of the component under measurement, also called the planned budget: the cost that we originally estimated in the program management plan. We use this variable in defining almost all the following variables. In our example, the value of BAC is $500,000.

Earned value (EV)   This is the value of the actually performed work expressed in terms of the approved budget for the component or a component activity for a given time period. In this variable, you see the relationship of schedule (or the scheduled work) and cost in action. As you already know, BAC represents the total value of the budget for the component. But when you perform some work on the component, you have earned some of that value, and the earned value is proportional to the fraction of the total work performed, as shown by the formula here:

```
EV = BAC x (work completed ÷ total work required)
```

So, in our example, EV can be calculated as follows:

```
EV = $500,000 (3 miles ÷ 12 miles) = $125,000
```

This is the earned value of the work, which may or may not be equal to the actual money that you spent to perform this work.

Actual cost (AC)   This is the total cost actually incurred until a specific point on the time scale in performing the work for a component. In our running example, let's say $150,000 has already been used up to this point. So the actual cost at this point in time is $150,000. This cost is to be compared with the earned value to calculate the cost variance and cost performance.

Cost variance (CV)   This is a measure of cost performance in terms of deviation of reality from the plan, and is obtained by subtracting the actual cost (AC) from the earned value (EV), as shown in the formula here:

```
CV = EV - AC
```

So, in our example, CV can be calculated as shown here:

```
CV = $125,000 - $150,000 = -$25,000
```

The expected value of CV is zero because we expect the earned value to be equal to the actual cost. The negative result indicates worse cost performance than expected, whereas a positive result would indicate better cost performance than expected. Deviation is one way of comparison, and ratio is another.

Cost performance index (CPI)   Earned value represents the portion of the work completed and actual cost represents the money spent. So the CPI indicates whether we are getting fair value for our money. This is a measure of cost efficiency of a component calculated by dividing earned value (EV) by actual cost (AC), as shown in the formula here:

```
CPI = EV ÷ AC
```

So, the CPI for our example can be calculated as follows:

```
CPI = $125,000 ÷ $150,000 = 0.83
```

This means you are getting $0.83 worth of performance for every $1.0 spent. A CPI value less than 1 indicates bad performance, whereas a value greater than 1 indicates good performance. The expected value of CPI is 1.

So, in our example, both CV and CPI indicate that you are getting less value for each dollar spent. Hold back a little before getting all blue. If you read the text of our example again, note that only 3 out of 18 weeks have passed, and you have finished one quarter of the work. You should get some credit for that somewhere. Clearly, you are ahead in your schedule. So, schedule performance needs to be investigated, too.

Schedule Performance in Terms of Cost

Schedule performance refers to how efficiently you are executing your program (or a component) schedule as measured against the expectations set in the program management plan. It can be measured by comparing the earned value with the planned value, just as cost performance is measured by comparing the earned value with the actual cost. *Planned value* refers to the value that we planned to create in the time spent so far.

Planned value (PV)   This is the authorized cost for the scheduled work on the program, program component, or a component activity up to a given point on the time scale. PV is basically how much we were authorized to spend in the fraction of schedule time spent so far, as shown in the formula here:

```
PV = BAC x (time passed ÷ total schedule time)
```

Therefore, the planned value for the component in our example at the end of first four weeks is calculated as shown here:

```
PV = $500,000 x (3 weeks ÷ 18 weeks) = $83,333
```

So, PV represents the planned schedule in terms of cost. We can calculate the schedule performance by comparing the planned schedule with the performed schedule in terms of cost.

Exam Spotlight

Remember the alternative names for some of the variables discussed here: actual cost of work performed (ACWP) for actual cost (AC), budgeted cost for the work scheduled (BCWS) for planned value (PV), and budgeted cost of work performed (BCWP) for earned value (EV).

Schedule variance (SV)   This is the deviation of the performed schedule from the planned schedule in terms of cost. No confusion is allowed here because we already know that the schedule can be translated to cost. SV is calculated as the difference between EV and PV, as shown in the formula here:

```
SV = EV - PV
```

So, the SV in our example can be calculated as:

```
SV = $125,000 - $83,333 = $41,667
```

The positive value means we are ahead of schedule, whereas a negative value would mean we were behind schedule. Deviation is one way of comparison, and ratio is another.

Schedule performance index (SPI) Earned value represents the portion of the work completed in terms of cost, and planned value represents how much work was planned by this point in terms of cost. So, the SPI indicates how the performed work compares with the planned work. This is a measure of schedule efficiency of a component calculated by dividing earned value (EV) with planned value (PV), as shown in the formula here:

$$SPI = EV \div PV$$

So, the SPI for our example can be calculated as shown here:

$$SPI = \$125,000 \div \$83,333 = 1.50$$

This indicates that the component is progressing at 150% of the planned pace. Congratulations!

You should note that all these performance variables except BAC are calculated at a given point in time. As shown in Figure 8.10, you can maintain a graphic that presents the values of these variables against points in time as the component progresses. Note that the value of BAC does not change with time because it is the cost at completion time. Further note that given BAC, PV can be calculated at any point in time before even the component execution starts. EV and EC are cumulated as the program (or the component) execution progresses.

FIGURE 8.10 Behavior of some performance variables as the program (or component) progresses in time. The variable BAC is independent of time.

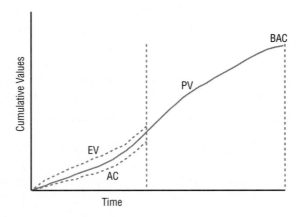

By using the variables discussed so far, you can monitor program performance as time progresses. Not only that; you can also make predictions about the future performance based on the past performance.

Forecasting Techniques

Forecasting refers to predicting some information about the future based on performance in the past. The forecasting is regularly updated as the program progresses and more data of the past performance becomes available.

Estimate to complete (ETC)   This is the prediction about the expected cost to complete the remaining work of the program, program component, or a component activity. This is basically how much value remains to be earned in terms of BAC. Therefore the value of ETC is obtained by subtracting the earned value (EV) from the budget at completion (BAC), as shown in the formula here:

```
ETC = BAC - EV
```

So, in our example, the value of ETC can be calculated as follows:

```
ETC = $500,000 - $125,000 = $375,000
```

Note that in this calculation, we are making an assumption that things will go in the future as planned; that is, the variation in the EV and PV that happened so far was atypical, and will not happen again. If we assume that the variation was typical and will happen again, then the formula to calculate ETC is the following:

```
ETC = (BAC - EV) ÷ CPI
```

Therefore, in our example the equation is as follows:

```
ETC = ($500,000 - $125,000) ÷ 0.83 = $451,807
```

The next question that can be asked about the future is how much it will cost to complete the whole component.

The variables AC, EV, and CPI are cumulative by definition. In the PMBOK Guide, this is at some places emphasized by placing a postscript C with these variables. I have avoided doing so in writing the formulae. However, as long as you understand these definitions, it does not change anything.

Estimate at completion (EAC)   This is the estimate made at the current point in time of how much it will cost to complete the component or a component activity. The value of EAC is obtained by adding the value of ETC to AC, as shown in the formula here:

```
EAC = ETC + AC
```

Accordingly, the value of EAC for our example can be calculated as the following:

For atypical variation:

```
EAC = $375,000 + $150,000 = $525,000
```

For typical variation:

```
EAC = $451,807 + $150,000 = $601,807
```

Now, consider the situation in which your manager says, "I don't care what happened so far. I would like to see the remaining work finished within the remaining cost." In this situation, a useful prediction is how much performance we need in the future to complete the remaining work within budget.

To-complete performance index (TCPI)   This is the variable to predict the future performance needed to finish the work within budget at the end of the road. It is calculated as the ratio of the remaining work to the remaining budget, as shown in the formula here:

```
TCPI = remaining work ÷ remaining funds = (BAC - BCWP) ÷ (BAC - ACWP) =
(BAC - EV) ÷ (BAC - AC)
```

Therefore, the value of TCPI in our example can be calculated as follows:

```
TCPI = ($500,000 - $125,000)  ($500,000 - $150,000) = 375,000 ÷ 350,000 = 1.07
```

A value greater than 1 means you have spent more than you have accomplished in terms of cost. So, you will need to accomplish more with less money in the future.

In a nutshell, during the executing stage, the obvious items that need to be executed are the schedule activities, and while these activities are being executed, the attached cost, schedule, and scope needs to be monitored and controlled largely through performance measurements. However, there is another important element of the program that needs to be monitored and controlled: the risk.

Controlling Quality and Risk

The program deliverables and results must meet the planned quality requirements. While the program is being executed to produce deliverables, the risks will be lurking around in the uncertainties. So, both the program quality and risk need to be controlled.

Controlling Quality

The program quality is controlled by using the Perform Quality Control process, which is the process of monitoring and controlling specific program deliverables (products, services, or results) to ensure they meet the planned quality standards. The goal of the Perform Quality Control process is two-prong:

- Identify the faulty outcome
- Make recommendations (change requests) to fix the faults

The program outcome that can be monitored in the process of performing quality control includes the following:

- Deliverables, including products, services, and results
- Management results
- Cost and schedule performance

The Perform Quality Control process at the program level includes quality reviews and project management health checks to ensure that the quality plans at the project level are executed.

 The Perform Quality Control process is performed throughout the program.

The Perform Quality Control process is shown in Figure 8.11.

FIGURE 8.11   The Perform Quality Control process: input and output

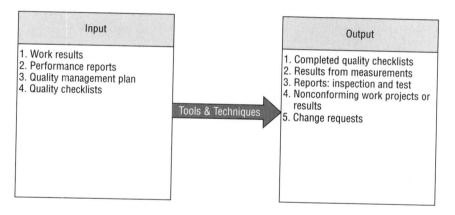

Input	Output
1. Work results 2. Performance reports 3. Quality management plan 4. Quality checklists	1. Completed quality checklists 2. Results from measurements 3. Reports: inspection and test 4. Nonconforming work projects or results 5. Change requests

Tools & Techniques

Input to Quality Control

Quality control is performed on the program work results according to the quality management plan. Therefore the work results and quality management plan are obvious input to the Perform Quality Control process. These and other input items are discussed in the following.

Work results   The work results generated by the Direct and Manage Program Execution process are the raw data for performing quality control. Some work results will tell you right away the status of quality, while other results will need to be analyzed and processed through the Performance Reporting process to get a clear picture of the quality status.

Performance reports   Cost and schedule performance are parts of the results that are monitored by the Perform Quality Control process. Therefore, performance reports that contain this information are essential input to quality control. Performance reports are generated by the Performance Reporting process, which takes work results as an input.

Quality management plan   The quality management plan, an output of the Quality Planning process, describes how the quality policies and standards will be implemented. It acts as a guideline for performing quality control.

Quality checklists   The quality checklists, prepared as an output of the Quality Planning process, are used to verify that a predetermined set of required quality-related steps has been performed.

Quality control is very involved and has a plethora of tools and techniques, discussed next.

Tools and Techniques for Quality Control

The tools and techniques used for quality control include inspection, defect repair reviews, and the so-called seven basic tools of quality. These tools can be used to control the quality of the program and its components, such as projects.

The Seven Basic Tools of Quality

The seven kinds of charts used in quality control are known as the seven basic tools of quality, and are introduced in Table 8.2. I describe these tools in the following sections.

TABLE 8.2   The Seven Basic Tools of Quality

Chart	Purpose
Flowchart	To anticipate what and where quality problems might occur.
Run chart	To perform trend analysis: predict future results based on past performance.
Scatter diagram	To find the relationship between two variables, such as cause and effect, or between two causes.
Histogram	To display the relative importance of different variables.
Pareto diagram	To identify and rank the errors based on the frequency of defects caused by them.
Control chart	To monitor whether the variance of a specified variable is within the acceptable limits dictated by quality control.
Cause-and-effect diagram	To explore all the potential causes of a problem, not just the obvious ones.

Flowcharts

A flowchart is a diagram that depicts inputs, actions, and outputs of one or more processes in a system. Commonly used in many disciplines of knowledge, flowcharts show the activities, decision points, and order of processing. They help to understand how a problem occurs. You can also use flowcharts to anticipate what and where the quality problems might occur, and to develop approaches to deal with them.

Run Charts

Run charts are used to perform trend analysis, which is the science of predicting future performance based on past results. In quality control, trend analysis can be used to predict such things as the number of defects and the cost to repair them. You can use the results of the trend analysis to recommend preventive actions if needed.

Scatter Diagrams

A scatter diagram is used to see the pattern of relationship between two variables: an independent variable, and another variable that depends on the independent variable. The dependent variable is plotted corresponding to the independent variable. For example, a variable representing a cause can be the independent variable and a variable representing the effect may be a dependent variable. The closer the data points are to a diagonal line, the stronger the relationship (called *correlation*) is between the two variables.

Histograms

A histogram is a bar chart that shows a distribution of variables. Each bar can represent an attribute such as defects due to a specific cause, and its height can represent the frequency of the attribute, such as number of defects. This tool helps to identify and rate the causes of defects.

You may wonder how the defects can be repaired efficiently. Pareto diagrams, which are examples of histograms, have the answer for you.

Pareto Diagrams

A Pareto diagram is used to rank the importance of each error (problem) based on the frequency of its occurrence over time in the form of defects. A defect is an imperfection or deficiency that keeps a component from meeting its requirements or specifications. A defect is caused by an error (problem), and can be repaired by fixing the error. An error in a product can give rise to multiple defects, and by fixing the error you repair all the defects caused by that error.

However all errors are not equal. Some errors cause more defects than others. According to Pareto's law, which is also known as the 80/20 rule, 80 percent of defects are caused by 20 percent of errors (or types of errors). Qualitatively, it means that most of the defects are caused by a small set of errors. The Pareto diagram lets you rank the errors based on the frequency of defects they cause. You begin by having the error that causes most of the defects fixed and you make your way to other errors that cause a smaller number of defects. This way the efforts of the team are optimized: you get the maximum number of defects repaired with minimal effort.

Pareto's Law, in its original form, was presented as an economic theory by Vilfredo Pareto, a 19th-century Italian economist, and it states that 80 percent of income is earned by 20 percent of the population. Since then it has been applied to other fields, such as project and program management.

Chapter 8 · Monitoring and Controlling the Program

So, the advantage of a Pareto diagram is twofold:

- Rank the errors according to the frequency of defects they cause.
- Optimize the efforts to repair the defects by working on the errors that cause most of the defects.

As an example, Table 8.3 presents data on the frequency of defects caused by certain errors. The data is displayed in Figure 8.12 in the form of a Pareto diagram. In this example, 300 defects are caused by 7 errors, and error A alone causes 111 defects, or 37 percent of all the defects. You can understand the impact of all 7 errors by looking at Table 8.3 and Figure 8.12. The Pareto diagram tells you that you should address error A first, error B second, and so on.

TABLE 8.3 An Example of Frequency of Defects Corresponding to Errors Causing the Defects

Error Causing the Defects	Number of Defects	Percentage of Defects Caused by This Error	Cumulative Percentage
A	111	37.0	37.0
B	75	25.0	62.0
C	45	15.0	77.0
D	30	10.0	87.0
E	23	7.7	94.7
F	10	3.3	98.0
G	6	2.0	100.0

You can ask, How many defects are acceptable? To find an answer to this question you need to understand another tool: the control chart.

Control Charts

Control charts are used to monitor whether the variance of a specified variable is within the acceptable limits dictated by quality control. A variance is a measurable deviation in the value of a program variable, such as cost from a known baseline or expected value. This is a way to monitor the deviations and determine if the corresponding variable is in control or out of control. The values are taken at different times to measure the behavior of a variable over time. The mean value in the control chart represents the expected value, and a predetermined spread from the mean value (usually ±3 σ) is used to define the limits within which an acceptable value can fall. The symbol σ represents standard deviation, described in Chapter 1.

Control charts can be used to monitor the values of any type of output variables. To illustrate its main feature, let's consider an example of a control chart, shown in Figure 8.13. In this example, assume that a manufacturer produces 100 units of a product each day and it is

expected that 90 out of 100 units should have no defect; that is, the expected number of defective units is equal to 10. The control limits are set to be ±5. In other words, 90 units out of 100
must be correct, give or take 5. That puts the lower limit at 85 and the upper limit at 95. Crossing the lower limit is not acceptable to the customer, and crossing the upper limit may require
unjustifiable cost.

Controlling quality includes dealing with the defects and problems that cause them. So,
studying causes of a problem is very critical to quality control.

FIGURE 8.12   A Pareto diagram

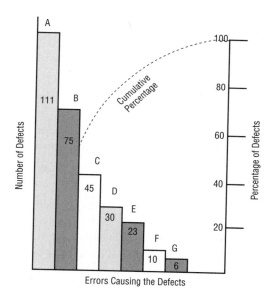

FIGURE 8.13   A control chart

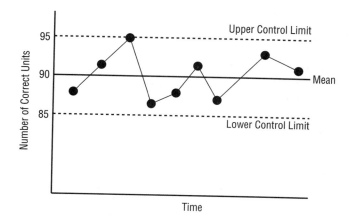

Cause-and-Effect Diagrams

A cause and effect diagram is used to explore all the potential causes (inputs) that result in a single effect (output), such as a problem or a defect. This type of diagram is the brainchild of Kaoru Ishikawa, who pioneered quality management processes in the Kawasaki shipyards, and therefore these diagrams are also called Ishikawa diagrams. Due to the shape of these diagrams, they are also known as fishbone diagrams. To construct and use the cause-and-effect diagrams effectively, perform the following simple steps:

Identify the problem   Write down the problem in the box drawn on the right-hand side of a large sheet of paper. This represents the head of the fish. Starting from the box, draw a horizontal line across the paper. This represents the spine of the fish.

Identify the possible areas of causes   Identify the areas or factors from where the potential causes of the problem may come. Environment, people, material, measurements, and methods are some examples of areas (factors) of causes. For each factor relevant to the problem under study, draw a line off the spine and label it with the name of the factor. These lines represent the fish bones.

Identify the possible causes   For each factor, identify possible causes. Represent each possible cause by a line coming off the bone that represents the corresponding factor.

Analyze the diagram   Analyzing the diagram includes narrowing down to the most likely causes and investigating them further.

Figure 8.14 shows a cause-and-effect diagram. The problem in this example is the delay in the release of a software application. The factors considered are environment, methods, people, and time. Of course, the diagram is incomplete in the sense that more factors and related causes could be explored, and causes for each factor could be explored further. The goal here is to give you some feel about this diagram.

FIGURE 8.14   A cause-and-effect diagram for exploring the causes for the delay in an application release

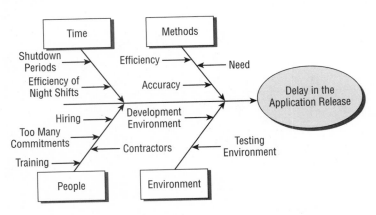

While constructing the cause-and-effect diagram, you can use the brainstorming method for identifying the potential factors of causes and potential causes for each factor.

So, a cause-and-effect diagram offers a structured way to think through all possible causes of a problem. You can use these diagrams to carry out a thorough analysis of a problematic situation. This kind of analysis is useful in complex situations where in order to discover the real causes, you need to explore all the potential causes and not just the obvious ones.

In addition to the seven quality tools we have discussed, there are some other tools that you can use for quality control.

Other Quality-Control Tools

In addition to the seven quality tools, the following tools can be used for controlling quality:

Statistical sampling   Statistical sampling involves randomly selecting a part of the population for study. In quality control, you can select a subset of features for inspection. This can save a substantial amount of resources.

Inspection   This is a technique to examine whether an activity, component, product, service, or result conforms to specific requirements. Inspections can be conducted at various levels of program execution. For example, you can inspect the results of a single project activity, the final product of a project in the program, or the results (benefits) of a program. Nevertheless, inspection generally includes measurements. There are various forms of inspections, such as reviews, peer reviews, audits, and walkthroughs.

Defect repair review   This review is conducted by the quality control (QC) department or body to ensure that the defects are repaired to bring the defective product, service, or results in conformance with the specified requirements.

These tools can be used to make quality control measurements, which in turn can be used to recommend preventive and corrective actions. Now we are talking about the output of the Perform Quality Control process.

Output of Quality Control

Quality control includes inspections and quality audits which will identify the faulty program outcome. Also the quality-control tools and techniques will generate some quality-control measurements. These and other output items are discussed in the following.

Completed quality checklists   These are the checklists that you'll have after verifying that a pre-determined set of required quality-related steps has been performed.

Results from measurements   The Perform Quality Control process involves some quality control measurements, which are the results of the quality control activities. These measurements are fed back to the Perform Quality Assurance process.

Reports   The tools and techniques used to monitor and control quality can produce two kinds of reports:

- Inspection reports; for example, as result of quality audits
- Test reports from various quality-control tests and analyses

Nonconforming work products and results   The Perform Quality Control process identifies the faulty outcome of the program; that is, the work results and products that are not conforming to the planned quality standards.

Change requests   The change requests largely originate from the response to the faulty outcome; for example, to eliminate the causes of faults and unsatisfactory performance.

So, during the executing stage, the obvious items that need to be executed are the schedule activities, and while these activities are being executed, the attached cost, schedule, and scope needs to be monitored and controlled. However, there is another important aspect of the program that needs to be monitored and controlled: the risk.

Monitoring and Controlling Risks

The program risks are monitored and controlled by using the Risk Monitoring and Control process, which includes the following:

- Track identified program risks.
- Identify new risks to the program as they emerge during the program execution.
- Execute the risk response plans.
- Evaluate the effectiveness of the risk response plans as they are executed.

Accomplishing these tasks at the program level also includes overlooking risks and responses at the level of the constituent projects within the program. You will find that some risks that emerge at the project level cannot be resolved at the project level. These risks will be resolved at the program level. An example of such risks will be a risk that has its impact on more than one project. Like Quality Control, Risk Monitoring and Control, shown in Figure 8.15, is an ongoing process.

Input to Risk Monitoring and Control

The risk register, which contains the list of identified risks, is an obvious input to the Risk Monitoring and Control process. This and other input items are discussed in the following.

Performance reports   These reports may contain risk-related information, such as the results from an analysis, that may influence risk monitoring and control.

Program work breakdown structure (PWBS)   The PWBS presents the program scope in terms of its deliverables. It also shows the relationships among different components of the program and therefore is necessary to evaluate the overall impact of a given risk, and is also helpful in identifying the risks by looking at the relationships.

Risk register   The risk register contains the list of risks, the risk priorities, and possibly the risk response plans. Therefore it is an essential input to the Risk Monitoring and Control process.

You apply some tools and techniques on these input items to generate the output.

FIGURE 8.15   The Risk Monitoring and Control process: input and output

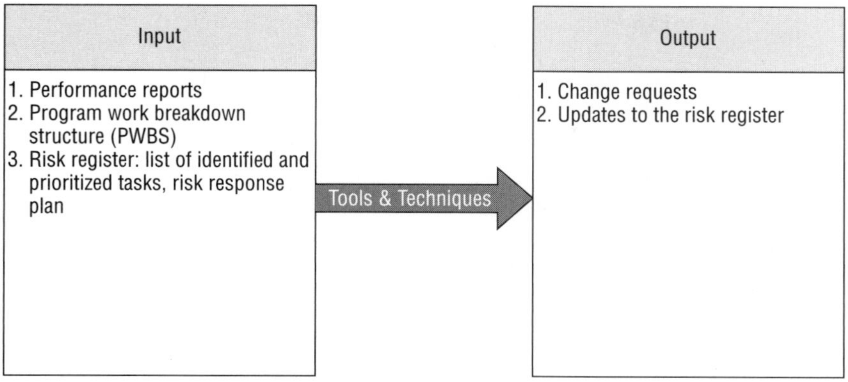

Input		Output

1. Performance reports
2. Program work breakdown
   structure (PWBS)
3. Risk register: list of identified and
   prioritized tasks, risk response
   plan
	Tools & Techniques →	1. Change requests
		2. Updates to the risk register

Tools and Techniques for Risk Monitoring and Control

There are some tools and techniques available to detect the risk triggers, to respond effectively to the risks that have occurred, and to identify new risks.

Risk audits   A risk audit is conducted to examine the following:

- Root causes of the identified risks
- Effectiveness of responses to the identified risks
- Effectiveness of the risk management processes

Risk reassessment and analysis   The risks should be continually reassessed as the program progresses. For example, a risk on the watch list may become important enough that you may need to prepare a response plan for it.

Risk analyses are necessary to effectively respond to the risks that have occurred, to detect the risk triggers, and to identify new risks. The following two kinds of analyses are appropriate for risk monitoring:

Variance and trend analysis   Trends in the program performance should be reviewed on a regular basis as the program execution progresses. These trends can be determined by analyzing the performance data based on various performance control techniques, such as variance and earned value analysis, discussed earlier in this chapter. This analysis can help in detecting new risks.

Reserve analysis   Recall that the contingency reserve is the amount of funds or time (in the schedule) in addition to the planned budget reserved to keep the impact of risks to an acceptable level when the program is executing. The risks occurring during the program execution may have positive or negative effects on the contingency reserve. You perform the reserve analysis at a given time to compare the remaining reserve amount to the remaining risk to determine if the remaining reserve amount is adequate.

Technical performance measurements   Technical performance measurements compare actual versus planned parameters related to the overall technical progress of the project. The deviation determines the degree to which system requirements are met in terms of performance, cost, schedule, and progress in implementing risk handling. The parameters chosen to measure technical performance could be any parameters that represent something important related to the program objectives and requirements: software performance, human resource performance, and system test performance are some examples. These measurements can be helpful in detecting the risk triggers and new risks.

Program risk reviews   You should hold program risk review meetings in a periodic fashion. You can also put risk management as an agenda item at the program status meetings. The time spent on this item will depend on the number of identified risks, their priorities, and the complexity of the responses planned for them. Nevertheless, keeping risks on your agenda and discussing them with the team on a regular basis helps make risk management smoother and more effective.

Contingency planning   The execution of risk responses may impact the contingency reserves. As a result, you may need to update your contingency plan. An important factor to consider here is the amount of current contingency reserve as compared to the amount of remaining risk.

These tools and techniques are used to monitor the risks that may generate change requests, such as recommendations for actions, which are parts of the output of the Risk Monitoring and Control process.

Output of Risk Monitoring and Control

As a result of risk monitoring and control the status of risks will change over time, and therefore updates to the risk register is an obvious output of this process. This and other output items are discussed in the following.

Change requests   You will need to make some change requests as a result of the Risk Monitoring and Control process. For example, the recommended actions, such as contingency plans and workarounds, may result in requirements to change some elements of the project management plan to respond to certain risks. Of course, the change requests will need to go through the Integrated Change Control process for approval, and the approved change requests will become the input to the Direct and Manage Program Execution process for implementation.

Updates to the risk register   Risk control focuses on risks that have developed into actual problems (or opportunities) or are at the point of doing so. At that point you need to implement the corresponding risk response plans that include response actions and contingency plans. You, as a program manager, also want to ensure that the unresolved risks are progressively escalated to higher authority levels until they reach a resolution. These kinds of developments and changes will require updates to the risk register.

You must ensure that the governance structure in the form of processes and procedures is in place to facilitate the assessment of risks for their potential impact across the organization; that is, across multiple projects and multiple programs.

A common thread runs through all the monitoring and controlling processes, and that is communication. All these processes will fail without effective communication. However, communication also needs to be controlled.

Monitoring and Controlling Communication

Communication is monitored and controlled by using two processes: Communication Control and Performance Reporting.

Controlling Communication

As you learned in the previous chapter, the necessary information is communicated to the program stakeholders in a timely fashion by using the Information Distribution process. This communication is monitored and controlled by using the Communication Control process. In other words, the Communication Control process is used to manage communication with the stakeholders for the purpose of information distribution and for resolving issues that are of interest to them.

> The Communication Control process includes ensuring that the relevant policies and procedures are received (or determined), documented, and distributed to the relevant parties (stakeholders) by using the Information Distribution process.

The counterpart of the Communication Control process at the project level is the manage stakeholders process. However, the scope of Communication Control at the program level is much wider in the following aspects:

- The stakeholders involved in a program can include financial managers, product managers, and senior management personnel, including those involved in strategic planning.

- Proactive communication is often required with the community at large. Such external communication can include the following:

  - Address issues which are relevant to the program and are of interest to the public, such as environmental issues related to the program.

  - Manage media and public relations of the program at the political and social levels.

The Communication Control process is shown in Figure 8.16.

FIGURE 8.16 The Communication Control process: input and output

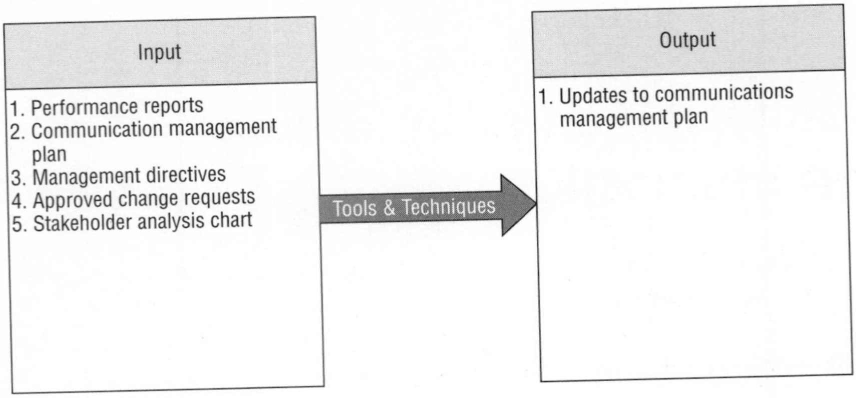

Input	Output
1. Performance reports 2. Communication management plan 3. Management directives 4. Approved change requests 5. Stakeholder analysis chart	1. Updates to communications management plan

Tools & Techniques

Input to Communication Control

A main task of communication control is to ensure that the performance information is being communicated to the stakeholders according to the communication management plan. Therefore, the performance reports and the communication management plan are the obvious input items to the Communication Control process. These and other input items are discussed in the following.

Performance reports   The performance reports contain information about the program performance. These reports are useful to ensure that all the necessary information is being communicated to the stakeholders.

Communication management plan   The Communication Control process is performed according to the communication management plan. The communication management plan is also used to ensure that the other communication processes, such as Information Distribution, are also being performed according to the plan.

Management directives   While controlling the communication, you need to follow any management directives that may exist in your organization.

Approved change requests   There may be some approved change requests regarding communication. These request are input to the Communication Control process, so this process ensures that these changes are implemented.

Stakeholder analysis chart   The stakeholder analysis chart contains stakeholders' requirements regarding communication. It is used to ensure that those communication requirements are being met.

These input items are used to generate the output of the Communication Control process.

Tools and Techniques for Communication Control

The tools and techniques used in communication control are discussed in the following.

Communication methods   Communication methods determined in the communication management plan are used to deliver information to and manage communication with stakeholders. These methods can also be used to resolve issues of concern to stakeholders.

Action items log   An action item (or issue) log is a tool used to document and monitor the actions that need to be taken or the issues that need to be resolved. This is a useful tool to ensure that important items do not fall through the cracks of communication. These issues or action items are generally not included in the program components, but it's important to address them effectively to maintain a good relationship with stakeholders. The following are some useful points about the issues (or the action items):

- Define an issue in such a way that it can be resolved.
- Assign an owner to a well-defined issue.
- Establish a target resolution or closure date.

An unresolved issue can grow into a major source of conflict and delay in completion of program components.

These tools and techniques can be used to generate the output of the Communication Control process.

Output of Communication Control

The main goal of the Communication Control process is to ensure that the needed communication is performed according to the communication management plan, which may be updated due to the approved change requests.

Communication Control, like most of the other processes in the Monitoring and Controlling process group, uses performance reports as an important input. Where do these performance reports come from? They are generated by using the Performance Reporting process.

Performance Reporting

While you are directing and managing the program, the work results (such as program deliverables) are produced. Just producing the results is no guarantee of success. The success is determined by the performance with which the results are being produced. The stakeholders need to know with what efficiency and performance the resources are being used to deliver the program benefits. For this you need to consolidate the program performance data, and you do that by using the Performance Reporting process.

The purpose of performance reporting is to present a clear performance picture of the whole program. It accomplishes this by aggregating the following information:

- Performance information across the constituent projects
- Performance information of the non-project activities related to the program

This performance information is then distributed to the following stakeholders by using the Information Distribution process:

- The program stakeholders
- The stakeholders of the constituent projects

Figure 8.17 shows the Performance Reporting process.

FIGURE 8.17   The Performance Reporting Process: input and output

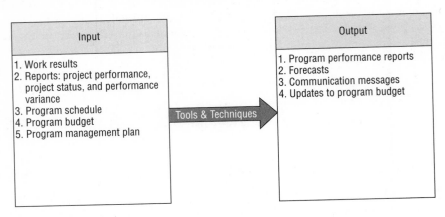

Input	Output
1. Work results 2. Reports: project performance, project status, and performance variance 3. Program schedule 4. Program budget 5. Program management plan	1. Program performance reports 2. Forecasts 3. Communication messages 4. Updates to program budget

Tools & Techniques

Input to Performance Reporting

To measure the program performance, you need to know the program work results and you need the performance reports from the constituent projects. Therefore work results and performance reports from the constituent projects are the obvious input items to the Performance Reporting process. These and other input items are discussed in the following.

Work results   Work results, which are an output of the Direct and Manage Program Execution process, are the raw data for performance reporting. These results include program deliverables.

Reports   The following reports are input to the Performance Reporting process:

- Performance reports about the constituent projects
- Status reports about the constituent projects
- Variance reports that present the variance of actual performance from the planned performance in areas such as schedule and cost

Program schedule   To determine the schedule performance, you need to compare the actual schedule performance from the work results against the planned schedule performance in the program schedule.

Program budget   To determine the cost performance, you need to compare the actual cost performance from the work results against the planned cost performance in the program budget.

Program management plan   The program management plan contains the performance baseline against which the actual work performance is compared.

You apply appropriate tools and techniques on these input items to generate the output.

Tools and Techniques for Performance Reporting

Tools and techniques used in performance reporting include the following.

Information distribution tools and techniques   These include the information distribution methods discussed in Chapter 7, and the presentation tools that include the following:

- The presentation preparation tools to present data in an easy-to-understand format, such as graphics and histograms
- The analysis tools, such as spreadsheet analysis
- The presentation tools, such as PowerPoint

Performance and status review meetings   The performance and status review meetings are generally the regularly scheduled meetings to review the program status and performance. There can be different levels of status review meetings—for example, the meetings of the program team and the meetings of the program manager with the program board, and so on. The frequency of these meetings can be determined based on need.

Performance analyses   To report performance, you need to get the performance information, which comes from performance analyses. These analyses include earned value analysis, trend analysis, and variance, analysis already discussed in this chapter.

Reporting systems   There can be specialized reporting systems to support performance reporting, including the following:

Cost reporting system   This system can store and report the cost expended on the program and on its different components.

Time reporting system   This system can store and report how much time has been expended on the program and on its different components.

WARNING   Different stakeholders will need different kinds of information at different levels of detail.

These tools and techniques can be used to generate the output of the Performance Reporting process.

Output of Performance Reporting

The performance report is an obvious output of the Performance Reporting process. This and other output items are discussed in the following.

Program performance reports   The performance reports can contain the following:

- Summary of work performance information.
- The program status and progress. The status refers to where the things are right now, and the progress refers to what has been accomplished in the past.
- Results from the comparison of the actual work results with the planned performance.

Forecasts   Performance reporting includes making forecasts based on the past performance. These forecasts include estimates such as what will be the total cost incurred at the program completion, called estimate at completion (EAC), and how much cost will be incurred to complete the remaining program, called estimate to complete (ETC). These forecasts can be updated as more performance information comes in.

Communication messages   The performance reports need to be communicated to the program stakeholders. For this purpose, this information is organized into communication messages that become input to the Information Distribution process.

Updates to program budget   Performance reports may include updates to the program budget based on the approved changes.

Effective performance reporting supports recommendations for corrective and preventive actions, especially during the benefits delivery phase (phase four) of the program life cycle. This means that performance reports are used as input to some processes that generate recommendations for preventive and corrective actions.

Performance reports generated by the Performance Reporting process are an input to many Monitoring and Controlling processes, including Program Contract Administration.

Administering the Program Contract

When you select sellers for procuring some items, you negotiate and sign contracts with the sellers. These contracts need to be administered. We have a Contract Administration process at both the project level and the program level. The contract administration process at the program level is called Program Contract Administration and includes the following:

- Manage the relationships with sellers and buyers at the program level without duplicating the efforts being made at the constituent projects level.
- Administer the procurements that span across the program domain and are not covered by a specific constituent project.
- Manage the procurement contract–related issues at the interface of the program with other programs and at the interfaces of one constituent project with other projects.

The Program Contract Administration process is shown in Figure 8.18.

FIGURE 8.18   The Program Contract Administration process: input and output

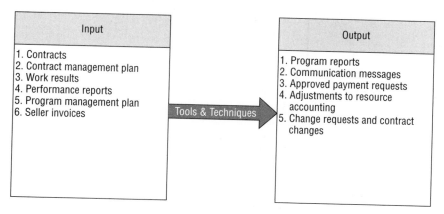

Input to Contract Administration

The Program Contract Administration process is all about administering the contracts according to the contract management plan. Therefore the contracts and the contract management plan are obvious input to the Contract Administration process. These and other input items are discussed in the following.

Contracts   Contracts are the essential input to the Program Contract Administration process. You need the contracts to administer them.

Contract management plan   The contracts are administered according to the contract management plan.

Work results   The work results from the seller will expose any potential issue regarding the contract. You need to take a look at the work results to determine if the contract is being honored.

Performance reports   The performance reports from the seller will indicate if the performance is being made according to the contract. For example, the performance information will reveal which deliverables have been completed, to what extent the planned quality standards are being met, what cost are being incurred, and so on.

Program management plan   The program management plan contains subsidiary plans such as the cost management plan, quality management plan, and procurement management plan, all of which may be useful for administering the contract.

Seller invoices   The seller invoices are part of administering the contract and are needed to approve the payments, which are an output of this process.

With these input items in place, you need some tools and techniques to generate the output of the Program Contract Administration process.

Tools and Techniques for Contract Administration

The tools and techniques used in contract administration include the following.

Contract change control system   The contract change control system, documented in the contract management plan, defines the process by which changes to the contract can be made. It can include the documentation, dispute-resolution procedures, and approval levels to facilitate the authorization of changes.

Procurement performance reviews   A procurement performance review is a buyer-conducted review to asses the seller's progress in delivering the scope and quality within cost and on schedule as determined in the contract or statement of work. The purpose of such a review is to identify the following:

- Progress made with respect to the contract and statement of work
- Performance successes and failures
- Contract noncompliance, if any

Inspections and audits   Inspections and audits that may be required by the buyer and agreed upon by the seller in the contract can be conducted during the execution of the procured work to identify any weakness or noncompliance in the seller's work processes or deliverables.

Payment system   Payment to the seller is usually processed through a payment system, which includes the review and approval of the payment. The payments are made in accordance with the terms in the contract.

Claims administration system   A *claim*, also called a *dispute* or an *appeal*, is a requested change on which the buyer and the seller disagree. Such a change is also called the *contested change*. Usually the claim management is specified in the contract, and the claims are accordingly managed throughout the life cycle of the contract. The claims are resolved according to the terms specified in the contract.

   You use these tools and techniques to generate the output of the Program Contract Administration process.

Output of Contract Administration

The output items generated by the Program Contract Administration process are discussed in the following.

Program reports   The Program Contract Administration process may generate various reports on the program that provide the results, reviews, status, and progress on various aspects of the program.

Communication messages   The program reports and other results from the Program Contract Administration process need to be communicated to the stakeholders in the form of communication messages.

Approved payment requests   The payment requests from the seller will need to be approved or disapproved.

Adjustments to resource accounting   The Program Contract Administration process may require adjustment to resource accounting, which means how the resources are being used and accounted for.

Change requests and contract changes   The contract administration may cause changes to the program management plan and its subsidiary plans, such as the procurement management plan and the program schedule. Such changes must go through the Integrated Change Control process.

> During the implementation of the contract, the program management team must be aware of the legal, managerial, and political implications of the contractual issues, which can affect the program deadlines, generate adverse publicity, and have legal and costly consequences. So the program management team must effectively communicate with sponsors, sellers, governing bodies, and the constituent project management teams.

The Three Big Takeaways

The three most important takeaways from this chapter are the following:

- A program is monitored by continually measuring its performance as it progresses.

- Based on the performance measurements, actions can be recommended and changes can be requested to control the program and thereby bring it in line with the program management plan.

- The forecasts are made and continually modified based on the past program performance.

Summary

Program phase four, the benefits delivery phase, is closely related to program monitoring and control. A general task during this phase is to continually manage the transition from the as-is state to the to-be state; that is, from the actual performance to the expected performance. This and most of the other activities in this phase are performed as part of the Monitoring and Controlling processes. The main purpose of monitoring and controlling the program is to ensure that the program is executed as planned. To accomplish this, the actual performance is measured against the planned performance and changes are requested to bring the performance in line with the plan. The Integrated Change Control process is used to approve or disapprove the change requests generated by other Monitoring and Controlling processes: Resource Control, Monitor and Control Program Work, Issue Management and Control, Scope Control, Schedule Control, Cost Control, Perform Quality Control, Risk Monitoring and Control, and Program Contract

Administration. The change requests will be made based on the performance reports, which are input to these processes. Performance reports are created by the Performance Reporting process. Another important aspect of monitoring and controlling the program is to make forecasts based on past performance. These forecasts are made by using the Performance Reporting process and the Monitor and Control Program Work process.

You execute a program and monitor and control it. At some point, hopefully at its completion, the program will need to be closed. I explore this topic in the next chapter.

Exam's-Eye View

Comprehend

- Change requests, which are input to the Integrated Change Control process, can be generated as an output by most of the other Monitoring and Controlling processes: Resource Control, Monitor and Control Program Work, Issue Management and Control, Scope Control, Schedule Control, Cost Control, Perform Quality Control, Risk Monitoring and Control, and Program Contract Administration.

- Performance reports, generated by the Performance Reporting process as an output, are input to most of the other Monitoring and Controlling processes: Integrated Change Control, Resource Control, Monitor and Control Program Work, Issue Management Control, Scope Control, Schedule Control, Cost Control, Perform Quality Control, Risk Monitoring and Control, and Program Contract Administration.

- Forecasts, an output of the Performance Reporting process and the Monitor and Control Program Work process, are input to the Schedule Control and Cost Control processes.

Look Out

- Lease agreements are an input to the Resource Control process, whereas the expenditure and utilization reports are output of the Resource Control process.

- The communication management plan is an input to the Monitor and Control Program process, whereas communication messages are part of the output.

- The issue register is an input to the Issue Management and Control process, whereas updates to the issue register are part of the output of this process.

- Project performance and status reports are input to the Performance Reporting process.

Memorize

The Monitoring and Controlling processes in the Integration Management knowledge area are as follows:

- Integrated Change Control

- Resource Control

- Monitor and Control Program Work

- Issue Management Control

For cost performance analysis you use the following formulae:

```
EV = BAC x (work completed ÷ total work required)
CV = EV - AC
CPI = EV ÷ AC
```

For schedule performance analysis you use the following formulae:

```
PV = BAC × (time passed ÷ total schedule time)
SV = EV - PV
SPI = EV ÷ PV
```

Estimate to complete has two versions—atypical variances and typical variances:

- For atypical variances the formula is as follows:

```
ETC = BAC - EV
```

- For typical variances the formula is:

```
ETC = (BAC - EV) ÷ CPI
```

Estimate at completion is calculated using the following formula:

```
EAC = ETC + AC
```

Exam Essentials

Integrated change control   The main purpose of the Integrated Change Control process is to approve or reject the change requests and recommendations for corrective and preventive actions. The program goals and objectives should be a major component of the approval criteria.

Program performance measurement   The performance of a program and its constituent projects is measured by using techniques such as earned value and metrics such as cost variance, cost performance index, schedule variance, and schedule performance index. The actual performance is evaluated by comparing it to the planned performance or the performance measurement baseline, which consists of the cost baseline, the schedule baseline, and the scope baseline.

Trend analysis   Trend analysis is the science of predicting future performance based on past results. In program management, it is closely tied to variance analysis—that is, performance analysis—because the variances can show a trend. Trend analysis can be used in several aspects of a program and its constituent projects, such as cost, schedule, quality, and risk. For example, in quality control the trend analysis can be used to predict such things as the number of defects and the cost to repair them. You can use the results of the trend analysis to recommend preventive actions if needed.

Key Terms and Definitions

actual cost (AC)   The total cost actually incurred until a specific point on the time scale for performing the program work, a program component, or a component activity.

baseline   A reference plan for components, such as schedule, scope, and cost, against which performance deviations are measured. The reference plan can be the original or the modified plan.

budget at completion (BAC)   The total budget authorized for performing the work under consideration. This is the planned budget for the program or for one of its component—the cost that you originally estimated.

change control system   A collection of formal documented procedures that specifies how the program deliverables and documents will be changed, controlled, and approved.

change request   A request for a change in some component of a program, such as adding a new feature to the program product, changing the scope of the program, etc.

Communication Control   A process used to manage communication to keep the stakeholders informed about the program progress and status.

corrective actions   Directions for executing the program work to bring expected program performance in conformance with the program management plan.

Cost Control   A process used to control changes to the program budget and generate the information on the variance from the planned budget.

cost performance index (CPI)   A measure of cost efficiency of a program calculated by dividing earned value (EV) by actual cost (AC).

cost variance (CV)   A measure of cost performance obtained by subtracting actual value (AV) from earned value (EV). A positive result indicates good performance, whereas a negative result indicates bad performance.

earned value (EV) or budgeted cost of work performed (BCWP)   The value of the actually performed work expressed in terms of the approved budget for a program, program component, or a component activity for a given time period.

estimate at completion (EAC)   The estimate from the current point in time of how much it will cost to complete the work under consideration (program, program component, or a component activity). The value of EAC is obtained by adding the value of ETC to AC.

estimate to complete (ETC)   The expected cost, estimated from CPI, to complete the remaining work.

Integrated Change Control   A process used to coordinate changes in various areas, including cost, schedule, scope, and quality, across the entire program.

Issue Management and Control   A process used to identify, track, and close the stakeholders' issues to ensure that their expectations are aligned with the program deliverables and activities.

Monitor and Control Program Work   A process used to generate, gather, and consolidate performance information and to measure performance and trends to make improvements.

Pareto diagram   A diagram used to rank the importance of each error (problem) based on the frequency of its occurrence over time in form of defects.

Perform Quality Control   A process used to monitor specific program deliverables (benefits, products, services, and results) to determine if they meet the quality requirements.

Performance Reporting   A process used to consolidate performance data on how program resources are being used to deliver program benefits. This information is provided to the stakeholders by using the Information Distribution process.

planned value (PV) or budgeted cost for the work scheduled (BCWS)   The authorized cost for the scheduled work of the program, program component, or a component activity up to a given point on the time scale.

preventive actions   Directions to perform activities that will reduce the probability of negative consequences associated with risks.

Program Contract Administration   A process used to manage the relationship with sellers and buyers at the program level for the procurement that is not being managed at the project level.

Resource Control   A process used to manage all program resources and the associated cost according to the program management plan.

Risk Monitoring and Control   A process used to track identified risks, identify new risks as they emerge, execute risk response plans, and evaluate the effectiveness of the responses.

Schedule Control   A process used to ensure that the program is completed in time according to the approved schedule.

schedule performance index (SPI)   A measure of the schedule efficiency of a program calculated by dividing earned value (EV) by planned value (PV).

schedule variance (SV)   The deviation of the performed schedule from the planned schedule in terms of cost.

Scope Control   A process used to control changes to the program scope.

trend analysis   The science of predicting future performance based on past results.

Review Questions

1. The infrastructure for monitoring and controlling the constituent projects in a program is established in phase:

   A. One

   B. Two

   C. Three

   D. Four

2. Performance reporting belongs to which of the following process groups?

   A. Planning

   B. Executing

   C. Monitoring and Controlling

   D. Performance

3. Which of the following is not part of the Integrated Change Control process?

   A. Escalate the change requests

   B. Determine if a change has occurred

   C. Implement the approved change requests

   D. Approve change requests

4. Which of the following items is not an input to the Resource Control process?

   A. Program management plan

   B. Cross-charges

   C. Lease agreements

   D. Performance reports

5. All of the following are output of the Monitor and Control Program Work process except:

   A. Change requests

   B. Forecasts

   C. Communication messages

   D. Performance reports

6. All of the following are input to the Issue Management and Control process except:

   A. Program management plan

   B. Escalated issues

   C. Issue register

   D. Performance reports

7. Which of the following is not part of the Scope Control process?

    A. Capture a change request

    B. Ensure that each change request goes through the Integrated Change Control process

    C. Watch out for scope creep

    D. Approve or disapprove change requests

8. All of the following documents are input to the Scope Control process except:

    A. Program scope

    B. Performance reports

    C. Program schedule

    D. Program budget

9. Which of the following items is not an output of the Schedule Control process?

    A. Information for stakeholders

    B. Performance reports

    C. Change requests

    D. Updates to the program schedule

10. All of the following items are input to the Perform Quality Control process except:

    A. Work results

    B. Performance reports

    C. Quality checklists

    D. Inspection reports

11. All of the following items are included in the input to the Perform Quality Control process except:

    A. Risk register

    B. Performance reports

    C. Change requests

    D. Risk response plan

12. Which of the following is not an input to the Performance Reporting process?

    A. Forecasts

    B. Work results

    C. Project performance reports

    D. Program schedule

13. The program sponsor has asked you to put together the performance measurement baseline for a program for which you are the program manager. Which of the following are three components of a performance measurement baseline?

   A. Cost baseline, schedule baseline, and scope baseline

   B. Quality baseline, scope baseline, and cost baseline

   C. Risk baseline, schedule baseline, and cost baseline

   D. Timeline, cost baseline, and scope baseline

14. A junior project manager is trying to compose a list of seven basic tools of quality control. You are going to help him. Which of the following should not be included in this list?

   A. Run chart

   B. Scatter diagram

   C. Earned value technique

   D. Ishikawa diagram

15. You went to a program management class. You were late for the class and when you entered the classroom, the instructor was talking about the action items technique. Which Monitoring and Controlling process was the instructor most likely covering at that time?

   A. Review Meetings

   B. Communication Control

   C. Performance Reporting

   D. Monitor and Control Program Work

16. You have collected the data in the following table from a constituent project of your program; the project is named Project Gap. (Use this data to answer questions 16 through 18.) How much money has actually been spent on Project Gap?

Parameter	Value
BAC	$50,000
PV	$5,500
EV	$4,000
CV	–$500

   A. $4,500

   B. $3,500

   C. $6,000

   D. $5,000

17. What is the current value of the schedule performance index (SPI) for Project Gap?

    A. $40 \div 45$

    B. $55 \div 40$

    C. $40 \div 55$

    D. $9,500

18. Project Gap is:

    A. Underrunning cost and ahead of schedule

    B. Overrunning cost and ahead of schedule

    C. Underrunning cost and behind schedule

    D. Overrunning cost and behind schedule

Answers to Review Questions

1. D.

   D is the correct answer because establishing project governance structure (part of infrastructure) to monitor and control the constituent projects in a program is part of phase four.

   A is an incorrect answer because phase one is the pre-program setup phase.

   B is an incorrect answer because phase two is the program setup phase.

   C is an incorrect answer because phase three establishes the program infrastructure.

2. C.

   C is the correct answer because performance reporting belongs to the Monitoring and Controlling process group.

   A and B are incorrect answers because the Planning and Executing process groups do not include performance reporting.

   D is an incorrect answer because there is no process group called Performance.

3. C.

   C is the correct answer because implementing the change requests is not part of the Integrated Change Control process.

   A, B, and D are incorrect answers because all these are part of the Integrated Change Control process.

4. B.

   B is the correct answer because cross-charges are an output of the Resource Control process.

   A, C, and D are incorrect answers because all these are input to the Resource Control process.

5. D.

   D is the correct answer because performance reports are an input to the Monitor and Control Program Work process.

   A, B, and C are incorrect answers because all these are included in the output of the Monitor and Control Program Work process.

6. B.

   B is the correct answer because escalated issues is an output of the Issue Management and Control process.

   A, C, and D are incorrect answers because all these are included in the input to the Issue Management and Control process.

7. D.

D is the correct answer because approving or disapproving change requests is a function of the Integrated Change Control process.

A, B, and C are incorrect answers because all these are parts of the Scope Control process.

8. A.

A is the correct answer because there is no standard document called program scope. The scope is defined in the program scope statement and in the PWBS.

B, C, and D are incorrect answers because all of these are included in the input to the Scope Control process.

9. B.

B is the correct answer because performance reports are included in the input to the Schedule Control process.

A, C, and D are incorrect answers because all these are included in the output of the Scope Control process.

10. D.

D is the correct answer because inspection reports are included in the output of the Perform Quality Control process.

A, B, and C are incorrect answers because all these are included in the input of the Perform Quality Control process.

11. C.

C is the correct answer because change requests are included in the output of the Perform Quality Control process.

A, B, and D are incorrect answers because all these are included in the input of the Perform Quality Control process.

12. A.

A is the correct answer because forecasts are included in the output of performance reporting.

B, C, and D are incorrect answers because all these items are included in the input of performance reporting.

13. A.

A is the correct answer because the performance measurement baseline basically consists of planned cost, schedule, and scope, against which the execution performance is measured.

B is incorrect because you can include some quality metrics in the performance baseline, but you must include planned cost, scope, and schedule. Here schedule is missing.

C is incorrect because there is no standard term called risk baseline, and because scope baseline is missing.

D is incorrect because there is no standard project management baseline called timeline, and because schedule baseline is missing.

14. C.

C is the correct answer because the earned value technique is used in measuring performance and forecasting, but it's not included in the seven basic quality tools.

A, B, and D are incorrect because the seven basic quality tools are flowchart, run chart, scatter diagram, histogram, Pareto diagram, control chart, and cause-and-effect diagram. A cause-and-effect diagram is also called an Ishikawa diagram or a fishbone diagram.

15. B.

B is the correct answer because action items are a tool or technique used in the Communication Control process.

A is incorrect because there is no standard process called Review Meetings.

C and D are incorrect because these processes do not have action items as a tool or technique.

16. A.

A is the correct answer because actual cost (AC) is calculated as below:

```
CV = EV - AC => AC = EV - CV
AC = $4,000 - (-$500) = $4,000 + $500 = $4,500
```

B is incorrect because the result of subtracting −500 from 4,000 is 4,500 and not 3,500.

C and D are incorrect because the CV is given by $EV - AC$ and not by $PV - AC$.

17. C.

C is the correct answer because SPI is calculated by $EV \div PV$.

A is incorrect because SPI is not calculated by $EV \div AC$; that would be CPI.

B is incorrect because SPI is not calculated by $PV \div EV$.

D is incorrect because SPI is not calculated by $EV + PV$.

18. D.

D is the correct answer because the negative value of CV means the project is overrunning the cost. As the answer to question 17 shows, the value of SPI is less than 1, which means the project is behind schedule.

A and C are incorrect because negative value of CV means the project is overrunning the cost.

B is incorrect because less than 1 value of SPI means the project is behind schedule.

chapter

9

Closing the Program

THE PGMP EXAM CONTENT FROM THE
EXECUTING AND CLOSING THE PROGRAM
PERFORMANCE DOMAIN COVERED IN THIS
CHAPTER INCLUDES THE FOLLOWING
OBJECTIVES:

✓ 4.7 Approve closure of constituent projects upon completion
through appropriate processes and procedures in order to
obtain acceptance.

✓ 6.1 Complete a performance analysis report by gathering
final values and comparing to planned values for quality,
cost, schedule, and resource data in order to determine
program performance.

✓ 6.2 Manage program completion by executing the transition
plan (initiate benefits realization measurement, release
resources and acknowledge individual performance, perform
administrative closure, obtain acceptance, transfer ongoing
activities to functional organization) in order to close out the
program.

✓ 6.3 Conduct the stakeholder post-review meeting by
presenting the program performance report in order to
obtain feedback and capture lessons learned.

✓ 6.4 Report lessons learned via appropriate methodologies to
support future program or organizational improvement.

Once a program has been started, it must be closed properly when completed or canceled. For example, there are benefits from the program that need to be transferred to a proper group within the performing organization. There is an infrastructure that was established to run the program. You cannot simply walk away from that. How about the contracts that were signed during the course of the program? You need to take care of these and other factors of the program and give them a proper closure. So, the core issue in this chapter is how to close a program. To understand this issue, we explore three avenues: closing the program, closing the program components, and closing program contracts.

Closing the Program: The Big Picture

Assume that all the program work has been completed and the program benefits have been obtained. Everybody is happy. All you need to do now is open the champagne, have a party, throw your hats, and go home or move to other assignments. Right? Wrong, because this would be an uncontrolled program closure—or would you even call it a closure? What you need is a controlled closure, and you perform it by using the processes from the Closing process group.

The topics related to the program closure are included in the exam objectives covered in this chapter.

The Exam Roadmap

The following table presents each PgMP exam objective covered in this chapter, along with its explanation:

Exam Objective	What It Really Means
4.7 Approve closure of constituent projects upon completion through appropriate processes and procedures in order to obtain acceptance.	You must understand the Component Closure process. You must also know what tasks are completed in phase five, the last program phase, called close the program. You must also understand the Contract Closure process. You should know that the organization's budget closure procedure must be followed in closing the program and its components.

Exam Objective	What It Really Means
6.1 Complete a performance analysis report by gathering final values and comparing to planned values for quality, cost, schedule, and resource data in order to determine program performance.	Understand the Close Program process. You must also understand the performance analysis techniques discussed in Chapter 8 including earned value analysis.
6.2 Manage program completion by executing the transition plan (initiate benefits realization measurement, release resources and acknowledge individual performance, perform administrative closure, obtain acceptance, transfer ongoing activities to functional organization) in order to close out the program.	Understand what tasks are performed during the last phase of a program, phase five. You should also know how to monitor the closure of the constituent projects in the program.
6.3 Conduct the stakeholder post-review meeting by presenting the program performance report in order to obtain feedback and capture lessons learned. 6.4 Report lessons learned via appropriate methodologies to support future program or organizational improvement.	Understand the Close Program process. You must understand what the final performance report and post-review meetings are. You must also understand the significance of capturing lessons learned.

The topics from these exam objectives covered in this chapter fall into two knowledge management areas: Integration Management and Procurement Management.

Understanding Program Closure

Closing the program means completing the program by obtaining a formal acceptance of the program outcome. This is accomplished by using the processes of the Closing process group shown in Table 9.1 along with their main outputs and the knowledge areas to which they belong. These processes will be discussed one by one in detail further on in this chapter.

TABLE 9.1   The Processes and Knowledge Areas of the Closing Process Group

Knowledge area	Program Closing Process	Major Output
Integration Management	1. Close Program 2. Component Closure	1. Certificate of program completion 2. Certification of component completion
Procurement Management	Contract Closure	Certification of contract completion

These processes are used to accomplish the following:

- Finalize the closure of constituent projects of the program
- Close a canceled project within the program
- Close all the activities of the program
- Close all contracts executed during the program

The purposes of the Closing process group include the following:

Benefits   Accomplish one of the following:

- If the program has been completed, demonstrate that the program scope has been fulfilled and that all the planned program benefits have been delivered.
- If the program has been terminated before completion, document the current state of the program.

Procurement   Accomplish one of the following:

- If the program has been completed, demonstrate that the contractual agreement with the seller, the buyer, or both has been met.
- If the program has been terminated before completion, document the current state of meeting the contractual agreement.

Payments   Accomplish one of the following:

- If the program has been completed, demonstrate that all the payments have been made to the seller, collected from the buyer, or both.
- If the program has been terminated before completion, document the current state of payments to sellers, from buyers, or both.

Release of resources   Accomplish the following:

- Demonstrate that all the human resources have been released.
- Demonstrate that all other resources have been made available to other activities, discarded or disposed of, returned to the owner, transferred to the customer, or transferred to the organization that will maintain the program output.

Intellectual property   Demonstrate that all the intellectual property developed during the program has been captured and legally protected.

Archive   Accomplish one of the following:

- If the program has been completed, demonstrate that all the documentation has been archived according to the program management plan.
- If the program has been terminated before completion, document the current state of the program.

Transition   Ensure that the appropriate transition from the program to an appropriate support function has been performed to facilitate product support, service management, and customer support. This is accomplished according to the transition plan discussed in Chapter 4, "Planning the Program."

Legacy   Ensure that a legacy of operational benefit sustainment is left in place to derive optimum value from the work accomplished by the program.

Because closing the constituent projects is included in the program closure, the program closure activities are performed throughout the program, not just at the program completion.

Figure 9.1 shows three processes in the Closing process group used to close a program: Close Program, Component Closure, and Contract Closure. Next we'll examine these three processes.

FIGURE 9.1   Processes in the Closing process group, used to close a program

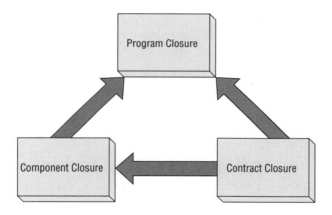

Program closure is performed during phase five of the program, the last program phase.

Close the Program: The Last Program Phase

Phase five, the last phase of a program, begins after the program has passed the phase gate review, G4—that is, the program has qualified to exit phase four. The purpose of this last phase is to perform a controlled closure of the program by accomplishing the following:

- Disband the program organization: goodbye time
- Shut down the program infrastructure
- Perform the transition of program artifacts, benefits monitoring, and ongoing operations to the appropriate groups

The activities performed to ensure safe and smooth program closure include the following:

Review   Review the status of program benefits delivery with the program sponsor and other appropriate stakeholders.

Learn and Document   The learning and documenting part of the closure includes the following:

- Capture the lessons learned and archive them in the performing organization's database for use in future programs. The lessons learned include both the strengths and the weaknesses experienced during the program.

- Provide feedback in the form of recommendations based on the experience, including changes identified during the program life cycle which were out of the program's scope. The purpose here is that the organization can benefit from the program's experience.

- Archive and index (for access) all the program-related documents so that they could be used in future programs.

Transition   The transition part of the program closure includes the following:

- Manage the transition of program artifacts, benefits monitoring, and ongoing operations to the appropriate groups.

- During the transition, ensure that the required customer support will be provided. The assurance for customer support may be part of a contract.

- The transition is performed according to the transition plan discussed in Chapter 4.

Shutdown   The shutdown to be managed during the program closure includes the following:

- Disband the program organization, including the program team.

- Dismantle the program infrastructure.

- Ensure that the redeployment of human resources has been arranged. Also ensure that the arrangements for the redeployment of physical resources such as equipment and facilities are in place.

The purpose of the lessons learned is to use the strengths and best practices from this program in future programs and to improve in the areas that were discovered to be weak.

Most of the critical tasks in the program closure are accomplished by using the processes of the Closing process group.

Performing the Program Closure

You close a program properly by putting together the closure document and reviewing them with the program sponsor, the customer, or both to obtain their acceptance of the program outcome. The process used to close the program is called the Close Program process, and is depicted in Figure 9.2.

FIGURE 9.2   The Close Program process: input and output

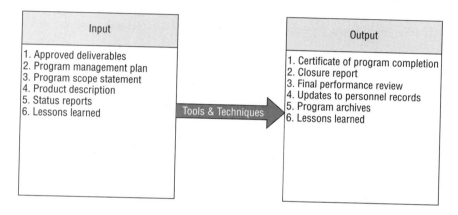

Input	Output
1. Approved deliverables 2. Program management plan 3. Program scope statement 4. Product description 5. Status reports 6. Lessons learned	1. Certificate of program completion 2. Closure report 3. Final performance review 4. Updates to personnel records 5. Program archives 6. Lessons learned

Tools & Techniques

Input to Closing the Program

The program management plan, against which the program outcome is to be evaluated, and the approved deliverables from the constituent projects are the obvious inputs to the Close Program process. These and other input items are discussed in the following.

Approved deliverables   These refer to the deliverables from the constituent projects that have been closed, and that means their deliverables have been approved (or accepted) during the project management process called Close Project, performed at the project level. Recall that all the projects must be closed before the program can be closed. Therefore, the approved deliverables from these projects become an input to closing the program.

The program management plan   The Close Program process is performed in accordance with the program management plan. The program management plan is also used to evaluate and approve the program outcome.

The program scope statement   The program scope statement is an input to the Close Program process because the scope of the completed program needs to be verified against the program scope statement.

Product description   Product descriptions will be needed to get the formal acceptance of the products.

Status reports   Status reports will indicate if we are ready for the closure. You need to review the status of program benefits delivery with the program sponsor and other appropriate stakeholders.

Lessons learned   During the program life cycle, several program management processes can generate lessons learned as an output. This output becomes an input to the Close Program process. The lessons learned from the closure of the constituent projects should also be used as an input to the program closure.

With these input items in place, you can use some tools and techniques to generate the output.

Tools and Techniques for Closing the Program

The following tools and techniques can be used in closing the program.

Management information system   A project/program management information system can be used to facilitate the program closure. It may have automated tools to help the program team in performing various closure tasks, such as creating a closure report, collecting and archiving lessons learned, and so on. This system is also used to update the records, making and storing program archives including lessons learned.

Performance reporting tools and techniques   The performance reporting tools and techniques discussed in Chapter 8, "Monitoring and Controlling the Program," (such as information distribution tools and review meetings) are used for closing the program. You will need to perform the final performance review and prepare performance and closure reports.

Post-review meeting   You should conduct a post-review meeting of the stakeholders in which you do the following:

- Present the program performance report
- Obtain feedback
- Discuss and capture lessons learned

Obviously, you use the appropriate communication tools and techniques to organize and conduct the post-review meeting.

Expert judgment   Help from the relevant experts can be used in different matters related to the program closure. For example, your program involves a product in a specific application area. You may need an expert from that application area to review with the customer or sponsor that all the planned requirements for this product are met in order to obtain acceptance.

You can use these tools and techniques to generate the output of the Close Program process.

Output of Closing the Program

A certification of the program completion is an obvious output of the Close Program process. This and other output items are discussed in the following.

Certificate of program completion   The main goal of the program closure is to obtain formal acceptance of the program's outcome. The program closure documents contain the signoff from the sponsor, the customer, or both on the projects and on the non-project program activities. These signoffs verify deliverables against requirements.

Closure report   The closure report consists of the closure documents of the constituent projects and non-project activities included in the program. These documents carry the signoff from the sponsor, the customer, or both. These documents also contain the results of verifications of deliverables against requirements and the lessons learned.

Final performance review   The performance review includes the review within the program team and the review to obtain acceptance of the program outcome. One of the purposes of the team review is to candidly learn from the successes and failures encountered during the program execution.

The closure documents and the performance of the program are also reviewed with the sponsor, the customer, or both as part of obtaining the formal acceptance of the program outcome. The performance measurements and analysis, including earned value analysis, are discussed in Chapter 8. The final performance analysis report should include the following:

- Consolidate the overall performance analysis results, including program metrics.
- Compile the performance results about different aspects of the program, such as cost, scope, schedule, quality, and risk.
- Summarize the achieved results in context of the strategic goals and objectives of the organization.
- Summarize the trends identified from the performance analysis during the life cycle of the program.

After the completion of this review, you ask the sponsor, the customer, or both to acknowledge the acceptance of the program outcome by signing the closure documents.

Updates to personnel records   Closing the program ensures releasing the human resources. The personnel records are updated accordingly.

Program archives   When a project (or a non-project activity) is closed, the Close Program process is performed to capture the useful information and archive it. You need to accomplish one of the following:

- If the program has been completed, demonstrate that all the documentation has been archived according to the program management plan.
- If the program has been terminated before completion, document the current state of the program.

The archive includes lessons learned.

Lessons learned   Lessons learned are compiled during the program review. This is also an output of several other program management processes. You also capture the lessons learned from the constituent project closures. These lessons learned are analyzed and integrated. The significant conclusions are incorporated into the closure report and are archived.

WARNING   The constituent projects in a program need to be closed by using the project management processes before the program can be closed. The closure event needs to be communicated to the project stakeholders.

A program consists of projects and non-project activities. The constituent projects must be closed before the program closure can be completed.

 Real World Scenario

Lessons Learned

You are in the process of closing a program for which you are the program manager. The program has met its goal of developing a social networking website that offers services to professionals in the field of project and program management. One of the objectives of the program was to have at minimum 100,000 professionals subscribe to the services the website offers. You have conducted several review meetings with different stakeholders to capture the lessons learned. In your meeting with the project managers who managed the constituent projects of the program, you made it clear that the purpose of the meeting is to capture the successes, failures, strengths, and the weaknesses so that future programs can benefit from the experience. You also assured them that the purpose of the meeting was not to assign responsibility for mistakes to individuals with the intention of disciplining or punishing them.

The following is a list of some of the lessons learned that you captured during the review meetings:

Don't just build; build and tell. You started your review meeting with the project managers by reviewing your decision made earlier in the program to delay and minimize the marketing efforts for the website. You reminded the attendees how you forecast: if you build it they will come. But your forecast did not come true, because you built it and they did not come. The marketing efforts were started late, and it delayed the program because it took more time for the website membership to reach the objective of 100,000. So the lesson learned is, do not assume that if you build it they will come. If you build, you need to tell people what you have built, and you need to sell to them what you have built before they can decide if they want to come.

Differences of opinion are good. John Forest, the development project manager, cited many situations in which there was a difference in opinion about how a component would be built. The differences were managed properly by staying focused on the goal and not on the people involved in the differences. As a result, in each case a solution was selected that turned out to be a far better solution than the default, which would have been selected if there were no difference of opinion. Lesson learned: differences in opinions, if managed properly, can produce better results.

Look out for scope creep. Alan Gill, a software developer, implemented some features that were not in the scope of the software application he was developing. But he implemented those features because he thought the customers would think they were cool. This implementation interacted with the implementation of features that were included in the scope, resulting in the delay of the scoped features' implementation. Because the implementations of some of these features was on the critical path, it delayed the development project. Lesson learned: raise the awareness of scope creep among the programmers and look out for scope creep more closely.

More is not always better. Ann Taylor, the data-warehouse project manager, told the meeting that she put two extra engineers on a task that was on a critical path because she wanted to make sure the task was completed in time. But because these two engineers were relative beginners to the data-warehouse technology, they slowed down the engineer originally assigned to the task. As a result the task took even longer than Ann feared it would if she had not assigned the additional engineers. Lesson learned: the time required to complete a task does not always decrease linearly with an increase in the number of individuals assigned to it.

These and other lessons learned are going to be archived for the benefit of future programs.

Closing the Program Components

A program consists of projects and non-project activities. These program components are closed by using the Component Closure process. Each project is originally closed by using the Closing processes at the project management level. The Component Closure process, depicted in Figure 9.3, is used to oversee the closure at the project level; that is, to ensure that the projects have been properly closed by using the project management processes.

FIGURE 9.3   The Component Closure process: input and output

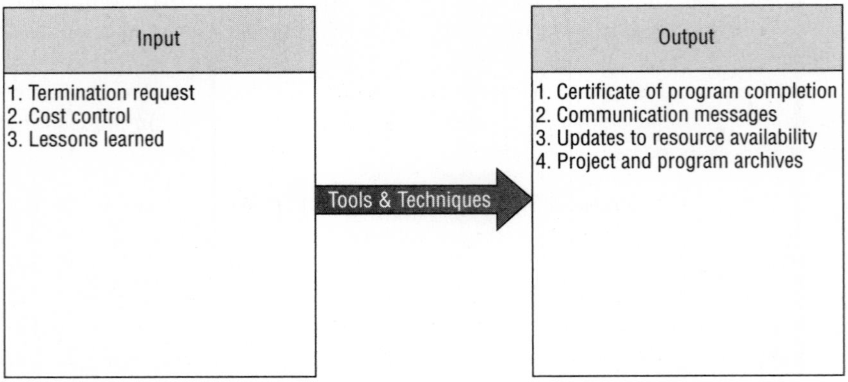

Input	Output
1. Termination request 2. Cost control 3. Lessons learned	1. Certificate of program completion 2. Communication messages 3. Updates to resource availability 4. Project and program archives

Tools & Techniques

Input to Component Closure

The items that are input to the Component Closure process are discussed in the following.

Termination request   The termination request for a project may originate at the program level. For example, a program benefits review may have concluded that because a specific project is not contributing to the planned program benefits, it must be terminated.

Cost control   It's possible that a component is being closed to control the cost; that is, to complete the program within the budget.

Lessons learned   When a component is closed the lessons learned from the work performed on that component must be captured. These lessons learned are the output of the closure at the project level and become an input to the closure at the program level.

With this input in place, you use some tools and techniques to generate the output.

Tools and Techniques for Component Closure

The following tools and techniques can be used in closing the program components.

Management information system   A project/program management information system can be used to facilitate the program component closure. It may have automated tools to help the program team in performing various closure tasks, such as creating communication messages, updating the resource availability, making the archives, and so on.

Meetings   Meetings can be held with the project managers to oversee the project closures.

Expert judgment   Help from the relevant experts can be used in different matters related to the program component closure. For example, an expert in an application area of the project's product can help determine if the product requirements are met.

You can use these tools and techniques to generate the output of the Component Closure process.

Output of Component Closure

You need to communicate the closure news to the appropriate stakeholders. Therefore communication messages are an obvious output of the Component Closure process. This and other input items are discussed in the following.

Certificate of program completion   You need to ensure that the component closure has been properly certified; that is, the outcome of the component completion has been accepted by the sponsor, the customer, or both. This will help in obtaining the certificate of program closure.

Communication messages   There will be stakeholders at the program level that are not included in the set of stakeholders at the project level. The information about the component closures will need to be communicated to those stakeholders at the program level.

Updates to resource availability   As the program components are closed, the resources assigned to those components will be released and the resource availability will be updated accordingly. The resources that have become available from one component closure can be allocated to another component within the program that is either active and needs more resources, or is waiting to be activated.

Project and program archives   As a project or a non-project activity of the program is closed, its records must be archived based on the need. The project records will go to the project archive and the records of the non-project activity will go to the program archive.

While monitoring the closure of a project, you should also accomplish the following:

- Apply the budget closure procedure of the performing organization while closing the finances. This procedure may include the following components:
  - Financial report
  - Compliance audit to verify that the finance-related contractual obligations were met
  - Financial closeout obligations included in the organization's policies
  - Financial metrics
- Assess the impact of the budget closure for the project on the program.
- Close project management authority levels properly. For example, the right individuals should sign the right documents.

  You will gather the financial reports and metrics from the projects to generate a consolidated financial report at the program level. There should also be a complete closure of contractual obligations. In other words, the program may include some contracts, which will need to be closed properly.

Closing the Contracts

The contracts executed during the program must be closed according to the contract terms and conditions by using the Contract Closure process shown in Figure 9.4.

FIGURE 9.4 The Contract Closure process: input and output

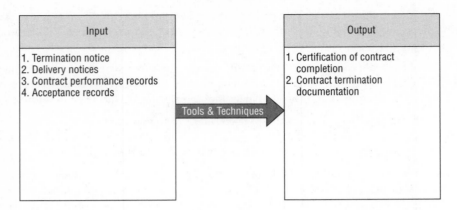

Input to Contract Closure

The input items that you need to perform the Contract Closure process are discussed in the following.

Termination notice If the contract is being terminated prematurely, a termination notice will be an important input to closing the contract.

Delivery notices The notices about the delivery of the outcome promised in the contract are essential input to closing the contract.

Contract performance records Contract performance records are input because they will need to be updated as part of the Contract Closure process.

Acceptance reports Contract closure involves verification of the work and the product related to the contract. Therefore, the product acceptance reports are an input to the Contract Closure process.

 With these input items in place, you can use some tools and techniques to generate the output of the Contract Closure process.

Tools and Techniques for Contract Closure

The tools and techniques for the Contract Closure process are the items that you need to facilitate the contract closure and are discussed here.

Procurement audits This is a structured review of the procurement process with the purpose of identifying successes and failures from the planning through the executing of the program. The lessons learned from the audit can be applied to other procurements.

The records management system   This is a part of the project/program management information system, and can be used to manage contract documentation and records. For example, you can use this system to archive the documents, maintain an index of contract and communication documents, and retrieve the documents.

> While closing the contracts, ensure that the contractual acceptance criteria for the project or its product is followed. The fulfillment of the acceptance criteria should be measured by using the agreed-upon mechanism described in the contract or in the contract management plan.

Now I'll ask you the easiest question in this book: what is the output of the Contract Closure process?

Output of Contract Closure

The Contract Closure output includes the completion certificate and documentation, discussed in the following.

Certification of contract completion   If the contract was completed, a completion certificate is an important output. The acceptance reports will be useful in obtaining the completion certificate.

Contract termination documentation   It is important to save the contract documentation, including the closure or termination documentation. It will be useful in case of a procurement audit or a legal action. Accurate and complete documentation is a key to the efficient resolution of various issues, including legal issues. The documentation may include the following:

- Contract
- Progress reports
- Financial records, including invoices and payments
- Work performed
- Work not performed
- Circumstances that led to the contract termination, if the contract is not completed

Contractual documents become part of the program archives.

> If a contract has been terminated before its full implementation, it still needs to be closed by using the Contract Closure process.

The Three Big Takeaways

The three most important takeaways from this chapter are the following:

- A program is closed by using the Close Program process. Before you can complete closing a program, you must close all the program components and the program contracts.

- A program component is closed by using the Component Closure process. Before you can complete the closure of a program component, all the contracts related to the component must be closed.

- A contract is closed by using the Contract Closure process.

Summary

The last phase in the life cycle of a program is the program closure, which includes disbanding the program organization; shutting down the program infrastructure; and transitioning program artifacts, benefits monitoring, and ongoing operations to the appropriate groups. Before the program closure is complete, all of its components, such as constituent projects, must be closed. Also, any contract involved in a project or the program must be closed before the closure of the corresponding project or program can be complete. The program performance data should be consolidated into the final performance analysis report, which should summarize the results in the context of the organization's strategic goals and objectives. Most of the tasks involved in closing the program are performed by using the processes from the Closing process group.

The Close Program process is used to close the program. The projects and other components of the program are closed by using the Component Closure process, whereas the program contracts are closed by using the Contract Closure process. It's important to review the program and document the lessons learned before disbanding the program team. This will benefit the future programs in the organization.

Exam's-Eye View

Comprehend

- All the contracts in a project or a program must be closed before the corresponding project or program can be closed, and all the projects in a program must be closed before the program can be closed.

- The Component Closure process is used to close a non-project component of a program and to oversee the closure of a project in the program.

- It's important to transfer ongoing program activities to the appropriate organization group before the program closure is complete.

Look Out

- Close Program, the name of the process in the Closing process group to close the program, is very similar to the name of the last phase of a program life cycle, close the program.

- Transition of program artifacts, benefits monitoring, and ongoing operations to the appropriate groups is part of the program closure.

- Lessons learned are included in the input to and output of the Close Program process, and include both the strengths and weaknesses of the program.

- If a contract has been terminated before its full implementation, it still needs to be closed by using the Contract Closure process.

Memorize

- The last program phase, phase five, is close the program, in which the program closure occurs.

- Lessons learned are an input to both the Close Program and Component Closure processes.

- The final performance analysis report is presented in the post-review meeting, in which feedback is obtained and lessons learned are captured.

Exam Essentials

The final performance analysis report   As a part of closing the program, the performance data is consolidated into the final performance analysis report. This report presents the overall performance of the program and accomplishes the following:

- Consolidates the overall performance analysis results, including program metrics
- Compiles the performance results about different aspects of the program, such as cost, scope, schedule, quality, and risk
- Summarizes the achieved results in the context of the strategic goals and objectives of the organization
- Summarizes the trends identified from the performance analysis during the life cycle of the program

The post-review meeting   As a part of closing the program, you conduct a post-review meeting of the stakeholders to accomplish the following:

- Present the program performance report
- Obtain feedback
- Discuss and capture lessons learned

Lessons learned   During the program closure it is important to capture lessons learned, both positive and negative. The purpose here is to support program and organizational improvements in the future. Lessons learned are archived by using the program/project management information system (PMIS).

Key Terms and Definitions

Close Program   A process of the Closing process group that is used to close a program.

Close the program   Phase five, the last program phase, in which the program is closed.

closure report   An output item of the Close Program process that consists of the closure documents of the constituent projects and non-project activities included in the program.

Component Closure   A process used to close a component or oversee the closure of a component of the program.

Contract Closure   A process used to close the program contracts according to the contract terms and conditions.

post-review meeting   A meeting conducted during the program closure with the stakeholders, in which the final performance analysis report is presented, feedback is obtained, and lessons learned are captured.

Review Questions

1. The Closing process group consists of the following set of processes:

   A. Administrative Closure, Contract Closure, and Close Program

   B. Close Project, Component Closure, and Contract Closure

   C. Close Program, Component Closure, and Contract Closure

   D. Review Program, Close Program, and Close Contract

2. Closing a program includes all of the following activities except:

   A. Disband the program organization

   B. Shut down the program infrastructure

   C. Perform the transition of program artifacts, benefits monitoring, and ongoing operations to the appropriate groups

   D. Ensure that all the projects in the program are closed after the program is closed

3. The input to the Close Program process includes of all of the following except:

   A. Approved deliverables

   B. Program management plan

   C. Certificate of program completion

   D. Product description

4. The output of the Component Closure process includes of all of the following except:

   A. Communication messages

   B. Termination request

   C. Project archive

   D. Program archive

5. The input to the Contract Closure process includes of all of the following except:

   A. Termination notice

   B. Delivery notices

   C. Acceptance reports

   D. Certificate of contract completion

6. In the program life cycle, closing the program is:

   A. Phase six

   B. Phase five

   C. Phase four

   D. Phase three

7. You overheard Delon, a program manager, saying he wanted to capture lessons learned before he could perform a certain process. Which process was Delon referring to?

   A. Component Closure

   B. Make Archive

   C. Contract Closure

   D. Administrative Closure

8. Your program is in phase five. You want to make archives of the information from the constituent projects. Which process should you perform?

   A. Close Program

   B. Contract Closure

   C. Component Closure

   D. Administrative Closure

9. Your program is in phase five. The sponsor has asked you to hold a post-review meeting. What do you need to accomplish before you could hold the post-review meeting?

   A. Capture lessons learned

   B. Make archives

   C. Prepare the final performance analysis report

   D. Close all the contracts

10. You are completing preparation for performing the processes to close the program. Which of the following is not a tool used in closing the program?

   A. Performance reporting tools and techniques

   B. Certificate of program completion

   C. PMIS

   D. Expert judgment

Answers to Review Questions

1.   C.

C is the correct answer because the three processes in the Closing process group are Close Program, Component Closure, and Contract Closure.

A is an incorrect answer because there is no process called Administrative Closure in the Closing process group.

B is an incorrect answer because there is no process called Close Project in program management.

D is an incorrect answer because there is no process called Review Program in the program Closing process group.

2.   D.

D is the correct answer because the program closure is not complete without closing the projects in it.

A, B, and C are incorrect answers because all these activities are included in closing the program.

3.   C.

C is the correct answer because the program management plan is an output of the Close Program process.

A, B, and D are incorrect because these items are included in the input to the Close Program process.

4.   B.

B is the correct answer because the termination request is included in the input to the Close Program process.

A, C, and D are incorrect because these processes are included in the output of the Close Program process.

5.   D.

D is the correct answer because the certificate of contract completion is an output of the Contract Closure process.

A, B, and C are incorrect because these items are included in the input to the Close Program process.

6.   B.

B is the correct answer because closing the program is phase five of the program life cycle.

A is incorrect because there are only five phases in the program life cycle.

C is incorrect because phase four is delivering the incremental benefits.

D is incorrect because phase three is establishing the program infrastructure.

7. A.

A is the correct answer because the Component Closure process takes lessons learned as an input.

B and D are incorrect because there are no standard processes called Make Archive and Administrative Closure.

C is incorrect because Contract Closure does not take lessons learned as an input.

8. C.

C is the correct answer because project archives are an output of the Component Closure process.

A and B are incorrect because Close Program and Contract Closure do not generate project archives as an output.

D is incorrect because there is no standard processes called Administrative Closure.

9. C.

C is the correct answer because the final analysis report is presented in the post-review meeting.

A is incorrect because one of the purposes of the post-review meeting is to get feedback and capture lessons learned.

B and D are incorrect because the completion of these tasks is not a requirement for conducting the post-review meeting.

10. B.

B is the correct answer because the certificate of program completion is an output of the Close Program process.

A, C, and D are incorrect because the key tools and techniques used in the Close Program process are performance reporting tools and techniques, program management information system (PMIS), and expert judgment.

About the Companion CD

In this appendix:

- What you'll find on the CD
- System requirements
- Using the CD
- Troubleshooting

What You'll Find on the CD

The following sections are arranged by category and provide a summary of the software and other goodies you'll find on the CD. If you need help with installing the items provided on the CD, refer to the installation instructions in the "Using the CD" section of this appendix.

Some programs on the CD might fall into one of these categories:

Shareware programs are fully functional, free, trial versions of copyrighted programs. If you like particular programs, register with their authors for a nominal fee and receive licenses, enhanced versions, and technical support.

Freeware programs are free, copyrighted games, applications, and utilities. You can copy them to as many computers as you like—for free—but they offer no technical support.

GNU software is governed by its own license, which is included inside the folder of the GNU software. There are no restrictions on distribution of GNU software. See the GNU license at the root of the CD for more details.

Trial, demo, or *evaluation* versions of software are usually limited either by time or functionality (such as not letting you save a project after you create it).

Sybex Test Engine

For Windows and Mac

The CD contains the Sybex Test Engine, which includes all of the Assessment Test and Chapter Review questions in electronic format, as well as two bonus exams located only on the CD.

PDF of the Book

For Windows and Mac

We have included an electronic version of the text in .pdf format. You can view the electronic version of the book with Adobe Reader.

Adobe Reader

For Windows and Mac

We've also included a copy of Adobe Reader, so you can view PDF files that accompany the book's content. For more information on Adobe Reader or to check for a newer version, visit Adobe's website at `http://www.adobe.com/products/reader/`.

Electronic Flashcards

For PC, Pocket PC and Palm

These handy electronic flashcards are just what they sound like. One side contains a question or fill in the blank, and the other side shows the answer.

System Requirements

Make sure that your computer meets the minimum system requirements shown in the following list. If your computer doesn't match up to most of these requirements, you may have problems using the software and files on the companion CD. For the latest and greatest information, please refer to the ReadMe file located at the root of the CD-ROM.

- A PC running Microsoft Windows 98, Windows 2000, Windows NT4 (with SP4 or later), Windows Me, Windows XP, or Windows Vista.

- An Internet connection

- A CD-ROM drive

Using the CD

To install the items from the CD to your hard drive, follow these steps.

1. Insert the CD into your computer's CD-ROM drive. The license agreement appears.

 Windows users: The interface won't launch if you have autorun disabled. In that case, click Start ➢ Run (for Windows Vista, Start ➢ All Programs ➢ Accessories ➢ Run). In the dialog box that appears, type **D:\Start.exe**. (Replace *D* with the proper letter if your CD drive uses a different letter. If you don't know the letter, see how your CD drive is listed under My Computer.) Click OK.

2. Read through the license agreement, and then click the Accept button if you want to use the CD.

The CD interface appears. The interface allows you to access the content with just one or two clicks.

Troubleshooting

Wiley has attempted to provide programs that work on most computers with the minimum system requirements. Alas, your computer may differ, and some programs may not work properly for some reason.

The two likeliest problems are that you don't have enough memory (RAM) for the programs you want to use, or you have other programs running that are affecting installation or running of a program. If you get an error message such as "Not enough memory" or "Setup cannot continue," try one or more of the following suggestions and then try using the software again:

Turn off any antivirus software running on your computer. Installation programs sometimes mimic virus activity and may make your computer incorrectly believe that it's being infected by a virus.

Close all running programs. The more programs you have running, the less memory is available to other programs. Installation programs typically update files and programs; so if you keep other programs running, installation may not work properly.

Have your local computer store add more RAM to your computer. This is, admittedly, a drastic and somewhat expensive step. However, adding more memory can really help the speed of your computer and allow more programs to run at the same time.

Customer Care

If you have trouble with the book's companion CD-ROM, please call the Wiley Product Technical Support phone number at (800) 762-2974. Outside the United States, call +1(317) 572-3994. You can also contact Wiley Product Technical Support at http://sybex.custhelp.com. John Wiley & Sons will provide technical support only for installation and other general quality control items. For technical support on the applications themselves, consult the program's vendor or author.

To place additional orders or to request information about other Wiley products, please call (877) 762-2974.

Glossary

Acquire Program Team   A process used to obtain the program team members needed to perform the program work.

actual cost (AC)   The total cost actually incurred until a specific point on the timescale for performing the program work, a program component, or a component activity.

alternatives identification   A technique used to apply nonstandard approaches, such as brainstorming and lateral thinking, to perform program (or project) tasks.

analogous estimation   A technique that is used to make an estimate of some quantities for an activity such as activity based on the actual values of these quantities for similar activities in a previous project or program. The quantities that can be estimated using this technique include activity duration, cost, and resource requirements.

arrow diagramming method (ADM)   A technique used to draw a network diagram in which an arrow represents an activity and also points to the successor activity through a junction represented by a node (box).

assumption   A factor that you consider to be true without any proof or verification.

asynchronous communication   A communication method in which the two communicating entities do not have to be present on both ends of the communication line at the same time. Email is an example of asynchronous communication because when the sender of the email pushes the Send button, the intended recipient of the e-mail message does not have to be logged on to the email server.

Authorize Projects   A program initiating process used to authorize projects in the program; includes obtaining project approval, issuing a program charter, and assigning a project manager.

baseline   A reference plan for components, such as schedule, scope, and cost, against which performance deviations are measured. The reference plan can be the original or the modified plan.

benchmarking   A technique that involves comparing practices, products, or services of a program (or program component) with those of some reference programs (or program components) for the purposes of learning, improvement, and creating the basis for measuring performance.

benefit   A positive contribution or improvement to the running of an organization such as increased revenues, reduced costs, and improved employee morale.

benefit cost ratio (BCR)   The value obtained by dividing the benefit by the cost.

benefits management   Part of management that includes activities and techniques for defining, creating, maximizing, and sustaining benefits from a program.

benefits realization plan   A document that contains definition of each expected program benefit and other information about it, such as how the benefit maps to program outcome and how it will be realized.

brainstorming   A creative technique generally used in a group environment to gather ideas as candidates for a solution to a problem or an issue, without any immediate evaluation of these ideas.

budget   An approved aggregated cost with a timeline.

budget at completion (BAC)   The total budget authorized for performing the work under consideration. This is the planned budget for the program or for one of its component—the cost that you originally estimated.

cash flow (CF)   Refers to both the money coming in and the money going out of an organization. Positive cash flow means more money coming in than going out.

change control system   A collection of formal documented procedures that specifies how the program deliverables and documents will be changed, controlled, and approved.

change request   A request for a change in some component of a program, such as adding a new feature to the program product, changing the scope of the program, etc.

Close Program   A process of the Closing process group that is used to close a program.

Close the Program   Phase five, the last program phase, in which the program is closed.

closure report   An output item of the Close Program process that consists of the closure documents of the constituent projects and non-project activities included in the program.

communication   An exchange of information between persons and groups by using an effectively common system of signs, symbols, and behavior.

communication control   The process of managing communication to ensure that the information needs of the program stakeholders are satisfied and resolve the issues that are of interest to the stakeholders.

communication planning   The process of determining the communication needs of the program stakeholders and planning to satisfy those needs. This includes determining what information is needed to be communicated and when, who will communicate it and to whom, and how it will be communicated.

Component Closure   A process used to close a component or oversee the closure of a component of the program.

conditional diagramming methods (CDM)   Network diagramming methods used to display dependency relationships among program components or activities when conditions, loops, or both are involved in these relationships.

constraint   A restriction (or a limitation) of available options that can affect the performance of the project or a program.

continuous process improvement   An iterative method for improving the quality of all processes.

contract   A mutually binding agreement between a buyer and a seller that obligates the seller to provide the specified product, service, or result and obligates the buyer to make the payment for it.

Contract Closure   A process used to close the program contracts according to the contract terms and conditions.

contract management plan   A document that specifies how a specific contract will be administered. This may include items such as performance requirements and delivery of certain documents.

contract statement of work (SOW)   A document that describes the procurement item in sufficient detail. This describes the scope of what will be delivered by the seller and becomes part of the contract.

control   Set of techniques used to control projects and programs by activities such as analyzing variances, assessing trends to improve processes, evaluating alternatives, comparing actual performance with planned performance, and recommending appropriate corrective and preventive actions and changes in order for the program or the project to succeed. These control activities include the monitoring element.

corrective actions   Directions for executing the program work to bring expected program performance in conformance with the program management plan.

cost   The value of the inputs that have been used up to perform a task or to produce an item: product, service, or result.

cost baseline   A time phased budget against which cost performance is measured, monitored, and controlled.

Cost Control   A process used to control changes to the program budget and generate the information on the variance from the planned budget.

cost estimating and budgeting   A process used to aggregate all cost at the program level and to put a timeline on it. The process is used to generate program budget and a cost management plan.

cost management plan   A plan used to manage and control the program cost.

cost performance index (CPI)   A measure of cost efficiency of a program calculated by dividing earned value (EV) by actual cost (AC).

cost variance (CV)   A measure of cost performance obtained by subtracting actual value (AV) from earned value (EV). A positive result indicates good performance, whereas a negative result indicates bad performance.

crashing   A schedule compression technique used to decrease the project duration with minimum additional cost. A number of alternatives are analyzed, including the assignment of additional resources.

critical path   The longest path (sequence of activities) in a project schedule network diagram. Because it is the longest path, it determines the duration of the project.

data   A raw fact or figure, such as cost equal to one million dollars.

database   An information system that contains a structured collection of records, such as student ID with the student name and the grades in different courses attached to the identification.

database management system (DBMS)   A set of software programs that allows a user to manage a database—that is, to store, manipulate, and retrieve the data in a database.

decision tree analysis   A technique that uses the decision tree diagram to choose from different options available; each option represented by a branch of the tree.

Delphi technique   An information-gathering technique used to reach consensus among the experts, who share their ideas and preferences anonymously.

Develop Program Team   A process used to improve individual and group competencies to enhance the program performance.

Direct and Manage Program Execution   A process used to manage various interfaces in the project to execute the program work smoothly with the goal of delivering the planned benefits.

earned value (EV) or budgeted cost of work performed (BCWP)   The value of the actually performed work expressed in terms of the approved budget for a program, program component, or a component activity for a given time period.

estimate at completion (EAC)   The estimate from the current point in time of how much it will cost to complete the work under consideration (program, program component, or a component activity). The value of EAC is obtained by adding the value of ETC to AC.

estimate to complete (ETC)   The expected cost, estimated from CPI, to complete the remaining work.

executive sponsor   An executive who is the key decision maker in the program board and is responsible for creating an environment that will ensure the program success.

expected monetary value (EMV) analysis   A statistical technique used to calculate the expected outcome when there are multiple possible outcome values with probabilities assigned to them.

fast tracking   A schedule-compression technique used to decrease the project duration by performing project phases or some schedule activities within a phase simultaneously when they would normally be performed in sequence.

float time   The positive difference between the late start date and the early start date of a schedule activity.

formalization   Making something official and putting it in the framework of proper rules and procedures.

free float (FF)   The maximum amount of time by which a given activity can be delayed without delaying the early start of any of the immediately following scheduling activities.

gate review   A program review, also called phase-gate review, that checks against the exit criteria of the phase that has just been completed and determines the readiness of the program for entering the next phase.

human resource planning   A process used to perform roles and responsibilities assignments and to generate a staffing management plan.

information distribution   The process of providing needed accurate information to the program stakeholders in a timely fashion.

Initiate Program   A process used to begin the program initiation by generating important documents, such as the program charter and preliminary program scope statement, and by identifying program manger.

Initiate Team   A program process used to put together a core program team.

intangible benefit   A benefit that may not be easy to quantify such as improved employee morale or increased customer satisfaction.

Integrated Change Control   A process used to coordinate changes in various areas including cost, schedule, scope, and quality across the entire program.

interface management plan   A document that is generated by the Interface Planning process and describes how to manage the interfaces of the program with other programs and with factors external to the program.

interface planning   A process used to identify and map the relationships of a program with other programs in the organization's active portfolio, and with other factors external to the program.

internal return rate (IRR)   An investment analysis method used to decide if a long-term investment should be made. It compares the expected benefit of investment in a project with benefits from other investment methods.

Issue Management and Control   A process used to identify, track, and close the stakeholders' issues to ensure that their expectations are aligned with the program deliverables and activities.

knowledge area   A knowledge area in project management is defined by its knowledge requirements related to managing a specific aspect of a project, such as cost, by using a set of processes. PMI recognizes a total of nine knowledge areas, such as Cost Management and Human Resource Management.

lateral thinking   Thinking outside the box, beyond the realm of your experience, to search for new solutions and methods rather than only better uses for the current solutions and methods.

matrix management   Management of a matrix team; that is, a team composed of individuals from different functional groups and departments.

milestone   A significant event happening at a specific point in the life cycle of a program. Some examples of program milestones are initiation of a project in the program, closure of a project in the program, and completion of a key deliverable.

mitigation   The process of taking actions to reduce or prevent the impact of a disaster that is expected to occur.

Monitor and Control Program Work   A process used to generate, gather, and consolidate performance information and to measure performance and trends to make improvements.

net present value (NPV)   The present value of the future cash inflows (benefits) minus the present value of the current and future cash outflows (cost). For a project to be worthwhile economically, the NPV must be positive.

network diagram   A schematic display of logical relationships among the program (or project) activities. The time flow in these diagrams is from left to right. Also called schedule network diagram.

operational definition   A description of an entity or a property of an entity in terms of measurable specifics which can be verified.

opportunity cost   Refers to selecting a project over another due to the scarcity of resources. Opportunity cost is the benefit missed by not selecting a project.

organization   A group of individuals organized to work for some purpose or mission.

parametric estimation   A quantitative technique used to calculate some quantities by using rates, historical information, and statistical relationships between some parameters. The quantities that can eb calculated by using this technique include activity duration, cost, and resource requirements.

Pareto diagram   A diagram used to rank the importance of each error (problem) based on the frequency of its occurrence over time in form of defects.

Perform Quality Assurance   In project management, a process used for applying the planned systematic quality activities to ensure that the project employs all the planned processes needed to meet all the project requirements.
  In program management, a process used to regularly evaluate the program performance to assure that the program complies with the planned quality standards.

Perform Quality Control   A process used to monitor specific program deliverables (benefits, products, services, and results) to determine if they meet the quality requirements.

performance reporting   A process used to consolidate performance data, collected from project and nonproject activities, about how program resources are being used to deliver program benefits. This information is provided to the stakeholders by using the Information Distribution process.

performing organization   The organization that is performing a project.

Plan Program Contracting   A process used to identify the type and determine the detail of documentation required to contract with the vendors who will supply the PWBS components that need to be acquired (procured). This process generates procurement documents and a contract management plan.

Plan Program Purchases and Acquisitions   A process used to determine what will be procured, when it will be procured, and how it will be procured. This process generates procurement management plan and a contract statement of work.

planned value (PV) or budgeted cost for the work scheduled (BCWS)   The authorized cost for the scheduled work of the program, program component, or a component activity up to a given point on the time scale.

post-review meeting   A meeting conducted during the program closure with the stakeholders, in which the final performance analysis report is presented, feedback is obtained, and lessons learned are captured.

precedence diagramming method (PDM)   A technique used to construct a network diagram in which a node (a box) represents an activity and an arrow represents the dependency relationship.

preliminary program scope statement   A document, generated as an output of the Initiate Program process, that defines the program scope at high level. For example it includes the program objectives and high-level deliverables.

present value (PV)   The present value of a future payment, that is, a future amount converted into the present time by taking into account the time value such as inflation and interest.

preventive actions   Directions to perform activities that will reduce the probability of negative consequences associated with risks.

process   A set of interrelated activities performed to obtain a specified set of products, results, or services.

procurement   The process of acquiring products, services, and results from outside the program team (and the constituent project teams) to complete the program.

procurement documents   The documents used to seek bids or proposals from the potential sellers.

procurement management   Execution of a set of processes used to obtain products, services, or results from outside the program team to complete the program.

procurement management plan   A document that specifies how the procurement processes will be performed and managed from preparing the procurement documents through closing contracts.

program   A set of related projects managed in a coordinated fashion to improve their overall efficiency and effectiveness, achieving benefits and control that cannot be achieved by managing these projects individually.

program artifacts   Objects created for the program, such as program documents, which include plans, procedures, and standards.

program board   An executive level forum to manage the issues of a program.

program charter   A document generated by the Initiate Program process; states the key objectives, expected benefits, and assumptions and constraints of the program.

Program Contract Administration   A process used to manage the relationship with sellers and buyers at the program level for the procurement that is not being managed at the project level.

program cost of quality   The total cost incurred in implementing conformance to the requirements and quality standards set for the program, the rework due to the defects resulting from the failure to meet the requirements, and updating the product or service to meet the requirements.

program governance   A management method that is used to develop, communicate, implement, and monitor the organizational structures, policies, procedures, practices, and other acts to run a program.

program management   The centralized management of a specific program performed in a coordinated fashion to achieve the strategic goals, objectives, and benefits of the program.

program management office (PMO)   An entity within an organization that holds the responsibility for defining and managing program-related governance elements such as processes, procedures, and templates for all the programs in the organization.

program management plan   The grand program plan, generated by using the Develop Program Management Plan process, that describes how to manage and execute the program to achieve its objectives. It consists of several subsidiary plans such as the cost management plan, the schedule management plan, and the scope management plan.

program office (PO)   An entity within an organization designed to handle the program administration functions of a program centrally by providing support to the program management team and program manager.

program package   A component at the lowest level of a branch of the PWBS.

program schedule   The planned dates for completing the PWBS components and the program milestones.

program scope management plan   A document that is generated by the Scope Definition process and describes how to manage the scope of the program, including how to create the PWBS and how to control the scope.

program scope statement   A document that is generated by the Scope Definition process and describes the scope of the program: what is included in the program and what is excluded.

program setup   Phase two of the program life cycle, which develops a detailed roadmap for the program by defining the deliverables and describing how to produce them. It uses the Program Planning processes to produce its key results.

program stakeholder management   Understanding and managing the influence and expectations of the program stakeholders.

program stakeholders   Individuals, organizations, or both whose interests may be affected—positively or negatively—by the outcomes of program execution and completion.

program team directory   A document that contains a list of program team members and information about them such as roles, responsibilities, and communication (e.g., contact info).

program work breakdown structure (PWBS)   A deliverable-oriented hierarchical structure that represents the program scope, including the deliverables to be produced by the constituent projects.

progressive elaboration   A technique to develop a plan in steps as more information becomes available. The detail and accuracy of the plan improves as it progresses with time.

project   A work effort made over a finite period of time with a start and a finish to create a unique product, service, or result. A process consists of three elements: input, tools and techniques, and output.

project charter   A document issued by the project initiator or the project sponsor that, when signed by an appropriate person in the performing organization, authorizes the project by naming the project manager and specifying the authority level of the project manager.

project management information system (PMIS)   An information system, also called program management information system, that consists of tools and techniques used to collect, integrate, store, and retrieve (to disseminate) the outputs of project management processes.

project management   Application of knowledge, skills, and tools and techniques to project activities in order to meet the project objectives. You do this by performing some processes at various stages of the project.

project management office (PMO)   An entity in an organization that is responsible for providing centralized coordinated management for projects in the organization.

project portfolio   A set of projects, programs, or both that is managed in a coordinated fashion to obtain control and benefits that would not be achieved if these projects and programs were managed individually.

project stakeholder   An individual or an organization that is positively or negatively affected by the project.

PWBS dictionary   A document that is generated by the Create PWBS process and contains information about the PWBS components.

quality   The degree to which a set of characteristics of program deliverables and program objectives fulfill the requirements.

quality assurance   The application of the planned systematic quality activities.

quality audit   A structured and independent review to determine whether program execution activities comply with the policies, processes, and procedures determined in the program management plan. It verifies the implementation of approved change requests, corrective actions, defect repairs, and preventive actions.

quality control   A process to monitor a specific set of program deliverables and results to ensure they meet the agreed upon quality standards.

quality metrics   An operational criterion that defines in specific terms what something (such as a characteristic or a feature) is and how the quality control process measures it.

Quality Planning   A process used to identify which quality standards are relevant to the project at hand, and determining how to meet them.

RACI chart   A responsibility assignment matrix (RAM) that assigns four roles to team members for various responsibilities/activities: responsible (R), accountable (A), consult (C), and inform (I).

Request Seller Responses   A process used to obtain responses in terms of quotations, bids, offers, and proposals from sellers outside the program team for their product or services needed for the program.

residual risk   A risk that remains after the risk response has been performed.

Resource Control   A process used to manage all program resources and the associated cost according to the program management plan.

resource leveling   A technique used to resolve over-allocation and conflicts in resource assignments.

resource management plan   A document that is generated by the Resource Planning process and describes at the program level how to manage the program resources. This includes determining the resource requirements and allocating the resources.

Resource Planning   A process that determines the type and quantity of resources needed for the program and the optimal use of these resources across the program

responsibility assignment matrix (RAM)   An accountability matrix used to specify the relationships between responsibilities, roles, and team members.

return on Investment (ROI)   The percentage profit from the investment in the project or program.

risk   An uncertain event or condition that, if it occurs, has a positive or negative effect on meeting the objectives of a program or its constituent projects.

Risk Management Planning and Analysis   The process used to determine the *how* of risk management: how to plan and execute the risk management activities for the given program. It includes identifying risks, analyzing risks, and planning responses for the risks.

risk mitigation   A technique for reducing the probability of risk occurring, reducing the impact of the risk if it does occur, or both. The risk-mitigation activities that impact the direction and delivery of multiple projects can play an important role in determining which project should go into a program.

Risk Monitoring and Control   The process used for tracking identified program risks, identifying new risks to the program, executing risk response plans, and evaluating the effectiveness of executing response plans throughout the lifecycle of the program.

Schedule Control   A process used to ensure that the program is completed in time according to the approved schedule.

Schedule Development   A process used to generate the program schedule and the schedule management plan.

schedule management plan   A plan used to manage and control the program schedule.

schedule performance index (SPI)   A measure of the schedule efficiency of a program calculated by dividing earned value (EV) by planned value (PV).

schedule variance (SV)   The deviation of the performed schedule from the planned schedule in terms of cost.

Scope Control   A process used to control changes to the program scope.

scope creep   The phenomenon of introducing uncontrolled changes, such as adding or modifying a feature, without going through the planned change-control system for approval.

Scope Definition   A process used to plan and define the program scope by creating the scope management plan and scope statement.

secondary risk   A risk that arises as a result of implementing a risk response.

Select Sellers   A process used to select sellers based on their responses and negotiate written contracts with the selected sellers.

social map   A map of an area that displays the social structures and institutions found in the area.

staffing management plan   A document that describes when and how human resource requirements for a program will be met.

stakeholder analysis   The procedure used to identify and understand the stakeholders and their needs and expectations.

Strengths, Weaknesses, Opportunities, and Threats (SWOT) analysis   An analysis used to gather information by examining the strengths, weaknesses, opportunities, and threats involved in an undertaking such as a program or a project.

synchronous communication   A communication method in which the two communicating entities have to be present on both ends of the communication line at the same time. An example is a phone conversation.

tangible benefit   A quantifiable benefit that may be directly related to the financial objectives such as a 10 percent increase in revenue.

total float (TF)   The maximum time by which a given activity can be delayed from its early start date without delaying the finish date of the project.

transition plan   A document that is generated by the Transition Planning process and describes how the program output after the program completion will be transferred to another organization or to a functional group within the performing organization.

Transition Planning   A process that plans for transferring the program outcome from the program team to the appropriate group, such as the operations group in the performing organization.

trend analysis   The science of predicting future performance based on past results.

virtual team   A team of members working on the same project (or program) with few or no face-to-face meetings. Various technologies, such video conferencing and the World Wide Web including email, web pages, and web bulletin boards are used to facilitate communication among team members.

work authorization system   A subsystem of the overall program management system that determines how the program work will be properly authorized in order to ensure that the work is performed in the right sequence by the right individuals or groups at the right time.

work breakdown structure (WBS)   A deliverable-oriented hierarchical decomposition of the work that must be performed to accomplish the objectives and create the project deliverables.

work package   A deliverable or a task at the lowest level of each branch of the WBS.

Index

Note to the reader: Throughout this index **boldfaced** page numbers indicate primary discussions of a topic. *Italicized* page numbers indicate illustrations.

cost-benefit analysis, in Quality Planning process, 242

cost budgeting, 17

cost change control system, 348

Cost Control process, 17, **347–349**, 378, 398
  performance measurement analysis for, **350–356**
    cost performance, **351–353**
    forecasting, **355–356**
    schedule performance in terms of cost, **353–354**

Cost Estimating and Budgeting process, 17, 196, 221
  input, **197–198**
  input and output, *197*
  output, **200–201**
  tools and techniques, 198–200

Cost Management knowledge area, 179

cost management plan, 200, 221
  in Integrated Change Control process, 330

cost overrun, 218

cost performance, **351–353**

cost performance index (CPI), 352–353, 378

cost-performance reports, 348

cost plus (CPF), 217

cost plus fixed fee (CPFF), 218

cost plus incentive fee (CPIF), 218

cost plus percentage of cost (CPPC), 217

cost-reimbursable contracts, 217

cost reporting system, in Performance Reporting process, 371

cost variance (CV), 352, 378

crashing, 185, 209, 221

Create Program Work Breakdown Structure (PWBS) process, 135, 158
  input, **158**
  input and output, *159*

output, **158–161**
tools and techniques, **161–162**
critical chain method, 194
critical path, 192–193, 222
cross-charges, 335
customer/user, as stakeholder, 23

D

data, 313
database, 303, 313
database management system (DBMS), 303, 313
decision tree analysis, 252, 265
  real world scenario, 253
decomposition, 161, 183
  for developing high-level program milestones, 99
defect repair review, for quality control, 363
deliverables, 9, 236
  in Closing process group, 393
  of program planning, 139–140
  of program, subdividing, 161
  quality of, 237
Delivering benefits phase, 71
delivery notices, in Contract Closure process, 400
Delphi technique, 124, 265
  for estimating resource requirements, 208
  in pre-program setup phase, 103
  for risk identification, 249
dependencies
  among projects in program, 54
  as Schedule Development input, 181
  types, **187–188**

K

Kaplan, Robert, 60
key performance indicators (KPIs), 72,
    74–76
key stakeholders, 62
kickoff meetings, **101–102**
knowledge areas, 2, 3, 37
    Program Initiating Process group
        mapped to, 93
    in program management, **16–22**
    Program Management processes
        mapped to process groups and,
        47–48
    Program Planning Process group
        mapped to, 136–137
    project management processes
        mapped to, 20–21
knowledge competence, 206
knowledge management, PMIS for, 261
known unknowns, 199

L

lag, applying to dependencies, 190
lateral thinking, 155, 168
lead, applying to dependencies, 190
leadership
    by project manager, 25
    in projects vs. programs, 55
    for team development, 288
learning, in Closing process group, 392
lease agreements, 299, 333
    termination requests, 335
lessons learned, 119, 120, 392, 396
    in Closing process group, 394
    in Component Closure process, 398
    as process output, 121
    real world scenario, 396–397

life cycle
    for benefits management, 59, 60
    of project, **9–15**
        stages, 10
        summary, 15
load balancing, 150
log, of issue resolution, 334
lump-sum contract, 217

M

make-or-buy analysis, 211–212
    and decisions, 213
Manage Stakeholders process, 367
management, 3
management directives, in Communi-
    cation Control process, 368
management information system, 143,
    151, 330
    in Closing process group, 394
    in Component Closure process, 398
    for developing high-level program
        milestones, 99
    for directing and managing
        program, 282
    in Issue Management and Control
        process, 340
    in Monitor and Control Program
        Work process, 338
management infrastructure, 278
management skills
    for directing and managing
        program, 282
    in Issue Management and Control
        process, 340
    in projects vs. programs, 55
    for team development, 288
management style, 30
mandatory dependencies, 181

projects, 3, 37
  identifying relationships, real world
    scenario, 52–53
  vs. operations, **6–7**
  vs. programs, 55–56
    determining need, 96
  relationship between programs, ben-
    efits and, 57
  relationship with portfolios and pro-
    grams, 4, 5
  selection, **115–116**
    benefit measurement methods, **116**
    constrained optimization methods,
      116–117
    expert judgment, **117**
  starting in program, 306
  what it is, **5–6**
proposal, 216
  evaluation techniques, 297
PWBS dictionary, 160, 168

Q

qualitative risk analysis, 244
quality, 234, 265
  controlling, **356–364**
  planning for, **235–236**
quality assurance, **291–294**, 314
quality audits, 292, 314
quality checklists, 244
  in Perform Quality Control
    process, 358
quality control, 265, **356–364**
  input, **357–358**
  input and output, *357*
  output, **363–364**
  tools and techniques, **358–363**
quality improvement plan, 243
Quality Management, **236–238**
  interaction with other processes, *237*

quality management plan, 243, 292
  in Perform Quality Control
    process, 358
quality metrics, 244, 265, 292
Quality Planning process, 237, **240–
    244**, 265
  input, **241–242**
  input and output, *241*
  output, **243–244**
  tools and techniques, **242–243**
quantitative analysis, 185
quantitative estimation of costs, 199
quantitative risk analysis, 245
quotation, 216

R

RACI chart, 114, 125
random variable, 34
ranking, 209
reactive approach, to cost control, 347
receiver in communication line, 302
recognition
  in staff management plan, 205
  in team development, 289
records management system, in Contract
    Closure process, 401
recruitment practices, 113
regulations, in program scope
    statement, 157
reliability of metrics, 73
reporting systems, in Performance
    Reporting process, 371
reports, in Performance Reporting
    process, 370
request for information (RFI), 294
request for proposal (RFP), 61, 216, 294

The Absolute Best PgMP: Program Management Professional Exam Book/CD Package on the Market!

Get ready for the new PgMP: Program Management Professional Exam with the most comprehensive and challenging sample tests anywhere!

The Sybex Test Engine features:

- All the review questions, as covered in each chapter of the book
- Challenging questions representative of those you'll find on the real exam
- Two bonus examlets (or one full-length bonus exam) available only on the CD
- An Assessment Test to narrow your focus to certain objective groups.

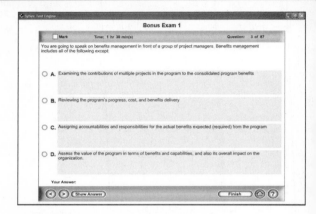

Use the Electronic Flashcards for PCs or Palm devices to jog your memory and prep last-minute for the exam!

- Reinforce your understanding of key concepts with these hardcore flashcard-style questions..
- Download the Flashcards to your Palm device and go on the road. Now you can study for the Program Management Professional exam any time, anywhere.

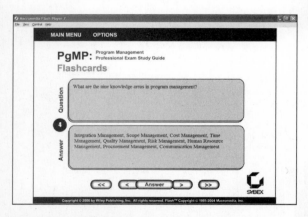

Search through the complete book in PDF!

- Access the entire *PgMP: Program Management Professional Exam Study Guide*, complete with figures and tables, in electronic format.
- Search the *PgMP: Program Management Professional Exam Study Guide* chapters to find information on any topic in seconds.

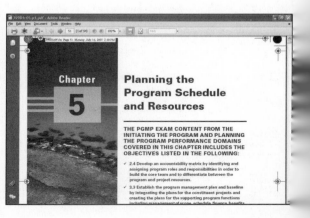